Christmas 2006

Austin

Remember, sometimes books are so much better than computers. We believe that you will find this interesting and useful.

Merry Christmas
&
Happy New Year!

Love

MaryAnn & Pop-Pop

ENCYCLOPEDIA OF
Animals

ENCYCLOPEDIA OF
Animals

KAREN MᶜGHEE • GEORGE MᶜKAY PH.D

NATIONAL GEOGRAPHIC

WASHINGTON, D.C.

Conceived and produced by Weldon Owen Pty Ltd

61 Victoria Street, McMahons Point

Sydney, NSW 2060, Australia

First published in North America in 2007 by the

National Geographic Society

1145 17th Street N.W.

Washington, D.C. 20036-4688

For information about special discounts for bulk purchases,
please contact National Geographic Books Special Sales:
ngspecsales@ngs.org

Chief Executive Officer John Owen

President Terry Newell

Publisher Sheena Coupe

Creative Director Sue Burk

Vice President International Sales Stuart Laurence

Administrator International Sales Kristine Ravn

Project Editor Jessica Cox

Project Designer Domenika Markovtzev

Editor Clara Finlay

Designers Kathryn Morgan, Juliana Titin

Editorial Coordinator Irene Mickaiel

Author Karen McGhee

Consultant Editor Dr. George McKay

Consultants Lucéia Bonora, Dr. Mark Hutchinson,
          Dr. Stephen Hutchinson, Dr. Noel Tait

Index Puddingburn Publishing Services

Production Director Chris Hemesath

Production Manager Louise Mitchell

Production Coordinator Monique Layt

Hardcover Edition:
ISBN-10: 0-7922-5936-X
ISBN-13: 978-0-7922-5936-7

Library Edition:
ISBN-10: 0-7922-5937-8
ISBN-13: 978-0-7922-5937-4

Direct Mail Expanded Edition:
ISBN-10: 0-7922-7458-X
ISBN-13: 978-0-7922-7458-2

Deluxe Direct Mail Expanded Edition:
ISBN-10: 0-7922-7460-1
ISBN-13: 978-0-7922-7460-5

Color reproduction by Colourscan Overseas Co Pte Ltd

Printed in China by SNP Leefung Printers Ltd

A Weldon Owen production

Contents

How to Use this Book

This book is divided into seven chapters. The first chapter explains the world of animals: how they are classified; their behavior; where they live; and threats to their survival. The remaining chapters present the major animal groups: mammals, birds, reptiles, amphibians, fish, and invertebrates. Each chapter starts with an introduction, followed by pages that describe the main groups that belong in that chapter. Special feature pages throughout the book highlight interesting animal characteristics. A glossary and list of animal sizes can be found at the back.

SCIENTIFIC NAMES

All known animals have a unique scientific name. The lion's name is *Panthera leo*. The two parts describe its genus (*Panthera*) and species (*leo*). The name shows that lions are closely related to cats, such as tigers, which share the same genus, but that lions form their own species.

ABBREVIATIONS

mm	millimeters	L	liters
cm	centimeters	in	inch
m	meters	ft	feet
km	kilometers	>	greater tha
km²	square	<	less than
	kilometers	°	degrees
g	grams	sp.	species
kg	kilograms	sing.	singular
t	tonnes	pl.	plural

Chapter name and classification data
This shows the group being discussed, as well as information about the group's classification.

Photo and caption
Captioned photos show one or more animals in the group.

Introductory text
This text introduces the group of animals in each chapter and describes what makes them unique.

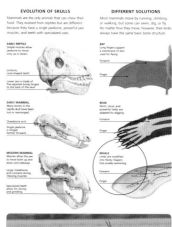

Color co
Each chap
color co

Feature
Important asp
of anat
reproductio
behavior ap
in feature b

Labeled dia
Detailed, lat
diagrams inc
cross section
animal skele

INTRODUCTORY PAGES
These pages introduce the animals to be explored in each chapter. They discuss the group's common features as well as their differences. The pages look at how these animals are built, the ways they reproduce, and why they behave as they do.

ICONS

Some animals have a conservation icon next to the arrow pointing from the species information to its illustration. The icons vary in color depending on that animal's conservation status. This information comes from the World Conservation Union Red List of Threatened Species (IUCN Red List).

Extinct 🔲 A species is extinct when it is known that the last individual has died. Species can be extinct in the wild but still survive in captivity or as domestic animals.

Critically endangered 🔲 Critically endangered species are at an extremely high risk of immediate extinction in the wild.

Endangered 🔲 Endangered species face a very high risk of extinction in the wild in the near future.

Vulnerable 🔲 Vulnerable species face a high risk of extinction in the wild in the future.

Other 🔲 Other conservation categories include near threatened species, which may become endangered in the future.

Male ♂   **Female** ♀ For species where the male and female look different, a male or female icon is placed next to its illustration.

ANIMAL SIZES

The maximum size of each of the illustrated animals is given on pages 246–5 The animals are listed according to where they appear in each chapter; fc example, primates are grouped together, as are frogs and toads, and worm The maximum size lies to the right of each animal's common name. A ke for each group notes how the animals have been measured.

Birds

Penguins	🐧
Adelie penguin	23¾ in (61 cm)
Emperor penguin	4 ft (1.2 m)
Jackass penguin	3¼ ft (1 m)
King penguin	3¼ ft (1 m)
Little penguin	17½ in (45 cm)
Royal penguin	27⅓ in (70 cm)
Snares penguin	23½ in (60 cm)

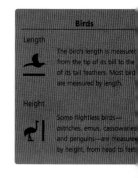

Birds

Length

The bird's length is measured from the tip of its bill to the of its tail feathers. Most bird are measured by length.

Height

Some flightless birds— ostriches, emus, cassowaries and penguins—are measured by height, from head to feet

Main groups
The main animal groups within a chapter have a large heading and classification data.

Species illustration
Many species within the group are illustrated on the species page.

Conservation Watch and distribution map
These two elements are explained in detail at the bottom of this page.

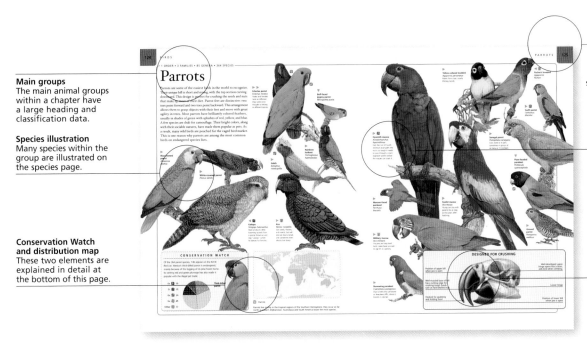

Running head
The right-hand running head shows different sections within the chapter.

Species information
Common and scientific names of each illustrated species are given. Many species also have extra information beneath.

Feature box
Feature boxes provide additional information about the group or individual species.

SPECIES PAGES
Within each chapter are a number of illustrated species pages. These pages explain why certain species are grouped together, and include galleries of individual species illustrations with their names and information.

Subgroups
Some of the main animal groups extend for several pages or are broken down into subgroups. These pages have a smaller heading and no classification data.

Arrows and icons
Arrows pinpoint each species. Conservation and gender icons are explained on page 8.

Fast Fact
An interesting fact about one or more species in the group can be found here.

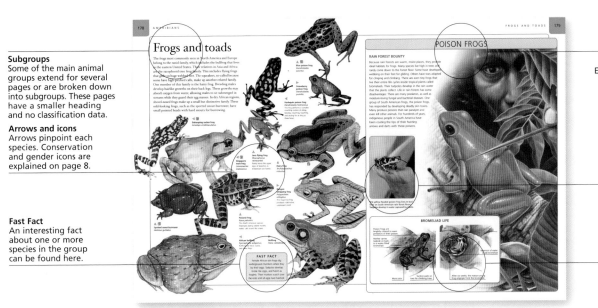

Full-page feature
Each full-page feature contains illustrations that are explained in the text.

Photo and caption
Captioned photos are also included in these features.

Inset box
Labeled illustrations or diagrams present more information.

FULL-PAGE FEATURES
Some species pages are accompanied by a full-page feature. These explore aspects of the group's anatomy or behavior in more detail. They may also show how humans interact with certain animals.

DISTRIBUTION MAP

ost major animal groups have distribution map, which shows here they can be found. This oes not include introduced or omestic species. The first group always yellow. A second group blue. Green indicates where e ranges overlap. Text explains e distribution in more detail.

Kingfishers
Mousebirds and trogons
Kingfishers, mousebirds, and trogons

Kingfishers are found in temperate areas, mostly in Africa and Southeast Asia. Mousebirds live in Africa. Trogons occur across Central America, Africa, and Asia.

CONSERVATION WATCH

Almost every major animal group in the book has a Conservation Watch box. The numbers of those species in the group that appear on the IUCN Red List are listed next to an icon. This data is also shown as a graph. An at-risk species is discussed in the text and illustrated.

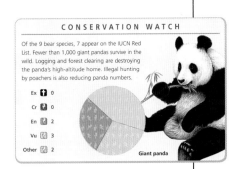

CONSERVATION WATCH

Of the 9 bear species, 7 appear on the IUCN Red List. Fewer than 1,000 giant pandas survive in the wild. Logging and forest clearing are destroying the panda's high-altitude home. Illegal hunting by poachers is also reducing panda numbers.

Ex	0
Cr	0
En	2
Vu	3
Other	2

Giant panda

Animal World

32 PHYLA • >1.5 MILLION SPECIES

The Animal Kingdom

Giraffes are the tallest land animals alive today, and African elephants are the heaviest. Most animals are rarely seen, and as many as 15 million species may still be unknown.

The living world consists of five groups called kingdoms. The five kingdoms are animals, plants, fungi, protists, and monerans. Unlike the single-celled protists and monerans, animals are made up of thousands of cells that work together as a living whole. The cells of most species are organized into tissues and organs, which each perform different tasks. Unlike plants and fungi, animals cannot produce their own food, so they need to eat other living things to survive. One reason there is such an enormous variety of animals is that species are constantly developing ways of finding and eating other animals while not being eaten themselves. Most animals have a central digestive system that takes food and breaks it down, supplying them with energy. To find food, most animals are mobile—they are able to walk, run, hop, fly, or swim—for at least part of their life cycles. Because animals can move, they have developed senses and nerves to be aware of and react to the world around them. As a result, animals have the most complex life cycles and behaviors of all living things. Almost all animals need separate male and female sex organs to create new life. This is known as sexual reproduction, and it usually occurs between two animals of different genders.

CLASSIFYING ANIMALS

Animals are sorted into groups based on how closely they relate to each other. This is called classification. It provides a way of organizing everything we know and discover about animals. Groups are arranged into levels that begin with the least related (the kingdom), with many organisms. Each level narrows down the groups, with fewer, increasingly similar animals. The diagram below shows all the groups to which a single species, the mallard, belongs.

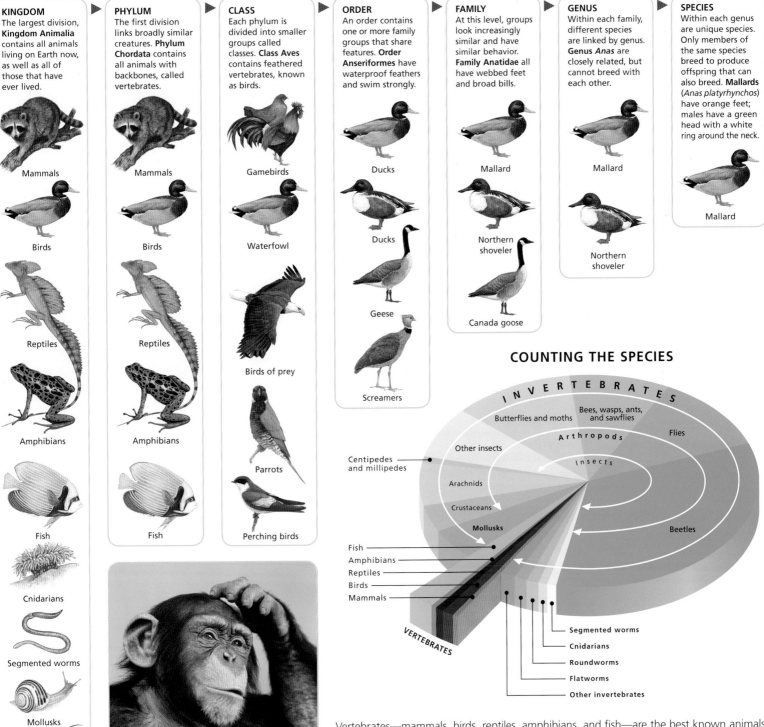

KINGDOM
The largest division, **Kingdom Animalia** contains all animals living on Earth now, as well as all of those that have ever lived.

Mammals
Birds
Reptiles
Amphibians
Fish
Cnidarians
Segmented worms
Mollusks
Arthropods

PHYLUM
The first division links broadly similar creatures. **Phylum Chordata** contains all animals with backbones, called vertebrates.

Mammals
Birds
Reptiles
Amphibians
Fish

CLASS
Each phylum is divided into smaller groups called classes. **Class Aves** contains feathered vertebrates, known as birds.

Gamebirds
Waterfowl
Birds of prey
Parrots
Perching birds

ORDER
An order contains one or more family groups that share features. **Order Anseriformes** have waterproof feathers and swim strongly.

Ducks
Ducks
Geese
Screamers

FAMILY
At this level, groups look increasingly similar and have similar behavior. **Family Anatidae** all have webbed feet and broad bills.

Mallard
Northern shoveler
Canada goose

GENUS
Within each family, different species are linked by genus. **Genus Anas** are closely related, but cannot breed with each other.

Mallard
Northern shoveler

SPECIES
Within each genus are unique species. Only members of the same species breed to produce offspring that can also breed. **Mallards** (*Anas platyrhynchos*) have orange feet; males have a green head with a white ring around the neck.

Mallard

Because chimpanzees share many features with humans, they are included in the same family.

COUNTING THE SPECIES

INVERTEBRATES
Butterflies and moths
Bees, wasps, ants, and sawflies
Arthropods
Flies
Other insects
Insects
Centipedes and millipedes
Arachnids
Crustaceans
Beetles
Mollusks
Fish
Amphibians
Reptiles
Birds
Mammals
Segmented worms
Cnidarians
Roundworms
Flatworms
Other invertebrates
VERTEBRATES

Vertebrates—mammals, birds, reptiles, amphibians, and fish—are the best known animals. But these classes make up only about 5 percent of animal species. By far, most members of the animal kingdom are invertebrates. These are animals that have no backbones, such as worms and arthropods. Arthropods, which include insects, are the most abundant invertebrates, both in numbers of species and individual animals.

Animal Behavior

Clown anemonefish escape predators by adaptations that let them live among the poisonous, stinging tentacles of sea anemones, which benefit by feeding on the fish's food scraps.

To survive each day in the wild, all animals behave in certain ways. Animals adapt their behavior to meet their basic needs, such as finding food, water, shelter, and a mate. The most important behaviors relate to the daily need to find food and to avoid being eaten. Lightning-fast reflexes and the ability to stalk silently are crucial for many predators, such as big cats, to catch prey. Prey, in turn, such as Africa's hoofed mammals, form herds or groups to deter and confuse predators. Many fish form schools for the same reason. Living together may bring other benefits, too. Young baboons in family troops learn to select the right foods by watching their mothers and aunts. In colonies of social insects, such as ants and honeybees, individuals share the workload by performing distinct tasks. Much of an animal's behavior is associated with choosing a mate. From rhinoceros beetles to elephant seals, males often show off to potential partners by battling each other. Other species impress females with special traits or skills: Male peacocks fan out their spectacular tails; male anoles flare colorful dewlaps. Many animals make regular journeys called migrations to find mates. Some birds and insects are thought to use the sun to navigate on such treks. Others may use Earth's magnetic field.

ANIMAL SENSES

Most animals can smell, see, taste, hear, and feel the world around them. These senses are developed to varying degrees in different species. Many kinds of dogs have an excellent sense of smell, while birds of prey, such as eagles, rely on highly developed vision. Some animals also have extra senses, which are like nothing humans have. Sharks, as well as the platypus, search out prey by detecting their electrical activity.

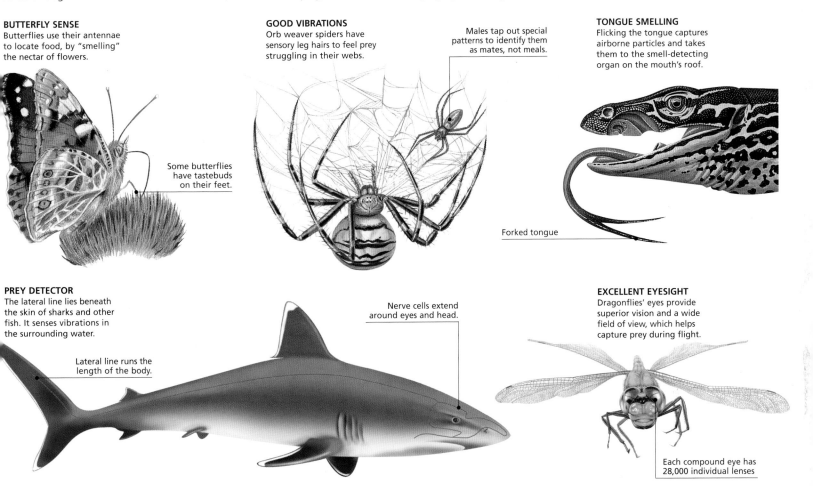

BUTTERFLY SENSE
Butterflies use their antennae to locate food, by "smelling" the nectar of flowers.

Some butterflies have tastebuds on their feet.

GOOD VIBRATIONS
Orb weaver spiders have sensory leg hairs to feel prey struggling in their webs.

Males tap out special patterns to identify them as mates, not meals.

TONGUE SMELLING
Flicking the tongue captures airborne particles and takes them to the smell-detecting organ on the mouth's roof.

Forked tongue

PREY DETECTOR
The lateral line lies beneath the skin of sharks and other fish. It senses vibrations in the surrounding water.

Lateral line runs the length of the body.

Nerve cells extend around eyes and head.

EXCELLENT EYESIGHT
Dragonflies' eyes provide superior vision and a wide field of view, which helps capture prey during flight.

Each compound eye has 28,000 individual lenses

ANIMAL COMMUNICATION

Animals communicate—send and receive messages—in many ways. They do so either to attract others or to warn them off. Species as different as ants and aardvarks mark their hunting or breeding territories with scent. Animals also use sound: They may call out to frighten enemies, warn of danger, or even attract mates. Communication by sight is also common. Males of many animal groups are brightly colored and adorned to appeal to females.

Pygmy sweepers swim in coordinated schools that move as a single unit. They use a number of senses to communicate with one another.

The nightingale's complex, melodic song has made it a popular pet for centuries.

Japanese macaques rely on grooming to help establish relationships and reinforce bonds within family groups.

HOW ANIMALS MOVE

The ways animals move depend on their body structure, where they live, and their reasons for moving. All fish can swim. But those that chase their food in the open water are usually more torpedo-shaped and faster than those that sit and wait for prey. Marine mammals can also swim, as can a surprising number of land mammals. Most mammals move by walking, crawling, running, or jumping. A few tree dwellers, such as possums and squirrels, can glide, but bats are the only mammals that can fly like birds. Some animals change the way they move during their life cycles. Tadpoles swim before changing into hopping adult frogs. Many insects begin their lives as crawling grubs before their bodies are transformed into adults that fly. Sea squirts swim freely as tadpole-like larvae, before attaching themselves to the seafloor as adults.

Orangutans have very long arms, which they use to climb and move among the trees.

INCHWORM
Geometrid moth caterpillars, also called inchworms, inch along by holding the ground firmly with their front legs and pulling their body into a loop. They stretch forward to straighten the loop, then start the process again.

ATTACK AND DEFENSE

The bright colors of this nudibranch, or sea slug, warn potential predators to leave it alone because its flesh is foul-tasting or even poisonous.

Freshwater leaffish avoid the attention of attackers by mimicking dead leaves lying on the water's surface.

The eyelash viper is a sit-and-wait predator; it strikes rapidly when it senses passing prey, such as this rodent.

GROWING UP

Whitetail does are protective of their fawns. Until they are four weeks old, fawns are hidden among the undergrowth while their mothers forage.

After leatherback turtles hatch, they must make their way down to the sea alone. These hatchlings grow up without any parental care.

WEAVER BIRDS

Male black-headed weaver birds push and pull grass into loops and knots to make basket-like nests. They then display themselves in front of their nests to attract a mate. After mating, the females care for the young alone.

Young Canada geese know instinctively to follow and keep close to their parents soon after hatching. They usually stay with the same flock as adults.

FINDING A MATE

Bluecheek butterflyfish are some of the only fish that have long-term mates. These relationships may last several years.

This male natterjack toad attracts females during the breeding season by inflating a special throat sac to call out loudly.

Male great egrets develop special ornamental plume feathers during the breeding season to impress potential mates.

Animal Habitats

Within the Torres del Paine National Park, in Chile, are habitats that range from forest to desert. The park is home to many different mammal species, including these guanacos.

Habitats are where animals find food and shelter, and where they mate and breed. They include all of the elements—including plant life, climate, and geology—that make up a particular environment. Some species live within just one habitat, but many use or move between different habitats. Emperor penguins breed, lay their eggs, and raise their young on the icy surface of Antarctica but return to the ocean to hunt fish. Habitats naturally change with time. Some are shaped by sudden geological events, such as earthquakes. Others shift more gradually in response to a persistent natural force, such as erosion. As Earth changed over time, so have animals. They developed in ancient seas then moved onto land more than 400 million years ago as plants began to grow. Climate patterns create seasonal changes. When conditions become severe, as they do during winter in the forests of eastern North America, animals may cope by hibernating or migrating to a warmer environment. Habitats can be altered by the animals that live in them. The dam-building activities of beavers can modify the areas where they live. Humans, however, cause the greatest change to habitats. Most land habitats, aside from deserts and urban areas, are shrinking because of human actions.

WHERE ANIMALS LIVE

On land, climate and soil determine the plants that grow in an area. In turn, the vegetation determines the number and variety of animals that an area supports. The map below shows the world's vegetation as it would occur naturally without human interference. The land habitat with the most species is tropical rain forest, which has consistently warm weather and high rainfall. In the oceans, tropical coral reefs have the most species.

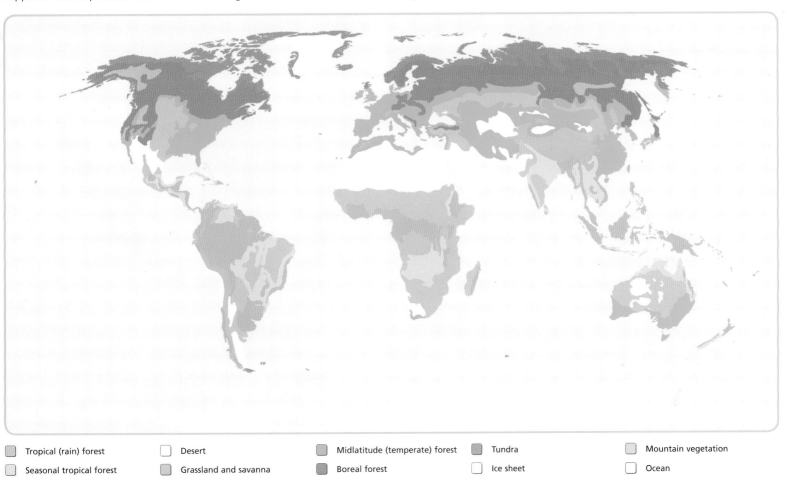

Tropical (rain) forest	Desert	Midlatitude (temperate) forest	Tundra
Seasonal tropical forest	Grassland and savanna	Boreal forest	Ice sheet
			Mountain vegetation
			Ocean

DESERTS

About one-third of Earth's land surface is covered by deserts. These can be extremely hot during the day and freezing at night. In such places, animals take advantage of any water, food, and shelter they can find. The hardy spinifex plant (left) can be home to lizards and insects, which attract small mammals and birds.

The gemsbok can go for days without drinking. It takes moisture from fruit and roots.

Ostriches cover great distances across inhospitable salt plains in Africa to search for food and water.

TROPICAL AND TEMPERATE FORESTS

Tropical forests contain an amazing variety of wildlife. The ocelot hunts small animals, camouflaged by its spotted coat among the dense vegetation of the tropical South American rain forest.

In temperate forests, summers are usually warm but winters can be severe. Many mammals hibernate during this time, but foxes remain active even during the coldest months.

GRASSLANDS

Termites survive the high temperatures in the grasslands of northern Australia by building huge mounds. These work like chimneys, allowing hot air to rise and cooler air to filter up from below.

URBAN AREAS

Urban areas often have a small number of animal species, but many individual animals. Those that eat a wide range of foods and find shelter in many locations do best. They include birds, such as sparrows; mice and rats; and cockroaches and other insect pests.

The peregrine falcon is normally a cliff-nesting species, but it has adapted to nesting on the ledges of high-rise buildings in many large cities throughout the world.

WATER WORLDS

Waterbirds, such as these snow geese, travel together from Arctic regions to spend winter on the salt marshes and marshy bays of North America's coasts.

RAIN FORESTS

Tropical rain forests receive more than 100 inches (250 cm) of rain each year. Life here exists in stories. Eagles patrol the tops of the tallest trees, often 130 feet (40 m) above the ground. Most trees are shorter, and their tops form a dense cover, or canopy, rich with insects, birds, and mammals that never go down to the ground. Shrubs and small trees form another story. The rain forest floor is home to insects and other invertebrates, as well as reptiles and amphibians.

Butterflyfish cruise the coral reefs of the tropical South Pacific Ocean. These reefs support a huge assortment of animal species, ranging from tiny marine worms to enormous sharks.

POLAR REGIONS

The short, dense, waterproof feathers of Adelie penguins provide protection from the windy, bitterly cold conditions of the Antarctic.

MOUNTAINS

Dall sheep are alpine mammals adapted to life in high mountain ranges. They escape predators by climbing steep cliffs and rugged outcrops.

Animals in Danger

Giant pandas are in danger of extinction in the wild. Large areas of the bamboo forests where they live in China have been cleared to make way for human activities such as farming.

Extinction—the complete dying out of a species—is a normal occurrence in nature. Most species that have ever existed are now extinct. But Earth is currently losing more animal species at a faster rate than ever before. Even the great mass extinction 65 million years ago that led to the end of the dinosaurs did not destroy as many species as are dying out now. The loss of so many species is in large part caused by humans and the impact of rapidly expanding populations. Animals are threatened by their habitats being destroyed and by the effects of pollution. Humans are also hunting and harvesting too many animals and are introducing diseases, plants, and animals into parts of the world where they would not normally occur, harming native wildlife. There is some good news: Concerned people are trying to stop or slow activities that threaten the future of so many animals. More species are now protected by international law. Some countries have introduced harsh penalties for people who hunt species illegally or damage sensitive environments. Land is being set aside as reserves and national parks to protect key habitats. Most importantly, education campaigns now teach children about how they can protect their planet's future.

HOT SPOTS OF DIVERSITY

Biodiversity refers to all life-forms on Earth, where they live, and how they interact with each other. Biodiversity hot spots are areas that have the richest and most threatened biodiversity. These places (in red on the map) have all been badly affected by human activity. They cover just 1.4 percent of Earth's land area, but they contain almost half of all plant species and more than one-third of all land vertebrates. The text discusses regions especially at risk (circled).

1. PACIFIC ISLANDS
Their isolation means that hundreds of unique bird and plant species exist only on individual islands. This makes them very vulnerable.

2. NORTH AMERICA
The Mediterranean areas of California, U.S.A., are under threat from agriculture and urban expansion. Mexico's mountain pine forests receive millions of monarch butterflies every winter but are being destroyed by logging.

3. SOUTH AMERICA
For its size, the tropical Andes is the most biodiverse region on Earth. Only a fifth of Brazil's coastal forests and inland savannas still remain. Most have been destroyed to make way for sugar plantations and urban sprawl.

4. AFRICA
Less than 5 percent of the Horn of Africa is untouched: Humans have exploited its rich mineral resources, and their livestock have overgrazed the arid grasslands, for centuries.

5. ASIA
New species are still being discovered in the many hot spots of Southeast Asia, a region which contains the rare orangutans and komodo dragons. These habitats are being cleared rapidly for human use.

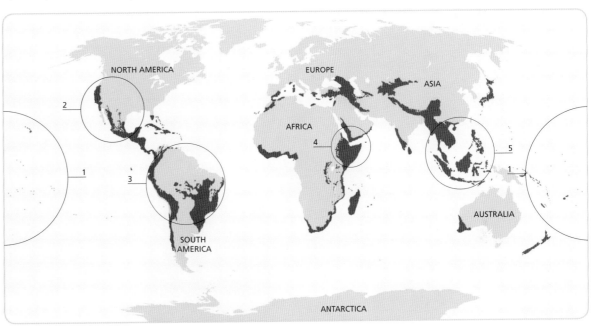

A POLLUTED WORLD

Unable to be freed by its mother from a tangle of discarded fishing net, an Antarctic fur seal pup faces a bleak future.

Oil spilled accidentally into the oceans from tankers coats the feathers of seabirds and ultimately kills them.

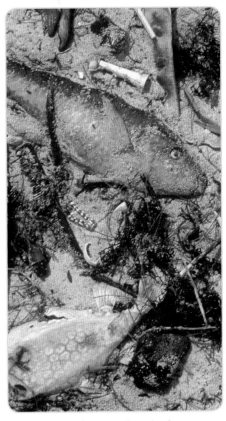

Pollution and overfishing are the major threats to biodiversity in oceans, lakes, and rivers.

Mammals

26 ORDERS • 137 FAMILIES • 1,142 GENERA • 4,785 SPECIES

Mammals

Jaguars are solitary hunters. Male jaguars remain with females only briefly during the mating season. Mothers are left to raise the cubs—numbering as many as four—on their own.

Mammals are vertebrates—the phylum of animals that have backbones. They are often the best known and most studied animals, in part because we humans are mammals. Mammals are warm-blooded, or endothermic, which means that they can control their internal body temperature. This allows them to remain active when their environment is very cold or hot. Except for echidnas and the platypus, mammals give birth to live young. They all have mammary glands that produce milk to nurse and nourish their young. Mammals have hair, even those species that spend most of their lives under the water.

Mammals evolved from reptiles about 195 million years ago. The first mammals were small, shrewlike creatures about an inch (2.5 cm) long. Today, they can be as small as field mice, the size of a human thumbnail, or as large as blue whales, which can reach 110 feet (33.5 m) in length. Mammals live in many habitats—on land, underground, in the air, and in both fresh and salt water—and the group has adapted to these habitats in different ways. Microbats fly like aerial acrobats, chasing insects on the wing; sleek-bodied cheetahs run prey to ground at breakneck speeds; and ungainly sloths climb trees in a painstakingly slow search for leaves.

EVOLUTION OF SKULLS

Mammals are the only animals that can chew their food. They evolved from reptiles but are different because they have a single jawbone, powerful jaw muscles, and teeth with specialized uses.

EARLY REPTILE
Simple muscles allow jawbone to move only up or down.

Uniform, cone-shaped teeth

Lower jaw is made of five separate bones hinged to the back of the skull.

EARLY MAMMAL
Many bones in the reptile skull have been lost or rearranged.

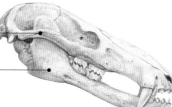

Cheekbone arch

Single jawbone is hinged farther forward.

MODERN MAMMAL
Muscles allow the jaw to move both up and down and sideways.

Large cheekbone arch contains strong chewing muscles.

Specialized teeth allow for slicing and grinding.

DIFFERENT SOLUTIONS

Most mammals move by running, climbing, or walking, but some can swim, dig, or fly. No matter how they move, however, their limbs always have the same basic bone structure.

BAT
Long fingers support a membrane of skin used for flying.

Forearm

Finger

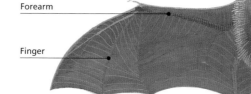

BEAR
Short, stout, and powerful limbs are adapted for digging.

Forearm

Finger

WHALE
Limbs are modified into fleshy flippers that enable swimming.

Forearm

Finger

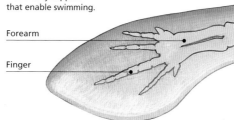

SKIN AND HAIR

The skin contains many different muscles, blood vessels, and glands. Sebaceous glands produce oils to protect and waterproof the fur. Sweat glands help control temperature, cooling mammals through evaporation of sweat. Hair is made of proteins and is found in no other kind of animal. Even mammals that appear to have none, such as dolphins and whales, have the remnants of fine hairs. Hair or fur can also form touch-sensitive whiskers, known as vibrissae.

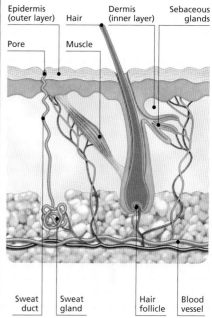

Epidermis (outer layer) Hair Dermis (inner layer) Sebaceous glands

Pore Muscle

Sweat duct Sweat gland Hair follicle Blood vessel

CROSS SECTION OF SKIN

The Arctic fox's thick, snow-white coat enables it to survive bitter winters and camouflages it from prey.

Blackbucks' legs are extended to form slender limbs with hooves. This allows them to run and to leap away from predators.

HOW MAMMALS REPRODUCE

There are three different kinds of mammals: monotremes, marsupials, and placental mammals. The eggs of all mammals are fertilized inside the female's body by sperm from the male. Monotremes—echidnas and the platypus—are the only mammals that lay eggs. They lay soft-shelled eggs just a few days after mating. These are kept warm by the mother until they hatch. Marsupials, such as kangaroos and opossums, give birth to live young that are poorly developed. The young complete their early growth inside a pouch of skin on the outside of their mother's body, where they suck her milk. For this reason, marsupials are sometimes called pouched mammals.

The young of placental mammals feed inside their mother's body through an organ called a placenta for a much longer period of time compared to marsupials. This time is known as gestation and varies in length between different species. Large elephants have a gestation time of about 22 months. Some tiny rodents have a gestation time of less than three weeks. Because they spend longer inside their mothers, placental mammals are far more developed than marsupials when they are born.

Male giraffes mate with as many females as they can during the breeding season.

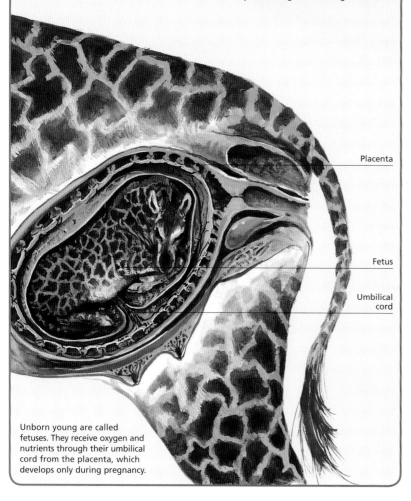

Unborn young are called fetuses. They receive oxygen and nutrients through their umbilical cord from the placenta, which develops only during pregnancy.

Placenta

Fetus

Umbilical cord

RAISING YOUNG

A parent's care is critical to the survival of young mammals after birth.

At first, most mammal babies feed only on milk from their mother's teats.

PREDATORS AND PREY

Predators hunt other animals for food. The animals they hunt are called their prey. Mammals have adapted in many ways to hunt, and to avoid being hunted and eaten themselves. This lion uses its strength and speed in a sprint to catch a gazelle. The smaller and lighter gazelle relies on endurance to outrun the easily tired lion.

Claws for grasping prey

Sideways-facing eyes for 180° vision

Slender back legs for power without weight

Toes modified into hooves for greater speed when running

MAMMAL BEHAVIOR

Male elephant seals, who fight for breeding territory, are larger than females.

Male gray wolves fight to establish dominance; the winners earn the right to mate.

Forward-facing eyes for sight in three dimensions

Sea otters are social mammals that live mostly in separate male and female groups, known as rafts.

Heavily muscled back legs for rapid acceleration

Male hippopotamuses are aggressive creatures that fight viciously over territory. They slash and bite each other with their teeth. Sometimes these bites are fatal.

For young Alaskan brown bear cubs, play is a way to practice skills needed for survival as adults.

1 ORDER • 2 FAMILIES • 3 GENERA • 3 SPECIES

Monotremes

Monotremes are an order of mammals that are similar to reptiles in some ways. They have a cloaca, an organ that is used to get rid of body waste as well as to reproduce, and they lay eggs. Monotremes ooze milk for their young from patches of skin on their abdomen. Only three monotreme species survive: the platypus and the short-nosed and long-nosed echidnas. Both platypuses and echidnas have a lower body temperature than other mammals, and echidnas hibernate in winter. Male platypuses and echidnas have a long spur on each back leg. The platypus's spur is poisonous—males use it to fight each other. Special organs in the rubbery skin of the platypus's bill can detect the electrical activity of shrimp, freshwater crabs, and other invertebrate prey in the water. Echidnas may also be able to sense their prey in this way.

Long-nosed echidna
Zaglossus bruijni
Tiny spines on its tongue help capture earthworms.

BIRTH CHAMBER
Female platypuses build nesting burrows in river banks, where they lay their eggs.

Short-nosed echidna
Tachyglossus aculeatus
Each spine is an individual hair. Its snout can be used like a snorkel so it can breathe when crossing water.

Echidnas eat termites, ants, or grubs.

Claws are strong enough to break into termite nests.

Long, sticky tongue

Platypus
Ornithorhynchus anatinus
Fat is stored in its broad tail. Partially webbed back feet are used as rudders.

CONSERVATION WATCH

Of the three species of monotremes, one appears on the IUCN Red List. The long-nosed echidna is listed as endangered; only 300,000 remain in the wild. They are hunted by humans for food and are threatened by habitat loss.

Ex		0
Cr		0
En		1
Vu		0
Other		0

Long-nosed echidna

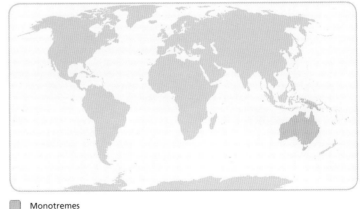

☐ Monotremes

The platypus lives in eastern Australia. The short-nosed echidna is found across Australia and the New Guinea lowlands, while its larger relative lives in the New Guinea highlands.

7 ORDERS • 19 FAMILIES • 83 GENERA • 295 SPECIES

Marsupials

All marsupials are born in an extremely immature state. Their gestation time can be as few as 9 days for the eastern quoll or as many as 38 days for the eastern gray kangaroo. They weigh only a few milligrams when they are born. Young marsupials then usually develop in a pouch or fold of skin, feeding on their mother's milk. This method of reproducing and raising young is the main difference between marsupials and placental mammals. Marsupials were once widespread across the Americas and Europe, as well as in Australia. Today, only 70 species of marsupials still survive in the Americas—opossums, shrew-opossums, and the monito del monte.

Ecuadorean shrew-opossum
Caenolestes fuliginosus

Monito del monte (colocolo)
Dromiciops gliroides
It uses bamboo leaves, moss, and twigs to build a round nest, where it may hibernate in winter.

Common opossum
Didelphis marsupialis
After living in her pouch for two months, young are carried on mother's back until they are three to four months old.

Little water opossum
Lutreolina crassicaudata
This opossum's thick tail has a hairless tip.

Patagonian opossum
Lestodelphys halli

Robinson's mouse opossum
Marmosa robinsoni
Opposable thumbs on all four paws help grip thin branches and vines.

Southern short-tailed opossum
Monodelphis dimidiata

Yapok (water opossum)
Chironectes minimus
The only aquatic marsupial, the yapok has webbed toes and oily fur.

Marsupials

Some marsupials occur in the Americas, but most are native only to Australia and New Guinea. They have been introduced to the islands of New Zealand, Hawaii, and Britain.

STARTING OUT

A newborn is little more than an embryo when it emerges from its mother's cloaca.

Using strong front legs, it crawls upward through its mother's hair toward her pouch.

The newborn attaches firmly to a teat in the pouch for weeks or months of rapid growth.

Possums and kangaroos

Possums and kangaroos belong to a large order of marsupials called diprotodonts that also includes wombats and the koala. Diprotodonts all have two large, protruding incisor teeth on the lower jaw. They are found only in the Australasian region. Most are grass- or leaf-eaters, but some possums eat insects or nectar. Very few species in this group are diurnal, or active during daylight hours, preferring to feed at twilight or at night. The largest living member of the group is also the largest marsupial—the male red kangaroo can reach heights of 4½ feet (1.5 m) and weights of 190 pounds (85 kg). Most kangaroos and wallabies move by hopping on well-developed back legs, although the tree kangaroos of northern Australia and New Guinea climb trees. Possums are mostly tree dwellers.

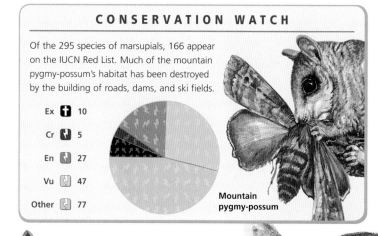

CONSERVATION WATCH

Of the 295 species of marsupials, 166 appear on the IUCN Red List. Much of the mountain pygmy-possum's habitat has been destroyed by the building of roads, dams, and ski fields.

Ex	✝	10
Cr		5
En		27
Vu		47
Other		77

Mountain pygmy-possum

▶ **Yellow-footed rock wallaby**
Petrogale xanthopus
Back feet have roughened soles for clinging to rocks.

◀ **Common wombat**
Vombatus ursinus

▶ **Goodfellow's tree kangaroo**
Dendrolagus goodfellowi
Has strong front legs for climbing trees

BOXING KANGAROOS

Male red kangaroos attempt to dominate others during the breeding season.

Front legs deliver scratches to the face and upper body.

The strong tail is used for balance.

Powerful back legs kick the opponent.

▲ **Red kangaroo**
Macropus rufus
This marsupial is active mainly at twilight or nighttime.

◀ **Western gray kangaroo**
Macropus fuliginosus
These kangaroos often form social groups, called mobs, which usually consist of related family members.

▶ **Rufous bettong**
Aepyprymnus rufescens

Common ringtail possum
Pseudocheirus peregrinus

Herbert River ringtail possum
Pseudochirulus herbertensis
This possum rarely leaves the safety of the trees for the ground.

Koala
Phascolarctos cinereus
Their diet of eucalyptus leaves is low in nutrients, but high in toxins. Koalas need to sleep 20 hours a day.

Striped possum
Dactylopsila trivirgata

Leadbeater's possum
Gymnobelideus leadbeateri
One of the most isolated marsupials: Its range is only 1,350 square miles (3,500 km²).

Musky rat-kangaroo
Hypsiprymnodon moschatus

Brushtail possum
Trichosurus vulpecula
This possum was once hunted for its fur; it is now a protected species in Australia.

Sugar glider
Petaurus breviceps
Each back foot has an opposable big toe.

Spotted cuscus
Spilocuscus maculatus

Feathertail glider
Acrobates pygmaeus
The feather-like fur on its tail acts as a rudder when gliding. A gliding membrane extends from wrist to knee.

Mountain pygmy-possum
Burramys parvus

Scaly-tailed possum
Wyulda squamicaudata

SIMILAR SOLUTIONS

Like the aye-aye of Madagascar, the Australian striped possum has a long, narrow finger for hooking grubs out of tree holes.

STRIPED POSSUM

AYE-AYE

Bandicoots and quolls

Some marsupials, including the catlike quolls and the Tasmanian devil, are meat-eaters. The dog-size thylacine was the largest member of this order. It was hunted into extinction in the early 1900s. These marsupials have different teeth from those of the plant-eating kangaroos and possums, because they capture other animals, tear flesh, and gnaw bone. The smaller dunnarts, phascogales, and antechinuses hunt mostly insects. In a separate order are the omnivorous bandicoots, which eat both plants and animals. They are often solitary creatures. Some species dig pits in their search for food. Marsupial moles burrow just underground for invertebrates. Unlike true moles, they leave no tunnels.

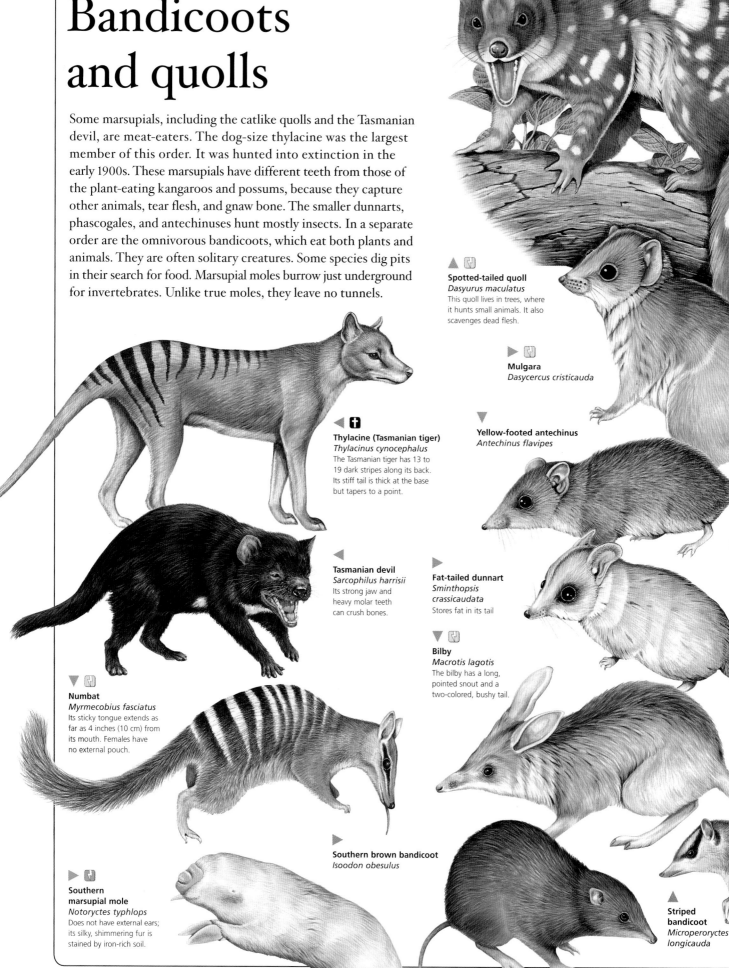

Spotted-tailed quoll
Dasyurus maculatus
This quoll lives in trees, where it hunts small animals. It also scavenges dead flesh.

Mulgara
Dasycercus cristicauda

Yellow-footed antechinus
Antechinus flavipes

Thylacine (Tasmanian tiger)
Thylacinus cynocephalus
The Tasmanian tiger has 13 to 19 dark stripes along its back. Its stiff tail is thick at the base but tapers to a point.

Tasmanian devil
Sarcophilus harrisii
Its strong jaw and heavy molar teeth can crush bones.

Fat-tailed dunnart
Sminthopsis crassicauda
Stores fat in its tail

Bilby
Macrotis lagotis
The bilby has a long, pointed snout and a two-colored, bushy tail.

Numbat
Myrmecobius fasciatus
Its sticky tongue extends as far as 4 inches (10 cm) from its mouth. Females have no external pouch.

Southern brown bandicoot
Isoodon obesulus

Southern marsupial mole
Notoryctes typhlops
Does not have external ears; its silky, shimmering fur is stained by iron-rich soil.

Striped bandicoot
Microperoryctes longicauda

2 ORDERS • 5 FAMILIES • 14 GENERA • 36 SPECIES

Anteaters and Pangolins

Anteaters, armadillos, and sloths are an order of placental mammals with small brains and few, or no, teeth. They have extra backbone joints that strengthen the lower back and hips. This is especially useful for diggers like anteaters and armadillos. Anteaters are toothless insect-eaters with a preference for termites, which they lap up with a long, sticky tongue. Armadillos also have sticky tongues for picking up insects, but most eat plants. They are powerful diggers and swimmers with a protective shell of large bony scales that extends over their backs. Sloths are known for their extremely sluggish movements, caused by their low-energy diet of leaves. Pangolins form their own order. They resemble armadillos with their armor of overlapping horny plates. Their tongue can be longer than the combined length of their head and body.

Pale-throated three-toed sloth
Bradypus tridactylus
Moths and beetles live in its shaggy fur.

Maned three-toed sloth
Bradypus torquatus

Collared anteater (tamandua)
Tamandua sp.

Giant anteater
Myrmecophaga tridactyla
Young may ride on mother's back for up to a year.

Southern three-banded armadillo
Tolypeutes matacus
Curls into a tight ball to defend itself from predators

Giant ground pangolin
Manis gigantea
Overlapping scales cover its entire body except for its underside.

Larger hairy armadillo
Chaetophractus villosus

CONSERVATION WATCH

Of the 36 species of anteaters, armadillos, sloths, and pangolins, 20 appear on the IUCN Red List. The lesser fairy armadillo, which lives in the grasslands of Argentina, is endangered. Much of its habitat has been lost because of increased agriculture, and many have been killed by domestic dogs.

Ex	✝	0
Cr		0
En		3
Vu		5
Other		12

Lesser fairy armadillo

☐ Pangolins   ☐ Anteaters, sloths, and armadillos

Anteaters, sloths, and armadillos are found in the Americas, particularly South America. Three pangolin species occur in southern Asia, while the other four live in Africa.

1 ORDER • 7 FAMILIES • 68 GENERA • 428 SPECIES

Insect-eating Mammals

Many of the earliest mammals were probably insect-eaters, or insectivores. Modern insect-eating mammals feed almost exclusively on insects and other small invertebrates. Some will also eat plants and even small fish and lizards, if they get the chance. The order includes shrews, tenrecs, hedgehogs, and moles. Insectivores have small, smooth brains and simple teeth that are primitive compared to those of other mammal groups. They are small, shy creatures, active only at night. While most live at ground level, some shrews and moles prefer the water. Most of them are small with long snouts and well-developed senses of smell and touch. Their vision is often poor—burrowing moles, in particular, can see little through their tiny eyes. Hedgehogs and some tenrecs have spines along their upper bodies to protect them from predators.

Himalayan water shrew
Chimarrogale himalayica

Eurasian common shrew
Sorex araneus

Elegant water shrew
Nectogale elegans
Has webbed feet with sticky pads for swimming and climbing on wet rocks

Giant otter shrew
Potamogale velox
Nostrils, eyes, and ears stay above the water's surface while its body is submerged. It locates prey using sensitive whiskers.

Mindanao moonrat
Podogymnura truei

Western European hedgehog
Erinaceus europaeus
This hedgehog raises its sharp spines when threatened. Its belly is covered with soft fur.

Cuban solenodon
Solenodon cubanus
Strong claws dig insects, worms, and small lizards out of leaf litter.

Hottentot golden mole
Amblysomus hottentotus
The horny pad on its nose and clawed toes on its front paws help this mole build tunnels.

European mole
Talpa europaea

CONSERVATION WATCH

Of the 428 species of insectivores, 173 appear on the IUCN Red List. This figure includes one of the world's rarest animals, South Africa's giant golden mole. The Ruwenzori otter shrew lives in rivers and streams around the Congo Basin in Africa. It is endangered because these streams are becoming polluted by waste and sewage as more humans settle in the area.

Ex ✝ 5
Cr 22
En 48
Vu 54
Other 44

Ruwenzori otter shrew

Insect-eating mammals

Hedgehogs, moonrats, moles, desmans, and shrews can be found throughout much of the world. Solenodons, tenrecs, and otter shrews live in more limited ranges.

2 ORDERS • 2 FAMILIES • 6 GENERA • 21 SPECIES

Flying Lemurs and Tree Shrews

There are just two living species of flying lemurs. Also known as colugos, both are leaf-eating tree dwellers that are active at night. They are small animals, with adults reaching as much as 4½ pounds (2 kg) in weight. Flying lemurs have a thin, but tough, membrane of skin that stretches between their front and back legs. They do not fly, but glide as far as 300 feet (91 m) between trees. Grace in the air does not equal grace on the ground, however; flying lemurs are clumsy and helpless walkers. Most of the 19 tree shrew species live in trees, scampering up and down in their search for small animals and fruit. They are active, territorial, and noisy creatures that look a little like squirrels. Although they are not related to squirrels, tree shrews have the same ability to hold food in their front paws while sitting up on their haunches.

FLYING LIKE A KITE

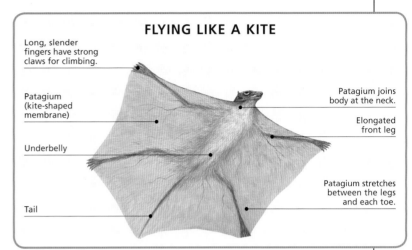

Long, slender fingers have strong claws for climbing.

Patagium (kite-shaped membrane)

Underbelly

Tail

Patagium joins body at the neck.

Elongated front leg

Patagium stretches between the legs and each toe.

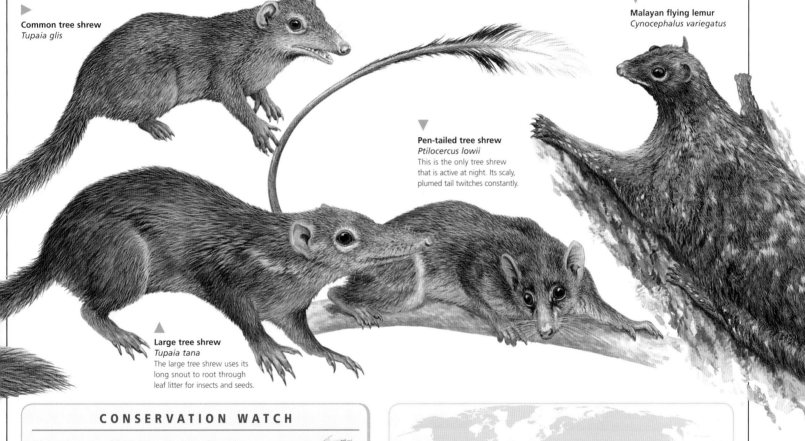

Common tree shrew
Tupaia glis

Malayan flying lemur
Cynocephalus variegatus

Pen-tailed tree shrew
Ptilocercus lowii
This is the only tree shrew that is active at night. Its scaly, plumed tail twitches constantly.

Large tree shrew
Tupaia tana
The large tree shrew uses its long snout to root through leaf litter for insects and seeds.

CONSERVATION WATCH

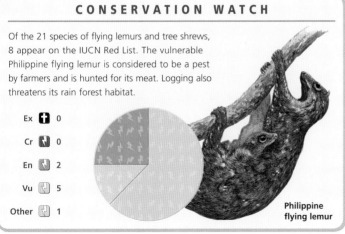

Of the 21 species of flying lemurs and tree shrews, 8 appear on the IUCN Red List. The vulnerable Philippine flying lemur is considered to be a pest by farmers and is hunted for its meat. Logging also threatens its rain forest habitat.

Ex	🐾	0
Cr	🐾	0
En	🐾	2
Vu	🐾	5
Other	🐾	1

Philippine flying lemur

☐ Tree shrews   ☐ Flying lemurs and tree shrews

Flying lemurs and tree shrews are found only in the tropical forests of southern and Southeast Asia. Most tree shrews live on the Indonesian island of Borneo.

1 ORDER • 18 FAMILIES • 177 GENERA • 993 SPECIES

Bats

Bats are the only mammals that can truly fly. They probably evolved from tree-dwelling ancestors that moved between high branches, first by leaping and later by gliding. Their wings are more flexible than those of birds, allowing more agility in flight. Bats form the second largest order of mammals; the group contains one-quarter of all mammal species. The smallest is the tiny Thai hog-nosed bat, also called the bumblebee bat. Its skull measures less than ½ inch (10 cm) across and its wingspan is 6 inches (15 cm). The largest bat is the Malayan flying fox, with a wingspan of almost 80 inches (2 m). There are two kinds of bats: the fruit bats, or flying foxes, and the microbats, most of which eat insects. Both groups of bats are usually social animals that live in colonies. Females may form special nursery colonies, where they roost and raise their young away from males and nonpregnant females.

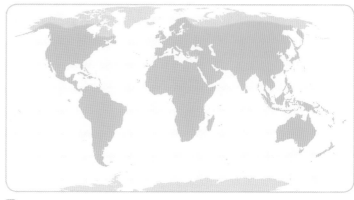

  Bats

Bats occur in all regions of the world except for the polar regions and a few isolated islands. They are most common in warmer areas, especially the tropics.

ROOSTING BATS

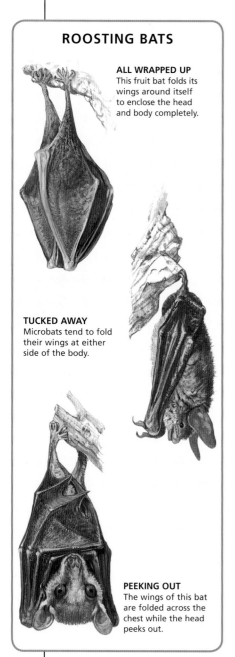

ALL WRAPPED UP
This fruit bat folds its wings around itself to enclose the head and body completely.

TUCKED AWAY
Microbats tend to fold their wings at either side of the body.

PEEKING OUT
The wings of this bat are folded across the chest while the head peeks out.

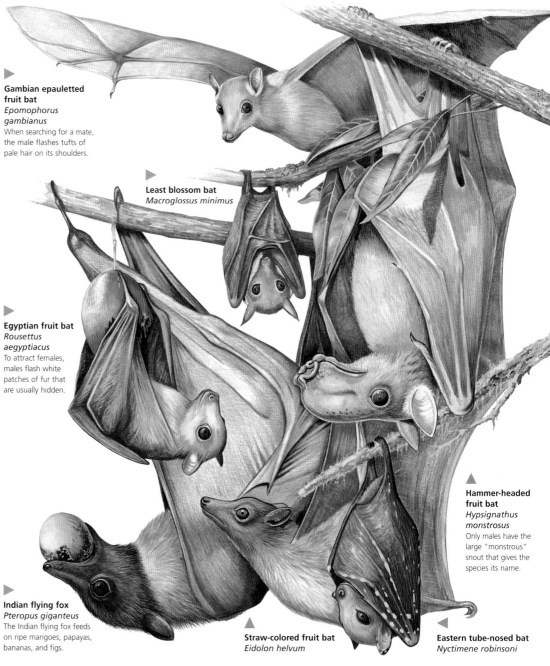

Gambian epauletted fruit bat
Epomophorus gambianus
When searching for a mate, the male flashes tufts of pale hair on its shoulders.

Least blossom bat
Macroglossus minimus

Egyptian fruit bat
Rousettus aegyptiacus
To attract females, males flash white patches of fur that are usually hidden.

Indian flying fox
Pteropus giganteus
The Indian flying fox feeds on ripe mangoes, papayas, bananas, and figs.

Hammer-headed fruit bat
Hypsignathus monstrosus
Only males have the large "monstrous" snout that gives the species its name.

Straw-colored fruit bat
Eidolon helvum

Eastern tube-nosed bat
Nyctimene robinsoni

SIGHT AND SOUND

ECHOLOCATION

Fruit bats rely on vision to get around. Microbats "see" by using a radar-like sense called echolocation. This enables many species to hunt in the dark. They send out high-pitched sounds, then assess what surrounds them by judging the echoes that bounce back off solid objects, such as insect bodies.

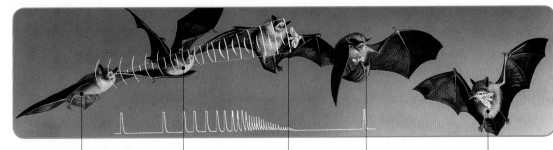

Bat emits rapid, high-pitched clicks of sound.

The clicks bounce off prey, revealing its location to the bat.

Frequency of clicks increases as it nears, pinpointing prey.

The bat seizes prey in its back claws.

The prey is then transferred to the bat's mouth.

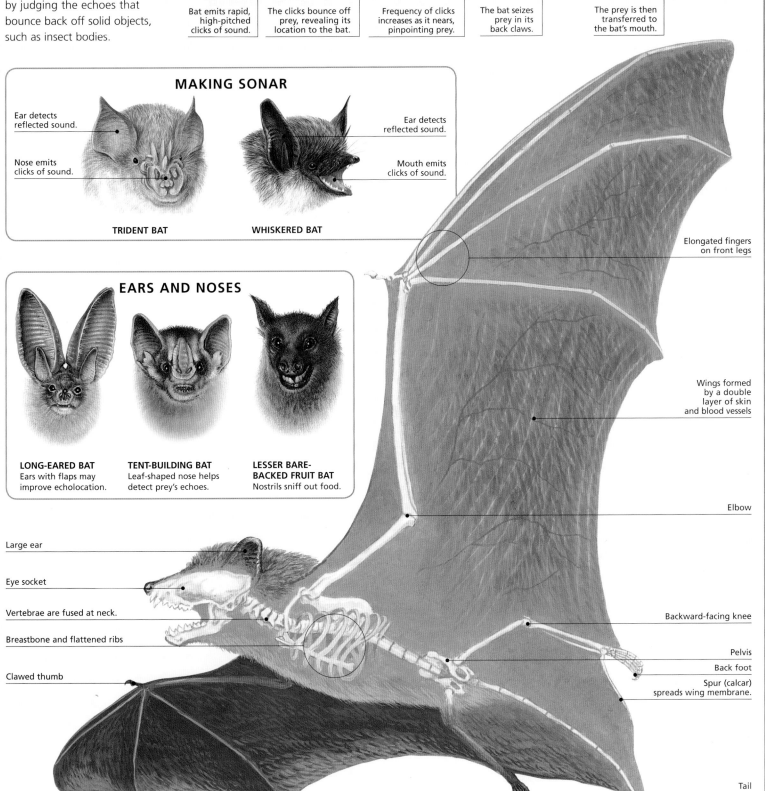

MAKING SONAR

Ear detects reflected sound.

Nose emits clicks of sound.

TRIDENT BAT

Ear detects reflected sound.

Mouth emits clicks of sound.

WHISKERED BAT

EARS AND NOSES

LONG-EARED BAT
Ears with flaps may improve echolocation.

TENT-BUILDING BAT
Leaf-shaped nose helps detect prey's echoes.

LESSER BARE-BACKED FRUIT BAT
Nostrils sniff out food.

Elongated fingers on front legs

Wings formed by a double layer of skin and blood vessels

Elbow

Large ear

Eye socket

Vertebrae are fused at neck.

Breastbone and flattened ribs

Clawed thumb

Backward-facing knee

Pelvis

Back foot

Spur (calcar) spreads wing membrane.

Tail

Microbats

The majority of bats are microbats. All use echolocation to find and capture their food. Most species eat flying insects that they pursue and capture on the wing at night. However, some of the larger species are meat-eaters, hunting small vertebrates such as fish, frogs, birds, lizards, and rodents. Others eat fruit, nectar, or flowers. Three species survive by lapping up fresh blood. As their name suggests, microbats tend to be smaller than fruit bats, with most reaching a body length of less than 6 inches (15 cm) when fully grown. Because they rely on echolocation, their eyes are usually small and ears more developed. The faces of some microbats are adorned with noseleaves, leaf-shaped flaps of skin and tissue that may help them find food.

▶

Wrinkle-faced bat
Centurio senex
This bat has strange-looking folds of skin around its face.

▲

Pocketed free-tailed bat
Nyctinomops femorosaccus
Its thick tail extends beyond the wing membrane.

▲

Diadem leaf-nosed bat
Hipposideros diadema

▲

Common vampire bat
Desmodus rotundus
Modified thumbs and back legs let it move on all fours as it hunts.

▲

American false vampire bat
Vampyrum spectrum

HONDURAN WHITE BATS

These small Central American fruit-eaters cut large leaves with their teeth in such a way that the leaves flop over to form protective "tents." Small colonies of as many as six bats shelter from heavy tropical downpours in these tents. When the sun shines through the rain forest leaves, the bats' soft white fur reflects the green light. This makes them appear almost invisible. At least 14 other bat species make leaf tents.

Veins of heliconia leaf are nibbled along the stem, making it flop over.

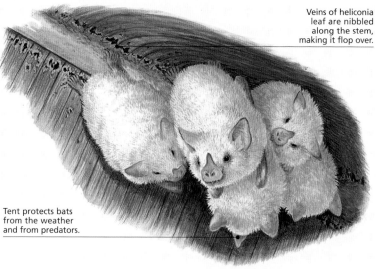

Tent protects bats from the weather and from predators.

▶

Greater bulldog bat
Noctilio leporinus
Long back legs with huge feet and strong claws snatch fish from the water. Cheek pouches store chewed fish so it can continue fishing.

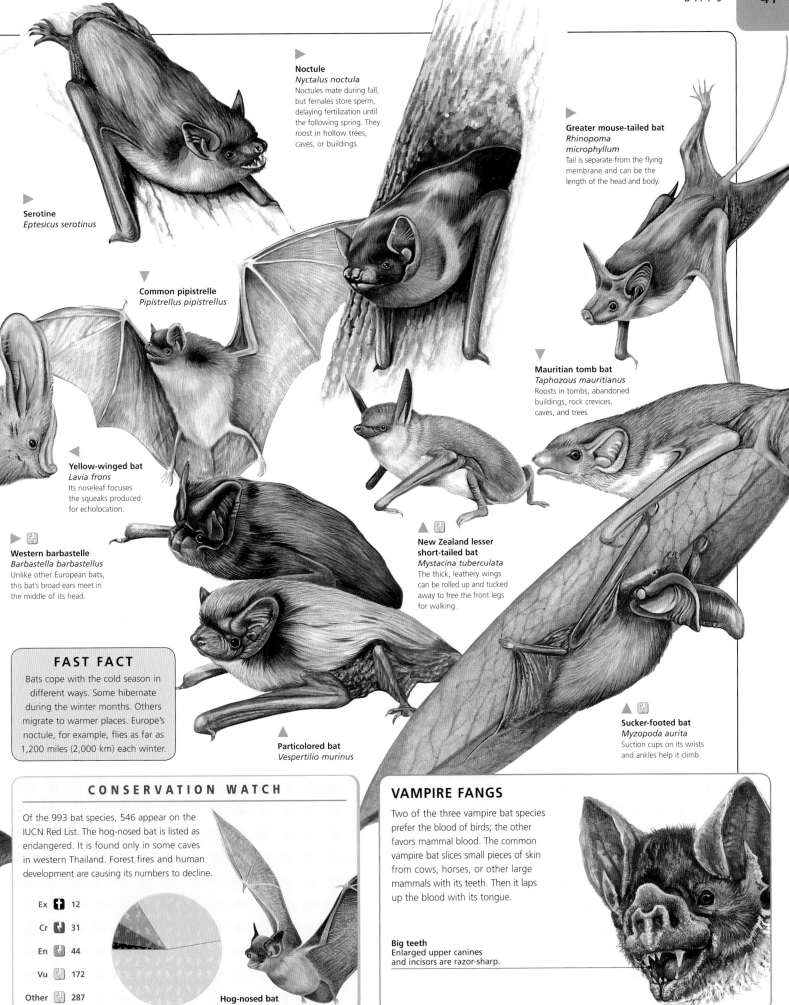

Serotine
Eptesicus serotinus

Noctule
Nyctalus noctula
Noctules mate during fall, but females store sperm, delaying fertilization until the following spring. They roost in hollow trees, caves, or buildings.

Greater mouse-tailed bat
Rhinopoma microphyllum
Tail is separate from the flying membrane and can be the length of the head and body.

Common pipistrelle
Pipistrellus pipistrellus

Mauritian tomb bat
Taphozous mauritianus
Roosts in tombs, abandoned buildings, rock crevices, caves, and trees

Yellow-winged bat
Lavia frons
Its noseleaf focuses the squeaks produced for echolocation.

Western barbastelle
Barbastella barbastellus
Unlike other European bats, this bat's broad ears meet in the middle of its head.

New Zealand lesser short-tailed bat
Mystacina tuberculata
The thick, leathery wings can be rolled up and tucked away to free the front legs for walking.

Sucker-footed bat
Myzopoda aurita
Suction cups on its wrists and ankles help it climb.

Particolored bat
Vespertilio murinus

FAST FACT

Bats cope with the cold season in different ways. Some hibernate during the winter months. Others migrate to warmer places. Europe's noctule, for example, flies as far as 1,200 miles (2,000 km) each winter.

CONSERVATION WATCH

Of the 993 bat species, 546 appear on the IUCN Red List. The hog-nosed bat is listed as endangered. It is found only in some caves in western Thailand. Forest fires and human development are causing its numbers to decline.

Ex	✝	12
Cr		31
En		44
Vu		172
Other		287

Hog-nosed bat

VAMPIRE FANGS

Two of the three vampire bat species prefer the blood of birds; the other favors mammal blood. The common vampire bat slices small pieces of skin from cows, horses, or other large mammals with its teeth. Then it laps up the blood with its tongue.

Big teeth
Enlarged upper canines and incisors are razor-sharp.

1 ORDER • 13 FAMILIES • 60 GENERA • 295 SPECIES

Primates

Gorillas live in family troops in eastern, central, and west-central Africa. Baby gorillas nurse for as long as 18 months and stay with their mothers for about three years.

rimates are intelligent mammals that live mostly in trees. Their forward-facing eyes let them see in three dimensions and judge distances. Their thumbs are opposable—they can reach around to touch the tips of the other fingers—which lets them hold objects. There are two main groups of primates: lower primates, or prosimians, and higher primates, or monkeys and apes.

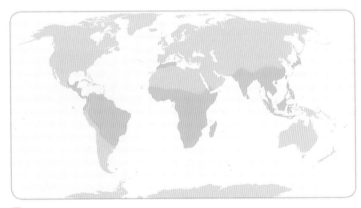

☐ Primates

Most primates live in rain forests, mainly in the tropical and subtropical regions of Africa, Asia, and South America. Only a few live in temperate areas.

PRIMATE FEATURES

UPRIGHT SKELETON
Apes sometimes sit and walk upright. Their arms, which are longer than their legs, help with balance as they walk.

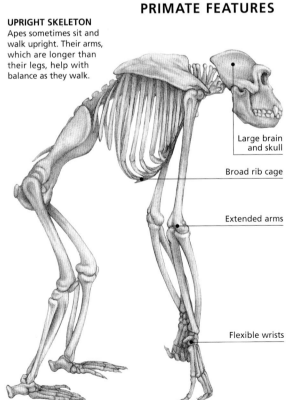

Large brain and skull

Broad rib cage

Extended arms

Flexible wrists

TARSIER
Disklike pads help when climbing trees.

AYE-AYE
Long third digit pulls grubs from holes.

GORILLA
Broad, flat feet (left) support heavy body.

Bushbabies and tarsiers

Bushbabies and tarsiers are lower primates, or prosimians. They have moist, doglike noses and faces covered with hair. Prosimians rely on smell—from their urine, feces, or scent glands—to mark territory and identify each other. Most are small tree dwellers that are nocturnal. They have large eyes to help them see in the dark, but they do not have full-color vision. Prosimians eat mostly insects, but some will also gather fruit, leaves, flowers, nectar, and plant gums. Bushbabies get their name from the childlike wails they make in the middle of the night. Tarsiers are named for the long tarsus bones in their feet.

Eastern needle-clawed bushbaby
Euoticus inustus
Dental comb is used to scrape sap off tree bark.

Potto
Perodicticus potto
Pottos leave messages for each other by giving off different scents.

Spectral tarsier
Tarsius spectrum
Its huge eyes are larger than its stomach.

Slender loris
Loris tardigradus
Enjoys play and wrestling sessions at dawn and dusk

Western tarsier
Tarsius bancanus
Its eyes are too big to move, but its head can rotate in almost a full circle.

Angwantibo (golden potto)
Arctocebus calabarensis

Lesser bushbaby
Galago senegalensis
Can leap as far as 12 feet (3.5 m) in a fraction of a second

Slow loris
Nycticebus coucang

Demidoff's galago
Galagoides demidoff

LOWER PRIMATE FEATURES

Reflective layer at back of eye helps night vision.

Large, pointed "toilet" claw on second finger is used for grooming.

Dental comb

DENTAL COMB
Enlarged front teeth on lower jaw project forward to form a dental "comb" used for grooming others.

Lemurs

Like bushbabies and tarsiers, lemurs are prosimians. Their ancestors once lived throughout Africa, Asia, and Europe, but became extinct because they were unable to compete as more advanced monkeys evolved. More than 50 million years ago, a few floated from the mainland of Africa on bits of wood and vegetation to Madagascar. About 50 species of lemurs currently live on Madagascar. The name lemur comes from the Latin word for "ghost," which suits their haunting stares and eerie nighttime cries. Most species live in eastern Madagascar's wet and monsoonal forests and eat fruit, leaves, insects, and small animals such as lizards. Eagles and hawks sometimes take young lemurs that stray. Adults and infants are hunted also by a catlike carnivore called the fossa.

CONSERVATION WATCH

Of the 63 species of prosimians, 49 appear on the IUCN Red List. The endangered aye-aye is threatened by the destruction of its forest home.

Ex	✝	0
Cr		3
En		9
Vu		11
Other		26

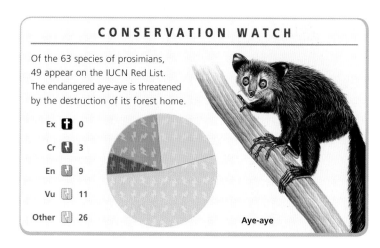

Aye-aye

Indri
Indri indri
The indri has large, black, tufted ears and a short tail.

Aye-aye
Daubentonia madagascariensis
The aye-aye uses echolocation to find grubs.

Brown lemur
Eulemur fulvus

Weasel sportive lem
Lepilemur mustelinu
Makes giant leaps on its strong back legs

Coquerel's dwarf lemur
Microcebus coquereli
Babies purr softly when licked by their mothers.

Ruffed lemur
Varecia variegata
Adult coat may be black and red or black and white. Mothers make nests in the trees where they can watch for predators.

Fork-marked lemur
Phaner furcifer
The fork-marked lemur eats tree sap that seeps out of insect holes.

FAST FACT

Lemurs communicate by smell. They have scent glands on their bottoms, feet, and sometimes arms, and leave smelly messages on every surface they pass to let other lemurs know they were there.

Diadem sifaka
Propithecus diadema

LEMURS OF MADAGASCAR

RING-TAILED LEMUR TROOP

Ring-tailed lemurs live in troops of as many as 30. Their distinctive tails are held high when traveling so all members can stay in contact. These lemurs prefer dry, rocky outcrops and spend half their time on the ground, more than any other lemur. They may sunbathe to warm up after a cold night. Females are dominant over males, unusual behavior for primates.

Tails always have 13 black and 13 white stripes.

They eat fruit, but sometimes flowers, sap, leaves, and occasionally insects.

Scent from wrist glands is rubbed on tails and thrown at opponents during "stink fights" over territory.

RED-TAILED SPORTIVE LEMUR
These nocturnal, tree-dwelling lemurs eat mainly leaves. They consume their own feces to aid digestion. Females carry young babies in their mouths.

INDRI
Indris may spring as high as 30 feet (9 m) in a single leap to reach a tree branch. Females feed in higher branches than males, where there is more food.

RED-BELLIED LEMUR
These lemurs form faithful bonds with just one mate. Pairs and as many as three offspring live together in family groups. Females are smaller than, but dominant over, males.

VERREAUX'S SIFAKA
These sifakas live in Madagascar's western dry forests. They hop and skip on their back legs when on the ground, possibly using small skin flaps on their arms to glide.

New World monkeys

There are two groups of monkeys—the New World and the Old World monkeys. New World monkeys are found in the tropical rain forests of Central and South America and as far north as Mexico. They include the spider, howler, and squirrel monkeys, as well as the tamarins, marmosets, and uakaris. All have broad, flat noses; nostrils that face sideways; and a distinctive arrangement of teeth. Many have a prehensile tail, which works like an extra limb. Most New World monkeys are diurnal and spend their lives in trees eating leaves, fruit, nuts, and other parts of plants. Some will also eat insects or small animals, such as lizards or baby birds. New World monkeys can live alone, in small bands or mating pairs, harems, family groups, or in troops of as many as 500 members.

Common woolly monkey
Lagothrix lagotricha

**Long-haired
spider monkey**
Ateles belzebuth
Thumbless fingers work together
like a hook for swinging.

Woolly spider mon
Brachyteles arachn
Likes to eat leaves whil
hanging only by its tai

Black howler
Alouatta caraya
Produces deep growls so loud
they can be heard more than
2 miles (3 km) away

White-faced saki
Pithecia pithecia
Long back legs let it leap
30 feet (9 m) between trees.

Golden lion tamarin
Leontopithecus rosalia
Sleeps in tree holes, such as
abandoned woodpecker nests

Mantled howler
Alouatta palliata

Geoffroy's tamarin
Saguinus geoffroy
Twins are common, an
males help to care fo
and carry the babies o
the whole troop.

Black-headed uakari
Cacajao melanocephalus

EXPERT SWINGERS

Spider monkeys rely on their prehensile tails for swooping through the treetops. The tail grasps tree branches like an extra arm or leg and helps spider monkey babies stay on their swinging mothers.

▶ **Common squirrel monkey**
Saimiri sciureus
Females give birth in the rainy season, when there is more food.

▶ **Northern
night monkey**
*Aotus
trivirgatus*
Large eyes help
this monkey see
at night.

ny
oset
hrix
naea

y titi
cebus moloch
s form strong,
g bonds with
e mate.

NEW AND OLD DIFFERENCES

NEW WORLD
Woolly monkey

OLD WORLD
Vervet monkey

Nostrils are close
together and
point downward.

Most have a grasping,
prehensile tail that works
like an extra limb.

Thumbs on both
limbs are highly
opposable—they
help grasp and
hold objects.

Broad flat noses
with sideways-
facing nostrils

Tail, if present,
is not prehensile.

Thumbs, when present,
are not highly opposable
to other fingers.

▲ **Common marmoset**
Callithrix jacchus

▲ **Brown capuchin**
Cebus apella

Old World monkeys

Old World monkeys are found only in Africa and Asia, aside from the Barbary ape, which was introduced to Gibraltar in Europe. All Old World monkeys have protruding nostrils that face downward. While these monkeys lack prehensile tails—a few lack tails entirely—they have strong hands with opposable thumbs that let them pick up objects precisely. Some have thick pads of bare skin called ischial callosities on their bottoms. Most species live in trees, but many forage on the ground. Old World monkeys are divided into two groups. The first group, including baboons, has cheek pouches in which they store their food while they are out in the open, so they can eat in safety. The second group, including colobuses, has a three-chambered stomach, which helps them fully digest their diet of plants.

CONSERVATION WATCH

Of the 214 species of monkeys, 119 appear on the IUCN Red List. The lion-tailed macaque, of India, survives in forest fragments, which are threatened by clearing.

Ex	0
Cr	14
En	32
Vu	32
Other	41

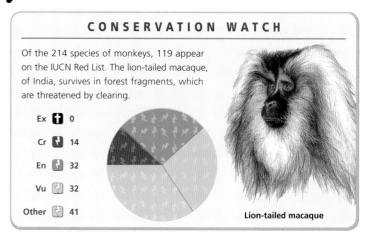

Lion-tailed macaque

Gelada
Theropithecus gelada

Hamadryas baboon (savanna baboon)
Papio hamadryas
As many as 750 animals sleep collectively for protection from predators. Bands of 100 animals travel and forage together.

Sykes's monkey (blue monkey)
Cercopithecus mitis
Coat is usually red-brown or gray-brown, but is sometimes blue.

Proboscis monkey
Nasalis larvatus
Big nose on males helps make their calls louder.

Barbary ape
Macaca sylvanus
Unusual among macaques because males help to raise young.

Allen's swamp monkey
Allenopithecus nigroviridis

Red colobus
Procolobus badius

**Chinese
snub-nosed monkey**
*Rhinopithecus
roxellana*
Lives in mountains more
than 14,500 feet (4,400 m)
above sea level

Douc langur
Pygathrix nemaeus

**Bear macaque
(stump-tailed macaque)**
Macaca arctoides
Bear macaques go bald
as they get old.

Hanuman langur
*Semnopithecus
entellus*
Considered sacred in
India; lives in troops
of 20 or 30, often
with a single male

**Vervet
monkey**
*Chlorocebus
aethiops*

**Redtail
monkey**
*Cercopithecus
ascanius*
Greet each other
before playing
or grooming by
rubbing noses

King colobus
*Colobus
polykomos*
Babies are white
for the first few
months of life.

White-cheeked mangabey
Lophocebus albigena
These monkeys make a high-
pitched chuckle when alarmed.

ill
illus

GRASS-EATING GELADAS

Geladas are the lawn mowers of the primate world—they eat almost nothing but
grass. They live only in Ethiopia, in eastern Africa, in groups of as many as 400. Fatty
padding on their bottoms allows them to sit eating for long periods each day. Their
thumbs and index fingers work together like pairs of tweezers, picking at single blades
of grass. Females also spend a lot of time grooming each other and ignoring the males.
Both sexes have a hairless, hourglass-shaped skin patch on the chest. This is always
bright red in adult males and is meant to be attractive to females while scaring off
other males. This patch only turns red in females when they are ready to mate.

Apes

Apes are the most intelligent primates. They are social animals that spend years looking after their young. While they have similar teeth and noses to Old World monkeys, apes have many different features. They can sit or stand upright, and have shorter spines, barrel chests, and no tail. Their arms are longer than their legs, and their shoulders and wrists are highly mobile. There are two families of apes. The chimpanzee, bonobo, and gorillas of Africa, and the orangutan of Asia are the great apes. The gibbons of Asia are the lesser apes. The two evolved into separate groups about 20 million years ago. The great apes are our closest relatives. They can solve problems with logic and recognize themselves in a mirror. Chimpanzees and orangutans use tools; gorillas have been taught sign language.

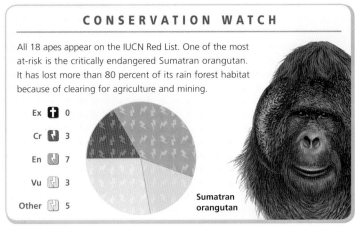

CONSERVATION WATCH

All 18 apes appear on the IUCN Red List. One of the most at-risk is the critically endangered Sumatran orangutan. It has lost more than 80 percent of its rain forest habitat because of clearing for agriculture and mining.

Ex   0
Cr   3
En   7
Vu   3
Other   5

Sumatran orangutan

◀
Chimpanzee
Pan troglodytes
Chimpanzees sometimes hunt monkeys in packs.

◀
Bonobo
Pan paniscus
Young bonobos play games similar to "blind man's bluff."

◀
Mountain gorilla
Gorilla beringei
Under stress, males produce a strong smell from glands in their armpits.

GORILLA SOCIETY

Gorillas live in eastern, central, and west-central Africa. They form family groups that consist of mainly females and their young. At the head of each family group is one large adult male, known as a silverback because of his silvery-white coat markings. He uses his size and aggression to protect his family and will stand upright, slap his chest, and roar to warn other adult male gorillas or predators to stay away.

▲
Western gorilla
Gorilla gorilla

Kloss's gibbon
Hylobates klossii
Its long hands form hooks for grasping branches.

▲ **Lar gibbon**
Hylobates lar

▶ **Hoolock**
Hylobates hoolock
Like humans, young hoolocks stay with their parents until after adolescence.

◀ **Siamang**
Hylobates syndactylus
This is the largest gibbon. When fully inflated, its throat sac is bigger than its head; this makes its calls louder.

▼ **Orangutan**
Pongo pygmaeus

▶ **Black gibbon**
Hylobates concolor
The black gibbon is born with a shiny coat that stays black in males but turns golden in females.

FAST FACT

Gibbons tend to avoid open water. They drink by scooping water in a cupped hand while hanging from a tree. Sometimes they rub their furry hands on wet leaves and suck the water from their fur.

GIBBON SONGS

Gibbons make long, loud calls, or songs. Each species of gibbon has its own songs. They often sing for half an hour first thing in the morning to identify their territory. Male and female pairs may sing complex duets. Such "love songs" probably make these pair bonds stronger.

SKULL COMPARISON

LEMUR SKULL
Lower primate

GORILLA SKULL
Higher primate

HUMAN SKULL
Higher primate

1 ORDER • 11 FAMILIES • 131 GENERA • 278 SPECIES

Carnivores

Brown bears that live in the coastal regions of North America will wait at waterfalls to catch salmon. Salmon hurdle the falls on their way upstream to breed.

Many animals eat meat, but the group of mammals called carnivores (or "meat-eaters") have features designed for hunting and eating other animals. Carnivores have two pairs of sharp-edged carnassial, or slicing, teeth. Their digestive system breaks down food quickly. Most carnivores eat meat; many eat both animals and plants; and some eat no meat at all.

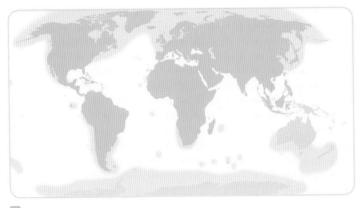

Carnivores

Carnivores can be found worldwide aside from Australia, New Guinea, New Zealand, some islands in the Pacific Ocean, and inland Antarctica.

CARNIVORE FEATURES

Sharp, slicing carnassial teeth shear meat.

Flexible spine provides greater speed and agility.

Long limbs allow for faster running.

Fused wrist bones improve strength.

Short collarbone allows longer strides.

Cats and dogs walk on toes and not sole of foot, unlike other carnivores.

CARNIVORE TEETH
Carnivores' teeth give clues to their diets. Strict meat-eaters have more developed slicing carnassials (red). Grinding molars (blue) are large and flat in those that eat plants.

Cat: eats only meat.

Giant panda: eats no meat.

Dog: eats mostly meat.

Brown bear: eats some meat.

Dogs and foxes

Dogs live on all continents except Antarctica—the dingo was introduced to Australia about 8,000 years ago. All dogs have good eyesight and hearing, as well as a well-developed sense of smell. Dogs eat meat, but some include plant matter, invertebrates, and dead animals in their diets. Members of this family generally live and hunt on open grasslands. Dogs hunt in one of two ways. They either surprise their prey by pouncing on it, or exhaust their prey by pursuing it. Some species, like wolves, hunt together to bring down bigger prey. They live in large social groups. Hunters of smaller prey live in smaller groups. Foxes tend to be slighter than wild dogs and wolves, with shorter limbs and bushier tails. They lead mainly solitary lives. At least one species, the kit fox, lives in burrows.

Gray fox
Urocyon cinereoargenteus
Produces a skunklike odor to mark its territory; strong, hooked claws help it scurry up trees with ease.

Culpeo fox
Pseudalopex culpaeus

Bush dog
Speothos venaticus

Pampas fox
Pseudalopex gymnocercus
Plays dead if threatened by a larger predator

Kit fox
Vulpes macrotis

Tibetan fox
Vulpes ferrilata

Swift fox
Vulpes velox
The swift fox can run faster than 25 miles per hour (40 km/h).

Red fox
North American form
Vulpes vulpes fulva

Pale fox
Vulpes pallida

Crab-eating fox
(common zorro)
Cerdocyon thous

Maned wolf
Chrysocyon brachyurus
When hunting, it taps the ground with its front paw to startle prey, then pounces.

Bengal fox
Vulpes bengalensis

Small-eared zorro
Atelocynus microtis

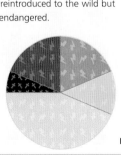

CONSERVATION WATCH

Of the 34 species of dogs and foxes, 16 appear on the IUCN Red List. In 1980, the red wolf was declared extinct in the wild because of hunting. It has since been reintroduced to the wild but remains critically endangered.

Ex	🕆	1
Cr		3
En		3
Vu		2
Other		7

Red wolf

DESIGNED FOR HUNTING

All dogs have elongated, pointed muzzles with large olfactory, or scent, organs. Their excellent sense of smell allows them to track prey over long distances. Large ears stand erect to aid their acute hearing.

Pricked-up ears to pinpoint sound

Forward-facing eyes to perceive depth

Sensitive nose to detect prey

Teeth with shearing edges to slice flesh

Dogs and foxes

Wild dogs and wolves tend to be larger than foxes. Their bodies are built for running, with long limbs and deep, narrow chests. Dogs communicate with each other using scent, posture, facial expressions, and a range of barks, yelps, and howls. They live mostly in groups called packs that have well-organized social structures. There is usually one pack leader, or sometimes a mating pair, that is dominant; the rest are followers that know their rank within the pack. Packs often work together to care for their young and wounded and to defend their territory. The largest packs are among species, such as the Cape wild dogs of southern Africa, that hunt together to bring down large animals. These dogs form packs of as many as 40 members.

Coyote
Canis latrans
The coyote's high-pitched howls carry over long distances. It can breed with wolves and domestic dogs.

Red wolf
Canis rufus
Adult pairs form lifelong bonds.

Cape wild dog
(African wild dog,
African hunting dog)
Lycaon pictus
Each dog has a different coat pattern.

Gray wolf
Scandinavian form
Canis lupus lupus

Gray wolf
Alaskan f
Canis lup
tundrarun
This subspe
gray wolf li
the Arctic o
North Ame
is protected

Arctic fox
Alopex lagopus
The Arctic fox burrows into snow to escape cold Arctic winds. It has a dark summer coat and a white winter coat that blends with the snow.

Ethiopian wolf
(Simien jackal)
Canis simensis
The disease rabies has reduced its numbers.

Bat-eared fox
Otocyon megalotis
Eats mostly insects, such as termites

Raccoon dog
Nyctereutes procyonoides
Puts on extra weight to survive cold winters

Dingo
Canis lupus dingo

COYOTE EXPRESSIONS

SUBMISSIVE   **AGGRESSIVE**   **DEFENSIVE**   **FRIENDLY**   **PLAYFUL**

Black-backed
jackal
Canis mesomelas
Male and female pairs share the care of pups.

DOMESTIC DOGS

TAMING THE BEASTS

Dogs were the first animals to become tame, or be domesticated. The earliest domesticated dogs probably descended from Eurasian gray wolves at least 14,000 years ago. These wolves lingered around villages, scavenging food scraps. Gradually, with successive generations, they lost their fear of the villagers and began living closely with them. Wolves are intelligent, social, and adaptable. Humans were able to influence their behavior by acting like dominant pack members. Those wolves with the most valued characteristics were encouraged to breed together, as were their pups. This selective breeding has resulted in the domestic dogs we see today.

DOG BREEDS

Today there are as many as 800 separate breeds of dogs worldwide. Each was bred originally for particular roles or reasons. Some are intended to work for people. Others have been developed for their companionship. Most dogs have been bred for both reasons.

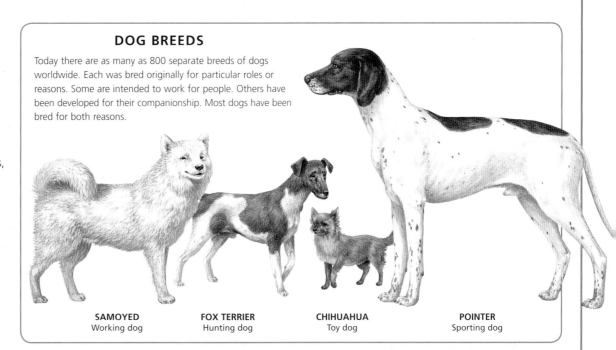

SAMOYED
Working dog

FOX TERRIER
Hunting dog

CHIHUAHUA
Toy dog

POINTER
Sporting dog

Bears

Bears have the reputation of being solidly built, powerful, and ferocious predators. Only the polar bear, however, eats meat almost exclusively. Most bears hunt prey but also forage for food such as fruit, nuts, and leaves. Three-quarters of the European brown bear's diet is plant matter, and China's giant panda eats only bamboo shoots and grass. Smell is the best developed sense in bears, which is why they have large snouts. Their eyes and ears are small. Some bears are found in temperate regions of the Northern Hemisphere. When the weather cools, a few species retreat to dens or caves and sleep for as long as six months, living only on stored body fat. This is not true hibernation but is similar to it. Bears live solitary lives, but cubs stay with their protective mothers until her next pregnancy.

Himalayan brown bear
Ursus arctos isabellinus

European brown bear
Ursus arctos arctos
Can stand up on back legs for long periods; ears are so small they can be hidden by long winter coat.

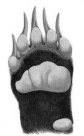

Sun bear
Helarctos malayanus
The sun bear's long tongue laps up honey and insect larvae.

Asiatic black bear
Ursus thibetanus

Sloth bear
Melursus ursinus
Has hair-free lips and a gap in its teeth for sucking up termites; the sound of its slurping can be heard 330 feet (100 m) away.

Giant panda
Ailuropoda melanoleuca
Has a special bone near the thumb of its front paws to grasp bamboo shoots

FAST FACT

All bear cubs are born tiny, defenseless, blind, and deaf, and most are bald. But they grow fast. Polar bear cubs are just 21 ounces (600 g) at birth but are 20 pounds (9 kg) after a few months.

BEAR FEET

Black bears dig up roots with long claws on their front feet (left). They walk flat on their back feet (right). Giant pandas are the only bears with a "thumb" on their front feet (left), which they use to hold bamboo. They also walk on the toes of their back feet (right).

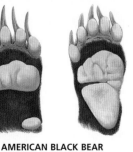

AMERICAN BLACK BEAR

GIANT PANDA

CONSERVATION WATCH

Of the 9 bear species, 7 appear on the IUCN Red List. Fewer than 1,000 giant pandas survive in the wild. Logging and forest clearing are destroying the panda's high-altitude home. Illegal hunting by poachers is also reducing panda numbers.

Ex 0
Cr 0
En 2
Vu 3
Other 2

Giant panda

TREE CLIMBERS

Many bears scramble up trees to sunbathe and sleep in the branches. Sun bears are the best climbers, reaching as high as 22 feet (7 m) above ground.

American black bear
Ursus americanus
The black bear's coat can be black or brown.

Polar bear
Ursus maritimus
The polar bear has large, paddle-like front paws for swimming.

Red panda
Ailurus fulgens
The smallest bear, and the only one with a long tail

Spectacled bear
Tremarctos ornatus
The only bear that lives in South America

Kodiak bear
Ursus arctos middendorffi
Cubs spend three years with mothers, learning to survive.

BEAR FEATURES

Long, massive skull

Sturdy frame

Short tail

Powerful limbs

Walks flat-footed on entire sole of foot

Strong, curved claws that cannot be pulled back

BROWN BEAR
Bears can run as fast as 40 miles per hour (65 km/h) if hunting or threatened.

A BEAR'S LIFE

YEAR OF THE POLAR BEAR

Polar bears live on the pack ice that forms off the coasts and islands of the Arctic. It is also home to the ringed seal, the polar bear's main prey. Male polar bears are solitary hunters; females form small family groups with their cubs. Males and females only come together during a short mating season in spring. While most cold-climate bears, such as American black bears, enter a deep sleep, or hibernate, during winter, polar bears tend to stay active. However, they can hibernate at any time of year if food becomes scarce.

YEAR OF THE BLACK BEAR

MARCH–MAY
Young are brought out of den for the first time as mother keeps watch.

JUNE–AUGUST
Adults mate, but embryos are not yet implanted in the mother's womb.

SEPTEMBER–NOVEMBER
Adults feed intensely. If mother has enough fat stored, embryo implants.

DECEMBER–FEBRUARY
As many as five young are born in midwinter while their mother hibernates.

April–May
Cubs stay with their mothers for more than two years. This means that females mate only every three years, which leads to intense battles between males for mates.

November–January
Pregnant polar bears dig and retreat into a snow den to give birth. Cubs, usually two but sometimes three, are born in an underdeveloped state but grow rapidly with constant nursing.

February–April
At three to four months of age, cubs are old enough to venture out of the den. They will stay with their mother for two and a half years. It takes that long for them to learn the hunting skills needed for the Arctic environment.

April–July
Food is hard to find in winter, so polar bears gorge themselves on the pups of ringed seals that are plentiful in late spring. They often eat only the blubber and leave the rest.

Badgers and skunks

Badgers and skunks are mustelids. Mustelids are the most successful family of carnivores. They can be found in almost every habitat on Earth and may dwell above ground, below ground, or in the water. They have long bodies with short limbs. Their faces are flattened with small eyes and ears, but they have well-developed noses. Almost all mustelids secrete an unpleasant scent from glands around their anus to mark territories and communicate. When threatened, skunks lift their tails and spray this substance at potential predators. Badgers are slow-moving creatures that feed on the small mammals they dig out of the ground using well-built shoulders and strong claws.

Spotted skunk
Spilogale putorius
This is the only skunk that can climb.

Striped skunk
Mephitis mephitis
Its bold colors are a warning to predators of its nasty smell.

Chinese ferret badger
Melogale moschata
Often sleeps in tree branches

Hog badger
Arctonyx collaris
Uses its piglike snout to search for worms, insects, and roots

FAST FACT
Skunks spray would-be attackers with a sulfur compound that smells a little like rotten eggs. They can squirt this either as an invisible mist or as a powerful stream aimed directly at the attacker's face.

Striped hog-nosed skunk
Conepatus semistriatus

Andean hog-nosed skunk
Conepatus chinga
Like all skunks, the Andean hog-nosed skunk has very poor eyesight.

American badger
Taxidea taxus
Unlike most carnivores, badgers find their prey by digging.

BURROWING BADGERS
Eurasian badgers create elaborate burrows called setts. Setts typically extend about 10 feet (3 m) below ground and include tunnels as long as 30 feet (9 m). They have a number of entrances, nesting chambers, and toilets. Badgers live in these burrows in small family groups of about six members, usually a dominant male and female and their offspring. Setts are passed on from one generation to the next, and can be hundreds of years old. Badgers leave the sett at night to forage for food.

Eurasian badger
Meles meles
Hair is often used to make brushes.

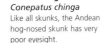

Entrance   Shared chamber   Individual badger's nesting chamber

Otters and weasels

Otters and weasels are closely related to badgers and skunks.
Their bodies tend to be longer and thinner, with a flexible spine
that allows them to scamper and leap. This makes them more
agile and fleet of foot than other mustelids. Otters and weasels
are found on all continents except Australia and Antarctica.
Otters are well adapted for swimming. Their feet are webbed
and their ears and nostrils close when underwater. They have
stiff whiskers called vibrissae on their snouts that help detect
their prey: frogs, crayfish, and waterbirds. Weasels are highly
active animals that are cunning, intelligent, and adaptable. They
eat mainly small animals that they will pursue relentlessly, even
following them down burrows and up trees. They can carry as
much as half their body weight in meat as they run.

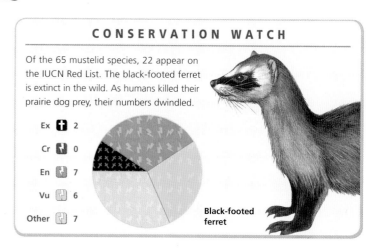

CONSERVATION WATCH

Of the 65 mustelid species, 22 appear on
the IUCN Red List. The black-footed ferret
is extinct in the wild. As humans killed their
prairie dog prey, their numbers dwindled.

Ex	✝	2
Cr		0
En		7
Vu		6
Other		7

**Black-footed
ferret**

Cape clawless otter
Aonyx capensis
Makes a loud, high-pitched
scream when attacked

Fisher
Martes pennanti
Babies are born in dens
high in hollow trees.

Yellow-throated marten
Martes flavigula
Also called the honey dog,
because it prefers sweet food

European otter
Lutra lutra
Lives in both freshwater
and saltwater habitats

Giant otter
*Pteronura
brasiliensis*
Lives beside
streams in
family groups
of as many
as eight

Japanese marten
Martes melampus
Eats small mammals, fish,
earthworms, insects, and fruit

Sea otter
Enhydra lutris
Spends almost its entire
life in the water

frican easel
ecilogale
oinucha

Stoat (ermine)
Mustela erminea
The stoat's summer coat is brown. Its white winter coat helps it blend in with snow.

American mink
Mustela vison
Partially webbed toes for swimming

riped polecat (zorilla)
onyx striatus
roduced into Britain, here it has slaughtered al wildlife.

Siberian weasel
Mustela sibirica

Long-tailed weasel
Mustela frenata
Goes on killing sprees when food is available, and stores leftovers for leaner times

Marbled polecat
Vormela peregusna

Grison
Galictis vittata

lecat
ustela putorius
ales can be twice as avy and a third longer an female polecats.

Ratel (honey badger)
Mellivora capensis
Tough skin is so loose that ratel can swing around to attack a predator that has bitten down on its neck.

Tayra
Eira barbara
Size of a medium dog; lives in trees

ropean mink
ustela lutreola
ebbed feet help it swim t hunts underwater.

SEA OTTER FEEDING

Like some primates and dolphins, sea otters can use tools. They use rocks like hammers to smash through the shells of abalone, sea urchins, and other prey to reach the soft meat inside. They dive to forage on the seafloor, sometimes as deep as 330 feet (100 m), before they return to the surface to eat, floating on their backs.

Seals and sea lions

Seals, sea lions, and the walrus are called pinnipeds. Their limbs are modified to form flippers—pinniped means "fin foot" in Latin. Their sleek, streamlined bodies help them swim through the oceans with ease, but on land they move with much less grace. Pinnipeds are excellent divers, with some species able to remain submerged for as long as two hours. When they swim underwater the pupils of their eyes open wide to improve their eyesight in the low light. Seals lack external ears and swim using their back flippers, which they cannot bend forward. Sea lions and fur seals have external ears and swim using their front flippers. They can bend their back flippers forward to act as feet on land. The walrus is in a group of its own. It lacks external ears and swims using its back flippers like seals, but can bend them forward like sea lions.

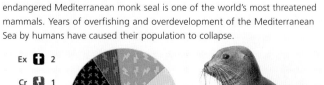

CONSERVATION WATCH

Of the 36 species of pinnipeds, 13 appear on the IUCN Red List. The critically endangered Mediterranean monk seal is one of the world's most threatened mammals. Years of overfishing and overdevelopment of the Mediterranean Sea by humans have caused their population to collapse.

Ex ✝ 2
Cr 1
En 2
Vu 7
Other 1

Mediterranean monk seal

Hooded seal
Cystophora cristata
Lining of left nostril inflates as part of a mating display.

Steller's sea lion
Eumetopias jubatus
The largest sea lion, it hunts and eats fish and otters, as well as the pups of other seals.

Ribbon seal
Phoca fasciata

Northern fur seal
Callorhinus ursinus
Males lose almost 120 pounds (55 kg) in the breeding season as they fight other males.

Southern elephant seal
Mirounga leonina
This is the largest seal; male elephant seals can weigh more than 2 tons (1.8 t).

Weddell seal
Leptonychotes weddellii

Leopard seal
Hydrurga leptonyx
The leopard seal is a fearsome Antarctic predator of other seals and penguins.

New Zealand fur seal
Arctocephalus forsteri
Hunts mainly at night, for squid, octopuses, and fish

Walrus
Odobenus rosmarus

Ringed seal
Phoca hispida
The smallest of the pinnipeds

Harp seal
Phoca groenlandica
Pups shed their pure white coats by three weeks of age.

Baikal seal
Phoca sibirica
The only seal that lives mainly in fresh water

California sea lion
Zalophus californianus
The sea lion's adaptable and intelligent nature makes it easy to train by humans.

Mediterranean monk seal
Monachus monachus
Hunts in shallow coastal waters, among reefs, caves, and crevices

COLONY OF SEA LIONS

Sea lions gather together in large numbers during the breeding season. Like all pinnipeds, they leave the sea to breed on land, where they form large, noisy colonies, called rookeries, on offshore islands. The strongest males maintain territories containing groups of females, called harems, with which they mate.

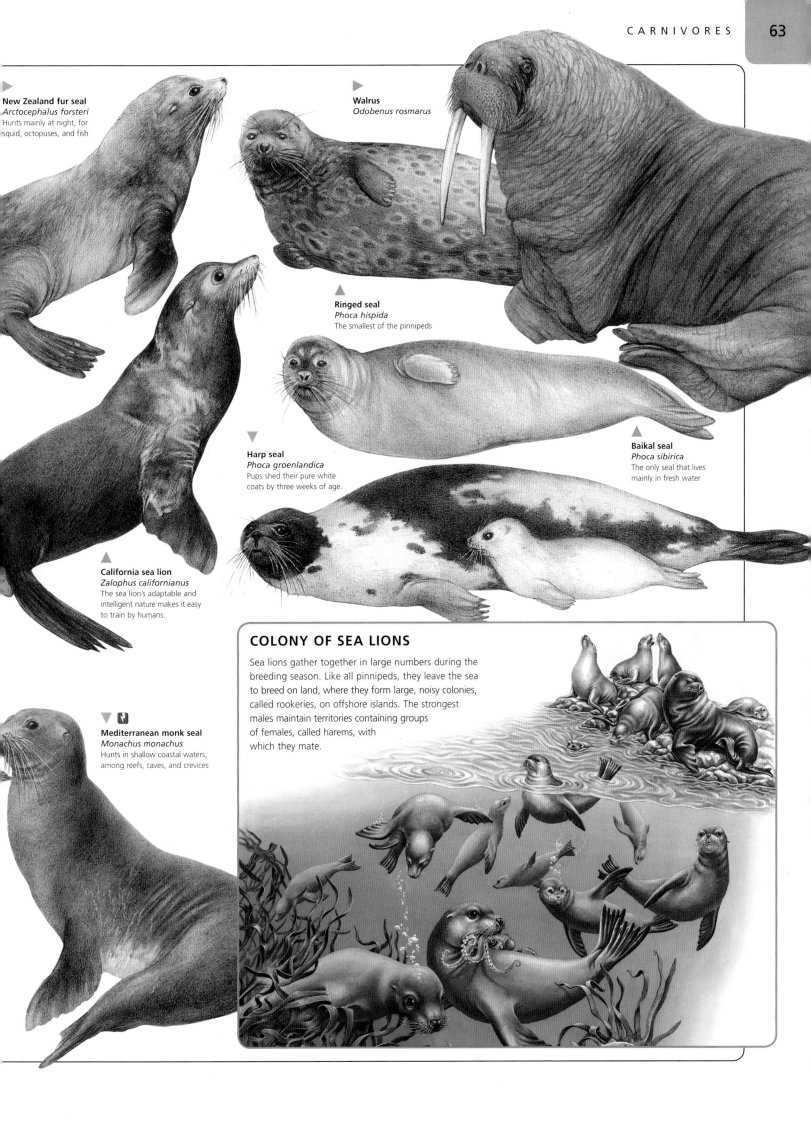

Raccoons and mongooses

Raccoons belong to a family that includes ringtails, coatis, kinkajous, and olingos. This highly social group communicates with each other using noisy barks and squeaks. Feeding on whatever food is available, they thrive in many habitats, even urban areas. Hyenas and the aardwolf look like dogs but have more in common with cats. Hyenas hunt large prey in packs but will also scavenge from the kills of other hunters, such as lions. The solitary, shy aardwolf feeds mainly on termites. Civets, genets, and linsangs are catlike. Most are nocturnal tree dwellers with long tails, claws that pull back into their paws, and pointed, upright ears. Mongooses are relatives of civets. Some are known to kill venomous cobras with their speed and agility. Most live alone but some live in sociable groups.

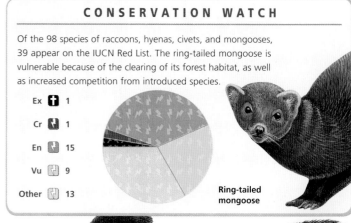

CONSERVATION WATCH

Of the 98 species of raccoons, hyenas, civets, and mongooses, 39 appear on the IUCN Red List. The ring-tailed mongoose is vulnerable because of the clearing of its forest habitat, as well as increased competition from introduced species.

Ex 🕈 1
Cr 🐾 1
En 🐾 15
Vu 🐾 9
Other 🐾 13

Ring-tailed mongoose

Ringtail
Bassariscus astutus
Able to clamber up vertical walls

Kinkajou
Potos flavus
Uses prehensile tail to balance on and swing between tree branches

Raccoon
Procyon lotor
Raids trash cans in North America for food scraps

Spotted hyena
Crocuta crocuta
Unlike most mammals, hyenas can digest skin and bone.

Suricate (meerkat)
Suricata suricatta
Stands upright to check for danger

Striped hyena
Hyaena hyaena
Spine slopes from large shoulders down to the tail. Its powerful jaws crush the bones of large animals.

White-nosed coati
Nasua narica
Tail is used for balance.

Aardwolf
Proteles cristatus
Mane stands up on back when stressed to make aardwolf appear larger.

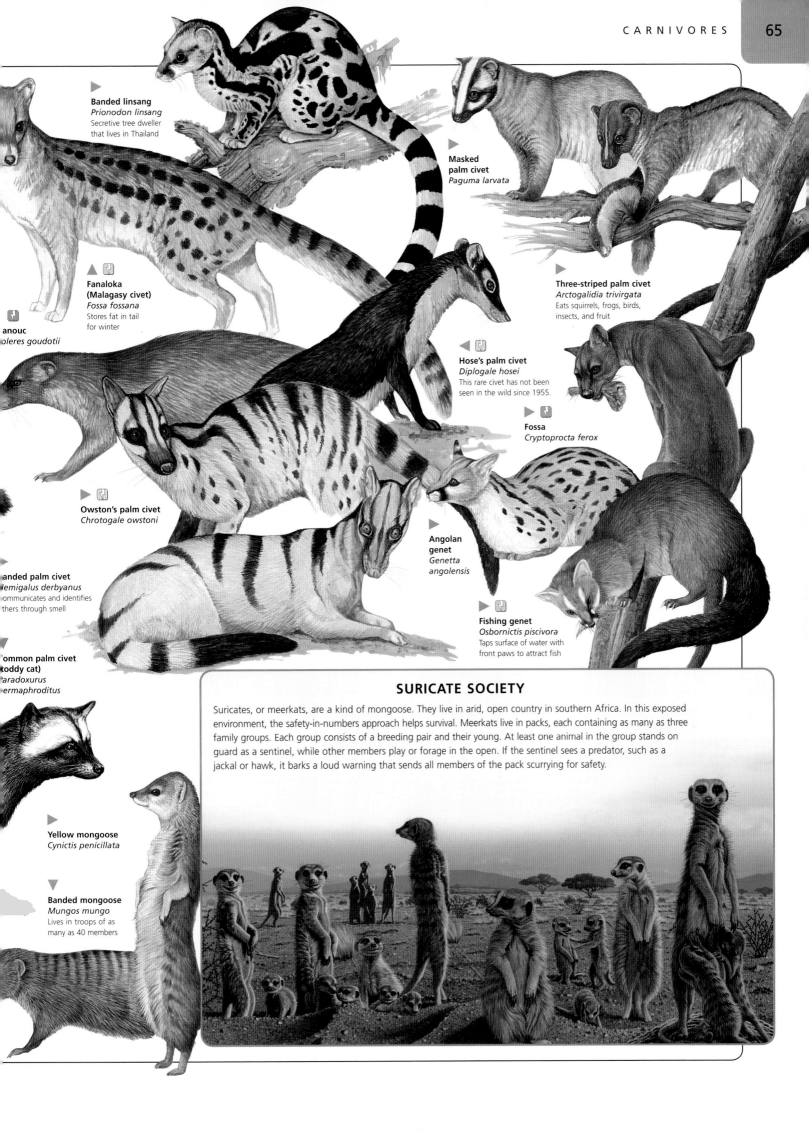

Banded linsang
Prionodon linsang
Secretive tree dweller
that lives in Thailand

**Masked
palm civet**
Paguma larvata

Three-striped palm civet
Arctogalidia trivirgata
Eats squirrels, frogs, birds,
insects, and fruit

**Fanaloka
(Malagasy civet)**
Fossa fossana
Stores fat in tail
for winter

anouc
oleres goudotii

Hose's palm civet
Diplogale hosei
This rare civet has not been
seen in the wild since 1955.

Fossa
Cryptoprocta ferox

Owston's palm civet
Chrotogale owstoni

**Angolan
genet**
*Genetta
angolensis*

anded palm civet
emigalus derbyanus
ommunicates and identifies
thers through smell

Fishing genet
Osbornictis piscivora
Taps surface of water with
front paws to attract fish

ommon palm civet
oddy cat)
aradoxurus
ermaphroditus

Yellow mongoose
Cynictis penicillata

Banded mongoose
Mungos mungo
Lives in troops of as
many as 40 members

SURICATE SOCIETY

Suricates, or meerkats, are a kind of mongoose. They live in arid, open country in southern Africa. In this exposed environment, the safety-in-numbers approach helps survival. Meerkats live in packs, each containing as many as three family groups. Each group consists of a breeding pair and their young. At least one animal in the group stands on guard as a sentinel, while other members play or forage in the open. If the sentinel sees a predator, such as a jackal or hawk, it barks a loud warning that sends all members of the pack scurrying for safety.

Great cats

Cats are the ultimate hunters. They have a strong, muscular body with forward-facing eyes, razor-like teeth, and sharp claws. They have quick reflexes and keen senses. Most eat nothing but meat; many live alone; and they are often active at night. Cats are land dwellers, but all can climb and many are good swimmers. There are three groups of cats: the great cats, the small cats, and the cheetah. Lions, tigers, leopards, and jaguars are the great cats. The small cats include lynxes, bobcats, and ocelots. Great cats are grouped together because they roar. They cannot purr like the small cats or the cheetah.

Jaguar
Panthera onca
Excellent climber, fast runner, and good swimmer

Tiger
Panthera tigris
This solitary hunter is the largest cat. Each tiger has its own pattern of stripes.

Leopard
Panthera pardus
Leopards are covered in spots, or rosettes. Black panthers are leopards with only black pigment in their fur.

Cheetah
Acinonyx jubatus
The fastest animal on land, it can reach a top speed of 60 miles per hour (97 km/h).

Snow leopard
Uncia uncia

Lion
Panthera leo
Males are the on with manes; the twice as large a

LION PRIDE

Usually one but sometimes two related males (often brothers) dominate the family group, or pride.

Lionesses are the pride's main hunters. They hunt together to provide meat for the group.

As many as three generations of females can live in a pride. This may consist of 30 lions.

Cubs nurse for as long as six months before being weaned. They are always the last to feed at kills.

STALKING AND STRIKING

SILENT HUNTERS

All cats hunt in similar ways, depending on their eyesight and hearing to judge distances accurately and pick up the faintest sounds. Cats stalk their prey in silence, remaining hidden while creeping toward their prey. Once the cats are close enough, or if they are spotted, they pounce. If they capture prey, they wrestle it to the ground and kill it with a bite to the neck or throat. The prey can die of suffocation before bleeding to death as the cat's powerful jaws cut off air to the windpipe.

Tigers steal up to deer, pigs, or porcupines before pouncing. Their stripes conceal them in the long grass to help them ambush prey. After eating their fill—as much as 85 pounds (39 kg) at once—tigers hide the remains of their kill to eat later. They do this because 9 out of every 10 hunts fail.

While lionesses hunt for their pride, male lions hunt for themselves. This band of males is attacking a water buffalo. Each lion clutches at part of the buffalo's body, and they drag it down together.

Stripes provide camouflage, letting tigers hide in grass.

Tiger stalks prey before suddenly pouncing.

Tiger grabs prey by the neck, cutting off air to the prey's windpipe.

Prey dies from bite, either by suffocation or loss of blood.

KNIFELIKE CLAWS

Almost all cats have claws that pull back into their paws, or sheathe. They are unsheathed only to climb trees or capture prey. This helps to keep them sharp.

Small cats

The small cats are not only smaller than the great cats, but also have a better developed voice box, or larynx. This lets them purr constantly. Like the great cats, small cats have well-developed shearing teeth, or carnassials, and lack grinding back teeth, or molars. This is because cats feed by tearing flesh, not by grinding plant matter. Small cats have large eyes with pupils that are generally vertical, but can sometimes be rounded. Their coats can be plain, like those of pumas and golden cats; consist of spots or rosettes, like ocelots, bobcats, and servals; contain faint stripes, like wildcats; or be a mixture of all these markings. The main purpose of their coat markings is to blend into their surroundings, or to be camouflaged, which is important for animals that rely on stalking and surprising prey.

CONSERVATION WATCH

Of the 36 species of cats, 25 appear on the IUCN Red List. This includes the Siberian tiger, which is critically endangered. Poachers threaten the largest remaining Siberian tiger population in Russia.

Ex	✝	0
Cr		1
En		4
Vu		12
Other		8

Siberian tiger

▲ **Bobcat**
Lynx rufus

▶ **Wildcat**
Felis silvestris
Wildcats rub objects with scent from tail and head glands; they also mark territory with urine.

▶ **Caracal**
Caracal caracal
Uses old porcupine burrows as dens for young

◀ **Puma**
(cougar, mountain lion)
Puma concolor

◀ **Canada lynx**
Lynx canadensis

▶ **Marbled cat**
Pardofelis marmorata
Lives in rain forests of Southeast Asia

FROM THE WILD

Cats were first tamed by the ancient Egyptians. Even after thousands of years of domestication, pet cats have not lost their hunting instincts, and some go back to the wild. These are known as feral cats. There are more than 100 million domestic or feral cats in North America alone.

▶ **Andean cat**
Oreailurus jacobita
Long, thick hair protects cat from cold and wind in high mountains.

Margay
Leopardus wiedii

Ocelot
Leopardus pardalis

Kodkod
Oncifelis guigna

African golden cat
Profelis aurata
Night hunter of small antelope,
monkeys, and rodents

Jaguarundi
Herpailurus yaguarondi
Kittens have spots at birth
but lose them as they mature.

Serval
Leptailurus serval
Can leap 10 feet (3 m)
in the air and change
direction mid-leap

Asiatic golden cat
Catopuma temminckii
Known as the "fire tiger"
by local Thai tribes

Leopard cat
*Prionailurus
bengalensis*

Iberian lynx
Lynx pardinus

Eurasian lynx
Lynx lynx
Furry feet act like
snowshoes to help the
lynx travel over soft snow.

Jungle cat
Felis chaus

Fishing cat
*Prionailurus
viverrinus*
Webbed toes
on front paws

DEFENSE SIGNALS

BACK OFF
Cats use facial expressions when threatened. The
margay, of Central and South America, signals it
can defend itself by staring with wide eyes.

READY TO ATTACK
The margay tucks its ears out of the way, opens
its mouth wide, and bares its sharp teeth to give
a final warning signal before attacking.

7 ORDERS • 28 FAMILIES • 139 GENERA • 329 SPECIES

Hoofed Mammals

Zebras and wildebeest surge through the Mara River together as they complete their annual migration across the Serengeti. Their large herds offer protection from predators.

Hard hooves evolved to help plant-eating mammals survive on grasslands. They make it easier to run fast and escape predators. Only two groups of hoofed mammals, or ungulates, have true hooves: odd-toed ungulates—tapirs, rhinoceroses, and horses—and even-toed ungulates—pigs, hippopotamuses, camels, deer, cattle, and giraffes. The other ungulates have their own specializations.

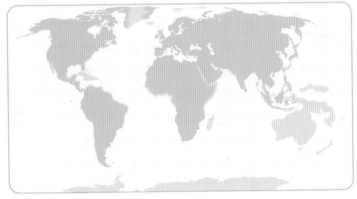

Hoofed mammals

Hoofed mammals occur on all landmasses except Australia, Antarctica, and some islands. Sirenians live in shallow waters off the coasts of the Americas, Africa, Asia, and Australia.

HORNS

Antelope horns have a bony core encased in keratin.

Deer antlers are made of bone that is shed each year.

Rhinoceros horns are made of modified hair.

Horns and antlers are used by males as weapons; they fight each other for the right to mate with females.

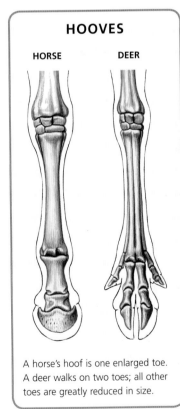

HOOVES

HORSE   DEER

A horse's hoof is one enlarged toe. A deer walks on two toes; all other toes are greatly reduced in size.

Elephants

Elephants are the world's biggest land animals. There are just two living species: the Asiatic elephant and the African elephant. Both species live in hot, tropical climates. An elephant's trunk is a combination of the upper lip and nose. It is made up of more than 150,000 muscle bands. The trunk is strong enough to carry heavy objects but agile enough to pick up a delicate twig. They have limbs like pillars and broad feet to support their huge bulk. Heat from their bodies is dispersed through their large, thin ears, which have many blood vessels running through them. Elephants are mostly social animals. Adult males gather in small bachelor herds, or they may live alone. Related adult females and their young live in strong family groups led by the oldest animals.

CONSERVATION WATCH

Both species of elephants appear on the IUCN Red List. African elephants have been hunted for their ivory tusks for centuries. An increase in hunting in recent years is the main cause of huge losses.

Ex	✝	0
Cr		0
En		1
Vu		1
Other		0

African elephant

Asiatic elephant
Elephas maximus
It has smaller ears than African elephant; one "finger" at tip of trunk; and four nails on back foot. Only males have large tusks: modified teeth that never stop growing.

♂

Adult

▶
African elephant
Loxodonta africana
Heavier and taller than Asiatic elephant, it has larger ears; three nails on its back foot; and its trunk has two "fingers" at tip. Both males and females can have large tusks.

Juvenile

ELEPHANT GROWTH

Newborn elephants are a fraction of their adult size. A male African elephant weighs 250 pounds (110 kg) at birth but will add almost 14,000 more pounds (6,400 kg) during its life. Elephants nurse for as long as 3 years. They are dependent on their mothers for 8 to 10 years. Like humans, they are adolescents at 12 to 14 years. Females can produce young at 16 years. Elephants grow rapidly when they are young. They achieve most of their growth by about 20 but will continue to grow throughout their lives. They live for 65 to 70 years.

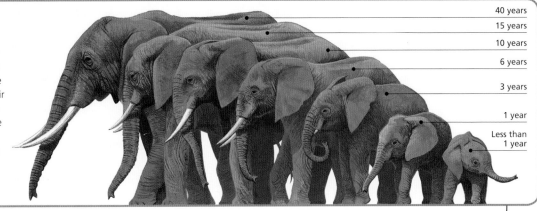

40 years
15 years
10 years
6 years
3 years
1 year
Less than 1 year

Horses, asses, and zebras

Horses, asses, and zebras are known as equids. Equids occur in the grasslands, savannas, and deserts of Africa and Asia, but feral herds live on most continents. Their ancestors evolved in North America, but equids vanished from there by the end of the last ice age. Equids commonly live in large female herds led by a harem male. All equids run on a single toe. Their teeth are highly specialized for eating plants: They have incisor teeth to snip at leaves and ridged cheek teeth to grind them. Eyes on the sides of their heads and sharp hearing help them keep alert for danger. Equids communicate with each other by moving their tails, ears, and mouths. Many also use sounds such as whinnies, brays, nickers, and squeals. Most species groom each other to reinforce herd relationships.

▶
Zebra
northern form
Equus burchelli
Every zebra has its own pattern of stripes, which probably helps herd members identify each other.

▼ ▶ 🔲
Mountain zebra
Equus zebra
Responds to alarm calls from wildebeest, as well as zebras

Adult

▲ ✝
Horse
wild form
Equus ferus
The horse is extinct in the wild, but lives on in domestic breeds.

▲
Kiang
Equus kiang
Forms family groups of as many as 400 members, led by a mature female

▲
Onager
Equus onager
This equid can reach speeds of 40 miles per hour (65 km/h) in short bursts.

▼ 🔲
Mongolian wild as
Equus hemionus
Grazes on grass but w shrubs and trees when is scarce

▶ 🔲
Ass
wild form
Equus africanus
Domestic donkey was bred from this species.

CONSERVATION WATCH

Of the nine equid species, six appear on the IUCN Red List. This includes the endangered Grevy's zebra, which was once hunted extensively for its striking pelt. It now faces threats from habitat loss and competition from domestic livestock.

Ex ✝	2	
Cr 🔲	1	
En 🔲	2	
Vu 🔲	1	
Other 🔲	0	

Grevy's zebra

HORSES AND HISTORY

SUSPENDED IN MIDAIR
Nobody knew how horses galloped until photography captured their motion in the late 1870s. It showed that there is a moment mid-stride when all four hooves are off the ground.

TRUSTED STEEDS

Horses were domesticated by people to provide meat and milk, carry heavy loads, and to move people. For at least 1,500 years, until the invention of the steam engine, horses were the fastest and most reliable form of transport. They played a critical role in the spread of human culture and a decisive role in warfare. The Huns, led by Attila, conquered half of Europe and defeated the mighty Roman Army, using the speed and agility of their warhorses.

DOMESTIC USES

Horses are used by the military and police.

They work alongside humans on farms.

Horses are also ridden for sport and pleasure.

Dugong and manatees

There are only four living sirenians, the dugong and three species of manatees. These marine mammals spend their entire lives in water. They live in tropical and subtropical regions, grazing on the seagrasses and plants that grow in shallow seas. Their ancestors would have been land dwellers; the closest living relatives of sirenians are probably elephants and hyraxes. Today, their front legs have become flippers and their back legs have almost disappeared. The dugong's tail is fluked like a whale's. Manatees have a tail like a large, flat paddle. The vegetarian diet of sirenians produces a lot of gas. To stop them from floating too high in the water, their heavy bones weigh them down. Fleeting glimpses of sirenians by confused sailors inspired the myth of the mermaid, or siren, for which they are named.

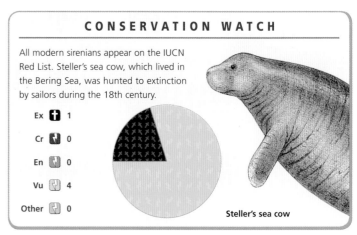

CONSERVATION WATCH

All modern sirenians appear on the IUCN Red List. Steller's sea cow, which lived in the Bering Sea, was hunted to extinction by sailors during the 18th century.

Ex		1
Cr		0
En		0
Vu		4
Other		0

Steller's sea cow

GRIZZLED GRAZERS

Sirenians graze on algae and seagrasses growing in shallow, warm waters. Their poor eyesight means they locate food by touch, with sensitive, bristle-like hairs on their piglike snouts. Their mobile, muscular lips grasp plant material and pull it from the sediment. Sirenians may use their flippers to pass food to the mouth. The disturbed sediment can form a murky feeding trail behind them.

Dugong
Dugong dugon
Dugongs have no nails on their flippers; these have calluses on them from crawling across the seabed.

Caribbean manatee
Trichechus manatus
Has nails on its flippers; algae and barnacles grow on its skin; it lives in both salt and fresh water.

Amazonian manatee
Trichechus inunguis
This species lives in lagoons and lakes among dense vegetation, where it feeds on floating grasses.

African manatee
Trichechus senegalensis
This manatee lives in rivers and coastal waters off the west coast of Africa.

Hyraxes, tapirs, and aardvark

Hyraxes are rabbit-size mammals that look like guinea pigs. These distant relatives of elephants and sirenians live in Africa and the Middle East. They have flattened, hooflike nails on their feet. Their upper incisor teeth grow constantly and look like small tusks. Hyraxes keep warm by huddling together in groups and basking in the sun. Tapirs have a trunklike nose similar to elephants, but they are more closely related to rhinoceroses. There are four living species. Three inhabit the tropical rain forests of Central and South America; one lives in Southeast Asia. All are shy plant-eaters with poor vision but excellent senses of hearing and smell. Unlike most hoofed mammals, the aardvark is not herbivorous. It eats ants and termites instead, and can gulp as many as 50,000 of them in one nighttime feeding session.

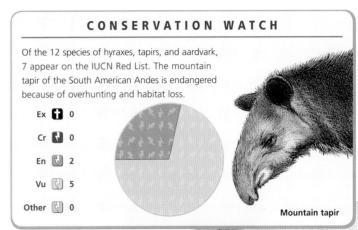

CONSERVATION WATCH

Of the 12 species of hyraxes, tapirs, and aardvark, 7 appear on the IUCN Red List. The mountain tapir of the South American Andes is endangered because of overhunting and habitat loss.

Ex		0
Cr		0
En		2
Vu		5
Other		0

Mountain tapir

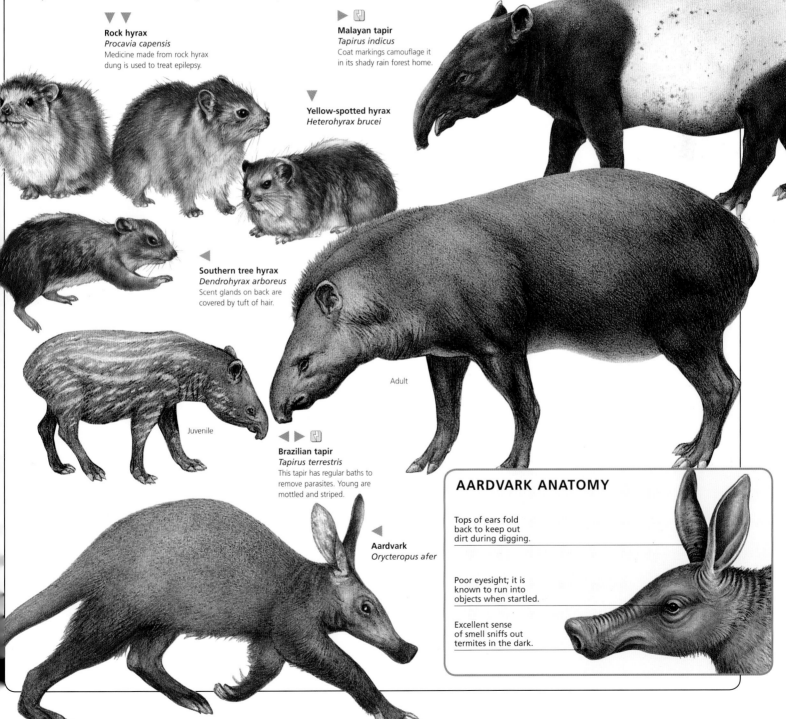

Rock hyrax
Procavia capensis
Medicine made from rock hyrax dung is used to treat epilepsy.

Malayan tapir
Tapirus indicus
Coat markings camouflage it in its shady rain forest home.

Yellow-spotted hyrax
Heterohyrax brucei

Southern tree hyrax
Dendrohyrax arboreus
Scent glands on back are covered by tuft of hair.

Juvenile

Adult

Brazilian tapir
Tapirus terrestris
This tapir has regular baths to remove parasites. Young are mottled and striped.

Aardvark
Orycteropus afer

AARDVARK ANATOMY

Tops of ears fold back to keep out dirt during digging.

Poor eyesight; it is known to run into objects when startled.

Excellent sense of smell sniffs out termites in the dark.

Rhinoceroses

Rhinoceroses might look similar to elephants, but they are more closely related to tapirs and horses. There are just five living rhinoceros species. Three live in Asia; two are found in Africa. Africa's white rhinoceros is the third largest living land animal after the elephants. All rhinoceroses have one or two large horns protruding from their snouts. Males use these to fight each other for females. Females use them to guide their young with gentle nudges. Both sexes use their horns to defend against predators or to push dung into scented signposts. Their bodies are large and stumpy; their three-toed feet leave tracks like the "ace of clubs" playing card. Rhinoceroses are generally solitary herbivores that come together for a few months to breed. Females or young males may form temporary herds.

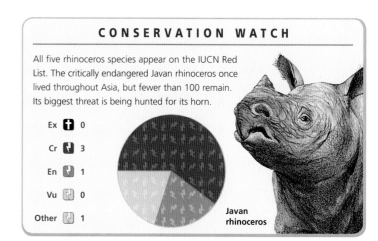

CONSERVATION WATCH

All five rhinoceros species appear on the IUCN Red List. The critically endangered Javan rhinoceros once lived throughout Asia, but fewer than 100 remain. Its biggest threat is being hunted for its horn.

Ex 0
Cr 3
En 1
Vu 0
Other 1

Javan rhinoceros

Javan rhinoceros
Rhinoceros sondaicus
Browses on leaves using prehensile upper lip

Indian rhinoceros
Rhinoceros unicornis

Sumatran rhinoceros
Dicerorhinus sumatrensis

Adult

Black rhinoceros
Diceros bicornis
Calf may stay with its mother for almost four years.

Juvenile

White rhinoceros
Ceratotherium simum
Its name comes from Afrikaans word "widje," which describes its wide mouth. A large hump helps support the massive head. Male sprays urine, spreads dung, and tramples plants to mark territory.

CHARGING RHINO

Black rhinoceroses can be aggressive and charge when threatened or startled. They are capable of surprising bursts of speed over short distances. Loud snorts add to the terrifying display. Adults can weigh almost 3,000 pounds (1,400 kg). With this weight charging at speed, horns cause serious damage when they connect with attackers.

Black rhinoceroses will gore and toss attackers with their horns.

Horns are made of keratin, the same substance as human fingernails.

Spotted hyena

FAST FACT

The largest land animal ever was a rhinoceros that lived about 40 million years ago, called *Indricotherium*. It stood 18 feet (5.5 m) tall at the shoulder and may have weighed over 22 tons (20 t).

Cattle, goats, and sheep

Cattle, goats, and sheep belong to the bovid family. This is a diverse group that also includes buffalo, bison, antelope, and gazelles. The males, and many females, of all wild species have horns made of bone and covered in keratin. These are never shed. Bovids bear their weight on the two middle toes of each foot. These toes form a split, or cloven, hoof. All bovids are plant-eaters; many eat nothing but grasses. Such foods are low in nutrients, but bovids extract the most they can with their specialized digestive system. A bovid's stomach has four chambers, in which food, especially the tough walls of plant cells that many other mammals are unable to digest, is broken down by bacteria. Bovids do not occur naturally in South America or Australia, but domestic species can be found worldwide.

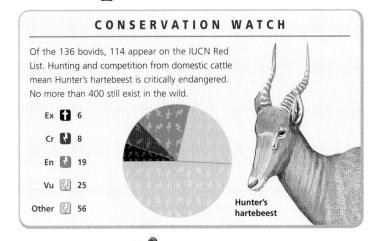

CONSERVATION WATCH

Of the 136 bovids, 114 appear on the IUCN Red List. Hunting and competition from domestic cattle mean Hunter's hartebeest is critically endangered. No more than 400 still exist in the wild.

Ex	6
Cr	8
En	19
Vu	25
Other	56

Hunter's hartebeest

Dall sheep
Ovis dalli
Migrates between summer and winter pastures

Mountain goat
Oreamnos americanus
Lives in steep, rocky, high mountain regions

Chamois
Rupicapra rupicapra
Flexible hoof pads grip the ground.

Mountain anoa
Bubalus quarlesi
A kind of water buffalo that looks more like a deer

Markhor
Capra falconeri
Massive horns as long as 5 feet (1.5 m)

Aoudad (Barbary sheep)
Ammotragus lervia

Spanish ibex
Capra pyrenaica

Arabian tahr
Hemitragus jayakari

Musk ox
Ovibos moschatus

Serow
Capricornis sumatraensis

Saola (Vu Quang ox)
Pseudoryx nghetinhensis

Yak
Bos grunniens

Bison
Bison bison

Antelope

Antelope are a group of bovids with hollow horns. They live in Africa. They are ruminants and have four-chambered stomachs. After they swallow, food passes through the first two stomachs. The partially digested meal, called cud, is returned to the mouth to be chewed and swallowed again. It then enters the final two stomachs. Antelope have slender bodies and lightweight frames; short tails; and well-developed, muscular back legs. Their ability to bound and dart in different directions when running helps them dodge predators. The North American pronghorn looks similar to antelope, but it is in a group of its own. Its horns are made of bone and keratin like bovids' horns, but the keratin is shed every year like deer's horns. One of the fastest mammals on land, it can reach speeds of 40 miles per hour (65 km/h).

Bongo
Tragelaphus eurycerus

Giant eland
Taurotragus derbianus
Breaks branches with long horns to reach leaves

Steenbok
Raphicerus campestris

Mountain reedbuck
Redunca fulvorufula

Impala
Aepyceros melampus
Only males have long, ridged horns. Impalas can leap as high as 10 feet (3 m) off the ground as they bound away from predators.

Chiru (Tibetan antelope)
Pantholops hodgsonii

Wildebeest
Connochaetes taurinus
When startled, it runs away, tossing its head and kicking its heels before turning to face the threat.

Thomson's gazelle
Gazella thomsonii
Usually lives in small groups, but thousands may migrate together to grasslands in the rainy season.

Gemsbok
Oryx gazella
Horns of a male gemsbok can be as long as 5 feet (1.5 m). Gemsbok mothers hide calves for first six weeks, returning to them daily to feed them.

Common hartebeest
Alcelaphus buselaphus
Can graze together in loose groups of as many as 10,000 members, sometimes with other antelope and zebras

Greater kudu
Tragelaphus strepsiceros
Males bark loudly to establish dominance and whine, hum, grunt, and gasp during courtship.

Common duiker
Sylvicapra grimmia

▶ Springbok
Antidorcas marsupialis
Leaps, or "pronks,"
as high as 13 feet
(4 m) in the air
when alarmed

Klipspringer
Oreotragus oreotragus

◀ **Ader's duiker**
Cephalophus adersi

sbok (bontebok)
maliscus pygargus
le uses dunghills to
rk out territory.

◀ **Pronghorn**
Antilocapra americana
Lives in deserts and open plains
of North America; its sharp eyes
can detect small movements as
far as 4 miles (6.5 km) away.

Blackbuck
Antilope cervicapra

Saiga
Saiga tatarica
Large, fleshy nose filters
dust from air in summer
and warms air in winter.

▼ **Waterbuck**
Kobus ellipsiprymnus
Sweat of waterbucks tastes
unpleasant as they grow older.
Only males have horns; these
form at eight to nine months.

FINICKY EATERS

Gerenuks can stand on their back legs
for long periods of time. Together with
their long, slender necks, this helps
them reach the most tender, nutritious
leaves. They use their front legs to
steady themselves against shrubs
and trees, and to pull down
branches as high as 8 feet
(2.5 m) off the ground.
When browsing on prickly
plants, such as acacia
shrubs, their narrow
mouths and long top
lips and tongues allow
them to pluck leaves
from between thorns.

Spine curves to let
gerenuk stand erect.

Weight is distributed evenly
on back legs and hooves.

ON THE MOVE

Millions of bison once migrated across the Great Plains of North America. They were hunted almost to extinction during the 19th century. Today they survive only in protected areas.

ACROSS THE SERENGETI

Many animals move from one place to another at regular times in the year. Such movements, known as migrations, can be linked with the changing seasons. Mammals migrate through the air, over land, or in water. They do so for many reasons: better quality and abundance of food; warmer weather conditions; or safer locations to give birth and raise young. Some of the greatest migrants are hoofed mammals, such as the caribou of the Arctic, the springbok of Africa, and the Himalayan tahr of Asia.

The annual migration of wildebeest is one of the world's largest mass movements. More than 1.3 million wildebeest travel the 1,800-mile (2,900-km) round trip from the Serengeti plains in Tanzania to the open grasslands of the Masai Mara region in Kenya. At the end of May, bellies filled with the grass of the Serengeti, the wildebeest travel in a loosely connected herd toward the Masai Mara. Once there, they mate, feast on new grass, and drink from permanent rivers. They return to the Serengeti in November.

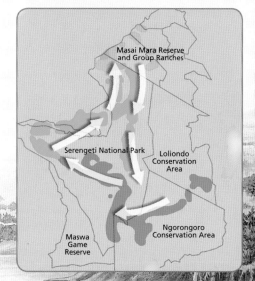

Wildebeest migrate with the wet and dry seasons. They follow a circular route through Serengeti National Park and neighboring reserves.

- Dry season
- Wet season
- Between seasons

MIGRATING HUMPBACKS

Humpback whales make some of the longest migrations in the world. Each year, these huge marine mammals follow a pattern that is mirrored at either end of the globe. They spend their summers in the icy waters of the Arctic and Antarctic. There they gorge on the explosion of life, such as tiny crustaceans called krill, which appears as the days lengthen and the seawater warms. As the days shorten, the whales migrate to spend the winter in warmer waters. This is where they breed and raise their calves. There are a number of isolated populations of humpback whales, and each migrates separately. One population does not migrate at all.

Breeding   Feeding   Breeding and feeding   ⟶ Migration route

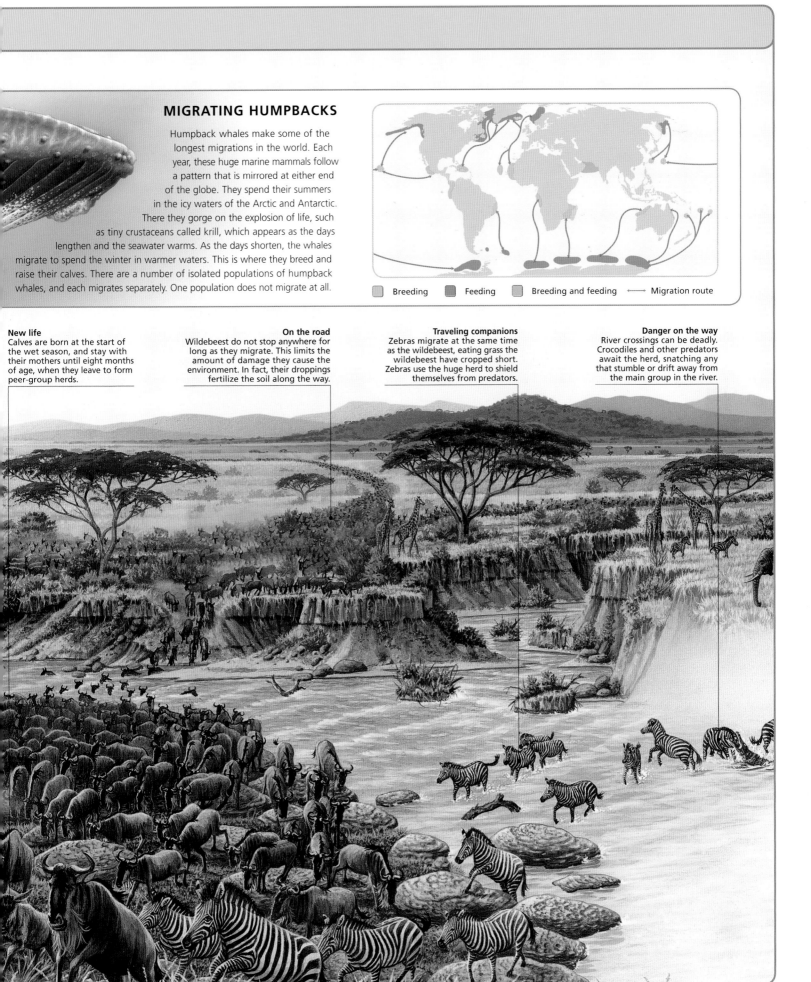

New life
Calves are born at the start of the wet season, and stay with their mothers until eight months of age, when they leave to form peer-group herds.

On the road
Wildebeest do not stop anywhere for long as they migrate. This limits the amount of damage they cause the environment. In fact, their droppings fertilize the soil along the way.

Traveling companions
Zebras migrate at the same time as the wildebeest, eating grass the wildebeest have cropped short. Zebras use the huge herd to shield themselves from predators.

Danger on the way
River crossings can be deadly. Crocodiles and other predators await the herd, snatching any that stumble or drift away from the main group in the river.

Deer

Deer, moose, caribou, and elk belong to the cervid family. Two related families include the chevrotains and musk deer, which both have long canine teeth. Deer resemble antelope, with long bodies and necks, slender limbs, short tails, large eyes on the side of the head, and high-set ears. Unlike antelope, however, most male deer (and some female deer) have antlers instead of horns. Antlers are made of bone and are grown then shed every year. They can be small simple spikes, as occurs in Asia's tufted deer, or enormous branched structures like those of the moose. The moose's antlers can measure 6½ feet (2 m) across. All deer are ruminants; they generally eat shoots, young leaves, new grasses, and fruit. Deer are great escape artists. Some leap and dodge into hiding spots to escape enemies. Others rely on speed and stamina.

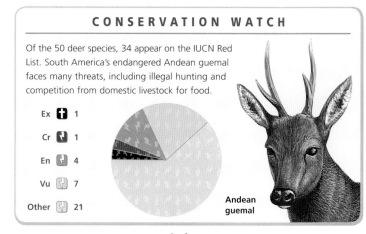

CONSERVATION WATCH

Of the 50 deer species, 34 appear on the IUCN Red List. South America's endangered Andean guemal faces many threats, including illegal hunting and competition from domestic livestock for food.

Ex	🕇	1
Cr		1
En		4
Vu		7
Other		21

Andean guemal

CYCLE OF GROWTH

SPRING
New antlers begin to grow in late spring. They are covered in sensitive skin known as velvet.

SUMMER
By late summer, the antlers are fully grown and hardened. The velvet begins to dry and loosen.

FALL
Male rubs the velvet onto shrubs and small trees. Its antlers are now ready for the mating season contests with other males.

WINTER
After the mating season has finished, both antlers are shed within days of each other.

Little red brocket
Mazama rufina

White-tailed deer
Odocoileus virginianus

Southern pudu
Pudu puda
Can stand on back legs to reach food

Chinese water deer
Hydropotes inermis
Canine teeth are like tusks; males use them to wound each other when fighting.

Peruvian guemal
Hippocamelus antisensis

Tufted deer
Elaphodus cephalophus
Tuft of hair on head hides male's antlers.

Water chevrotain
Hyemoschus aquaticus
Active only at night; rests in vegetation during the day

Lesser Malay chevrotain
Tragulus javanicus

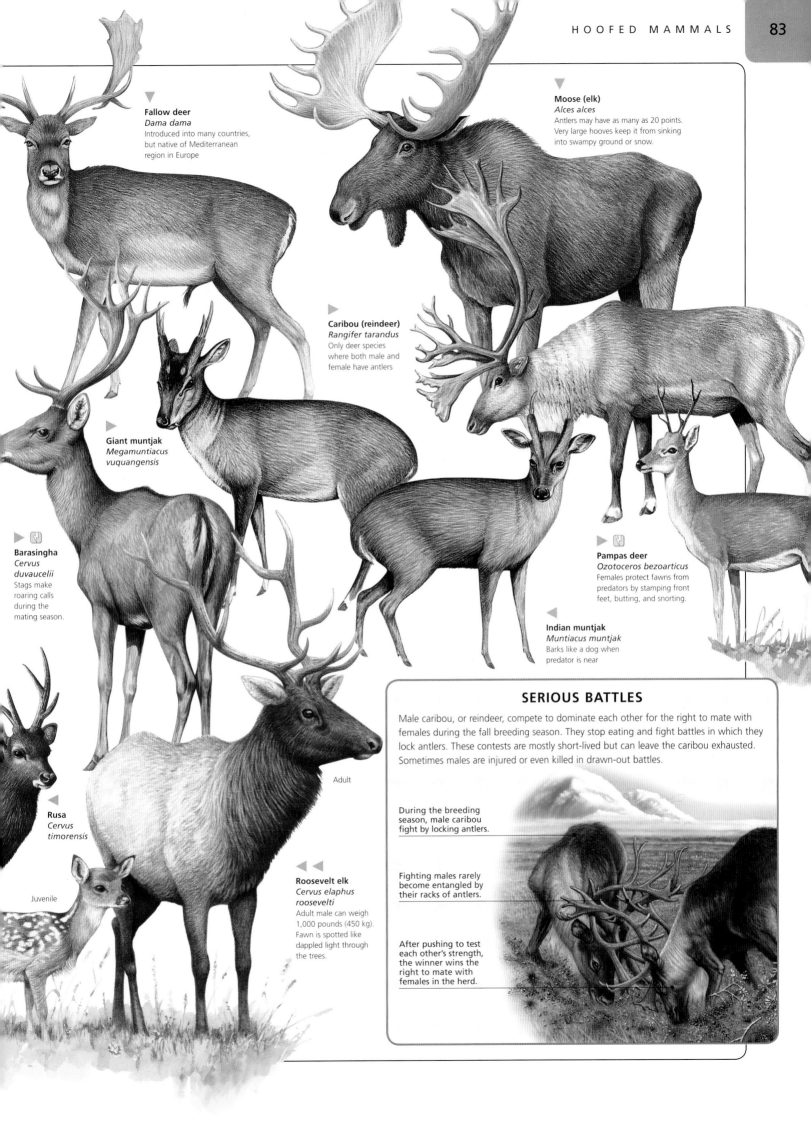

Fallow deer
Dama dama
Introduced into many countries, but native of Mediterranean region in Europe

Moose (elk)
Alces alces
Antlers may have as many as 20 points. Very large hooves keep it from sinking into swampy ground or snow.

Caribou (reindeer)
Rangifer tarandus
Only deer species where both male and female have antlers

Giant muntjak
Megamuntiacus vuquangensis

Barasingha
Cervus duvaucelii
Stags make roaring calls during the mating season.

Pampas deer
Ozotoceros bezoarticus
Females protect fawns from predators by stamping front feet, butting, and snorting.

Indian muntjak
Muntiacus muntjak
Barks like a dog when predator is near

Rusa
Cervus timorensis

Adult

Juvenile

Roosevelt elk
Cervus elaphus roosevelti
Adult male can weigh 1,000 pounds (450 kg). Fawn is spotted like dappled light through the trees.

SERIOUS BATTLES

Male caribou, or reindeer, compete to dominate each other for the right to mate with females during the fall breeding season. They stop eating and fight battles in which they lock antlers. These contests are mostly short-lived but can leave the caribou exhausted. Sometimes males are injured or even killed in drawn-out battles.

During the breeding season, male caribou fight by locking antlers.

Fighting males rarely become entangled by their racks of antlers.

After pushing to test each other's strength, the winner wins the right to mate with females in the herd.

Giraffes and okapi

Giraffes and the okapi are the only living members of the giraffe family. They are distantly related to cattle, sheep, and antelope. Both have long necks, tails, and limbs. Their front legs are longer than their back legs. This causes their backs to slope down toward the tail. A fully grown giraffe's neck is so long that it can reach as high as 18 feet (5.5 m) above the ground. This makes it the tallest animal in the world. Giraffes and the okapi have small bony horns covered by furred skin; thin, movable lips; and large eyes and ears. Giraffes live in small herds in wooded areas of Africa's savannas. Their striking coats mimic the dappled light of these regions. The okapi prefers to live alone in the dark rain forests of central Africa. The distinctive stripes on its rear break up its outline in the dense undergrowth.

Reticulated giraffe
Giraffa camelopardalis reticulata
Has seven neck bones, like humans, only longer; young males have contests with their necks, much like arm wrestling.

Southern giraffe
Giraffa camelopardalis giraffa
A giraffe's coat pattern provides for excellent camouflage on open savannas. These markings fade along lower limbs.

Okapi
Okapia johnstoni
Has poor vision, but sharp hearing and good sense of smell

Kenyan giraffe
Giraffa camelopardalis tippelskirschi
Kicks with front legs to defend itself

Nubian giraffe
Giraffa camelopardalis camelopardalis
Spreads its front legs wide and bends down to reach the water, making it easy prey for predators

PICKING AT ACACIAS

Acacia leaves contain poisons and the branches have sharp thorns. Giraffes have special adaptations that allow them to eat these leaves in large quantities.

Giraffes select the most tender, and least poisonous, new leaves from acacia trees.

Mobile, grasping tongue can be 21 inches (53 cm) long in adults.

Acacia thorns

Camels

Two kinds of camels, together with the guanaco, vicuña, and the domesticated llama and alpaca, are known as camelids. Camelids are social animals. In the wild, they live in female groups, or harems, that have one dominant male. Young males sometimes form small bachelor herds. All camelids are well adapted to life in desert or semidesert conditions. Their three-chambered stomachs extract nutrients from the leaves and stems that they eat. The two camels also have a fatty hump that stores food. Only the front of a camelid's hoof touches the ground. Its weight rests instead on a fleshy pad on the foot's sole. When they walk, camelids move the front and back legs of one side together, creating a rolling gait. This has led some domestic camels to be called "ships of the desert."

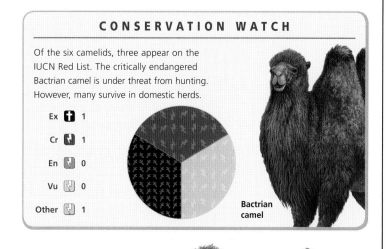

CONSERVATION WATCH

Of the six camelids, three appear on the IUCN Red List. The critically endangered Bactrian camel is under threat from hunting. However, many survive in domestic herds.

Ex ✝ 1
Cr 🗡 1
En 〽 0
Vu 🗒 0
Other 🗒 1

Bactrian camel

Dromedary
Camelus dromedarius
Can drink 30 gallons (110 L) of water in 10 minutes, but can go for days without drinking

Bactrian camel
Camelus bactrianus
Long winter coat sheds in summer. Its humps are mainly stored fat, and shrink during food shortages.

Alpaca
Lama pacos
Probably a cross between wild vicuña and tame llama; its silky wool is used to make clothing.

Llama
Lama glama

Vicuña
Vicugna vicugna

Guanaco
Lama guanicoe
Spits when threatened

INSIDE A CAMEL'S HUMP

Shaggy fur

Fatty tissue, connective tissue, and blood vessels

Skin

Woolly fur

Pigs and hippopotamuses

Pigs, hogs, boars, and the babirusa are all hoofed mammals but are not strict herbivores. While they eat plant matter, they also eat grubs, earthworms, eggs, and small animals. They forage for food in leaf litter and dirt with their long snouts. A pig's snout is surrounded by tough cartilage, which is similar to flexible bone. The upper and lower canines form sharp tusks that are used as weapons and for displaying status. Social peccaries look like pigs but have long, slender limbs; a scent gland on the rump; and a complex stomach to digest the plant matter they eat. Hippopotamuses also look like pigs, but their closest relatives are probably whales. These barrel-shaped herbivores are strong swimmers and spend most of the day resting in water before emerging at night to feed.

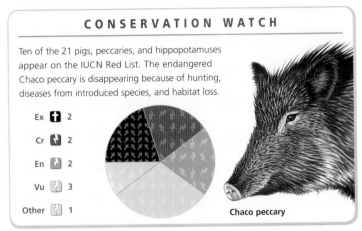

CONSERVATION WATCH

Ten of the 21 pigs, peccaries, and hippopotamuses appear on the IUCN Red List. The endangered Chaco peccary is disappearing because of hunting, diseases from introduced species, and habitat loss.

Ex ✝ 2
Cr ⚐ 2
En ⚐ 2
Vu ⚐ 3
Other ⚐ 1

Chaco peccary

▼ **Babirusa**
Babyrousa babyrussa
Skin is mostly hairless, with large folds and wrinkles.

▲ **Giant hog**
Hylocherus meinertzhageni
Males have puffy cheek pads that contain scent glands.

▲ **Red river hog**
Potamochoerus porcus
Butt heads and whip each other with tails during fights

◄ ⚐ **Pygmy hog**
Sus salvanius
Smallest pig: Males reach maximum weight of only 20 pounds (9 kg).

Adults

► **Hippopotamus**
Hippopotamus amphibius
Although this mammal does not have sweat glands, its skin is protected by mucus glands that stain the skin red.

♀

♂

◄ ▲ **Wild boar**
Sus scrofa
Wild boars wallow in mud or water for protection from sun and insects. Piglets' camouflaging stripes fade with age.

Juveniles

▶ **White-lipped peccary**
Tayassu pecari

▼ **Chaco peccary**
Catagonus wagneri
Communicates by grunts
and chattering teeth

▶ **Warthog**
Phacochoerus
africanus
Both male and female
warthogs have tusks.
Their padded knees
are for kneeling
during feeding.

▼ **Bush pig**
Potamochoerus
larvatus

▶ **Collared peccary (javelina)**
Pecari tajacu
Group members greet by
rubbing heads on rumps;
they also groom each other.

OPEN WIDE

Hippopotamuses can open their jaws wide because they are hinged
together far back in the skull. They are lined with sharp teeth. The lower
canine teeth of males can grow longer than a foot (30 cm) and are used
to do battle with each other. Sound waves travel through the jaws,
allowing hippopotamuses to hear underwater.

▲ **Pygmy hippopotamus**
Hexaprotodon liberiensis
Mostly lives alone and is
active at night

Baleen whales

Whales, dolphins, and porpoises are called cetaceans. Whale ancestors lived entirely on land, and were probably also those of hippopotamuses. Over time, whales became as streamlined as fish, modifying their front legs into flippers, losing their back legs entirely, and developing a powerful tail with two flattened flukes. All cetaceans now feed, rest, mate, give birth, and raise young entirely in the water. There are two groups of cetaceans: baleen whales and toothed whales. Baleen whales, the giants of the ocean, feed on tiny prey. They have thin, meshlike plates of a bony substance called baleen that hang down from their top jaw. This strains the water for tiny animals that are then swallowed. Many baleen whales communicate with moaning sounds. Some species form long and complicated songs.

Humpback whale
Megaptera novaeangliae

Bowhead whale
Balaena mysticetus
Kept warm by a 24-inch (60-cm) layer of blubber just under skin

Gray whale
Eschrichtius robustus
Adults are covered in lice and barnacles. They feed by straining sediment scooped from the seafloor.

Fin whale
Balaenoptera physalus
Fin whales can swim as fast as 23 miles per hour (37 km/h).

Minke whale
Balaenoptera acutorostrata
Both the smallest and most abundant baleen whale

Blue whale
Balaenoptera musculus
Largest animal ever to live on Earth

Northern right whale
Eubalaena glacialis
This whale has been hunted by humans for at least 1,000 years.

CONSERVATION WATCH

Of 13 baleen whale species, 12 appear on the IUCN Red List. The endangered fin whale was overhunted in the 20th century by commercial whalers. Thanks to whaling bans, the species is recovering.

Ex 🕆 0
Cr 0
En 5
Vu 1
Other 6

Fin whale

Whales, dolphins, and porpoises

Whales, dolphins, and porpoises live in all the world's oceans and seas, except under the ice caps and in the Caspian Sea. River dolphins live in some of the world's major rivers.

CATCH OF THE DAY

HUNTING TACTICS

Whales use strategies and tricks when hunting. Baleen whales have enormous mouths to engulf huge quantities of tiny animals. Toothed whales pursue single prey, using sonar to find it. Many whales hunt together, calling out their next move as they swim. Humpback whales use bubbles as a group hunting tactic. One humpback swims around a school of fish to herd them together. While circling upward, it breathes out to produce a "net" of bubbles, which the prey cannot swim through. The whales then take turns swimming through the trapped school with their mouths open, eating the fish.

Orcas regularly patrol sites where their favorite prey dwell. Here an orca lunges right up onto the beach to snatch a sea lion pup.

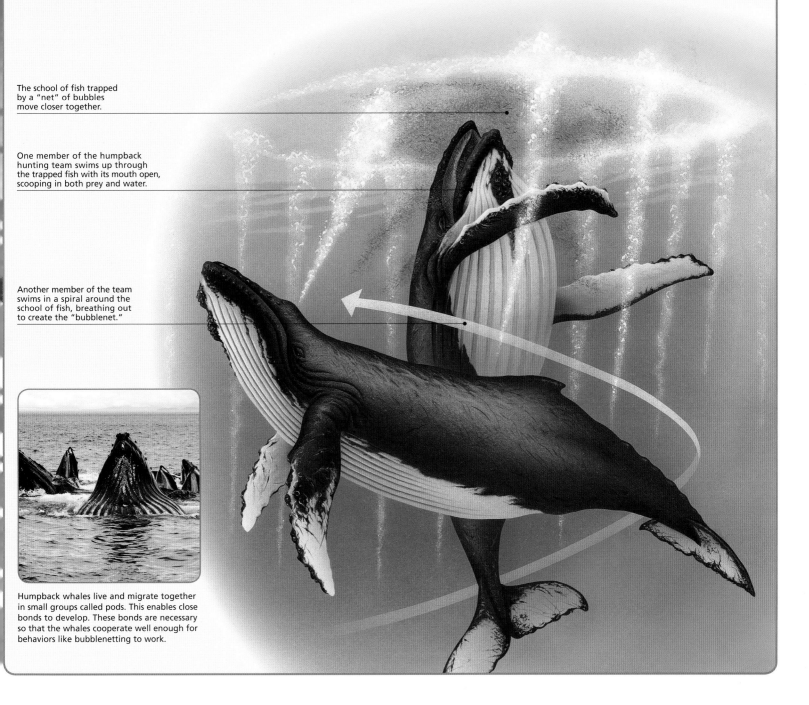

The school of fish trapped by a "net" of bubbles move closer together.

One member of the humpback hunting team swims up through the trapped fish with its mouth open, scooping in both prey and water.

Another member of the team swims in a spiral around the school of fish, breathing out to create the "bubblenet."

Humpback whales live and migrate together in small groups called pods. This enables close bonds to develop. These bonds are necessary so that the whales cooperate well enough for behaviors like bubblenetting to work.

Toothed whales

Most cetaceans are toothed whales. The group includes sperm whales, narwhals and belugas, beaked whales, dolphins, porpoises, and river dolphins. Compared to the massive baleen whales, most toothed whales are medium-size. They also tend to live in larger groups and have more complex relationships. Toothed whales are among the most intelligent mammals. They are vocal when they communicate and can be very playful. Toothed whales use echolocation to "see" underwater with sound. They emit high-pitched clicks, then use the echoes that bounce back from objects in the water around them to determine their location. Fish and squid are their preferred prey. Toothed whales' jaws are lined with sharp, cone-shaped teeth that allow them to grasp prey firmly, but not to chew it.

CONSERVATION WATCH

Of the 69 species of toothed whales, 35 appear on the IUCN Red List. China's baiji is critically endangered. Fishermen often catch and kill baijis by accident. Its habitat is being destroyed by pollution and other causes.

Ex	✝	0
Cr		2
En		2
Vu		1
Other		30

Baiji

Common porpoise (harbor porpoise)
Phocoena phocoena

Spectacled porpoise
Australophocaena dioptrica
Lives with one or two others, or alone

Finless porpoise
Neophocaena phocaenoides
Has no dorsal fin

Common dolphin
Delphinus delphis
Lives in herds of several hundred, or even a thousand, members

Risso's dolphin
Grampus griseus
Crisscross scars from battles with squid prey

False killer whale
Pseudorca crassidens
Mothers nurse calves for two years.

Pygmy sperm whale
Kogia breviceps

Sperm whale
Physeter catodon
Large "melon" on head is filled with oil.

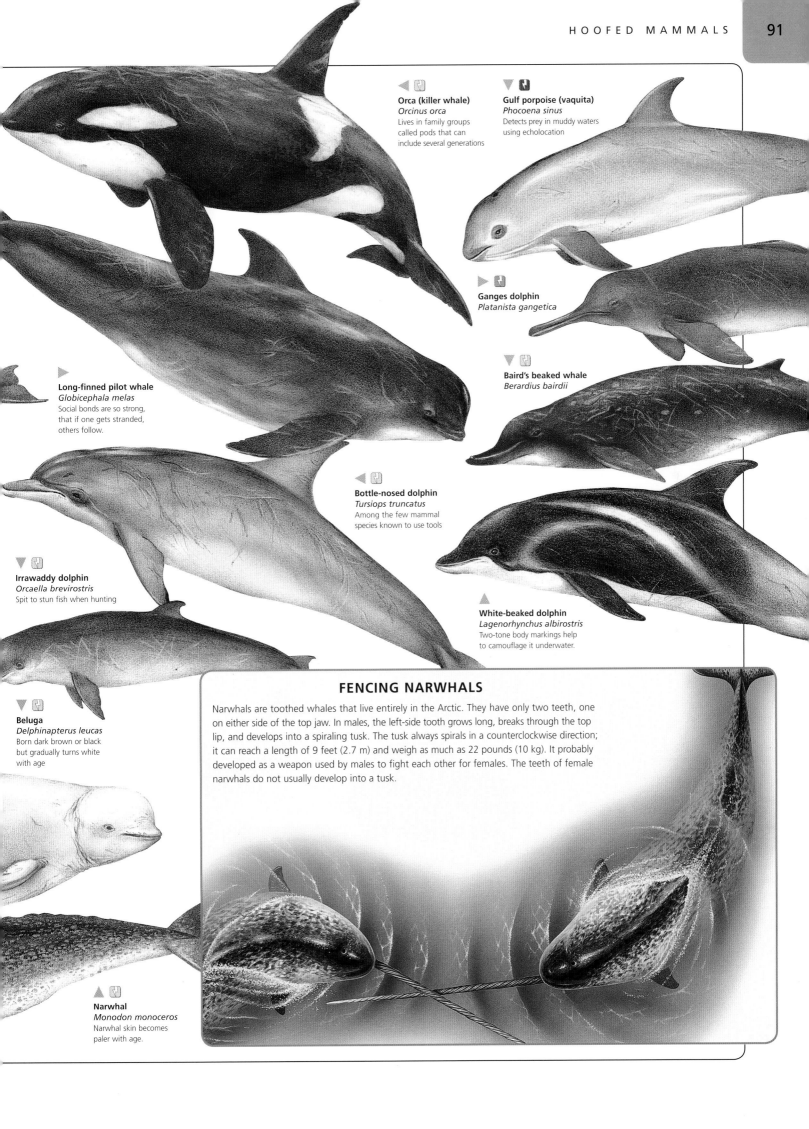

Orca (killer whale)
Orcinus orca
Lives in family groups called pods that can include several generations

Gulf porpoise (vaquita)
Phocoena sinus
Detects prey in muddy waters using echolocation

Ganges dolphin
Platanista gangetica

Baird's beaked whale
Berardius bairdii

Long-finned pilot whale
Globicephala melas
Social bonds are so strong, that if one gets stranded, others follow.

Bottle-nosed dolphin
Tursiops truncatus
Among the few mammal species known to use tools

Irrawaddy dolphin
Orcaella brevirostris
Spit to stun fish when hunting

White-beaked dolphin
Lagenorhynchus albirostris
Two-tone body markings help to camouflage it underwater.

Beluga
Delphinapterus leucas
Born dark brown or black but gradually turns white with age

FENCING NARWHALS

Narwhals are toothed whales that live entirely in the Arctic. They have only two teeth, one on either side of the top jaw. In males, the left-side tooth grows long, breaks through the top lip, and develops into a spiraling tusk. The tusk always spirals in a counterclockwise direction; it can reach a length of 9 feet (2.7 m) and weigh as much as 22 pounds (10 kg). It probably developed as a weapon used by males to fight each other for females. The teeth of female narwhals do not usually develop into a tusk.

Narwhal
Monodon monoceros
Narwhal skin becomes paler with age.

1 ORDER • 29 FAMILIES • 442 GENERA • 2,010 SPECIES

Rodents

Almost half of all mammal species are rodents. One reason they are so successful is that they produce large numbers of offspring very quickly. Rodents tend to be small animals with stocky bodies and short limbs and tails. Their small size has helped them adapt to many habitats and conditions. Rodents all have a pair of chisel-like incisor teeth in each jaw, which continue to grow throughout their lives. There are three main groups of rodents: the squirrel-like rodents, mice, and cavies. All squirrel-like rodents have jaw muscles arranged to give them a strong bite. Many squirrels live in trees, feeding on fruit, nuts, leaves, and insects. Ground-dwelling squirrels, prairie dogs, marmots, and chipmunks prefer to eat grasses and small plants. Pocket gophers and mice, as well as mountain beavers and springhares, live underground in burrows. Beavers live mostly in water.

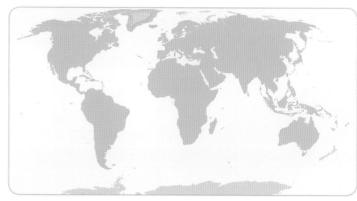

Rodents

Rodents occur in the wild on every continent except Antarctica. They can live in the freezing cold of the Arctic or in the heat of the world's deserts.

Long-tailed pocket mouse
Chaetodipus formosus
This aggressive and territorial mouse lives alone.

Black-tailed prairie dog
Cynomys ludovicianus

Hoary marmot
Marmota caligata
Hibernates in burrows during winter months

European souslik
Spermophilus citellus
Looks for predators by standing on back legs

Mountain beaver
Aplodontia rufa
Never strays far from its home burrow

Eurasian beaver
Castor fiber

Striped ground squirrel
Xerus erythropus
Stores food to survive dry season

Desert kangaroo rat
Dipodomys deserti

Botta's pocket gopher
Thomomys bottae
This gopher lives alone and mostly underground.

Gundi
Ctenodactylus gundi
Colonies of gundis lie on top of each other to keep warm during winter.

Eastern chipmunk
Tamias striatus
Stores gathered food in cheek pouches

Springhare
Pedetes capensis
Jumps on strong back legs like a kangaroo

Eurasian red squirrel
Sciurus vulgaris
Stores acorns and nuts in the ground

Southern flying squirrel
Glaucomys volans
Thin piece of skin between and wrist allows it to glide

Prevost's squirrel
Callosciurus prevostii

BUSY BEAVERS

LODGES AND DAMS

Beavers are the engineers of the animal world. They change their environment by building dams, canals, and lodges. Beavers live in family groups made up of a male and female pair and their offspring. The pair stay together for life. Families may live in a riverbank burrow system, or they may build a lodge. A lodge is a dome of sticks and mud, with underwater entrances that lead to a raised living area. The living area is lined with plant material. Beavers create a calm pond for their lodge by building dams to stop the flow of water around it. They also dig canals to link their dam to nearby sources of food. Several generations of a beaver family may use and look after a dam. Eventually, however, it will fill up with silt and the family will need to find somewhere else to build a new home.

Beavers paddle through the water using their webbed back feet. They steer with their flat, scaly tails. Clear eyelids keep water out of their eyes while allowing them to see.

TEETH AND JAWS

Like all rodents, beavers have two pairs of large, sharp incisor teeth. These teeth never stop growing, and wear in a way that ensures they stay sharp. The outside surface is covered by a tough enamel that protects the teeth. But the inside surface is softer. It wears away as the beaver gnaws; this creates an edge like a chisel. A gap, called the diastema, lets the lips close behind the incisors. This keeps inedible material, like wood, out of the mouth when gnawing.

Incisor teeth are at the front of the mouth.

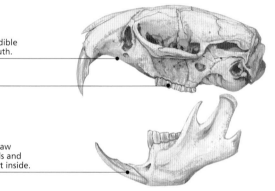

Diastema keeps inedible material out of mouth.

Molars grind food.

Incisors slice and gnaw through tough shells and seeds to get to meat inside.

Chew and cut
Beavers eat bark and use their strong incisor teeth to chew through tree trunks.

Carry away
After felling trees and saplings for cross-braces, beavers carry smaller logs in their mouths.

The way in
The lodge's entrance is underwater to protect the beavers from predators.

Warm indoors
Temperatures inside the lodge are much more constant than the changeable climate outside.

Beaver lodge

Mice and cavies

Mice and their relatives, or mouse-like rodents, mainly have pointed faces with long whiskers. They all have chewing muscles that let them gnaw readily. Most are seed-eaters that live on the ground, but some spend time in trees, underground, or in water. Dormice are mouse-like rodents that often live in trees. They survive harsh winters by hibernating. Jumping mice and jerboas have long back feet and tails, which let them move by hopping. Compared to the mouse-like rodents, most cavies and their relatives, or cavy-like rodents, have large heads, plump bodies, short limbs, and small tails. They tend to have smaller litters, and babies are born in a more advanced state. Cavy-like rodents, such as guinea pigs and porcupines, have chewing muscles that give them a strong bite.

CONSERVATION WATCH

Of the 2,010 rodent species, 698 appear on the IUCN Red List. This includes the golden hamster, which is endangered in the wild. Large numbers survive in captivity as pets throughout the world.

Ex ✝ 31
Cr 56
En 98
Vu 161
Other 352

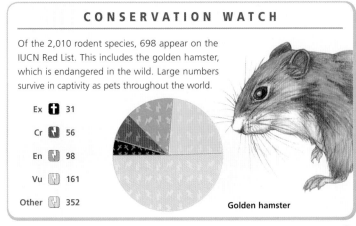

Golden hamster

Harvest mouse
Micromys minutus
Climbs using tail like a fifth limb

Meadow jumping mouse
Zapus hudsonius

Vlei rat
Otomys irroratus

Gray climbing mouse
Dendromus melanotis

Hispid cotton rat
Sigmodon hispidus

Deer mouse
Peromyscus maniculatus

Northern three-toed jerboa
Dipus sagitta

Long-clawed mole-vole
Prometheomys schaposchnikowi

Muskrat
Ondatra zibethicus

Fawn hopping mouse
Notomys cervinus

Garden dormouse
Eliomys quercinus
Can hibernate for more than half the year

European hamster (common hamster)
Cricetus cricetus

Black rat (roof rat, ship rat)
Rattus rattus

DISEASE SPREADERS

Black and brown rats have lived alongside humans for thousands of years. They forage in often great numbers among crops, food stores, and rubbish dumps. Not only do they cause untold damage, they also spread disease. Brown rats triggered the bubonic plague, which killed more than a third of Europe's population in the Middle Ages. By spreading disease, they have caused more deaths than all the wars in history.

Greater bandicoot rat
Bandicota indica

Great gerbil
Rhombomys opimus

Greater stick-nest rat
Leporillus conditor

Smooth-tailed giant rat
Mallomys rothschildi

Siberian collared lemmi (Arctic lemming)
Dicrostonyx torquatus
Brown summer coat change to white in the winter mont

Striped grass mouse
Lemniscomys striatus

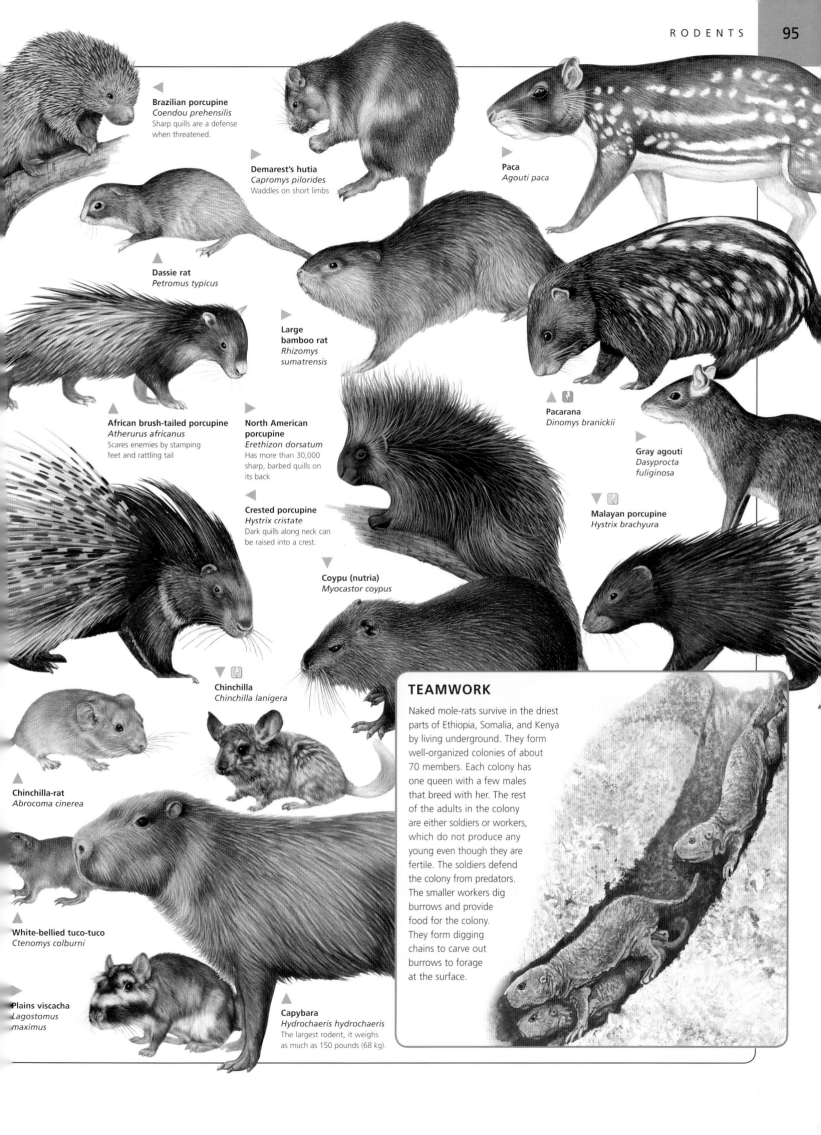

Brazilian porcupine
Coendou prehensilis
Sharp quills are a defense
when threatened.

Demarest's hutia
Capromys pilorides
Waddles on short limbs

Paca
Agouti paca

Dassie rat
Petromus typicus

**Large
bamboo rat**
*Rhizomys
sumatrensis*

African brush-tailed porcupine
Atherurus africanus
Scares enemies by stamping
feet and rattling tail

**North American
porcupine**
Erethizon dorsatum
Has more than 30,000
sharp, barbed quills on
its back

Pacarana
Dinomys branickii

Gray agouti
*Dasyprocta
fuliginosa*

Crested porcupine
Hystrix cristate
Dark quills along neck can
be raised into a crest.

Malayan porcupine
Hystrix brachyura

Coypu (nutria)
Myocastor coypus

Chinchilla
Chinchilla lanigera

Chinchilla-rat
Abrocoma cinerea

White-bellied tuco-tuco
Ctenomys colburni

Plains viscacha
*Lagostomus
maximus*

Capybara
Hydrochaeris hydrochaeris
The largest rodent, it weighs
as much as 150 pounds (68 kg).

TEAMWORK

Naked mole-rats survive in the driest
parts of Ethiopia, Somalia, and Kenya
by living underground. They form
well-organized colonies of about
70 members. Each colony has
one queen with a few males
that breed with her. The rest
of the adults in the colony
are either soldiers or workers,
which do not produce any
young even though they are
fertile. The soldiers defend
the colony from predators.
The smaller workers dig
burrows and provide
food for the colony.
They form digging
chains to carve out
burrows to forage
at the surface.

2 ORDERS • 3 FAMILIES • 19 GENERA • 97 SPECIES

Rabbits and Elephant Shrews

Rabbits, hares, and pikas look similar to large rodents, but they belong to an order called the lagomorphs. Like rodents, they have large, constantly growing incisors and produce many offspring quickly. Unlike rodents, a second pair of incisors, known as peg teeth, sit behind the first. Plant-eaters, lagomorphs all have eyes on the sides of their heads to keep on the lookout for predators. Rabbits and hares have large ears for sharp hearing; pikas have shorter, rounded ears. With their powerful back legs, many species can outrun predators. Elephant shrews are named for their long, mobile snouts. They live on the ground, eat insects, and have excellent sight and hearing. They scamper or leap away from predators on their slender limbs. Most elephant shrews share a territory with a lifelong mate.

Arctic hare
Lepus timidus
Brown summer coat blends in with the tundra vegetation. This coat turns white in winter, for camouflage in the snow.

Central African hare
Poelagus marjorita

Pygmy rabbit
Brachylagus idahoensis

Hispid hare
Caprolagus hispidus

Brown hare
Lepus europaeus
Can run at speeds of 35 miles per hour (56 km/h)

Sumatran rabbit
Nesolagus netscheri

Eastern cottontail
Sylvilagus floridanus

Forest rabbit
Sylvilagus brasiliensis

European rabbit
Oryctolagus cuniculus

CONSERVATION WATCH

Of the 97 species of lagomorphs and elephant shrews, 34 appear on the IUCN Red List. South Africa's riverine rabbit is critically endangered because of the clearing of its habitat. Feral cats and dogs, as well as illegal trapping by hunters, are other threats.

Ex		1
Cr		4
En		10
Vu		7
Other		12

Riverine rabbit

Lagomorphs   Lagomorphs and elephant shrews

Lagomorphs occur naturally worldwide except Australia, Antarctica, southern South America, and parts of Southeast Asia. Elephant shrews live throughout much of Africa.

Black-tailed jackrabbit
Lepus californicus
Enormous ears keep it cool in summer and can hear a predator's slightest sound.

Checkered elephant shrew
Rhynchocyon cirnei
Highly sensitive, flexible snout finds insects.

Rufous elephant shrew (spectacled elephant shrew)
Elephantulus rufescens
Back legs are longer than front legs.

Asiatic brown hare
Lepus tolai

Volcano rabbit
Romerolagus diazi
This rabbit is found only in Mexico. Tail is almost impossible to see.

Four-toed elephant shrew
Petrodromus tetradactylus
Unlike most elephant shrews, it has four toes on its back feet, instead of five.

Snowshoe hare
Lepus americanus
Has brown coat and eats green plants and berries in summer; grows white coat and eats bark and buds in winter

Daurian pika
Ochotona daurica

Golden-rumped elephant shrew
Rhynchocyon chrysopygus

Northern pika
Ochotona alpina
When snow gets too deep in winter, pika retreats into tunnels.

American pika
Ochotona princeps
Makes two main sounds, an alarm call and a mating song

Royle's pika
Ochotona roylei
Stores "haypiles" of long grasses during summer to eat during harsh winters

ROCK ELEPHANT SHREW HABITAT

Rock elephant shrews nest in rock overhangs. Here they are protected from predators and the weather. Young are well developed when born and can walk soon after birth.

Like other elephant shrews, they have a long, sensitive, mobile snout. They use this to find insects, such as ants and termites, which they eat.

Their gray-brown colored coat acts as a good camouflage; it makes it hard for predators to see them in their rocky habitat.

Birds

31 ORDERS • 194 FAMILIES • 2,161 GENERA • 9,723 SPECIES

Birds

Easily startled, flamingos take flight to avoid danger. They need to run a few steps to gain enough speed to take off. In flight, they stretch out their long necks and trail their legs behind them.

Birds live in almost every habitat on Earth, from the freezing cold of the Antarctic to arid deserts and even urban areas. The ostrich, which can grow taller than 9 feet (2.7 m) and weigh more than 300 pounds (136 kg), is the largest bird. The smallest is the bee hummingbird, which weighs just ⅒ ounce (2.8 g). The first birds developed from dinosaurs more than 150 million years ago. These early species had feathers and could fly. Today, all birds still have feathers and most can fly, but some have lost this ability. Like their reptile ancestors, birds have scales on their limbs and lay eggs. Unlike reptiles, they are warm-blooded.

Flight has made many birds great travelers, migrating long distances every year to escape cold winters and find food. The need to react and maneuver quickly on the wing means that sight is the best developed sense in birds. Hearing is the next most important sense, even though birds do not have external ears. Birds mainly communicate by sound. More than half of all birds are called perching birds. They are known for their ability to sing or make complex calls. They sing to mark their territory, warn of danger, or find a mate. Some birds form lifelong pair bonds with their mate; many live and breed in large flocks; others are solitary.

BIRDS 101

Birds come in all shapes and sizes, but they all share similar body features. Their front limbs are modified into wings. Birds have no sweat glands in their skin, but most produce an oily substance from a preen gland at the base of the tail. This helps keep the feathers in good condition. The bodies of flying birds are designed to let them move through the air with ease. Their weight is concentrated in the center of the body—a rather bullet-like shape that is streamlined to reduce the effort of flight. Birds have fewer bones than mammals, so their bodies are light as well as strong. Many bones have hollow spaces inside, which makes them even lighter. Some of these spaces are connected to the bird's breathing system. This allows room for more air to be taken in.

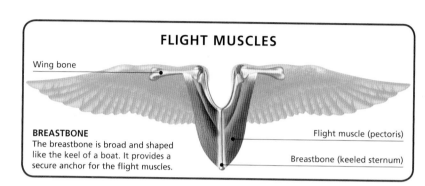

FLIGHT MUSCLES

Wing bone

BREASTBONE
The breastbone is broad and shaped like the keel of a boat. It provides a secure anchor for the flight muscles.

Flight muscle (pectoris)

Breastbone (keeled sternum)

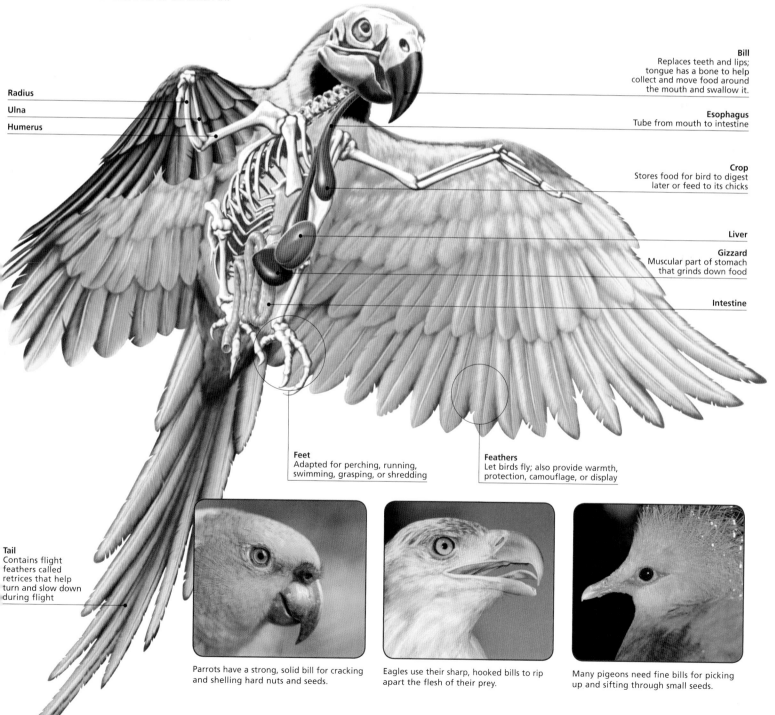

Radius

Ulna

Humerus

Bill
Replaces teeth and lips; tongue has a bone to help collect and move food around the mouth and swallow it.

Esophagus
Tube from mouth to intestine

Crop
Stores food for bird to digest later or feed to its chicks

Liver

Gizzard
Muscular part of stomach that grinds down food

Intestine

Feet
Adapted for perching, running, swimming, grasping, or shredding

Feathers
Let birds fly; also provide warmth, protection, camouflage, or display

Tail
Contains flight feathers called retrices that help turn and slow down during flight

Parrots have a strong, solid bill for cracking and shelling hard nuts and seeds.

Eagles use their sharp, hooked bills to rip apart the flesh of their prey.

Many pigeons need fine bills for picking up and sifting through small seeds.

KINDS OF FEATHERS

Feathers combine strength with lightness. They are made of keratin, the same material as mammal hair and claws, and reptile scales. Each feather consists of a central shaft with many paired vanes branching off it. In some feathers, the vane is made up of barbs, lined with hooked barbules that interlock to hold the vane stiff. There are three main kinds of feathers. Down feathers lie closest to the body. They provide protection from the cold. Contour feathers lie on top of the down. They keep the bird streamlined so it moves smoothly through air. Flight feathers on the bird's wing and tail allow the bird to take off, fly, maneuver, and land.

FLIGHT FEATHERS
Long, stiff, and smooth

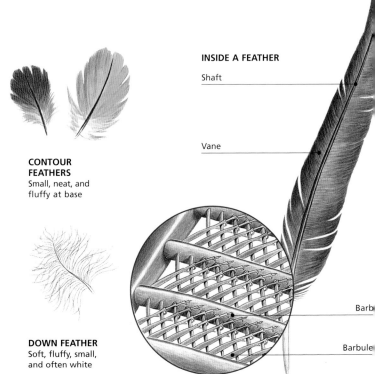

CONTOUR FEATHERS
Small, neat, and fluffy at base

DOWN FEATHER
Soft, fluffy, small, and often white

INSIDE A FEATHER
Shaft

Vane

Barb

Barbule

FROM EGG TO CHICK

Male birds fertilize eggs inside females' bodies. The albumen layers, yolk, membranes, and shell develop before the egg is laid. Inside the hard, protective shell, the developing embryo is nourished by the yolk and albumen. Eggs are usually laid in a nest. The parents often take turns sitting on the nest to keep the eggs warm. When the chick is ready to hatch, it has to crack the shell so it can break out.

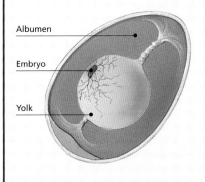

Albumen

Embryo

Yolk

NEWLY LAID EGG
Yolk provides food; albumen provides water.

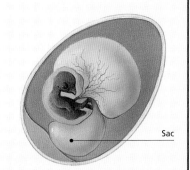

Sac

EMBRYONIC CHICK
A special sac stores the embryo's waste.

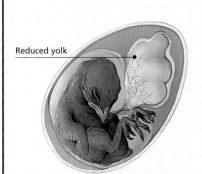

Reduced yolk

DEVELOPING CHICK
As the chick grows, it absorbs the yolk.

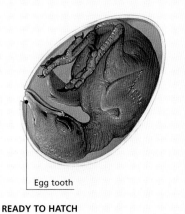

Egg tooth

READY TO HATCH
Chick uses "egg tooth" to crack through shell.

CATCHING PREY

Birds have adapted in various ways to find the food they eat. Many birds, such as swifts, eat insects. These insectivores, as they are called, catch bugs as they fly through the air. Woodpeckers bore through tree bark to get at grubs; birds of prey use their talons to seize larger prey; waders probe in the mud for worms; and herons spear fish with their bills. Pelicans use the stretchable pouch on their bills like a fishing net to catch prey. They have a clear third eyelid that lets them see underwater.

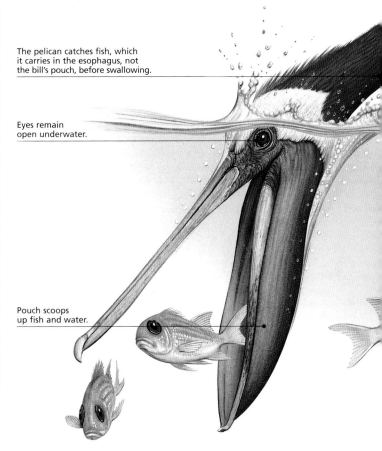

The pelican catches fish, which it carries in the esophagus, not the bill's pouch, before swallowing.

Eyes remain open underwater.

Pouch scoops up fish and water.

BIRD BEHAVIOR

A great gray owl feeds a mouse to its chick. Some owls change their breeding season to match food supplies.

King penguins form colonies of more than 100,000 pairs on islands off the coast of Antarctica. They do not build nests. Instead, adults incubate eggs on their feet. Despite the crowded conditions, king penguins rarely fight.

All pelicans have webbing that runs between their toes.

The green-backed heron stabs at fish and frogs with its long, sharp bill as it wades through wetlands.

Most birds have just one breeding partner. Red-crowned cranes attract and keep mates by dancing.

3 ORDERS • 5 FAMILIES • 15 GENERA • 60 SPECIES

Ratites and Tinamous

Most flightless birds—ostriches, rheas, emus, cassowaries, and kiwis—are known as ratites. Their breastbones lack the keel of flying birds because they do not have large flight muscles. Most have stubby wings and soft flight feathers. Ratites probably lost the ability to fly because they either lacked predators or could evade them more easily by other means. They are powerful runners that can use their strong, long legs for kicking. The ostrich is so fast it can outrun a racehorse. Rheas have large, cloaklike wings, which they sometimes spread to act like a sail as they run. Tinamous are small, plump flying birds, closely related to ratites. They have a keeled breastbone and many can fly, although not very well. They usually avoid predators either by standing still or by creeping through undergrowth.

Ostrich
Struthio camelus
Males raise their white tail feathers during courtship. Both males and females care for eggs.

Great tinamou
Tinamus major

Variegated tinamou
Crypturellus variegatus
Tinamous forage on the ground for their diet of seeds, roots, and insects.

Greater rhea
Rhea americana

Elegant crested tinamou
Eudromia elegans

Emu
Dromaius novaehollandiae
Emus have hairy, double feathers.

Southern cassowary
Casuarius casuarius
Helmet on head pushes through dense rain forest vegetation. Male builds a nest and incubates eggs.

Little spotted kiwi
Apteryx owenii
Nostrils are located at the tip of its bill.

FAST FACT

Kiwis are among the few birds that have a good sense of smell. They forage on the ground and use their long, sensitive bills to find prey, such as worms and insects, by their scent. Kiwis have very poor eyesight.

CONSERVATION WATCH

Of the 60 species of ratites and tinamous, 22 appear on the IUCN Red List. New Zealand's endangered brown kiwi has been devastated by introduced predators, such as dogs and cats. These predators, together with habitat loss, have killed most of the population on New Zealand's two main islands.

Ex	🕆	2
Cr		2
En		2
Vu		10
Other		6

Brown kiwi

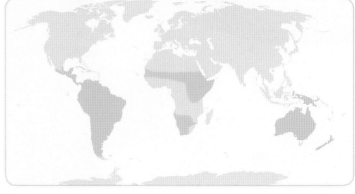

▢ Ratites and tinamous

Ostriches are found in Africa. Emus and cassowaries are strictly Australasian. Kiwis occur in New Zealand. Rheas and tinamous live in Central and South America.

1 ORDER • 5 FAMILIES • 80 GENERA • 290 SPECIES

Gamebirds

Pheasants, partridges, grouse, quail, and their relatives are called gamebirds because many of them are hunted by humans. They have stocky bodies, relatively small heads, and short, broad wings. While most can fly fast and low over short distances, many live mainly on the ground. Gamebirds usually have strong legs and can run well. The chicks of ground-dwelling species run quickly soon after hatching. Because they are the favored food of many predators, most gamebirds have dull-colored plumage that acts as camouflage. Others, like male pheasants and peafowl, are brilliantly colored. Males use their bright plumage, or elaborate feathery outgrowths, to make themselves stand out to females. They may court females with calls or complex dances.

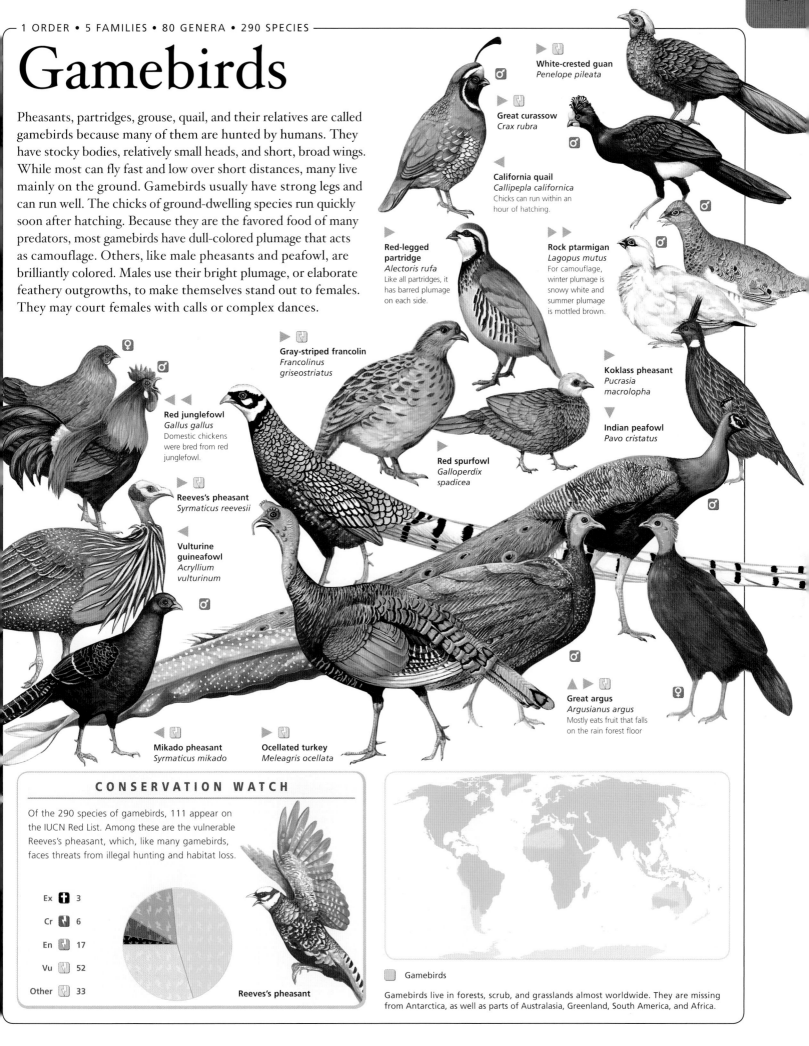

White-crested guan
Penelope pileata

Great curassow
Crax rubra

California quail
Callipepla californica
Chicks can run within an hour of hatching.

Red-legged partridge
Alectoris rufa
Like all partridges, it has barred plumage on each side.

Rock ptarmigan
Lagopus mutus
For camouflage, winter plumage is snowy white and summer plumage is mottled brown.

Koklass pheasant
Pucrasia macrolopha

Indian peafowl
Pavo cristatus

Gray-striped francolin
Francolinus griseostriatus

Red junglefowl
Gallus gallus
Domestic chickens were bred from red junglefowl.

Reeves's pheasant
Syrmaticus reevesii

Vulturine guineafowl
Acryllium vulturinum

Red spurfowl
Galloperdix spadicea

Great argus
Argusianus argus
Mostly eats fruit that falls on the rain forest floor

Mikado pheasant
Syrmaticus mikado

Ocellated turkey
Meleagris ocellata

CONSERVATION WATCH

Of the 290 species of gamebirds, 111 appear on the IUCN Red List. Among these are the vulnerable Reeves's pheasant, which, like many gamebirds, faces threats from illegal hunting and habitat loss.

Ex	✝	3
Cr		6
En		17
Vu		52
Other		33

Reeves's pheasant

☐ Gamebirds

Gamebirds live in forests, scrub, and grasslands almost worldwide. They are missing from Antarctica, as well as parts of Australasia, Greenland, South America, and Africa.

1 ORDER • 3 FAMILIES • 52 GENERA • 162 SPECIES

Waterfowl

Ducks, geese, and swans are known as waterfowl and often live on or near water. Waterfowl are excellent swimmers with short legs and webbed feet. Those that live on land have less webbing. Waterfowl have broad, flat bills and necks that are long compared to their bodies. Their bodies are covered in dense, waterproof feathers and a thick layer of down to protect them from cold water. These feathers can be brightly colored and patterned. Some waterfowl species do not fly, but most are strong fliers and many migrate between their summer and winter homes. They migrate in search of food, such as plant matter or fish and shellfish. Screamers are related to waterfowl. They live in South America on riverbanks and uproot aquatic vegetation with their hooked bills.

Common eider
Somateria mollissima
Lives on the coast and eats shellfish; its down is prized as a warm filling for bedding.

Red-crested pochard
Netta rufina

Common shelduck
Tadorna tadorna
Male has an orange knob on bill; female has white.

Freckled duck
Stictonetta naevosa
Eats plankton in freshly flooded, inland Australian swamps

Common pochard
Aythya ferina

Orinoco goose
Neochen jubata
Nests in tree hollows on riverbanks

Oldsquaw (long-tailed duck)
Clangula hyemalis

Mallard
Anas platyrhynchos

Comb duck
Sarkidiornis melanotos
The male has a large fleshy growth on top of its bill.

Torrent duck
Merganetta armata
Breeds in riverside caves in South America's Andes mountains

Wood duck
Aix sponsa
Ducklings sometimes leap from tree nests into water below.

CONSERVATION WATCH

Of the 162 species of waterfowl, 41 appear on the IUCN Red List. The white-headed duck is endangered from breeding with non-native ducks. Other threats include habitat clearing, pollution, hunting, and accidental drowning in fishing nets.

Ex ✝ 6
Cr 6
En 9
Vu 11
Other 9

White-headed duck

☐ Waterfowl

Waterfowl live in freshwater and ocean wetland habitats worldwide, except Antarctica and parts of Greenland and Africa. They occur in almost every kind of wetland.

Muscovy duck
Cairina moschata
Isolated groups live in South America and Africa.

White-faced whistling-duck
Dendrocygna viduata

Snow goose
Anser caerulescens
Breeds in North American tundra; migrates in winter to southern North America

Red-breasted goose
Branta ruficollis

Southern screamer
Chauna torquata
Alarm calls can be heard more than 2 miles (3.2 km) away.

Canada goose
Branta canadensis
Lives in flocks, aside from nesting time

Northern shoveler
Anas clypeata
Northern shovelers live in small groups of up to 20 birds, but larger numbers may migrate together.

Mute swan
Cygnus olor
Mute swans mate for life. Females incubate the eggs, but both parents care for young.

Whooper swan
Cygnus cygnus

Black-necked swan
Cygnus melanocoryphus

Bean goose
Anser fabalis
Breeds in Arctic during summer; flies south to the Mediterranean and China for winter

Magpie goose
Anseranas semipalmata
Lives in northern Australian swamps; it is a good swimmer although its feet are only partially webbed.

Coscoroba swan
Coscoroba coscoroba

MIGRATING GEESE

Barnacle geese breed in Greenland during summer, before flying south to Europe for the cold winter months. Like many waterfowl, flocks fly in a V-shaped formation when migrating. This is an efficient way to travel long distances. The lead goose breaks up the air, creating small updrafts that make flight easier for the birds behind it. The geese can also see clearly what is ahead of them. Each bird takes a turn at being in the lead.

1 ORDER • 1 FAMILY • 6 GENERA • 17 SPECIES

Penguins

Penguins are flightless birds that use their wings to swim rather than fly. They spend three-quarters of their lives in the sea and are well adapted to life in the water. Their dense, waterproof feathers protect them from cold by trapping warm air. Beneath the skin a layer of fat called blubber provides insulation from frigid waters. On land they molt old feathers and grow new ones, which may take more than a month. Most penguins live in large, noisy colonies, where they mate and lay eggs. Chicks have down feathers for warmth. They cannot enter the water until they grow their first waterproof feathers. Before then they are dependent on their parents for food. Skuas and gulls prey on eggs and chicks, but adults have few predators on land. In the ocean, they are hunted by sharks and leopard seals.

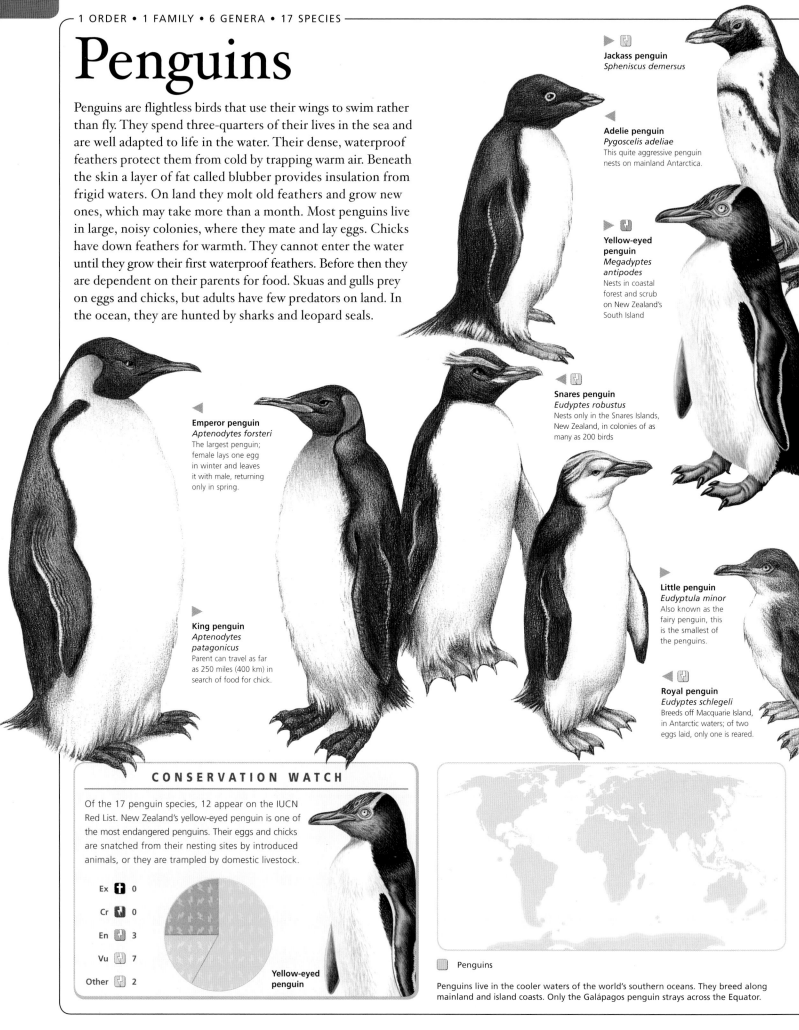

Jackass penguin
Spheniscus demersus

Adelie penguin
Pygoscelis adeliae
This quite aggressive penguin nests on mainland Antarctica.

Yellow-eyed penguin
Megadyptes antipodes
Nests in coastal forest and scrub on New Zealand's South Island

Snares penguin
Eudyptes robustus
Nests only in the Snares Islands, New Zealand, in colonies of as many as 200 birds

Emperor penguin
Aptenodytes forsteri
The largest penguin; female lays one egg in winter and leaves it with male, returning only in spring.

King penguin
Aptenodytes patagonicus
Parent can travel as far as 250 miles (400 km) in search of food for chick.

Little penguin
Eudyptula minor
Also known as the fairy penguin, this is the smallest of the penguins.

Royal penguin
Eudyptes schlegeli
Breeds off Macquarie Island, in Antarctic waters; of two eggs laid, only one is reared

CONSERVATION WATCH

Of the 17 penguin species, 12 appear on the IUCN Red List. New Zealand's yellow-eyed penguin is one of the most endangered penguins. Their eggs and chicks are snatched from their nesting sites by introduced animals, or they are trampled by domestic livestock.

Ex 🕇 0
Cr 🔲 0
En 🔲 3
Vu 🔲 7
Other 🔲 2

Yellow-eyed penguin

☐ Penguins

Penguins live in the cooler waters of the world's southern oceans. They breed along mainland and island coasts. Only the Galápagos penguin strays across the Equator.

IN AND OUT OF WATER

DIVING FOR FISH

Penguins look clumsy on land but are fast and agile in the sea, where they hunt fish and other small marine animals. They often toboggan on their stomachs down icy shores to enter the water. As they swim, penguins leap out of the water like dolphins. They breathe during these leaps. Their wings are flat, stiff paddles that let them swim much as other birds fly. They hunch their heads down into their shoulders and press their feet against their bodies to form a torpedo shape. Penguins can swim as fast as 20 miles per hour (32 km/h), and stay underwater for as long as 20 minutes.

Penguins waddle on short legs set well back on their bodies. They also jump and hop between rocks.

On land, penguins may hold their wings out to release heat from their bodies and prevent overheating.

3 ORDERS • 6 FAMILIES • 33 GENERA • 139 SPECIES

Albatrosses and Grebes

Albatrosses and petrels, or tubenoses, are well adapted to life at sea. They are called tubenoses because of their long, external, tubelike nostrils. They use their sense of smell to locate food, breeding sites, and each other. Tubenoses are excellent fliers, often flying hundreds of miles in search of squid, fish, and other marine animals. They may travel for days across open water without seeing or stopping on dry land. Grebes, too, spend their lives around water. They even nest on floating platform nests made of plant material. Larger grebes are slim and elegant; smaller species look like ducklings. Grebes have lobed toes that propel them rapidly in water. Distantly related to grebes, loons have webbed feet. Loons and grebes are both poor fliers, and prefer to dive underwater to avoid danger.

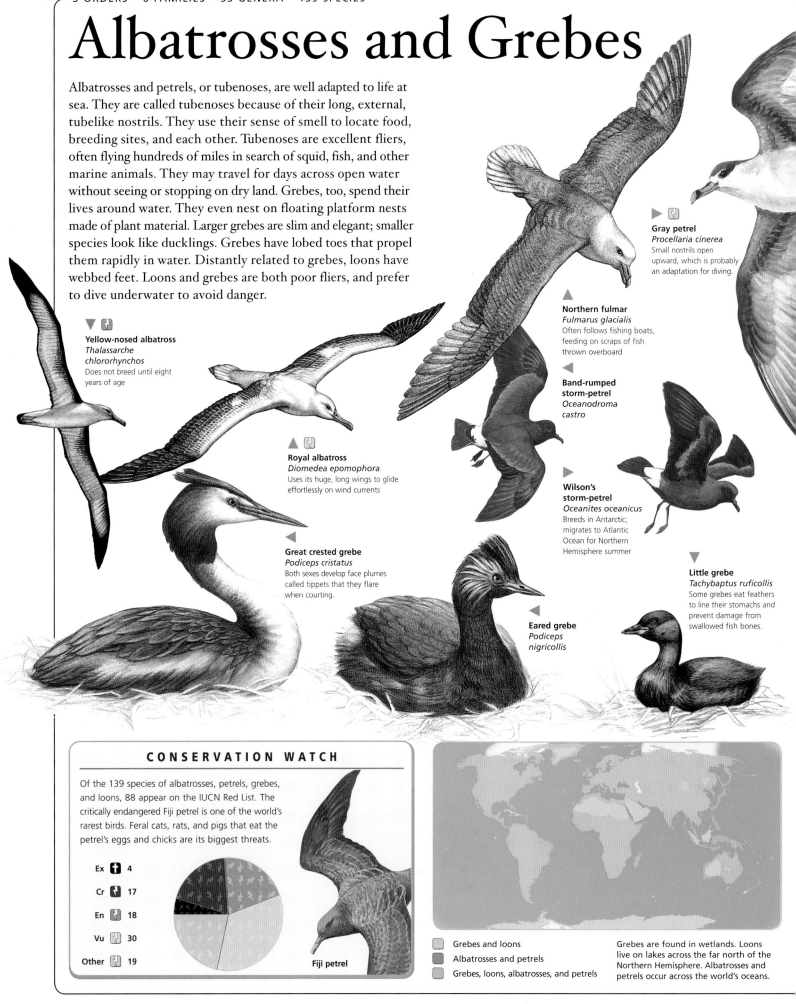

Gray petrel
Procellaria cinerea
Small nostrils open upward, which is probably an adaptation for diving.

Northern fulmar
Fulmarus glacialis
Often follows fishing boats, feeding on scraps of fish thrown overboard

Band-rumped storm-petrel
Oceanodroma castro

Wilson's storm-petrel
Oceanites oceanicus
Breeds in Antarctic; migrates to Atlantic Ocean for Northern Hemisphere summer

Yellow-nosed albatross
Thalassarche chlororhynchos
Does not breed until eight years of age

Royal albatross
Diomedea epomophora
Uses its huge, long wings to glide effortlessly on wind currents

Great crested grebe
Podiceps cristatus
Both sexes develop face plumes called tippets that they flare when courting.

Eared grebe
Podiceps nigricollis

Little grebe
Tachybaptus ruficollis
Some grebes eat feathers to line their stomachs and prevent damage from swallowed fish bones.

CONSERVATION WATCH

Of the 139 species of albatrosses, petrels, grebes, and loons, 88 appear on the IUCN Red List. The critically endangered Fiji petrel is one of the world's rarest birds. Feral cats, rats, and pigs that eat the petrel's eggs and chicks are its biggest threats.

Ex 4
Cr 17
En 18
Vu 30
Other 19

Fiji petrel

Grebes and loons
Albatrosses and petrels
Grebes, loons, albatrosses, and petrels

Grebes are found in wetlands. Loons live on lakes across the far north of the Northern Hemisphere. Albatrosses and petrels occur across the world's oceans.

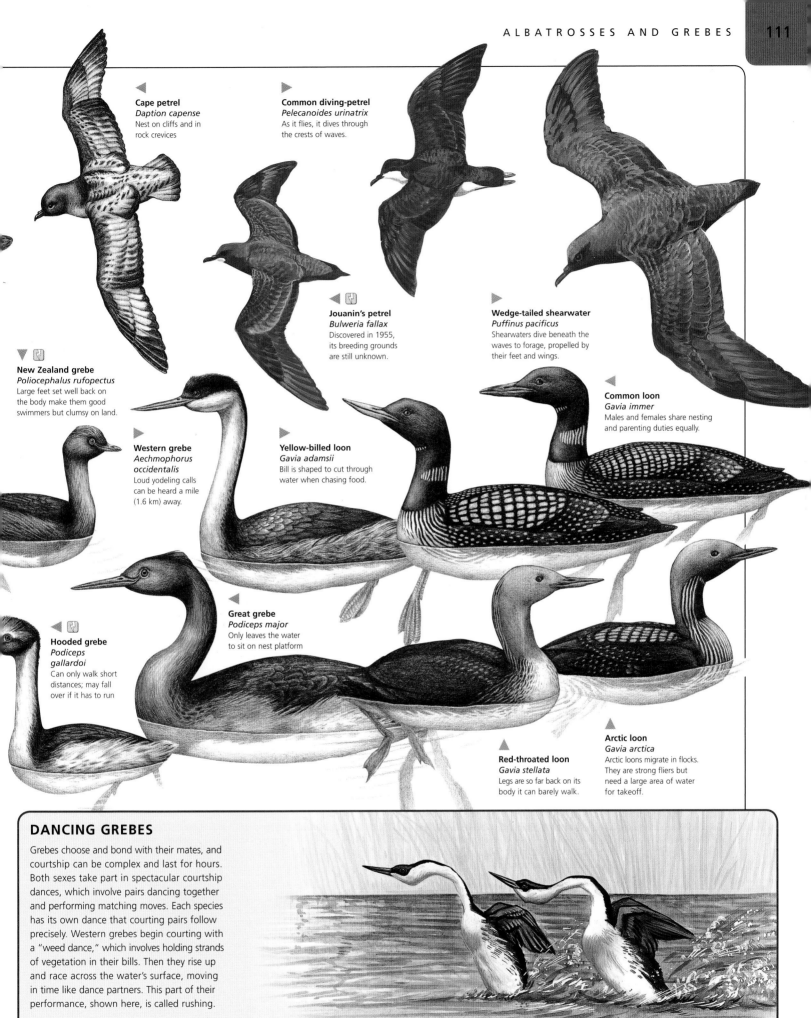

Cape petrel
Daption capense
Nest on cliffs and in
rock crevices

Common diving-petrel
Pelecanoides urinatrix
As it flies, it dives through
the crests of waves.

Jouanin's petrel
Bulweria fallax
Discovered in 1955,
its breeding grounds
are still unknown.

Wedge-tailed shearwater
Puffinus pacificus
Shearwaters dive beneath the
waves to forage, propelled by
their feet and wings.

New Zealand grebe
Poliocephalus rufopectus
Large feet set well back on
the body make them good
swimmers but clumsy on land.

Western grebe
*Aechmophorus
occidentalis*
Loud yodeling calls
can be heard a mile
(1.6 km) away.

Yellow-billed loon
Gavia adamsii
Bill is shaped to cut through
water when chasing food.

Common loon
Gavia immer
Males and females share nesting
and parenting duties equally.

Hooded grebe
*Podiceps
gallardoi*
Can only walk short
distances; may fall
over if it has to run

Great grebe
Podiceps major
Only leaves the water
to sit on nest platform

Red-throated loon
Gavia stellata
Legs are so far back on its
body it can barely walk.

Arctic loon
Gavia arctica
Arctic loons migrate in flocks.
They are strong fliers but
need a large area of water
for takeoff.

DANCING GREBES

Grebes choose and bond with their mates, and
courtship can be complex and last for hours.
Both sexes take part in spectacular courtship
dances, which involve pairs dancing together
and performing matching moves. Each species
has its own dance that courting pairs follow
precisely. Western grebes begin courting with
a "weed dance," which involves holding strands
of vegetation in their bills. Then they rise up
and race across the water's surface, moving
in time like dance partners. This part of their
performance, shown here, is called rushing.

2 ORDERS • 4 FAMILIES • 44 GENERA • 123 SPECIES

Herons and Flamingos

Herons and their relatives—storks, ibises, spoonbills, egrets, bitterns, and the hamerkop—wade in shallow water or swampy areas to hunt for fish, insects, and frogs. Their long legs let them stride through water without getting their feathers wet. All herons have long beaks and necks; they fold these back on their shoulders when they fly. Herons have patches of special feathers, called powder-down, that do not molt, but the tips fray into a fine powder, which the bird collects in its bill and uses to clean its feathers. Flamingos are also wading birds. Their distinctive reddish feathers come from pigments in the tiny plants and animals that they eat. These birds have a specially designed bill that strains this food from the surface of lakes, where they gather in huge numbers.

Greater flamingo
Phoenicopterus ruber

Great blue heron
Ardea herodias
Often seen stalking along the edges of lakes or marshes

Whistling heron
Syrigma sibilatrix

Boat-billed heron
Cochlearius cochlearius

White-crested bittern
Tigriornis leucolophus

Hamerkop
Scopus umbretta

Cattle egret
Bubulcus ibis
Often perches on cattle, eating insects that the cattle's hooves stir up

Andean flamingo
Phoenicoparrus andinus

Sacred ibis
Threskiornis aethiopicus
An important bird in ancient Egyptian mythology, sacred ibises were often mummified.

Wood stork
Mycteria americana
Sensitive bill finds prey by touch in muddy water.

CONSERVATION WATCH

Of the 123 species of herons, their relatives, and flamingos, 37 appear on the IUCN Red List. The crested ibis is endangered because of the destruction and pollution of its habitat. These birds are now found only in central China.

Ex	5
Cr	4
En	12
Vu	7
Other	9

Crested ibis

Herons

Herons and flamingos

Herons and their relatives can be found in freshwater habitats worldwide, except near the Poles. Flamingos live on most continents, around shallow lakes and coastal regions.

— 1 ORDER • 6 FAMILIES • 8 GENERA • 63 SPECIES ———————

Pelicans

Pelicans are related to five other families of waterbirds: gannets and boobies; tropicbirds; cormorants; anhingas and darters; and frigatebirds. All of these birds have four toes on each foot that are connected by webbing. Pelicans and their relatives are true waterbirds. They are all excellent swimmers, and some can barely walk on land. Most, except cormorants and darters, have waterproof feathers. Many species have a large throat sac that has no feathers. This sac is used to catch fish, as well as to impress mates during courtship displays. This group nests in colonies, often with other seabirds. They are long-lived birds, and may return to the same nesting sites and breed with the same partners every year for 20 years. The males and females of all species share nesting and parenting duties.

Great white pelican
Pelecanus onocrotalus

Red-tailed tropicbird
Phaethon rubricauda

Northern gannet
Morus bassanus

Lesser frigatebird
Fregata ariel

Dalmatian pelican
Pelecanus crispus
Chick puts entire head into parent's mouth for a meal of partly digested fish.

European shag
Phalacrocorax aristotelis
Communicates using grunts and clicks

Pelagic cormorant
Phalacrocorax pelagicus
Dives as deep as 100 feet (30 m) in coastal waters to feed on the sea bottom

Darter
Anhinga melanogaster

Double-crested cormorant
Phalacrocorax auritus
Perches with its wings spread out to dry them after diving

Great cormorant
Phalacrocorax carbo
White patches develop on the birds' legs at breeding time.

Peruvian booby
Sula variegata
Can dive from 50 feet (15 m) high to catch fish

Anhinga
Anhinga anhinga

Blue-footed booby
Sula nebouxii
The blue-footed booby incubates its eggs with its webbed feet.

CONSERVATION WATCH

Of the 63 species of pelicans and their relatives, 23 appear on the IUCN Red List. The vulnerable rough-faced shag is found only around four tiny New Zealand islands. In the past, it was hunted by indigenous people; now it is sometimes caught accidentally by commercial fishing operations.

Ex	🕊	1
Cr		2
En		3
Vu		11
Other		6

Rough-faced shag

☐ Pelicans

Pelicans and their relatives live in watery environments throughout much of the world. Most species tend to be found in tropical or temperate areas.

1 ORDER • 3 FAMILIES • 83 GENERA • 304 SPECIES

Birds of Prey

Eagles, kites, buzzards, condors, vultures, and hawks are all birds of prey. These diurnal hunters are known as raptors, a Latin word meaning "one who seizes and carries away." Many of these birds hunt by swooping down from the sky to snatch up prey. Raptors are one of the largest bird orders. This fierce group includes the world's fastest fliers—the falcons—as well as some of the ugliest scavengers—the vultures. All raptors are carnivorous, and most are well adapted to hunting live prey. Strong feet armed with sharp claws, called talons, seize onto struggling animals. Sharp, hooked bills tear through their prey's flesh. Most raptors have long, broad wings to soar high above open habitats looking for food far below. Those that dwell in forests have shorter, rounded wings that let them change direction quickly.

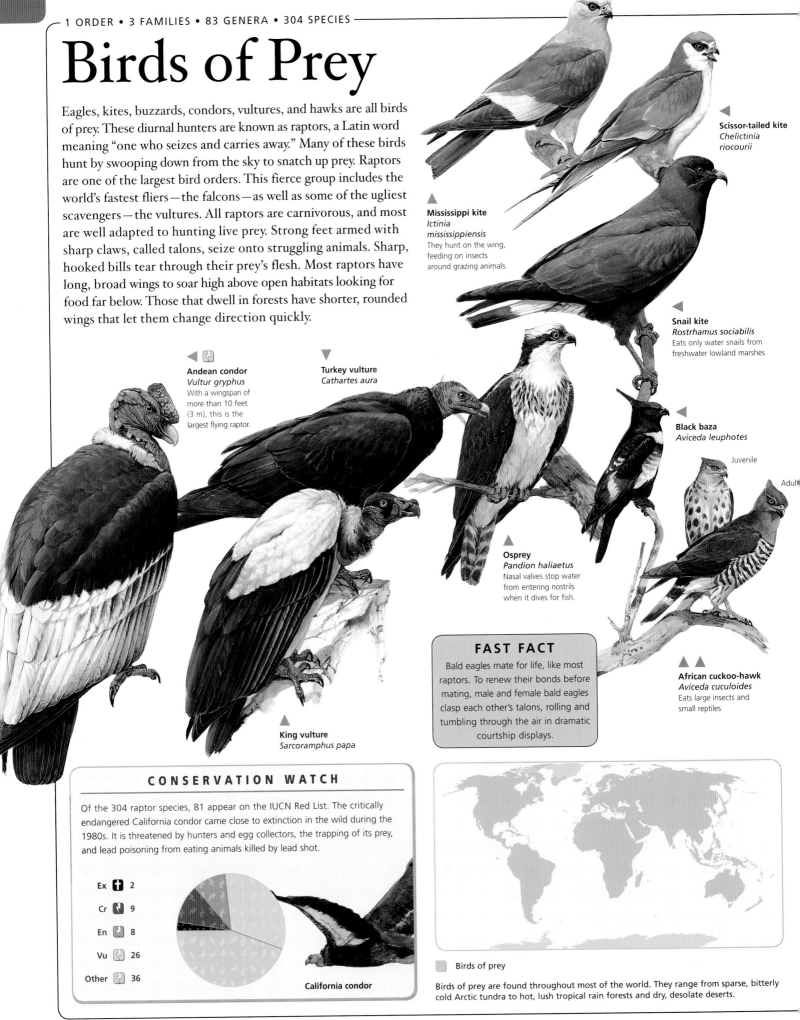

Scissor-tailed kite
Chelictinia riocourii

Mississippi kite
Ictinia mississippiensis
They hunt on the wing, feeding on insects around grazing animals.

Snail kite
Rostrhamus sociabilis
Eats only water snails from freshwater lowland marshes

Black baza
Aviceda leuphotes

Juvenile

Adult

Andean condor
Vultur gryphus
With a wingspan of more than 10 feet (3 m), this is the largest flying raptor.

Turkey vulture
Cathartes aura

Osprey
Pandion haliaetus
Nasal valves stop water from entering nostrils when it dives for fish.

African cuckoo-hawk
Aviceda cuculoides
Eats large insects and small reptiles

King vulture
Sarcoramphus papa

FAST FACT
Bald eagles mate for life, like most raptors. To renew their bonds before mating, male and female bald eagles clasp each other's talons, rolling and tumbling through the air in dramatic courtship displays.

CONSERVATION WATCH
Of the 304 raptor species, 81 appear on the IUCN Red List. The critically endangered California condor came close to extinction in the wild during the 1980s. It is threatened by hunters and egg collectors, the trapping of its prey, and lead poisoning from eating animals killed by lead shot.

Ex 🕆 2
Cr 🗓 9
En 🗓 8
Vu 🗓 26
Other 🗓 36

California condor

Birds of prey

Birds of prey are found throughout most of the world. They range from sparse, bitterly cold Arctic tundra to hot, lush tropical rain forests and dry, desolate deserts.

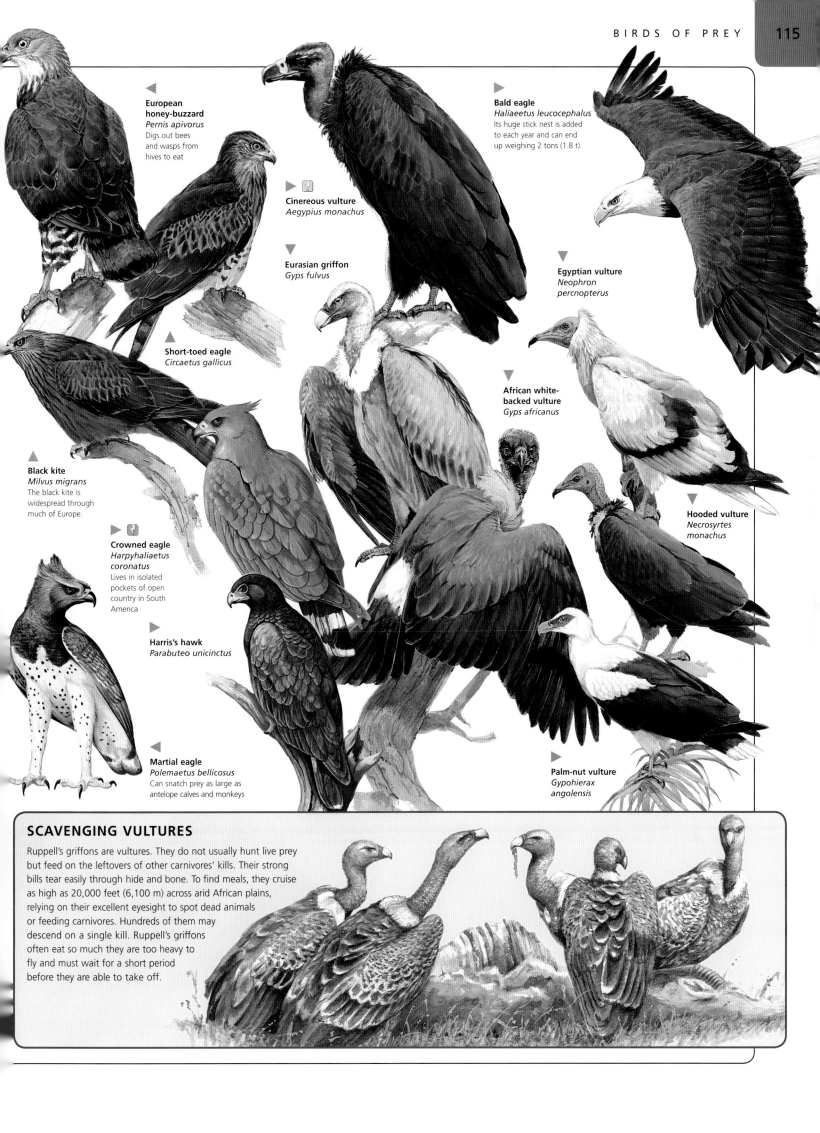

European honey-buzzard
Pernis apivorus
Digs out bees and wasps from hives to eat

Cinereous vulture
Aegypius monachus

Eurasian griffon
Gyps fulvus

Short-toed eagle
Circaetus gallicus

Bald eagle
Haliaeetus leucocephalus
Its huge stick nest is added to each year and can end up weighing 2 tons (1.8 t).

Egyptian vulture
Neophron percnopterus

African white-backed vulture
Gyps africanus

Black kite
Milvus migrans
The black kite is widespread through much of Europe.

Crowned eagle
Harpyhaliaetus coronatus
Lives in isolated pockets of open country in South America

Harris's hawk
Parabuteo unicinctus

Hooded vulture
Necrosyrtes monachus

Palm-nut vulture
Gypohierax angolensis

Martial eagle
Polemaetus bellicosus
Can snatch prey as large as antelope calves and monkeys

SCAVENGING VULTURES

Ruppell's griffons are vultures. They do not usually hunt live prey but feed on the leftovers of other carnivores' kills. Their strong bills tear easily through hide and bone. To find meals, they cruise as high as 20,000 feet (6,100 m) across arid African plains, relying on their excellent eyesight to spot dead animals or feeding carnivores. Hundreds of them may descend on a single kill. Ruppell's griffons often eat so much they are too heavy to fly and must wait for a short period before they are able to take off.

Birds of prey

One reason that raptors are such superb hunters is their exceptional eyesight. Many cruise at great heights, watching over large territories for the smallest movements of prey. A kestrel hovering 100 feet (30 m) above the grass can spot a grasshopper that a human would struggle to see at 10 feet (3 m). Once they spot a potential meal, raptors respond with lightning-fast reflexes, rapid speed, and great power. This lets them make their kill before their prey has time to escape. Falcons are aerial hunters that use sight in this way. Many falcons also rely on sound. They often have a ruff of feathers framing their face to assist their hearing. The secretary bird is the only raptor that actively hunts on the ground, stalking and flushing out prey with its long, graceful legs.

Crested serpent-eagle
Spilornis cheela
Eats tree snakes but will also hunt lizards

Variable goshawk
Accipiter novaehollandiae

Black harrier
Circus maurus
A small raptor found in southern Africa

Collared falconet
Microhierax caerulescens

Red-footed falcon
Falco vespertinus
This falcon migrates in winter from northwest Europe and Asia to southern Africa.

♂ ♀

Eurasian sparrowhawk
Accipiter nisus

Dark chanting-goshawk
Melierax metabates

Javan hawk-eagle
Spizaetus bartelsi
Lives in rain forests and eats birds and small mammals

Common kestrel
Falco tinnunculus

Secretary bird
Sagittarius serpentarius
Uses its long legs to kick its prey and subdue it

Yellow-headed caracara
Milvago chimachima
Often plucks ticks off the backs of cattle

BILLS AND TALONS

Raptors' diets can include other birds, mammals, fish, frogs, snakes, and even insects. Their bills and talons, or claws, vary to suit their food preference. Raptors generally hold their prey firmly in their talons while tearing flesh with their strong bills.

OSPREY: FISH-EATER
Reversible outer toe, long curved talons, and rough, spiny toes with barbs called spicules help grab and carry slippery prey.

EURASIAN SPARROWHAWK: BIRD-EATER
Long, sharp talons and forceful grip are designed for clutching at birds in flight. Its bill then plucks feathers and rips flesh.

WHITE-BACKED VULTURE: CARRION-EATER
Its talons are used for holding, rather than capturing, prey that is already dead or dying. Its powerful bill tears bone and flesh.

HARPY EAGLE: MAMMAL-EATER
Its massive legs and talons are used to capture and hold monkeys, sloths, and other large tree-dwelling mammals.

STRATEGIES FOR HUNTING

WAYS TO ATTACK

Although their powerful feet and sharp talons are their main weapons, raptors have many ways to search for and attack prey. Some, such as osprey and kestrels, hover with short, fast wingbeats before dropping suddenly when they spot a meal. Some kestrels also like to perch in prime positions, watching out for the movements of prey on the ground below. Hawks may adopt a similar perching method. Harriers are renowned for "coursing," which involves flying low and slowly over hunting grounds. Sea eagles "kite" over coastal areas, flapping slowly while keeping a lookout for fish in the water below. Kites catch insects in midair with their feet. "Stooping" describes the sudden and dramatic high-speed plunge-dives made by falcons. Falcons fold their wings back as they dive toward their target. Their claws rip into prey, killing it with the impact. The peregrine falcon can reach speeds as fast as 168 miles per hour (270 km/h) when it stoops.

Stooping
Falcons may use several different hunting strategies. The most dramatic is stooping. They begin by circling slowly in the air, watching out for movement below them.

Spotting prey
When they spot prey, they drop suddenly, head first with their wings folded back. They can plunge at speeds of more than 150 miles per hour (240 km/h), often much faster.

Ospreys are unusual raptors because they eat only fish. They snatch the fish from the water with their talons, before carrying it away to eat.

Carrying away
The falcon reaches its prey feet first with all four toes outstretched. The impact as the talons hit their target usually rips through the prey's flesh. The prey may not be grasped immediately, but collected moments later as it falls.

Egyptian vultures use "tools" such as twigs or stones to open ostrich eggs.

2 ORDERS • 12 FAMILIES • 62 GENERA • 213 SPECIES

Cranes

Cranes belong to a diverse order that includes limpkins and trumpeters, rails and crakes, bustards, and buttonquails. Many do not appear to have a lot in common: Cranes tend to be large, long-legged birds; buttonquails have small, plump bodies and short legs. But they are all descended from an ancient ground-dwelling shorebird. Cranes and their relatives spend much of their lives on the ground. Many prefer to walk rather than fly or swim. Some have even lost the ability to fly. Cranes usually make their nests on the ground or on platforms in shallow water. Their young can walk almost as soon as they hatch. Most cranes use sound to communicate. Males and females of many species sing together. They may also perform elaborate dances to form new mating pairs or renew old bonds.

Sunbittern
Eurypyga helias
As a courtship display, it fans its brightly colored wings and tail.

African finfoot
Podica senegalensis

Denham's bustard
Neotis denhami
This shy bird often crouches to avoid being seen.

Horned coot
Fulica cornuta

Hoatzin
Opisthocomus hoazin
Breaks down plant matter in its gut as cattle do

Lesser florican
Sypheotides indica

Corncrake
Crex crex

White-breasted mesite
Mesitornis variegatus

Limpkin
Aramus guarauna
Called the "crying bird" because of its eerie wails and screams

Demoiselle crane
Anthropoides virgo
Performs spectacular ballet-like courtship dances with mate

Barred buttonquail
Turnix suscitator

Black crowned crane
Balearica pavonina
Roosts in trees, unlike most other cranes

CONSERVATION WATCH

Of the 213 cranes and relatives, 101 appear on the IUCN Red List. Once thought extinct, the endangered takahe of New Zealand was rediscovered in 1948. Introduced species have been a major threat in recent years.

Ex	✝	22
Cr		4
En		20
Vu		30
Other		25

Takahe

Cranes

Every continent except Antarctica has at least one member of this bird group. They live in a wide range of habitats, from wetlands and forests to grasslands and deserts.

1 ORDER • 16 FAMILIES • 86 GENERA • 351 SPECIES

Waders and Shorebirds

Waders and shorebirds live near the sea or around lakes, pools, and puddles. They feed mainly on small animals. Many of these birds look different from each other because of the roles they fill in the environment, but they are all strong fliers. There are three main subgroups of waders and shorebirds: waders, gulls and terns, and auks. Waders, such as oystercatchers, curlews, and stilts, are often long-legged birds. They stride through shallow waters and along shorelines, foraging in sediment. Gulls are mostly seabirds. They scavenge along the shorelines but may also swim out to take prey in deeper water. Terns are plunge-divers that hover when they spot a fish, then plunge head first to catch their meal. Auks find food by swimming underwater, like penguins. Unlike penguins, they can also fly.

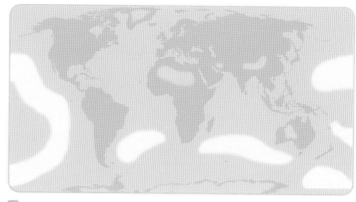

■ Waders and shorebirds

These birds live near lakes, rivers, and oceans. Some can live in semidesert regions.

Long-tailed jaeger
Stercorarius longicaudus
Hunts lemmings and other rodents during breeding season

Fairy tern (white tern)
Sterna nereis
Although they have webbed feet, terns rarely swim.

Little tern
Sterna albifrons
Feeds on small fish and shrimps

Common tern
Sterna hirundo
Nests in noisy colonies, where intruders are attacked from the air by angry terns

Atlantic puffin
Fratercula arctica
Nests in colonies, sometimes in burrows dug by rabbits

Crested auklet
Aethia cristatella

Great black-backed gull
Larus marinus
Eats almost anything, including smaller birds

Tufted puffin
Fratercula cirrhata
Nests in burrows as deep as 6 feet (1.8 m) on coastal shores

Herring gull
Larus argentatus
Often seen with groups of great black-backed gulls

Black skimmer
Rynchops niger
Flies low along surface of water with its bill open, scooping up any prey it finds

FAST FACT
The Arctic tern migrates farther than any other bird. Each year, it travels from its Arctic breeding grounds to spend the summer in the Antarctic, before returning. The trip is at least 12,400 miles (20,000 km) each way.

Waders and shorebirds

Curlews, sandpipers, and their relatives are typical waders. They tend to have long bodies and long, thin legs. Their narrow bills vary in length and how they curve. Curlew bills are long and curve slightly downward to probe for worms in the mud. Godwits use their long, straight bills to search through mud underwater. The small, stubby bills of stints have sensitive endings which "feel" for food that cannot be seen. Plovers and dotterels have short, stout bills for snatching prey. Most waders do not have webbed feet. Two exceptions are stilts and avocets, but they prefer to stride along shorelines and in shallow waters rather than to swim. The sheathbills of the Antarctic look more like large, white pigeons with plump bodies than waders. They are not good fliers but run well on their short, strong legs.

CONSERVATION WATCH

Of the 351 species of waders and shorebirds, 71 appear on the IUCN Red List. The flightless great auk was hunted into extinction. The last known living pair was found in Iceland in 1844.

Ex 4
Cr 8
En 8
Vu 21
Other 30

Great auk

FAST FACT

Many female shorebirds lay four eggs, each pointed at one end and placed in the nest with their points toward the center to take up the least amount of space. It probably makes their incubation easier, too.

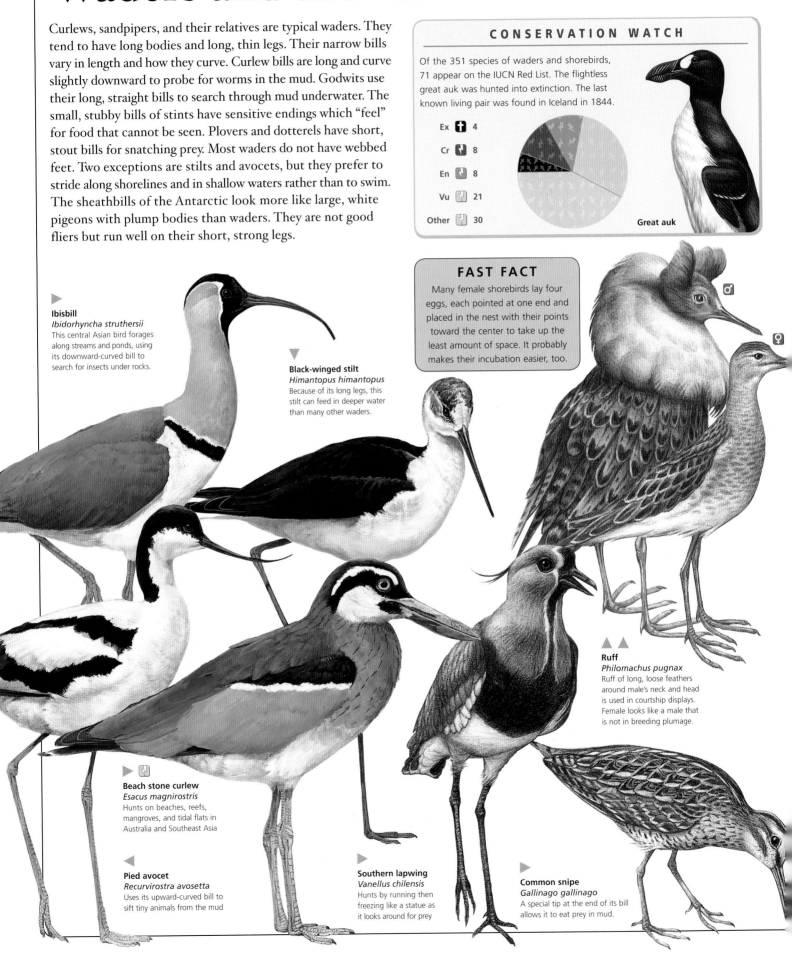

Ibisbill
Ibidorhyncha struthersii
This central Asian bird forages along streams and ponds, using its downward-curved bill to search for insects under rocks.

Black-winged stilt
Himantopus himantopus
Because of its long legs, this stilt can feed in deeper water than many other waders.

Ruff
Philomachus pugnax
Ruff of long, loose feathers around male's neck and head is used in courtship displays. Female looks like a male that is not in breeding plumage.

Beach stone curlew
Esacus magnirostris
Hunts on beaches, reefs, mangroves, and tidal flats in Australia and Southeast Asia

Pied avocet
Recurvirostra avosetta
Uses its upward-curved bill to sift tiny animals from the mud

Southern lapwing
Vanellus chilensis
Hunts by running then freezing like a statue as it looks around for prey

Common snipe
Gallinago gallinago
A special tip at the end of its bill allows it to eat prey in mud.

Curlew sandpiper
Calidris ferruginea
Forages for worms on tidal mudflats, washing them before eating

Collared pratincole
Glareola pratincola
Feeds on insects while flying in flocks at dawn and dusk

Eurasian curlew
Numenius arquata
Name comes from its haunting "curloo-oo" cry.

Black-tailed godwit
Limosa limosa
This sociable bird often forms large feeding flocks. Breeding pairs migrate separately but find each other at the breeding ground every year.

Spotted redshank
Tringa erythropus

Common redshank
Tringa totanus
Feeds day and night on coastal mudflats when the tide is out

Red-necked phalarope
Phalaropus lobatus
Swims gracefully, holding its head high and nodding

Black-faced sheathbill
Chionis minor
Uses small spur on wing as a weapon; a fatty layer keeps it warm in its Antarctic habitat.

ON THE SEASHORE

Many of the world's shorebirds breed in the Arctic during the short (June to July) but highly productive summer, when food resources explode. As winter approaches, millions migrate south to feed on coastal seashores throughout the world. Tens of thousands arrive in some places, such as the coasts of the Mediterranean Sea. Little terns lay their eggs on the pebbles of the shore, where they are well camouflaged. The cliffs provide excellent nesting sites. Plovers hide their nests, each with two or three eggs, between boulders or among plants. Gulls nest in colonies among the sand dunes. Some larger gulls may prey on the eggs or baby birds of other species, and sometimes even their own.

2 ORDERS • 3 FAMILIES • 46 GENERA • 327 SPECIES

Pigeons and Sandgrouse

Pigeons and sandgrouse forage in flocks and travel large distances between feeding and nesting areas every day. Pigeons and doves are tree-dwelling birds that eat seeds and fruit. The term "dove" is used for smaller birds; "pigeon" describes larger species. Pigeons and doves have bills that let them suck up water rather than sip it. They are able to produce "crop milk." The crop is a pouch at the beginning of the digestive system. Glands in the crops of both males and females produce a thick, milky substance that is fed to chicks. Desert-dwelling sandgrouse do not produce crop milk. These strong, fast fliers need to drink regularly and may fly more than 40 miles (65 km) between waterholes and feeding areas. They nest on the ground. Sandgrouse chicks leave the nest a few hours after hatching.

Victoria crowned pigeon
Goura victoria
Males repeatedly bow their elaborate crests to impress females during courtship.

Seychelles blue pigeon
Alectroenas pulcherrima
These striking birds became rare because they were once shot for food, but their numbers have since recovered.

Zebra dove
Geopelia striata
Scurry around like rodents, feeding on grass seeds

Pied imperial pigeon
Ducula bicolor

Chestnut-bellied sandgrouse
Pterocles exustus
Adults soak up water in their feathers; chicks drink from the wet feathers.

Emerald dove
Chalcophaps indica
Feeds on fallen rain forest fruit and sometimes termites

Pallas's sandgrouse
Syrrhaptes paradoxus

Rock dove
Columba livia
Known as the common pigeon, huge flocks are seen in cities worldwide.

Banded fruit dove
Ptilinopus cinctus
Fruit doves have a specialized digestive system to cope with a diet of fruit.

CONSERVATION WATCH

Of the 327 species of pigeons and sandgrouse, 112 appear on the IUCN Red List. The extinct flightless dodo lived only on the Indian Ocean island of Mauritius. Explorers in the late 1600s slaughtered it for food and sport.

Ex	✝	14
Cr		12
En		15
Vu		34
Other		37

Dodo

☐ Pigeons and sandgrouse

Pigeons and doves occur worldwide, but most species live in the tropics and subtropics. Sandgrouse are found only in regions of Africa and Eurasia that have low rainfall.

2 ORDERS • 2 FAMILIES • 41 GENERA • 161 SPECIES

Cuckoos and Turacos

Even though cuckoos and turacos are related, they look and behave differently. Cuckoos are infamous for laying their eggs in other birds' nests for those birds to raise. While about 50 species behave like this, most do not. These include the social anis and guiras, which live in distinct territories; the roadrunners and ground cuckoos, which rarely fly and prefer to run; and the couas and coucals. Most members of the cuckoo family have drab-colored feathers that provide them with good camouflage. In contrast, turacos are brightly colored birds with long tails and short wings. They are more agile running along branches than flapping among them. All except one species have crests on their heads. These noisy birds live in groups of as many as 10 and communicate with loud, barking calls.

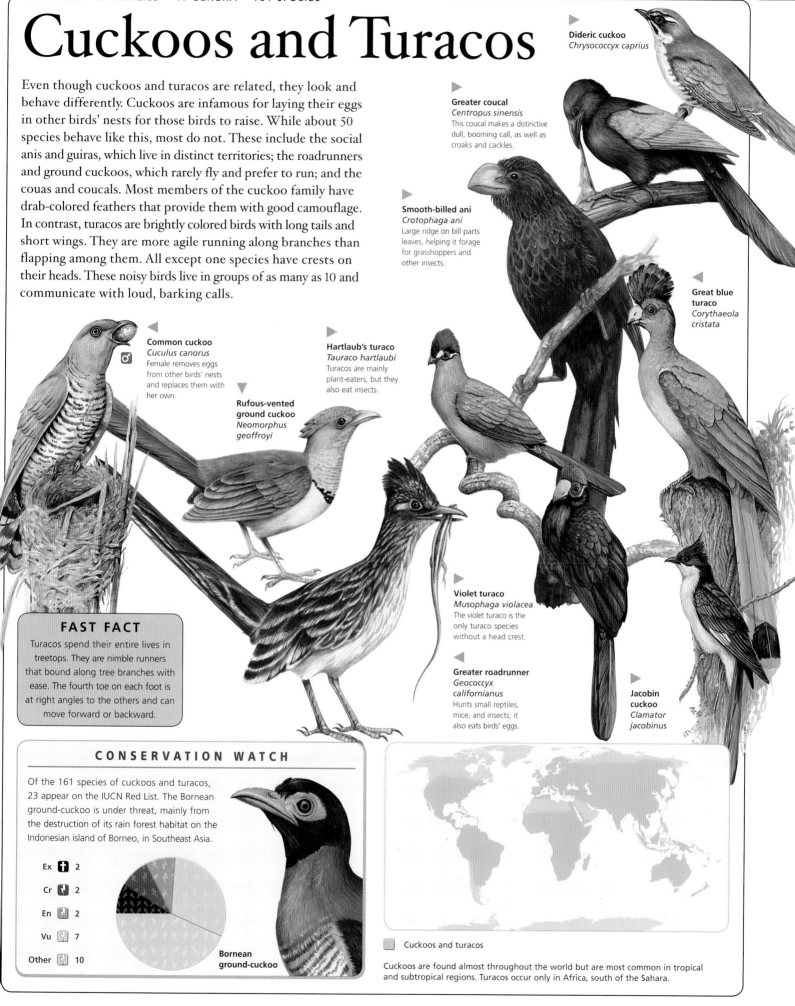

Dideric cuckoo
Chrysococcyx caprius

Greater coucal
Centropus sinensis
This coucal makes a distinctive dull, booming call, as well as croaks and cackles.

Smooth-billed ani
Crotophaga ani
Large ridge on bill parts leaves, helping it forage for grasshoppers and other insects.

Great blue turaco
Corythaeola cristata

Common cuckoo
Cuculus canorus
Female removes eggs from other birds' nests and replaces them with her own.

Hartlaub's turaco
Tauraco hartlaubi
Turacos are mainly plant-eaters, but they also eat insects.

Rufous-vented ground cuckoo
Neomorphus geoffroyi

Violet turaco
Musophaga violacea
The violet turaco is the only turaco species without a head crest.

Greater roadrunner
Geococcyx californianus
Hunts small reptiles, mice, and insects; it also eats birds' eggs.

Jacobin cuckoo
Clamator jacobinus

FAST FACT

Turacos spend their entire lives in treetops. They are nimble runners that bound along tree branches with ease. The fourth toe on each foot is at right angles to the others and can move forward or backward.

CONSERVATION WATCH

Of the 161 species of cuckoos and turacos, 23 appear on the IUCN Red List. The Bornean ground-cuckoo is under threat, mainly from the destruction of its rain forest habitat on the Indonesian island of Borneo, in Southeast Asia.

Ex		2
Cr		2
En		2
Vu		7
Other		10

Bornean ground-cuckoo

☐ Cuckoos and turacos

Cuckoos are found almost throughout the world but are most common in tropical and subtropical regions. Turacos occur only in Africa, south of the Sahara.

1 ORDER • 3 FAMILIES • 85 GENERA • 364 SPECIES

Parrots

Parrots are some of the easiest birds in the world to recognize. Their unique bill is short and strong, with the top section curving downward. This design is perfect for crushing the seeds and nuts that make up most of their diet. Parrot feet are distinctive: two toes point forward and two toes point backward. This arrangement allows them to grasp objects with their feet and move with great agility in trees. Most parrots have brilliantly colored feathers, usually in shades of green with splashes of red, yellow, and blue. A few species are drab for camouflage. Their bright colors, along with their sociable natures, have made them popular as pets. As a result, many wild birds are poached for the caged bird market. This is one reason why parrots are among the most common birds on endangered species lists.

Eclectus parrot
Eclectus roratus
Males and females look so different they were once thought to belong to different species.

Buff-faced pygmy parrot
Micropsitta pusio

Blue-fronted parrot
Amazona aestiva

White-crowned parrot
Pionus senilis

Galah
Eolophus roseicapilla

Rainbow lorikeet
Trichoglossus haematodus

Kakapo
Strigops habroptilus
Male produces deep booming sounds from a special throat sac and digs "arenas" where he dances for females.

Kea
Nestor notabilis
Eats seeds, flowers, and insects, but will also eat dead animals and sometimes even attacks live sheep

CONSERVATION WATCH

Of the 364 parrot species, 146 appear on the IUCN Red List. Mexico's thick-billed parrot is endangered, mainly because of the logging of its pine forest home. Its striking red and green plumage has also made it popular with the illegal pet trade.

Ex	✝	19
Cr		15
En		30
Vu		45
Other		37

Thick-billed parrot

Parrots

Parrots live mainly in the tropical regions of the Southern Hemisphere; they occur as far north as eastern Afghanistan. Australasia and South America boast the most species.

Yellow-collared lovebird
Agapornis personatus
Mates form close, usually
lifelong, bonds.

Fischer's lovebird
Agapornis fischeri

Swift parrot
Lathamus discolor

Hyacinth macaw
Anodorhynchus hyacinthinus
Eats the nut of South
America's acuri palm; the
nut is so tough it needs
to pass through a cow's
digestive system before
the macaw can crack it.

Senegal parrot
Poicephalus senegalus
Lives alone or in pairs,
sometimes in groups of
as many as 10 members

Plum-headed parakeet
Psittacula cyanocephala

Maroon-faced parakeet
Pyrrhura leucotis

Scarlet macaw
Ara macao
Young can stay with
parents for as long
as two years after
hatching.

Military macaw
Ara militaris
Macaws are long-lived
birds: some have survived
to age 65 in captivity.

Ground parrot
Pezoporus wallicus

Burrowing parakeet
Cyanoliseus patagonus
Digs tunnels into sandstone
or limestone cliffs, where it
breeds in colonies

DESIGNED FOR CRUSHING

Position of upper bill
when jaw is open

Well-developed upper
hinge opens like a lever;
aids bird when climbing.

Well-muscled base of bill
has a cutting edge for
cracking tough foods,
such as hard-shelled nuts.

Lower hinge

Hooked for grabbing
and holding food

Position of lower bill
when jaw is open

2 ORDERS • 7 FAMILIES • 51 GENERA • 314 SPECIES

Nightjars and Owls

Nightjars, their relatives, and owls are predators that hunt almost exclusively at night or twilight. Most have drab, mottled plumage that provides camouflage when they are at rest. Nightjars and their relatives are expert at striking poses that make them look like broken-off tree limbs. Owls have sharp, hooked bills to tear flesh; strong legs; and feet with talons to grasp and hold struggling prey. They have large, round eyes that face forward. This gives owls binocular vision, which helps them to judge distances. Their eyes are designed to work best at low light levels, with many light-sensitive cells known as rods. Similarly to owls, nightjars and their relatives have eyes adapted for seeing at low light levels. Unlike owls, these are not forward facing. They also do not have talons. Their hearing is excellent.

Tawny frogmouth
Podargus strigoides
Perches completely still, then pounces when it spots prey

Spotted nightjar
Eurostopodus argus

Common pauraque
Nyctidromus albicollis

Oilbird
Steatornis caripensis
Lives in dark caves and finds its way around using echolocation, like bats

Common potoo
Nyctibius griseus
Mottled feathers and habit of posing like a branch give excellent camouflage.

**European nightjar
(Eurasian nightjar)**
Caprimulgus europaeus

Common poorwill
Phalaenoptilus nuttallii

CONSERVATION WATCH

Of the 314 species of nightjars and owls, 81 appear on the IUCN Red List. The spotted owl, found in Central and North America, is near threatened. In many areas its forest habitat is being disrupted or destroyed by logging and clear-felling of trees.

Ex	✝	4
Cr		8
En		12
Vu		16
Other		41

Spotted owl

☐ Owls   ☐ Owls and nightjars

Owls live in forested areas throughout most of the world. Frogmouths are found in and around forests in Australasia. Nightjars occur in warm climates across the world.

Great horned owl
Bubo virginianus

Tropical screech owl
Otus choliba
Eats insects, small mammals, and reptiles; has a screeching cry

Verreaux's eagle-owl
Bubo lacteus

Barred owl
Strix varia
Young leave nest about four weeks after hatching but do not fly for another week.

Spectacled owl
Pulsatrix perscipillata

Ural owl
Strix uralensis
Nests in tree hollows and the abandoned nests of crows and raptors

Snowy owl
Nyctea scandiaca

Barn owl
Tyto alba

Eurasian pygmy owl
Glaucidium passerinum

Boreal owl
Aegolius funereus
Male leaves food in tree hollows for female. When he visits, he brings more food and they mate.

Long-eared owl
Asio otus

Elf owl
Micrathene whitneyi
Elf owls are the world's smallest owls. They bark to warn intruders away from their nests.

Northern saw-whet owl
Aegolius acadicus

Burrowing owl
Athene cunicularia

Black-banded owl
Ciccaba huhula

HEAD OF A HUNTER

Some owls' ears are not symmetrical—they are distinct sizes and in different positions on either side of the head. This creates small variations between the sound reaching each ear, which helps owls to locate prey. Owls may also have a "facial mask" of feathers, arranged to capture sound waves and direct them to the ears.

Higher and larger ear opening

Nostril

Eyes at front of head help judge distance better.

Lower and smaller ear opening

Bill

70° binocular vision range

110° field of vision range

1 ORDER • 3 FAMILIES • 124 GENERA • 429 SPECIES

Hummingbirds and Swifts

The wings of hummingbirds and swifts have a distinctive bone structure. This means they can beat their wings rapidly and fly in special ways that other birds cannot. Hummingbirds are noted for their beautifully colored feathers, which often sparkle in sunlight, as well as their small size. Most species weigh less than ⅓ ounce (9 g). They are nectar feeders with long, narrow bills that they poke into flowers as they hover in front of the blossoms. Swifts are slightly larger birds with narrow, swept-back wings that help make them fast fliers. They spend most of their time in the air, usually landing only at night to roost. They feed on swarms of mayflies and termites while flying and can even mate in the air. Many swifts migrate south over vast stretches of ocean to escape the Northern Hemisphere winter.

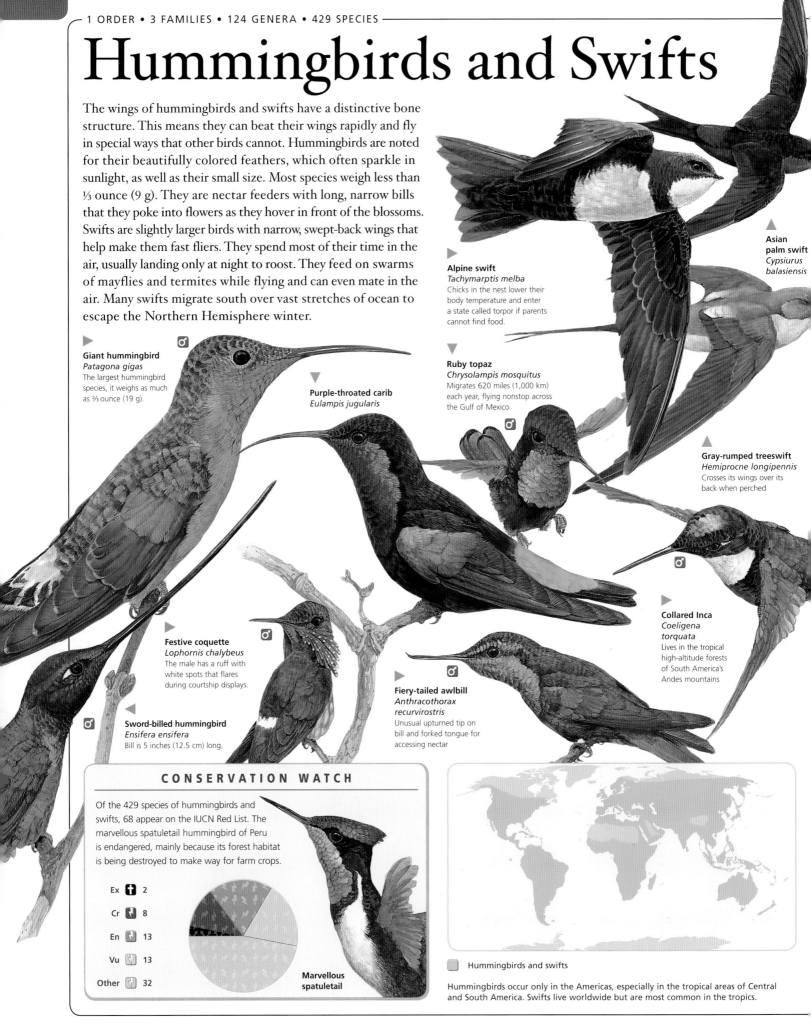

Asian palm swift
Cypsiurus balasiensis

Alpine swift
Tachymarptis melba
Chicks in the nest lower their body temperature and enter a state called torpor if parents cannot find food.

Giant hummingbird
Patagona gigas
The largest hummingbird species, it weighs as much as ⅔ ounce (19 g).

Purple-throated carib
Eulampis jugularis

Ruby topaz
Chrysolampis mosquitus
Migrates 620 miles (1,000 km) each year, flying nonstop across the Gulf of Mexico

Gray-rumped treeswift
Hemiprocne longipennis
Crosses its wings over its back when perched

Festive coquette
Lophornis chalybeus
The male has a ruff with white spots that flares during courtship displays.

Sword-billed hummingbird
Ensifera ensifera
Bill is 5 inches (12.5 cm) long.

Fiery-tailed awlbill
Anthracothorax recurvirostris
Unusual upturned tip on bill and forked tongue for accessing nectar

Collared Inca
Coeligena torquata
Lives in the tropical high-altitude forests of South America's Andes mountains

CONSERVATION WATCH

Of the 429 species of hummingbirds and swifts, 68 appear on the IUCN Red List. The marvellous spatuletail hummingbird of Peru is endangered, mainly because its forest habitat is being destroyed to make way for farm crops.

Ex	✝	2
Cr		8
En		13
Vu		13
Other		32

Marvellous spatuletail

Hummingbirds and swifts

Hummingbirds occur only in the Americas, especially in the tropical areas of Central and South America. Swifts live worldwide but are most common in the tropics.

FLIGHT OF THE HUMMINGBIRD

BUSY LIKE BEES

Most birds only fly forward, but hummingbirds can fly backward, forward, up and down, and hover, much like helicopters. Hummingbird wings beat as fast as 90 times a second, which can create a humming noise. The special structure of their wings lets them maneuver in this way. A bird's wing is like a human arm, with shoulder, elbow, wrist, and hand joints. While the hummingbird's shoulder joint moves, the permanently bent elbow and wrist joints do not. The hand is enlarged compared to the rest of the arm. This transfers enormous power to the flight feathers, which take up almost the entire wing. The breastbone is strong enough to support the muscles needed for high-energy flight. Hummingbirds need to produce a lot of energy to fuel the way they fly. They feed almost constantly throughout the day. At night, they reduce their needs by allowing their body temperatures to drop; this is called torpor.

INSIDE THE WING

The arrangement of the wing bones gives great power to the flight feathers. To fly forward, hummingbirds flap their wings up and down. To hover, they move their wings rapidly in a figure-eight shape.

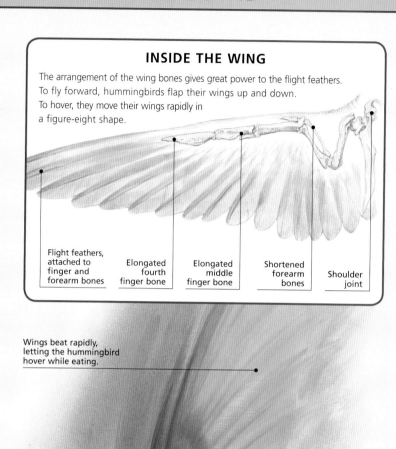

Flight feathers, attached to finger and forearm bones

Elongated fourth finger bone

Elongated middle finger bone

Shortened forearm bones

Shoulder joint

The scintillant hummingbird has such fine control over its flight that it can position itself at just the right angle to reach the nectar deep inside a flower.

To produce the energy they need to fly, hummingbirds must eat almost their body weight in nectar each day.

Bill is long and slender so it can reach deep inside flowers. Tongue is tipped with a brush to capture nectar.

Wings beat rapidly, letting the hummingbird hover while eating.

Flexible shoulder joint allows the wing to move in different directions.

Nectar-rich flower

This female green hermit feeds its nesting chicks in Costa Rica. Hummingbird hearts can beat more than 600 times a minute during activity such as this.

3 ORDERS • 13 FAMILIES • 59 GENERA • 254 SPECIES

Kingfishers

The kingfisher order includes many related birds—hornbills, todies, motmots, rollers, bee-eaters, wood-hoopoes, and the hoopoe. Trogons and mousebirds form two separate orders. All kingfishers have small feet with four toes. The three toes that point forward are fused together. They all use their large, strong, straight bills to dig nests in soil or rotten trees. Kingfishers usually sit on a perch, waiting and watching for small land or water animals, before swooping suddenly. The plumage of most kingfishers is brightly colored. Trogons, such as the resplendent quetzal, can be even more spectacular. These birds live in tropical forests and eat insects and small lizards. Some species also eat fruit. Mousebirds are far more drab. They creep among bushes like mice or hang upside down with their tails high in the air.

African pygmy kingfisher
Ceyx pictus

Green kingfisher
Chloroceryle americana
Green kingfishers often perch or fly just above the water's surface.

Banded kingfisher
Lacedo pulchella

Hook-billed kingfisher ♂
Melidora macrorrhina

Common kingfisher
Alcedo atthis

Lilac-cheeked kingfisher
Cittura cyanotis

Laughing kookaburra
Dacelo novaeguineae
Its distinctive loud cry sounds like laughter.

Belted kingfisher
Megaceryle alcyon
Defends its riverside territory from rival birds

Pied kingfisher
Ceryle rudis
Catches fish by plunge-diving into shallow water

CONSERVATION WATCH

Of the 254 species of kingfishers, mousebirds, and trogons, 66 appear on the IUCN Red List. Madagascar's long-tailed ground-roller is vulnerable, in part because its habitat is being cleared for firewood and making charcoal.

Ex	🕯	1
Cr		2
En		4
Vu		21
Other		38

Long-tailed ground-roller

- Kingfishers
- Mousebirds and trogons
- Kingfishers, mousebirds, and trogons

Kingfishers are found in temperate areas, mostly in Africa and Southeast Asia. Mousebirds live in Africa. Trogons occur across Central America, Africa, and Asia.

Resplendent quetzal
Pharomachrus mocinno

Speckled mousebird
Colius striatus

White-headed mousebird
Colius leucocephalus

Narina's trogon
Apaloderma narina

Red-headed trogon
Harpactes erythrocephalus
Male trogons are well known for the brilliant colors of their plumage.

White-tailed trogon
Trogon viridis

Dollarbird
Eurystomus orientalis
Acrobatic fliers that catch insects in midair

Cuban tody
Todus multicolor

Cuckoo-roller
Leptosomus discolor
Cuckoo-rollers make loud whistling and cackling cries.

Carmine bee-eater
Merops nubicus
This specialist eater rides on mammals' backs to catch bees.

European roller
Coracias garrulus

Common hoopoe
Upupa epops
Feeds by probing its long bill into soft earth and animal droppings for insects

Great hornbill
Buceros bicornis

DIVING FOR FISH

Kingfishers watch for fish while sitting on a high perch or hovering above the water. Some species have special light filters in their eyes to see prey beneath the water's surface.

Hovering
Female hovers above water in search of prey.

Spotting prey
Spotting a fish, she prepares to plunge-dive.

Plunge-diving
Wings back, she drops head first into the water.

Capture
She snaps her bill shut onto the fish.

Success
Holding the fish in her bill, she returns to the nest.

2 ORDERS • 5 FAMILIES • 68 GENERA • 398 SPECIES

Woodpeckers

Woodpeckers are related to honeyguides, jacamars, puffbirds, barbets, and toucans. All have two toes pointing forward and two pointing backward, which helps them grasp tree branches. Most are colorful birds that live in the tropics. They lay their eggs in trees, termite mounds, or the ground. Woodpeckers hang onto tree bark with strong toes and long claws. They use their chisel-like bills to break through tough bark to find insects. Honeyguides eat insects and beeswax. Females trick other birds to raise young honeyguides as their own. Jacamars and puffbirds are both insect-eaters: Jacamars have long, pointed bills; puffbirds have short, solid bills and big heads. Brightly colored barbets and toucans are fruit-eaters. Toucans are well camouflaged in rain forest trees despite their enormous bills.

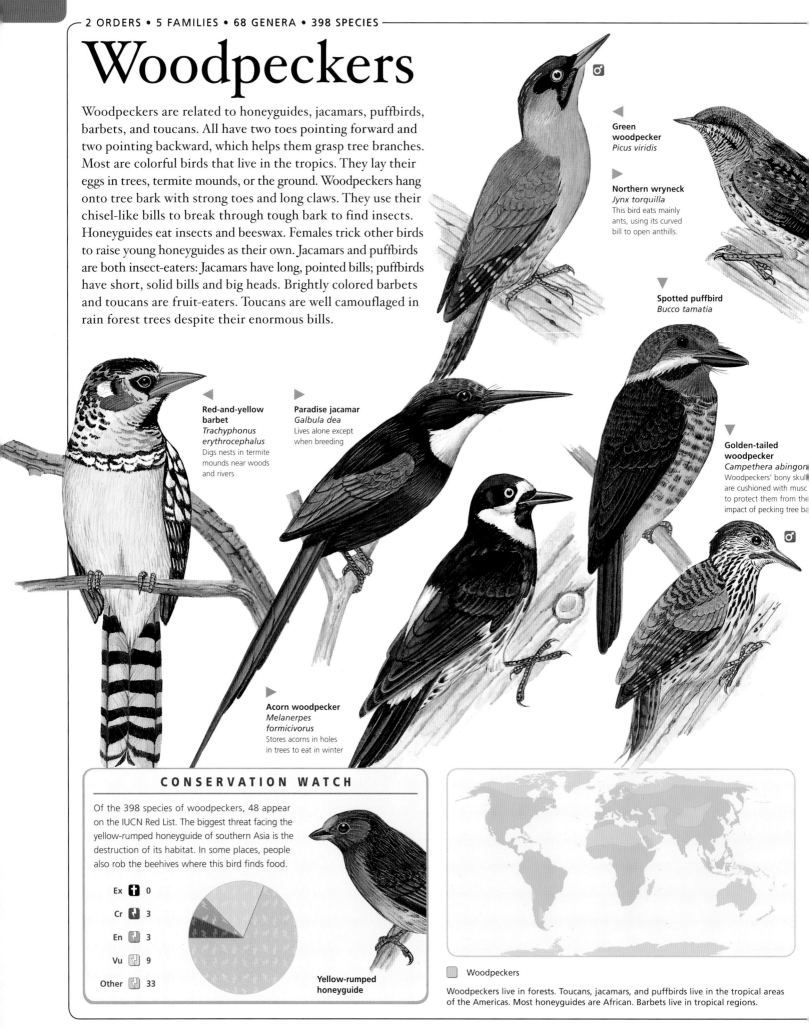

Green woodpecker
Picus viridis

Northern wryneck
Jynx torquilla
This bird eats mainly ants, using its curved bill to open anthills.

Spotted puffbird
Bucco tamatia

Red-and-yellow barbet
Trachyphonus erythrocephalus
Digs nests in termite mounds near woods and rivers

Paradise jacamar
Galbula dea
Lives alone except when breeding

Golden-tailed woodpecker
Campethera abingoni
Woodpeckers' bony skull are cushioned with musc to protect them from the impact of pecking tree ba

Acorn woodpecker
Melanerpes formicivorus
Stores acorns in holes in trees to eat in winter

CONSERVATION WATCH

Of the 398 species of woodpeckers, 48 appear on the IUCN Red List. The biggest threat facing the yellow-rumped honeyguide of southern Asia is the destruction of its habitat. In some places, people also rob the beehives where this bird finds food.

Ex	✝	0
Cr		3
En		3
Vu		9
Other		33

Yellow-rumped honeyguide

Woodpeckers

Woodpeckers live in forests. Toucans, jacamars, and puffbirds live in the tropical areas of the Americas. Most honeyguides are African. Barbets live in tropical regions.

Pileated woodpecker
Dryocopus pileatus
♀

Black-rumped woodpecker
Dinopium benghalense
Forages in trees for ants and other insects
♀

Gray woodpecker
Dendropicos goertae
♂

Yellow-bellied sapsucker
Sphyrapicus varius

TOCO TOUCAN

Large bill is light and mostly hollow but has a honeycomb structure that makes it strong.

Bill is used to pick off fruit, which is then tossed back in the mouth to be swallowed.

Two toes in the front and two at the back help to grasp tree branches firmly.

It sleeps by folding tail over its head and resting long bill over its back.

Greater honeyguide
Indicator indicator

Emerald toucanet
Aulacorhynchus prasinus

Blue-throated barbet
Megalaima asiatica

Rufous woodpecker
Celeus brachyurus

Gray-breasted mountain toucan
Andigena hypoglauca

Ground woodpecker
Geocolaptes olivaceus
Digs its bill into ant nests and sticks out its tongue to catch and eat the ants inside

Curl-crested aracari
Pteroglossus beauharnaesii

Channel-billed toucan
Ramphastos vitellinus
This bird drinks water from tropical plants or by holding its bill open in the rain.

1 ORDER • 96 FAMILIES • 1,218 GENERA • 5,754 SPECIES

Perching Birds

The canary is a finch from the Canary Islands in the Atlantic Ocean. Its beautiful songs have made it a prized pet for 400 years; it is now one of the most popular caged birds.

The largest order of birds is the perching birds, or passerines. This order contains more than half of all birds. Their flexible toes are well adapted for gripping perches, such as twigs and branches. The muscles and tendons of their legs are arranged so their toes grip tightly. Three toes face forward and one faces backward. The smallest perching birds can perch on blades of grass. A perching bird's syrinx, or voice box, is a structure at the base of its windpipe. It is well developed, allowing the birds to sing complex, musical songs. These songs can be used to mark out territory or to find mates. Most perching birds raise young with the same partner, usually working together to raise chicks. They eat insects and plants. During the breeding season, they tend to eat more insects for their protein.

CONSERVATION WATCH

Of 5,754 species of perching birds, 1,066 appear on the IUCN Red List. Southeast Asia's white-eyed river martin was discovered in 1968 and has not been seen since 1978. Hunting of this bird at its winter roosting sites has probably reduced its numbers.

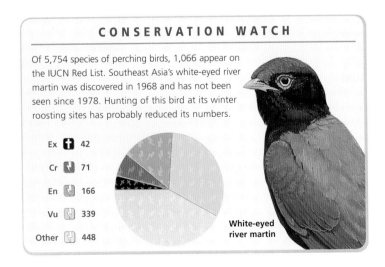

Ex	42
Cr	71
En	166
Vu	339
Other	448

White-eyed river martin

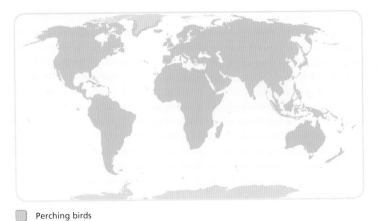

Perching birds

Perching birds are found throughout the world except Antarctica. They are adapted to live in a wide range of environments, from deserts to rain forests.

Perching birds

Woodcreepers, ovenbirds, antbirds, and tapaculos occur in the forests of South and Central America. Many prefer to live in dense foliage and hop between leaves, eating insects and spiders. A few species eat small frogs and snakes, eggs, and the chicks of other birds. Woodcreepers use their tails to brace themselves against tree trunks, similarly to woodpeckers. Antbirds feed on swarms of army ants. They avoid stings by darting in and out to pick off single ants. Manakins, cotingas, and tyrant flycatchers live in South and Central America, but many extend into North America. Manakins and cotingas are small fruit-eaters. Males can be brightly colored; most females are drab. Tyrant flycatchers eat insects or fruit. Many distinct species can live in one area because each species uses different resources.

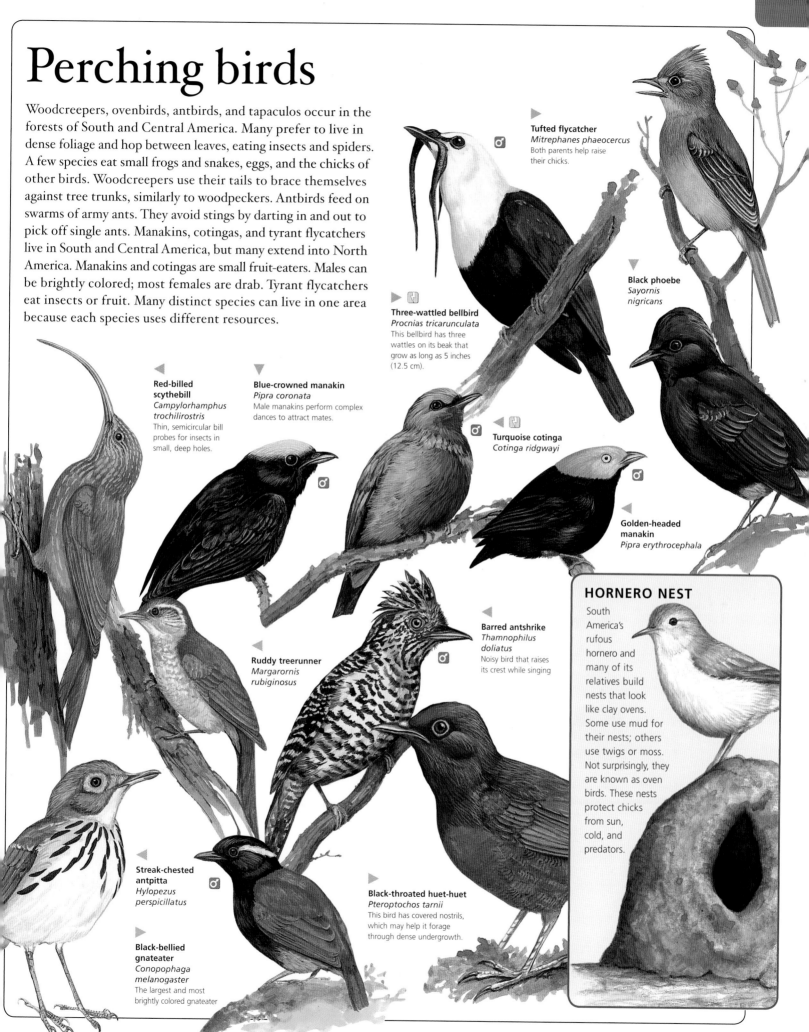

Tufted flycatcher
Mitrephanes phaeocercus
Both parents help raise their chicks.

Three-wattled bellbird
Procnias tricarunculata
This bellbird has three wattles on its beak that grow as long as 5 inches (12.5 cm).

Black phoebe
Sayornis nigricans

Red-billed scythebill
Campylorhamphus trochilirostris
Thin, semicircular bill probes for insects in small, deep holes.

Blue-crowned manakin
Pipra coronata
Male manakins perform complex dances to attract mates.

Turquoise cotinga
Cotinga ridgwayi

Golden-headed manakin
Pipra erythrocephala

Ruddy treerunner
Margarornis rubiginosus

Barred antshrike
Thamnophilus doliatus
Noisy bird that raises its crest while singing

Streak-chested antpitta
Hylopezus perspicillatus

Black-bellied gnateater
Conopophaga melanogaster
The largest and most brightly colored gnateater

Black-throated huet-huet
Pteroptochos tarnii
This bird has covered nostrils, which may help it forage through dense undergrowth.

HORNERO NEST

South America's rufous hornero and many of its relatives build nests that look like clay ovens. Some use mud for their nests; others use twigs or moss. Not surprisingly, they are known as oven birds. These nests protect chicks from sun, cold, and predators.

Perching birds

Brilliantly colored pittas are insect-eaters that live in tropical forests. They prefer to hop about rather than to fly. Honeyeaters and white-eyes are mainly Southern Hemisphere woodland birds. Honeyeaters have tongues with fringed tips to collect nectar. Insect-eating tits and flycatchers often use their tails in special ways: Fantails spread and wave their long tails like fans; monarch flycatchers flick their tails. Nuthatches are Northern Hemisphere bark-climbing birds that spend their lives looking for insects in trees. Crows—including choughs, nutcrackers, magpies, ravens, and jays—are found almost worldwide. Many hide food and are able to find it after a long time. Some are excellent singers.

Asian paradise-flycatcher
Terpsiphone paradisi

Oriental white-eye
Zosterops palpebrosus

Crimson chat
Epthianura tricolor

Red-headed honeyeater
Myzomela erythrocephala

Crimson-breasted flowerpecker
Prionochilus percussus

Cape sugarbird
Promerops cafer
Sugarbirds are nectar-eaters with long, curved bills and even longer tails.

Spotted pardalote
Pardalotus punctatus

Yellow-bellied fantail
Rhipidura hypoxantha

Brown-throated sunbird
Anthreptes malacensis

Fairy gerygone
Gerygone palpebrosa

Variegated fairy-wren
Malurus lamberti
This fairy-wren lives in family groups of as many as seven birds.

Green broadbill
Calyptomena viridis

Red-browed treecreeper
Climacteris erythrops

Superb lyrebird
Menura novaehollandiae
These expert mimics copy the sounds of birds, animals—even chainsaws.

Red-bellied pitta
Pitta erythrogaster

Crested tit
Parus cristatus

♂ White-browed
woodswallow
Artamus superciliosus

Red-backed shrike
Lanius collurio

♂ Eurasian golden
oriole
Oriolus oriolus

Red-billed
blue magpie
*Urocissa
erythrorhyncha*
Tail feathers are as
long as 17 inches
(43 cm).

♂ Australian magpie
Gymnorhina tibicen
This bird carols with other
members of its flock.

White-necked raven
Corvus albicollis
Drops tortoises to crack
their hard shells and eat
the meat inside

Penduline tit
Remiz pendulinus
Nest of feathers and plants
hangs like a paper bag from
a tree branch.

Wallcreeper
Tichodroma muraria
Nests in gaps between
rocks on cliff faces

SHARING THE LOAD

Some perching birds are known as cooperative breeders. This means that
other birds help raise the chicks of a nesting pair. The helpers might be chicks
of the pair that are almost fully grown. They can also be adult birds that have
tried, but failed, to raise their own chicks that season. Australia's superb
fairy-wrens commonly breed cooperatively.

Family affair
Young superb fairy-wrens from earlier broods
often stay with their parents to help raise the
brothers and sisters that are born after them.

Different tasks
A young male removes waste produced
by the chicks from the nest. Other helpers
tidy the nest or catch food. Some help
protect the chicks from predators.

Mother's help
The mother brings food to her
chicks in the nest. Her workload
is made much easier by helpers. Chicks
raised in communities like this are fed
insects more often than chicks looked
after by just their parents.

Father's role
The father of the brood perches
near the nest. Fathers also take
part in feeding the chicks.

Perching birds

Swallows are some of the most widespread perching birds. Many make long migrations. Like their relatives, the martins, they feed on insects caught in midair. They twitter and warble songs near their nests, but are mostly silent birds. Larks, in contrast, are impressive singers, which has led them to be introduced into many parts of the world. They walk, rather than hop, on their long legs and toes as they forage for insects. Bulbuls, known for their cheerful calls, can be rowdy when they gather in groups to feed. Dippers, the only family of perching birds that is closely associated with water, feed on the larvae of water insects and sometimes on small fish. Most catch prey by diving into a stream and walking along the bottom. They use their wings to help them move around underwater.

White-banded swallow
Atticora fasciata

White-winged swallow
Tachycineta albiventer

Greater short-toed lark
Calandrella brachydactyla

Standardwing
Semioptera wallacii

Black-crowned sparrow-lark
Eremopterix nigriceps

Western parotia
Parotia sefilata

Orange-bellied leafbird
Chloropsis hardwickei

Red-whiskered bulbul
Pycnonotus jocosus
Chicks are fed caterpillars, whereas adults eat fruit.

Marsh wren
Cistothorus palustris

Golden bowerbird
Prionodura newtoniana

Bohemian waxwing
Bombycilla garrulus

Scarlet minivet
Pericrocotus flammeus

Satin bowerbird
Ptilonorhynchus violaceus

Bar-bellied cuckoo-shrike
Coracina striata

White-capped dipper
Cinclus leucocephalus

Red-throated pipit
Anthus cervinus
Pipits mostly nest on the ground and feed on insects.

Madagascan wagtail
Motacilla flaviventris
Wagtails almost constantly wag their long tails up and down.

OUT TO IMPRESS

USING SIGHT

Because most birds have well-developed eyesight, they send each other messages using signals that can be seen. This is called visual communication. These visual signals can involve fancy feathers in bright colors or shapes; actions such as bobbing the head or dancing; building elaborate structures; or flying in a special way. Birds may use such actions to greet each other. They can also be used to threaten or warn others of danger. Males of many species use visual signals as part of their courtship displays, to impress females and hopefully win themselves a mate.

This male superb lyrebird spreads its fanlike tail to attract mates. He throws this over his head, twitches his feathers, dances, and sings.

Male bowerbirds impress females with bowers, decorating them with objects. Females then build nests elsewhere.

Showing off
New Guinea's raggiana birds of paradise are known for their beautiful feathers. Males perch together in groups, quivering their long, lacy feathers to win over watching females. They call loudly at the same time.

Human mimics
The raggiana bird of paradise is the national bird of Papua New Guinea. Indigenous people of eastern New Guinea copy the male birds' displays. They dress using the plumes of these birds, then perform ceremonial dances of their own.

Choosing a mate
The female raggiana bird of paradise is drab compared to the male. She chooses the dancer with the most spectacular feather display to be her mate. This ensures she has found the best possible father for her chicks.

Perching birds

Just as there are tyrant flycatchers in the Americas, the Old World flycatchers fill the same insect-eating roles in the rest of the world. Many sit on perches and dart out to snap up passing prey. Others hop through forests picking insects and caterpillars from leaves. Sparrows and finches rely on insects to feed their chicks. Adults eat mostly seeds with their short, cone-shaped bills. Thrushes eat fruit and small animals, usually found on the ground. Some of the best known perching birds are the thrushes, such as the European blackbird and the American robin. Starlings are common garden birds and are easily recognized. Less easy to identify by sight are the members of the warbler family, because of their dull plumage. However, each warbler species tends to have its own lovely, rich, loud song.

Shining starling
Aplonis metallica
Feathers are dark with a metallic sheen that glistens purple and green in the sun.

Southern red bishop
Euplectes orix

Black-thighed grosbeak
Pheucticus tibialis
Has a cone-shaped bill for eating seeds

Snow bunting
Plectrophenax nivalis

Eastern paradise whydah
Vidua paradisaea
Whydahs lay their eggs in waxbills' nests to be cared for by waxbills.

American goldfinch
Carduelis tristis

Tropical gnatcatcher
Polioptila plumbea
Flocks with other insect-eating birds

Goldcrest
Regulus regulus

Black-throated accentor
Prunella atrogularis
Eats mainly insects in summer and berries and seeds in winter

Icterine warbler
Hippolais icterina

White-browed shortwing
Brachypteryx montana

White-necked picathartes
Picathartes gymnocephalus

Northern scrub robin
Drymodes superciliaris
This bird looks like a robin but is more closely related to crows.

Collared redstart
Myioborus torquatus
Like most American wood warblers, this is a small woodland bird.

Bluethroat
Luscinia svecica

Eastern whipbird
Psophodes olivaceus

American robin
Turdus migratorius
The robin hops across the ground, feeding on fruit and berries, as well as worms and insects.

Black-throated thrush
Turdus atrogularis

Bananaquit
Coereba flaveola
Bananaquits are very small birds with slender, curved bills for taking nectar.

Red-winged blackbird
Agelaius phoeniceius

Scarlet tanager
Piranga olivacea

Fluffy-backed tit-babbler
Macronous ptilosus

Chestnut-crowned babbler
Pomatostomus ruficeps

Red-billed buffalo weaver
Bubalornis niger

Gouldian finch
Erythrura gouldiae

Blue-faced parrotfinch
Erythrura trichroa

Black-capped vireo
Vireo atricapilla
Vireos build their nests in trees or low shrubs. They suspend the woven nests from forked branches.

DIVERSE BILLS

1. CRESTED HONEYCREEPER

Rapid spread
Some honeycreepers eat insects (1 and 3) or seeds (2). They developed from one species of seed-eating finch that arrived in Hawaii long ago.

2. LAYSAN FINCH

3. ANIANIAU

Different appetites
Many honeycreepers are seed-eaters that have strong, stout bills to crack hard shells (4). Others have developed long, curved bills that let them probe flowers for nectar (5).

4. MAUI PARROTBILL

5. IIWI

Limitations
Despite bills that allowed them to eat well on the Hawaiian islands, many honeyeaters became extinct (6). They could not adapt fast enough to cope with introduced predators and other threats.

6. BLACK MAMO (EXTINCT)

The shape and size of a bird's bill relates to its diet and the way that it gathers food. Sometimes many bird species share the same habitat. This happens because each has a bill suited to eating a different food. There are more than 30 species of honeycreepers on the islands of Hawaii (although some are now extinct). They have the same ancestor, a finch species that settled in Hawaii millions of years ago. Some species kept the short, strong bills of their seed-eating ancestor, but many have developed bills designed to eat nectar from different-shaped flowers.

Reptiles

4 ORDERS • 60 FAMILIES • 1,012 GENERA • 8,163 SPECIES

Reptiles

Chameleons are a kind of lizard. They change their skin color for camouflage or to communicate. Some color changes warn enemies to stay away, and others attract potential mates.

Reptiles have lived on Earth for more than 300 million years. There are several groups of reptiles: scaly reptiles, including lizards, snakes, and tuatara; ruling reptiles, such as crocodiles; and turtles. Reptiles can be found in salt water, fresh water, on land, underground, and in trees. They are most common in tropical or temperate regions because they are cold-blooded, or ectothermic. Most of their body heat is drawn from their surroundings, not produced by themselves. Despite this, at least two species live in the Arctic, and some are found in the cold environment of high mountains. They survive by sitting in the sun to warm themselves. Most reptiles do not have to eat as often as mammals or birds, because they do not need to burn as much energy to warm their bodies. Some can go for days without eating. Like mammals and birds, reptiles have internal fertilization: Males deposit sperm inside females to fertilize eggs. Because of this, reptiles have developed many ways of finding each other, courting, and choosing mates. Reptiles differ from mammals and birds in the amount of care they give their young. While a few are devoted parents, many species leave their young to develop on their own. As a result, many die, and only a few survive to adulthood.

SKIN AND SCALES

Reptile skin is covered with scales. Like mammal hair, these are made of keratin. Some reptiles also have bony plates under their scales called osteoderms. Each species has a different shape and arrangement of scales to help them move and protect them from danger.

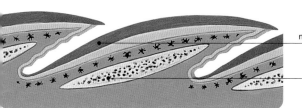

Horny layer made of keratin

Bony plate (osteoderm)

GRANULAR SCALES

KEELED SCALES

SMOOTH SCALES

REPTILE REPRODUCTION

Many female snakes stay with their clutch of eggs to keep predators away.

Crocodile eggs have soft, leathery shells and need to be buried to limit water loss.

Reptiles develop in eggs that are usually laid outside the mother's body. Some snakes and lizards keep eggs in their bodies and give birth to live young. To keep the embryo moist, the shell is waterproof. Oxygen enters through the chorion. The embryo is nourished by yolk and cushioned by fluid-filled sacs.

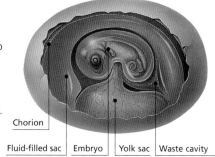

Chorion

Fluid-filled sac | Embryo | Yolk sac | Waste cavity

---

1 ORDER • 1 FAMILY • 1 GENUS • 2 SPECIES

Tuatara

The two species of tuatara are the only survivors of a group that roamed with the dinosaurs more than 225 million years ago. They look like lizards but have a different skeleton and no external ear openings. Their teeth are unique: A single row of lower teeth fits between two rows of upper teeth. Tuatara are nocturnal and spend their days in burrows. They eat insects and other small animals.

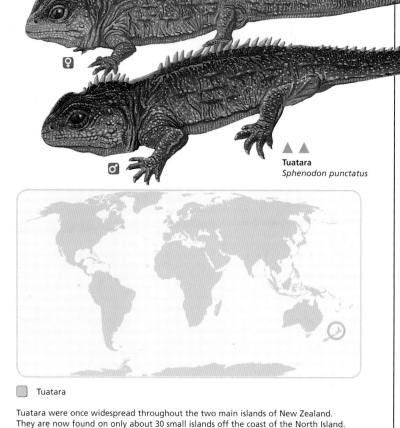

♀

♂

▲ ▲

Tuatara
Sphenodon punctatus

CONSERVATION WATCH

One tuatara species appears on the IUCN Red List as vulnerable. Land clearing, as well as introduced predators such as rats, which eat its eggs and young, have reduced its numbers during the past few centuries.

Ex	✝	0
Cr		0
En		0
Vu		1
Other		0

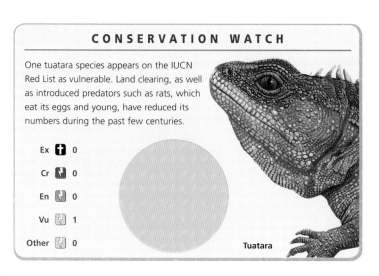

Tuatara

□ Tuatara

Tuatara were once widespread throughout the two main islands of New Zealand. They are now found on only about 30 small islands off the coast of the North Island.

1 ORDER • 14 FAMILIES • 99 GENERA • 293 SPECIES

Turtles and Tortoises

Turtles and tortoises are found mainly in tropical and temperate regions. Many divide their lives between water and land habitats. Some live almost their entire lives in water. The limbs of sea turtles have developed into paddles, making them fast and agile swimmers but slow and awkward walkers. Others have adapted to life in dry environments, such as deserts and savanna grasslands. There are species of land tortoises that have probably never encountered any open bodies of water in their lifetimes. The shells of turtles and tortoises are built into the skeleton, with the backbone running along the inside. They are made up of an inner layer of bones and an outer layer of horny plates. The shell's structure varies among species. Softshell turtles have soft, leathery, and flexible plates on their shells.

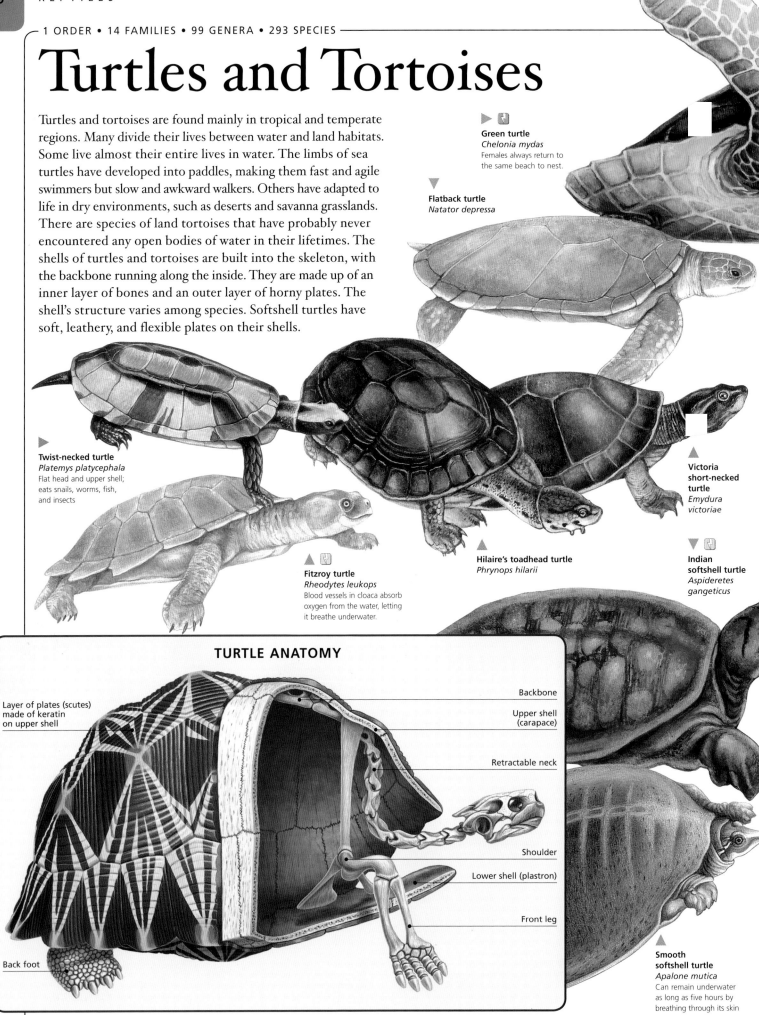

Green turtle
Chelonia mydas
Females always return to the same beach to nest.

Flatback turtle
Natator depressa

Twist-necked turtle
Platemys platycephala
Flat head and upper shell; eats snails, worms, fish, and insects

Victoria short-necked turtle
Emydura victoriae

Fitzroy turtle
Rheodytes leukops
Blood vessels in cloaca absorb oxygen from the water, letting it breathe underwater.

Hilaire's toadhead turtle
Phrynops hilarii

Indian softshell turtle
Aspideretes gangeticus

TURTLE ANATOMY

Layer of plates (scutes) made of keratin on upper shell

Backbone

Upper shell (carapace)

Retractable neck

Shoulder

Lower shell (plastron)

Front leg

Back foot

Smooth softshell turtle
Apalone mutica
Can remain underwater as long as five hours by breathing through its skin

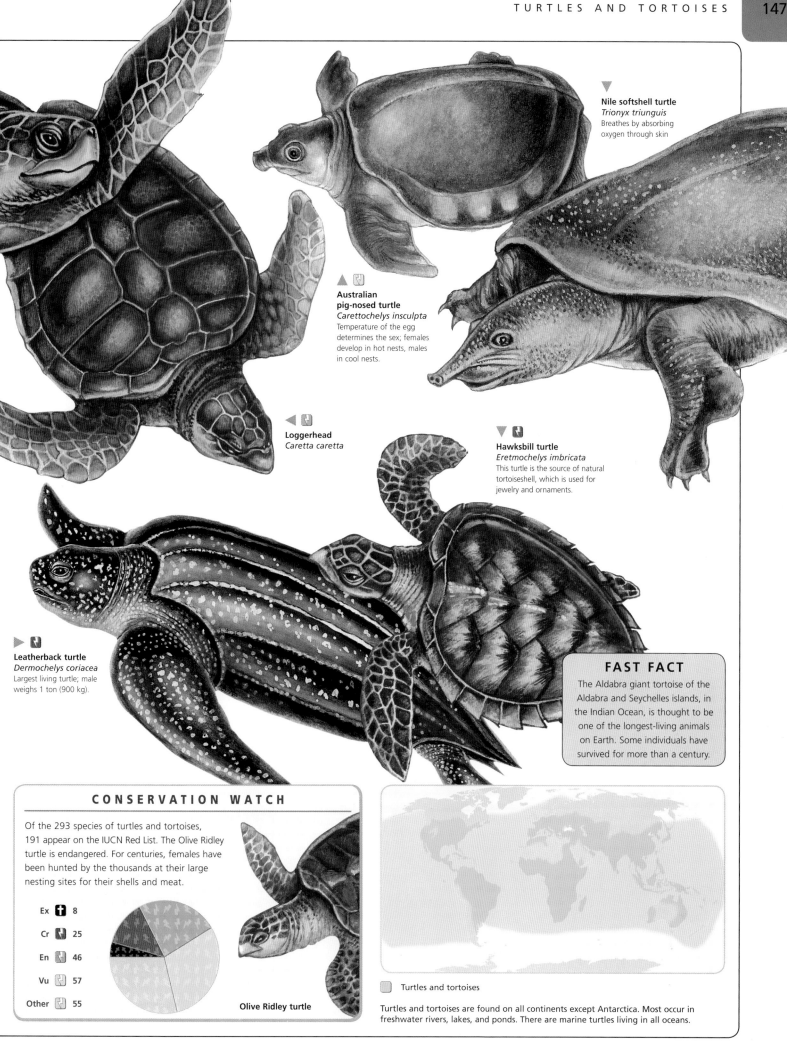

Nile softshell turtle
Trionyx triunguis
Breathes by absorbing oxygen through skin

Australian pig-nosed turtle
Carettochelys insculpta
Temperature of the egg determines the sex; females develop in hot nests, males in cool nests.

Loggerhead
Caretta caretta

Hawksbill turtle
Eretmochelys imbricata
This turtle is the source of natural tortoiseshell, which is used for jewelry and ornaments.

Leatherback turtle
Dermochelys coriacea
Largest living turtle; male weighs 1 ton (900 kg).

FAST FACT

The Aldabra giant tortoise of the Aldabra and Seychelles islands, in the Indian Ocean, is thought to be one of the longest-living animals on Earth. Some individuals have survived for more than a century.

CONSERVATION WATCH

Of the 293 species of turtles and tortoises, 191 appear on the IUCN Red List. The Olive Ridley turtle is endangered. For centuries, females have been hunted by the thousands at their large nesting sites for their shells and meat.

Ex	✝	8
Cr		25
En		46
Vu		57
Other		55

Olive Ridley turtle

☐ Turtles and tortoises

Turtles and tortoises are found on all continents except Antarctica. Most occur in freshwater rivers, lakes, and ponds. There are marine turtles living in all oceans.

Turtles and tortoises

There are two main groups of turtles and tortoises: side-necked turtles and hidden-necked turtles. Side-necked turtles use a sideways movement to fold their necks and bring their heads under the front edge of the upper shell. Hidden-necked turtles draw their necks directly back into the shell. Some cannot do this completely, so their heads always stick out a little. Tortoises are land-dwelling species of hidden-necked turtles. Turtles and tortoises do not have teeth. Instead, they all have hard ridges covering the top and bottom jaws. They eat a variety of foods: the soft parts of plants; small invertebrates like worms and insects; crayfish; and sometimes fish or birds. Meat-eating species have sharp ridges that work like shears. The ridges of plant-eaters have sawlike outer edges.

Diamondback terrapin
Malaclemys terrapin

European pond turtle
Emys orbicular

Alligator snapping turtle
Macrochelys temminckii

Big-headed turtle
Platysternon megacephalum

Common snapping turtle
Chelydra serpentina

Central Ameri river turtle
Dermatemys r

River terrapin
Batagur bask

HOW TURTLES REPRODUCE

Mating
Most tortoises sniff and butt each other before mating. Some mate at sea, but most mate on land.

Laying eggs
Almost all turtle eggs are laid in a nest chamber on land. Hatchlings usually appear after about a month.

Hatching
Turtle hatchlings look after themselves from birth and dig their own way out of the nest.

Ringed sawback
Graptemys oculifera

South American red-footed tortoise
Geochelone carbonaria
Bright red scales on limbs

Painted turtle
Chrysemys picta

African tent tortoise
Psammobates tentorius
This tortoise is named for the arched plates on its upper shell with patterns that look like tents.

Bell's hinge-back tortoise
Kinixys belliana
Upper shell has a hinge and can be closed around the back legs.

Gopher tortoise
Gopherus polyphemus
Lives in burrows as deep as 10 feet (3 m)

Painted terrapin
Callagur borneoensis
Male's head turns white with a red stripe in breeding season.

SADDLEBACK TORTOISES

The shells of Galápagos tortoises come in two varieties: dome and saddleback. Most Galápagos tortoises have dome-shaped shells and live in environments with many plants to eat. Those tortoises living on the drier parts of the islands, with few plants and hardly any water, have saddle-shaped shells (right). The raised front of the shell lets these tortoises stretch their heads as high as 5 feet (1.5 m) above the ground. This allows them to browse on higher parts of the cactus plants they eat. They also tend to have smaller shells and longer necks, limbs, and snouts compared to the tortoises with dome-shaped shells.

Malayan snail-eating turtle
Malayemys subtrijuga
This freshwater turtle nests on beaches; hatchlings can live in seawater for at least two weeks.

Black-breasted leaf turtle
Geoemyda spengleri

1 ORDER • 3 FAMILIES • 8 GENERA • 23 SPECIES

Crocodiles and Alligators

Crocodiles and alligators, along with caimans and gharials, are known as crocodilians. They all have long bodies with short, muscular limbs and tails flattened at the sides for swimming. Their massive skulls hold powerful jaws with sharp teeth. Crocodilians have lived on Earth for at least 220 million years. They are the survivors of an ancient reptile group that included the dinosaurs. Crocodilians spend much of their lives in the water and are often seen basking on the shorelines of estuaries, rivers, swamps, lakes, or streams. All crocodilians lay eggs in nests near the water. These can be in mounds of plant matter or dug into soil or sand. Unlike most reptiles, crocodilians can be noisy, especially males that are trying to attract a mate. Mothers are also unusually protective of eggs and hatchlings.

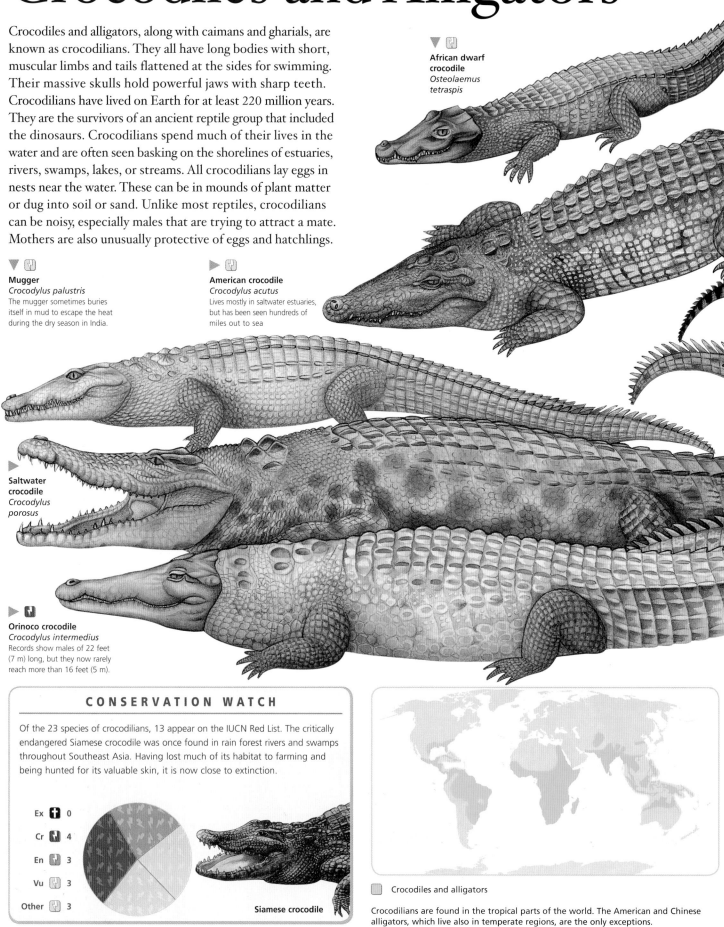

African dwarf crocodile
Osteolaemus tetraspis

Mugger
Crocodylus palustris
The mugger sometimes buries itself in mud to escape the heat during the dry season in India.

American crocodile
Crocodylus acutus
Lives mostly in saltwater estuaries, but has been seen hundreds of miles out to sea

Saltwater crocodile
Crocodylus porosus

Orinoco crocodile
Crocodylus intermedius
Records show males of 22 feet (7 m) long, but they now rarely reach more than 16 feet (5 m).

CONSERVATION WATCH

Of the 23 species of crocodilians, 13 appear on the IUCN Red List. The critically endangered Siamese crocodile was once found in rain forest rivers and swamps throughout Southeast Asia. Having lost much of its habitat to farming and being hunted for its valuable skin, it is now close to extinction.

Ex	0
Cr	4
En	3
Vu	3
Other	3

Siamese crocodile

Crocodiles and alligators

Crocodilians are found in the tropical parts of the world. The American and Chinese alligators, which live also in temperate regions, are the only exceptions.

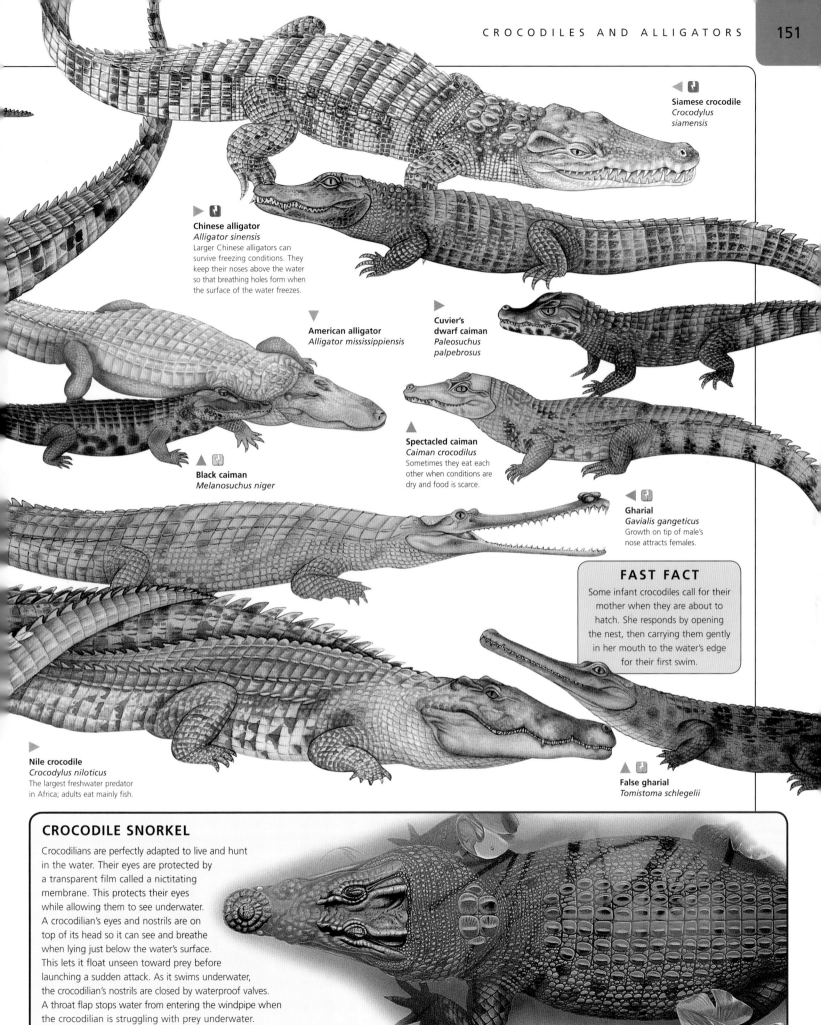

Siamese crocodile
Crocodylus siamensis

Chinese alligator
Alligator sinensis
Larger Chinese alligators can survive freezing conditions. They keep their noses above the water so that breathing holes form when the surface of the water freezes.

American alligator
Alligator mississippiensis

Cuvier's dwarf caiman
Paleosuchus palpebrosus

Black caiman
Melanosuchus niger

Spectacled caiman
Caiman crocodilus
Sometimes they eat each other when conditions are dry and food is scarce.

Gharial
Gavialis gangeticus
Growth on tip of male's nose attracts females.

FAST FACT

Some infant crocodiles call for their mother when they are about to hatch. She responds by opening the nest, then carrying them gently in her mouth to the water's edge for their first swim.

Nile crocodile
Crocodylus niloticus
The largest freshwater predator in Africa; adults eat mainly fish.

False gharial
Tomistoma schlegelii

CROCODILE SNORKEL

Crocodilians are perfectly adapted to live and hunt in the water. Their eyes are protected by a transparent film called a nictitating membrane. This protects their eyes while allowing them to see underwater. A crocodilian's eyes and nostrils are on top of its head so it can see and breathe when lying just below the water's surface. This lets it float unseen toward prey before launching a sudden attack. As it swims underwater, the crocodilian's nostrils are closed by waterproof valves. A throat flap stops water from entering the windpipe when the crocodilian is struggling with prey underwater.

1 SUBORDER • 27 FAMILIES • 442 GENERA • 4,560 SPECIES

Lizards

Most lizards prey on insects and other small animals, but the green iguana is strictly a plant-eater. It is almost perfectly camouflaged in the lush vegetation of its tropical home.

Lizards have existed for more than 100 million years. While dinosaurs and most other large reptiles died out about 65 million years ago, lizards survived. They now form the largest group of living reptiles. One reason why there are so many lizards is that they are small in size: Most are no bigger than a foot (30 cm) long. This means many species can exist in the same habitat. Their small size

also makes them the popular prey of mammals and birds. Many have developed ways of avoiding or escaping predators. Most are well camouflaged. The sharp spines of some can injure a predator's mouth. The slippery scales of others make them hard to grip. Iguanas and monitors use their tails like weapons to beat off attackers. Skinks and geckos lose their tails when attacked, which lets them escape with their lives.

CONSERVATION WATCH

Of the 4,560 lizard species, 179 appear on the IUCN Red List. The endangered Fiji banded iguana lives on the islands of Fiji. Introduced predators, such as mongooses and cats, are a major threat to its survival.

Ex	✝	11
Cr		22
En		16
Vu		72
Other		58

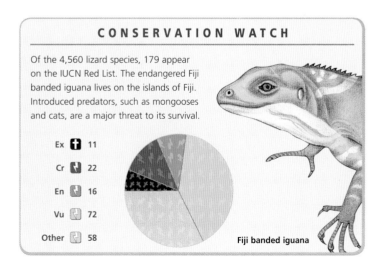

Fiji banded iguana

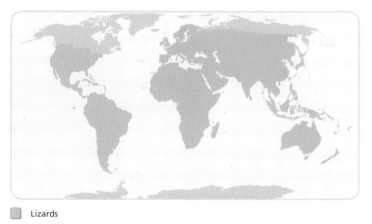

Lizards

Lizards can be found on almost all continents and islands. They are missing from Antarctica and some regions of North America, Europe, and Asia.

Iguanas

Iguanas live mainly in the tropical and subtropical parts of the Americas. All are diurnal, and most have camouflaging scales. Most species have a fold of skin called a dewlap underneath their heads and necks. Many have raised scales forming a crest along their backs. Young iguanas usually feed on insects and other small animals, but adults are often herbivores that eat flowers, fruit, and leaves. Most iguanas dwell on land, either on the ground or among rocks. Some live almost exclusively in trees and come down from the branches only to lay eggs. The marine iguana is the only lizard that spends large amounts of time in the sea. It dives to depths of 30 feet (9 m) and grazes on marine algae or submerged plants. A gland in its nose removes excess salt from its body in the form of salt crystals.

West Indian iguana
Iguana delicatissima
Males have head-pushing competitions to win the right to mate with females.

Leopard lizard
Gambelia sila
It often lives in abandoned burrows of ground squirrels.

Merrem's Madagascar swift
Oplurus cyclurus
This iguana lives in forested regions of Madagascar.

Collared lizard
Crotaphytus collaris
When scared, it rises up on its back legs to run faster.

Chuckwalla
Sauromalus obesus
Lives in the southwestern deserts of North America; it stops laying eggs when food is scarce.

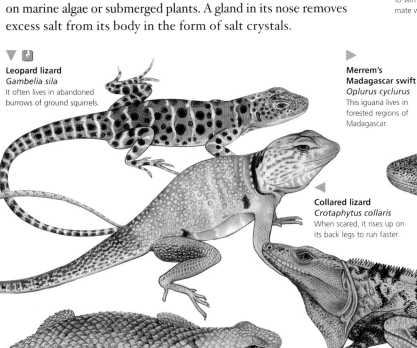

Desert spiny lizard
Sceloporus magister

Black iguana
Ctenosaura similis
By basking in sunlight this iguana lightens its color from dark (right) to lighter (top).

Rhinoceros iguana
Cyclura cornuta
Bacteria in its stomach helps to digest food.

Green iguana
Iguana iguana
This iguana can grow to be as long as 6½ feet (2 m), including its tail.

Anoles and agamids

Anoles and their relatives are small lizards with bodies that range in length from 1 to 4½ inches (2.5 to 12 cm). Most eat insects and other small animals. Tree-dwelling varieties have special sticky pads on their feet that make them good climbers. All lose their tails if they are grasped by predators. Anoles are found in South and Central America. One species, the green anole, lives in the southeastern United States. It can change color from bright green to dark brown, depending on light and temperature. Agamids, or chisel-toothed lizards, live in Africa, Asia, and Australia. They range in length from 1 inch to 4½ feet (2 cm to 1.4 m). Agamids have large heads, notched tongues, and well-developed limbs. They can live in environments from deserts to tropical forests. Some even live partly in fresh water.

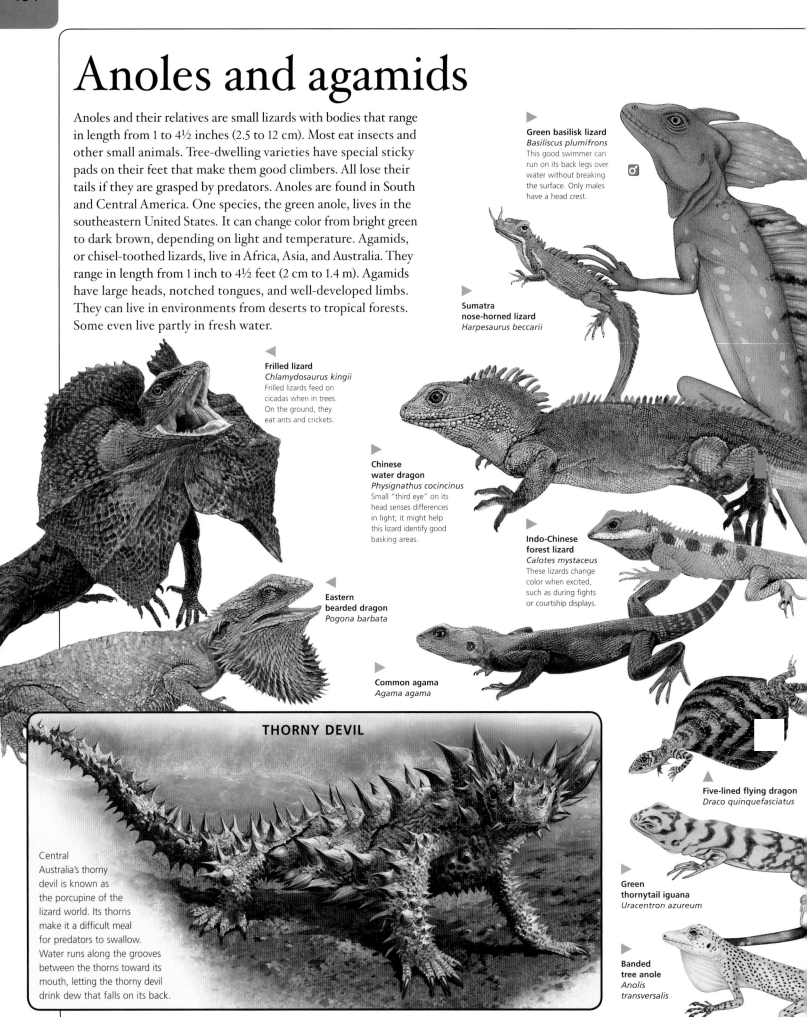

Green basilisk lizard
Basiliscus plumifrons
This good swimmer can run on its back legs over water without breaking the surface. Only males have a head crest.

Sumatra nose-horned lizard
Harpesaurus beccarii

Frilled lizard
Chlamydosaurus kingii
Frilled lizards feed on cicadas when in trees. On the ground, they eat ants and crickets.

Chinese water dragon
Physignathus cocincinus
Small "third eye" on its head senses differences in light; it might help this lizard identify good basking areas.

Indo-Chinese forest lizard
Calotes mystaceus
These lizards change color when excited, such as during fights or courtship displays.

Eastern bearded dragon
Pogona barbata

Common agama
Agama agama

Five-lined flying dragon
Draco quinquefasciatus

Green thornytail iguana
Uracentron azureum

Banded tree anole
Anolis transversalis

THORNY DEVIL

Central Australia's thorny devil is known as the porcupine of the lizard world. Its thorns make it a difficult meal for predators to swallow. Water runs along the grooves between the thorns toward its mouth, letting the thorny devil drink dew that falls on its back.

DISPLAYS AND COURTSHIP

Warning pose
The frilled lizard opens its mouth wide, hisses loudly, and pushes up on its front legs to frighten predators away.

Frilled threat
The lizard also flashes open the frills around its neck to appear larger.

DIFFERENT DISPLAYS

BOBBING RAPIDLY
The carpenter anole has a simple display. It opens its orange-colored dewlap, then bobs its head in a fast and regular rhythm.

VARIABLE BOBBING
The silk anole has a more varied display. It repeatedly opens and closes its colorful dewlap, bobbing its head fast then slow.

SLOW BOBBING
The lichen anole has a complex display. It bobs its head slowly as it opens and closes its dewlap. As the dewlap expands, more colored lines appear.

BODY LANGUAGE

Lizards can communicate by changing posture or moving body parts. Some, when threatened or courting a mate, raise crests on their heads. Others extend and curl dewlaps on their necks. Many lash their tails or raise their bodies up and down as if they are doing push-ups. Some young male lizards tell dominant males they are not a threat by standing on three limbs and waving the fourth in slow circles. Lizards can also change color to communicate messages to each other or scare predators. Male anoles court females by bobbing their heads and flaring the colorful dewlaps around their necks. Some lizards, such as Australia's frilled lizard, use scare tactics to warn off potential predators. The capelike frill that lies over the lizard's shoulders flares up when it is frightened or angry. This makes the lizard appear twice its actual size.

Chameleons

Chameleons are the most recognizable of all the lizard families. Their large eyes are covered by skin; only the pupil can be seen. Their eyes can move in different directions from each other. This helps chameleons judge distances, so they can aim their long tongues in the precise direction to catch prey. Most eat insects and other invertebrates. However, larger species will also eat small birds and mammals. Chameleons range in length from 1 inch (2.5 cm) to just over 26 inches (68 cm). Most chameleons have agile tails that work like an extra limb to grasp branches. Two or three of their toes are joined together to form pads, which help them move easily through trees. Chameleons are diurnal. Most species live in humid forests in the African highlands or on the island of Madagascar.

Lesser chameleon
Furcifer minor
Long tongue covered with sticky mucus shoots out like a slingshot, capturing prey. Unlike many lizards, it does not lose its tail when threatened.

Common Mediterranean chameleon
Chamaeleo chamaeleon

Knysna dwarf chameleon
Bradypodion damaranum
This chameleon gives birth to live young; it does not lay eggs.

Malthe's elephant-eared chameleon
Calumma malthe

CHANGING COLOR

Chameleons are able to change color. At cool temperatures, they turn almost white. Behavior also affects color. Male chameleons may flush with color to warn other males out of their territories. This species changes from a camouflaging green to an angry red.

Jackson's chameleon
Chamaeleo jacksonii
Males have three horns and use these to fight each other.

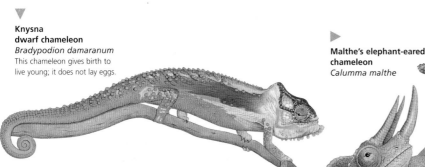

Carpet chameleon
Furcifer lateralis

Giant Madagascar chameleon
Furcifer oustaleti

Parson's chameleon
Calumma parsoni
One of the largest chameleons, it can grow to about the size of a small cat.

Horned leaf chameleon
Brookesia superciliaris

FAST FACT

The amazing tongues of chameleons are incredibly long and fast. They can travel at speeds faster than 16 feet (5 m) per second, reaching prey a body length away in less than one-hundredth of a second.

Geckos

Geckos are the second largest group of lizards. They live on all continents except Antarctica. They are most common in the tropics and subtropics. Some live in cooler areas, such as northern Italy or southern New Zealand, and a few even live in harsh alpine areas. Unusual for lizards, geckos are active mainly at night. Large eyes help them hunt prey in poor light. Their feet have special toe pads that stick to surfaces, which makes them good at climbing—some can run up smooth surfaces, such as glass, where there is nothing to cling to. Geckos rely on sound to communicate. Many chirp like birds. Others can growl. Some make high-pitched alarm squeals when threatened. Although many geckos use sound to find mates, the females of certain species can produce young without males.

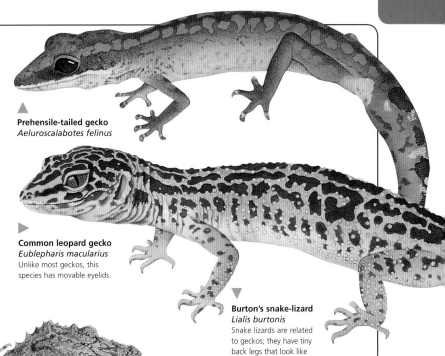

Prehensile-tailed gecko
Aeluroscalabotes felinus

Common leopard gecko
Eublepharis macularius
Unlike most geckos, this species has movable eyelids.

Burton's snake-lizard
Lialis burtonis
Snake lizards are related to geckos; they have tiny back legs that look like flaps and no front legs.

Northern leaf-tailed gecko
Saltuarius cornutus

Madagascar day gecko
Phelsuma madagascariensis
Unlike most geckos, it is active during the day.

Tokay gecko
Gekko gecko
To attract a mate, the male gecko makes a loud call that sounds like "to-kay."

Kuhl's flying gecko
Ptychozoon kuhli
Males are aggressive toward other males that come into their territories.

Northern spiny-tailed gecko
Strophurus ciliaris
Can squirt a foul-smelling liquid from the spines on its tail

FAST FACT
Most geckos have no eyelids. Instead, each eye is protected by a clear scale that does not move. This can become coated with dirt, so geckos clean their eyes by licking them regularly with their tongues.

FLYING HIGH

Kuhl's flying gecko lives in trees in Southeast Asia and can "fly" as well as climb. It has webbed feet and skin flaps along each side of its body and tail. By holding its limbs out from its body, it can glide short distances between branches.

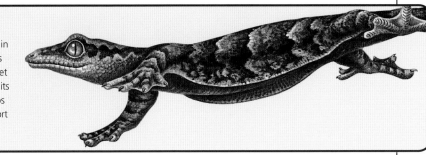

Common wall gecko
Tarentola mauritanica

Skinks

Skinks make up the largest of the lizard families. They are found throughout the world, except for the polar regions, but are more common in warmer areas. They range in length from 1 to 26 inches (2.5 to 67 cm), and almost all are covered by smooth overlapping scales. Skinks tend to be drab gray or brown in color. This provides good camouflage in the leaf litter, rock crevices, or rotting logs where they often live. Many skinks have either small or no limbs; limbless species usually live in burrows. Some species can climb trees. Like many lizards, skinks readily lose their tails to save themselves when attacked. This is called autotomy. The tail almost always grows back. Skinks themselves prey on insects and other small animals, such as spiders. They actively forage for food, using mostly sight and smell.

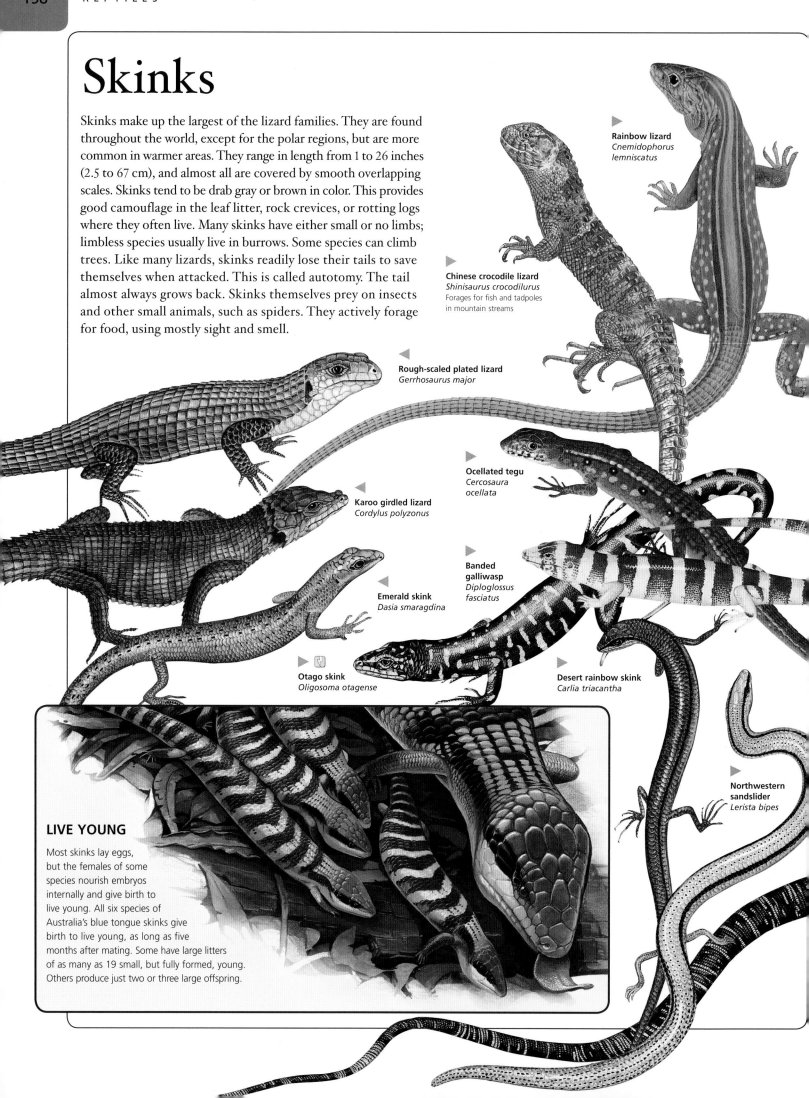

Rainbow lizard
Cnemidophorus lemniscatus

Chinese crocodile lizard
Shinisaurus crocodilurus
Forages for fish and tadpoles
in mountain streams

Rough-scaled plated lizard
Gerrhosaurus major

Ocellated tegu
Cercosaura ocellata

Karoo girdled lizard
Cordylus polyzonus

Banded galliwasp
Diploglossus fasciatus

Emerald skink
Dasia smaragdina

Otago skink
Oligosoma otagense

Desert rainbow skink
Carlia triacantha

Northwestern sandslider
Lerista bipes

LIVE YOUNG

Most skinks lay eggs, but the females of some species nourish embryos internally and give birth to live young. All six species of Australia's blue tongue skinks give birth to live young, as long as five months after mating. Some have large litters of as many as 19 small, but fully formed, young. Others produce just two or three large offspring.

Monitors

Monitors are found in Africa, Asia, Australia, and the Pacific Islands. They can be as small as 8 inches (20 cm) in length and half an ounce (14 g) in weight, or as large as the Komodo dragon, which reaches 10 feet (3 m) and 365 pounds (166 kg). Komodos are the world's largest lizards; they are predators that pounce on large mammal prey. Monitors have long necks, thick skin, and whiplike tails. Their forked tongues flick in and out of their mouths, "tasting" the air for chemical signals. These signals tell them the location of food, possible mates, or predators. Related to monitors are lacterids, which include the sawtail, wall, and tiger lizards. Lacterids are small lizards with tails that can be twice as long as their bodies. They are found in Africa, Europe, and Asia, where they live either on the ground or in trees.

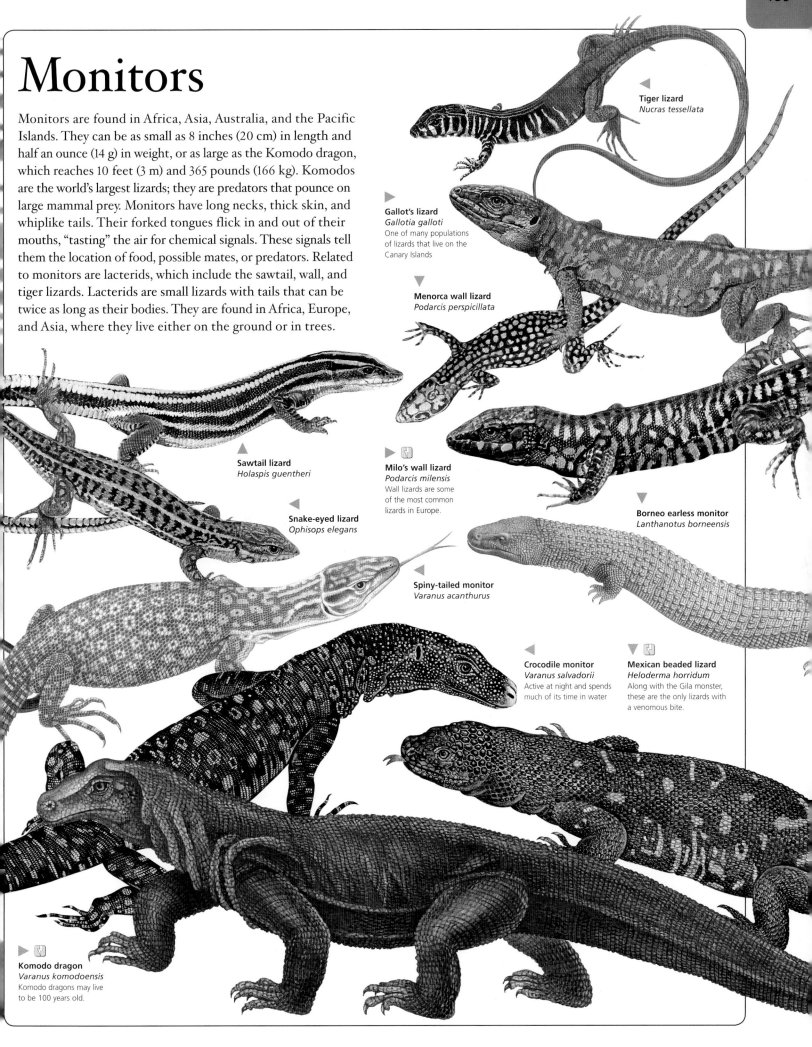

Tiger lizard
Nucras tessellata

Gallot's lizard
Gallotia galloti
One of many populations of lizards that live on the Canary Islands

Menorca wall lizard
Podarcis perspicillata

Sawtail lizard
Holaspis guentheri

Milo's wall lizard
Podarcis milensis
Wall lizards are some of the most common lizards in Europe.

Snake-eyed lizard
Ophisops elegans

Borneo earless monitor
Lanthanotus borneensis

Spiny-tailed monitor
Varanus acanthurus

Crocodile monitor
Varanus salvadorii
Active at night and spends much of its time in water

Mexican beaded lizard
Heloderma horridum
Along with the Gila monster, these are the only lizards with a venomous bite.

Komodo dragon
Varanus komodoensis
Komodo dragons may live to be 100 years old.

1 SUBORDER • 17 FAMILIES • 438 GENERA • 2,955 SPECIES

Snakes

A parrot snake in the rain forest of Costa Rica opens its mouth wide to startle a predator. The fangs are located at the back of its mouth and are used to pierce prey that it catches.

There are almost 3,000 species of snakes. They range from tiny burrowing blind snakes just 4 inches (10 cm) long to huge constrictors more than 30 feet (9 m) in length. Snakes evolved from lizards. As their bodies became long and narrow, so did their internal organs. The left lung is either missing or extremely small in all species. Snakes have no limbs, but some species still show signs of the limbs of their ancestors. Without limbs, snakes developed new ways of moving. They use special belly scales called scutes and tiny muscles attached to their ribs to move across surfaces. On the ground, they follow scent trails to mates and prey. All snakes are carnivores. The prey they eat depends on their size. Whereas some lizards tear prey apart with their teeth, snakes swallow their food whole.

CONSERVATION WATCH

There are 2,955 species of snakes, of which 79 appear on the IUCN Red List. Wagner's viper, which is found among rocks and grass in the high mountains around Lake Urmia, in northwest Iran and Turkey, is endangered. Its numbers have been reduced mainly by overenthusiastic reptile collectors.

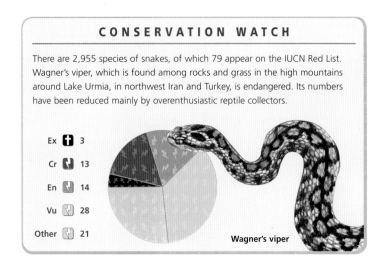

Ex	3
Cr	13
En	14
Vu	28
Other	21

Wagner's viper

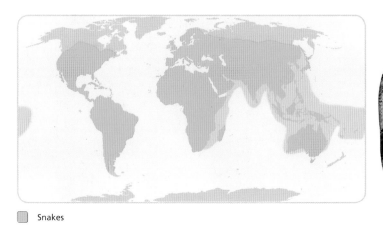

Snakes

Snakes are found on all landmasses except Antarctica and some islands, such as New Zealand, Ireland, and Iceland. Most snake species live in tropical or temperate regions.

Pythons and boas

Pythons and boas belong to the boid family. It has many small species but also includes the largest snakes. The longest snakes on record are Asia's reticulated python and South America's anaconda, which spends much of its time in the Amazon River. Individuals from both species can grow longer than 30 feet (9 m). Pythons are found mostly in Asia, Africa, and Australia. All species lay eggs. Unlike most reptiles, they protect their eggs. Females make nests and then coil around their developing broods. After hatching, the young snakes are left to look after themselves. Pythons and boas are not venomous. They kill their prey by constricting, or squeezing, and then suffocating it with their coiled bodies. Boas occur mainly throughout the Americas. They do not lay eggs but give birth to live young.

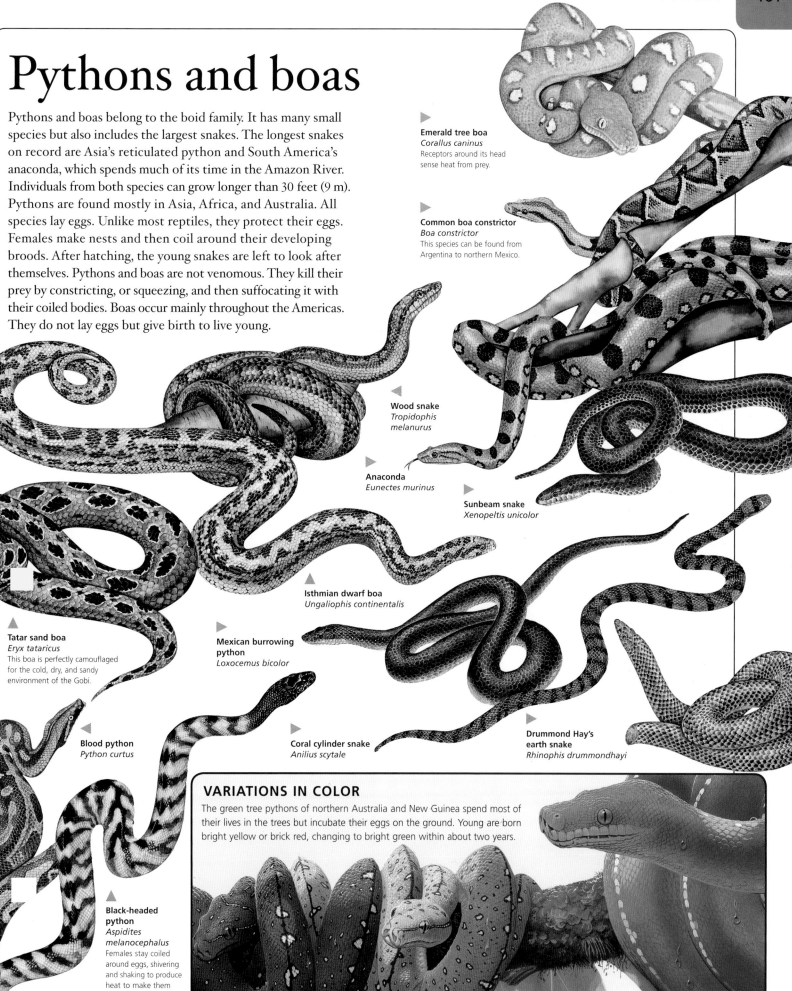

Emerald tree boa
Corallus caninus
Receptors around its head sense heat from prey.

Common boa constrictor
Boa constrictor
This species can be found from Argentina to northern Mexico.

Wood snake
Tropidophis melanurus

Anaconda
Eunectes murinus

Sunbeam snake
Xenopeltis unicolor

Isthmian dwarf boa
Ungaliophis continentalis

Tatar sand boa
Eryx tataricus
This boa is perfectly camouflaged for the cold, dry, and sandy environment of the Gobi.

Mexican burrowing python
Loxocemus bicolor

Blood python
Python curtus

Coral cylinder snake
Anilius scytale

Drummond Hay's earth snake
Rhinophis drummondhayi

VARIATIONS IN COLOR

The green tree pythons of northern Australia and New Guinea spend most of their lives in the trees but incubate their eggs on the ground. Young are born bright yellow or brick red, changing to bright green within about two years.

Black-headed python
Aspidites melanocephalus
Females stay coiled around eggs, shivering and shaking to produce heat to make them hatch faster.

Colubrid snakes

More than half of all snake species are colubrid snakes. They live on all continents except Antarctica. Colubrids are found in almost all habitats and are usually the most common snakes in areas where snakes occur. Some live mostly in fresh water and eat fish. Others spend much of their lives in trees and hunt small mammals or birds. Many live in grass or leaf litter on the ground and eat frogs, small reptiles, or large insects and spiders. Most colubrids produce venom, but they are often thought of as harmless snakes. Venom trickles down grooves on large fangs at the back of the mouth, so that only about half of it enters a wound during a bite. Their venom is not injected, as it is in snakes that are considered more dangerous. However, some colubrids have been known to kill humans with their venom.

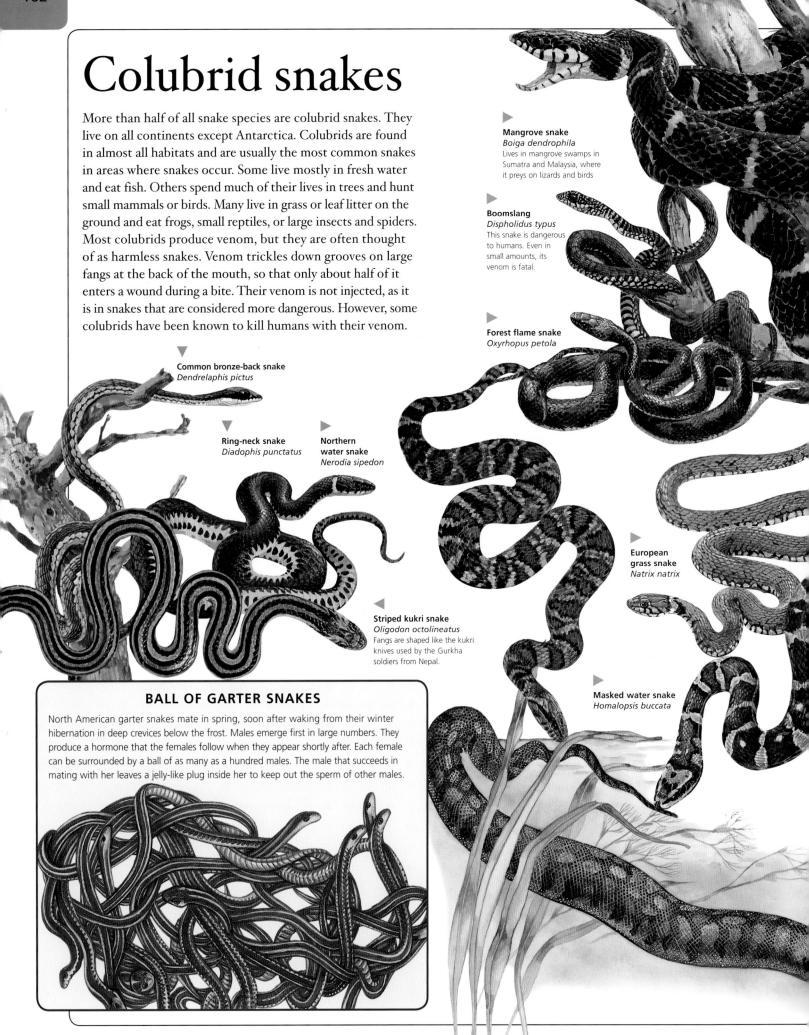

Mangrove snake
Boiga dendrophila
Lives in mangrove swamps in Sumatra and Malaysia, where it preys on lizards and birds

Boomslang
Dispholidus typus
This snake is dangerous to humans. Even in small amounts, its venom is fatal.

Forest flame snake
Oxyrhopus petola

Common bronze-back snake
Dendrelaphis pictus

Ring-neck snake
Diadophis punctatus

Northern water snake
Nerodia sipedon

European grass snake
Natrix natrix

Striped kukri snake
Oligodon octolineatus
Fangs are shaped like the kukri knives used by the Gurkha soldiers from Nepal.

Masked water snake
Homalopsis buccata

BALL OF GARTER SNAKES

North American garter snakes mate in spring, soon after waking from their winter hibernation in deep crevices below the frost. Males emerge first in large numbers. They produce a hormone that the females follow when they appear shortly after. Each female can be surrounded by a ball of as many as a hundred males. The male that succeeds in mating with her leaves a jelly-like plug inside her to keep out the sperm of other males.

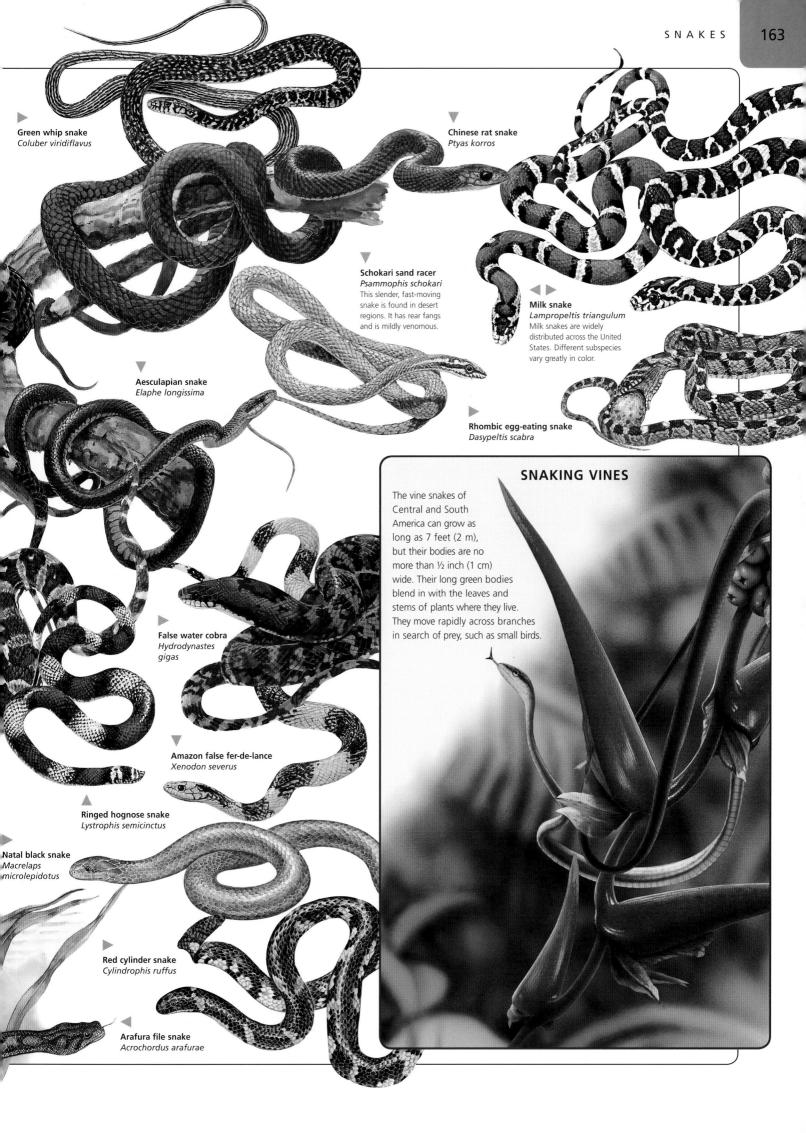

Green whip snake
Coluber viridiflavus

Chinese rat snake
Ptyas korros

Schokari sand racer
Psammophis schokari
This slender, fast-moving
snake is found in desert
regions. It has rear fangs
and is mildly venomous.

Milk snake
Lampropeltis triangulum
Milk snakes are widely
distributed across the United
States. Different subspecies
vary greatly in color.

Aesculapian snake
Elaphe longissima

Rhombic egg-eating snake
Dasypeltis scabra

False water cobra
*Hydrodynastes
gigas*

Amazon false fer-de-lance
Xenodon severus

Ringed hognose snake
Lystrophis semicinctus

Natal black snake
*Macrelaps
microlepidotus*

Red cylinder snake
Cylindrophis ruffus

Arafura file snake
Acrochordus arafurae

SNAKING VINES

The vine snakes of
Central and South
America can grow as
long as 7 feet (2 m),
but their bodies are no
more than ½ inch (1 cm)
wide. Their long green bodies
blend in with the leaves and
stems of plants where they live.
They move rapidly across branches
in search of prey, such as small birds.

ATTACK AND DEFENSE

THE HUNTERS AND THE HUNTED

Many snakes are aggressive predators with venomous bites. But snakes are often preyed on, too, especially by mammals and birds. Camouflage helps them hide from predators. Many tree snakes have long, slender heads and necks that blend in with their habitat. A cobra may use a threat display when challenged. To appear larger than its actual size, it raises half its body off the ground and flattens the ribs in its neck to form a hoodlike shape. A spitting cobra (left) avoids a fight that could injure its mouth by spitting poison at an attacker's eyes.

A venomous Florida cottonmouth reveals its startling white mouth. This warns potential predators to stay away.

The mild venom of this grass snake can paralyze a small fish, making it easier for the snake to swallow.

Cobras

Cobras belong to the elapid family, a venomous group that also includes kraits, sea snakes, mambas, coral snakes, and death adders. Elapids have hollow fangs located at the front of the mouth. They are fixed to the upper jawbone like normal teeth. They need to be small enough for the snake to close its mouth over them. Elapid venom acts on prey's nerves to stop the heart beating and damage the lungs. These snakes are found in Australia, Africa, South and Central America, and southeast North America. Many species live in burrows or leaf litter. Mambas and tree cobras live in trees. Sea snakes are found mainly in tropical parts of the Pacific and Indian Oceans. They have flattened bodies that are so well adapted to life in the water that it is almost impossible for them to move on land.

King cobra
Ophiophagus hannah

Black mamba
Dendroaspis polylepis
The fastest-moving snake, it has been recorded at speeds as fast as 12½ miles per hour (20 km/h).

Monocled cobra
Naja kaouthia
Markings on the back of the hood are thought to discourage predators attacking from behind.

Eastern coral snake
Micrurus fulvius
This venomous snake confuses would-be predators by moving its tail in the same way as it moves its head.

Common death adder
Acanthophis antarcticus

Taipan
Oxyuranus scutellatus

Arizona coral snake
Micruroides euryxanthus

Tiger snake
Notechis scutatus

Blue-lipped sea krait
Laticauda laticaudata

Western brown snake
Pseudonaja nuchalis

Mulga snake
Pseudechis australis

FAST FACT

Central Australia's fierce snake has the most poisonous venom of any snake. It is about 500 times more potent than that of an eastern diamondback rattlesnake. The venom in one bite could kill 250,000 mice.

Turtle-headed sea snake
Emydocephalus annulatus

Adders and vipers

The viper family includes rattlesnakes and adders. All have large, hollow fangs located at the front of the mouth that swing forward to inject potent venom when they bite. The fangs are tucked away at other times. Vipers and adders occur throughout the Americas, Africa, Europe, and Asia. Instead of stalking prey, they ambush it. Their bodies are often patterned in shades of brown and green that blend in with their surroundings. This allows them to remain unseen as they lie coiled up beside a trail used by small mammals, or in the branches of a fruit tree where birds gather. They wait for prey to come within range before they strike with lightning speed. Some lure prey into range by wriggling their tails to look like a worm.

Gaboon viper
Bitis gabonica

Saw-scaled viper
Echis carinatus

Copperhead
Agkistrodon contortix

Cantil
Agkistrodon bilineatus

Persian horned viper
Pseudocerastes persicus

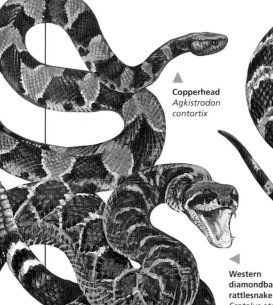

Western diamondback rattlesnake
Crotalus atrox

Rhinoceros viper
Bitis nasicornis

Massasauga
Sistrurus catenatus

ENTHRALLING PREY

The rattle at the end of a rattlesnake's tail is made of interlocking pieces of keratin, the same material as in reptile scales. Shaking it holds prey's attention until the snake strikes.

INSIDE A RATTLE

Body scales

Interlocking shells

Mojave rattlesnake
Crotalus scutulatus
This rattlesnake can be recognized by the black and white rings on its thick tail.

Timber rattlesnake
Crotalus horridus
Often gathers in large groups with other snake species to hibernate during winter

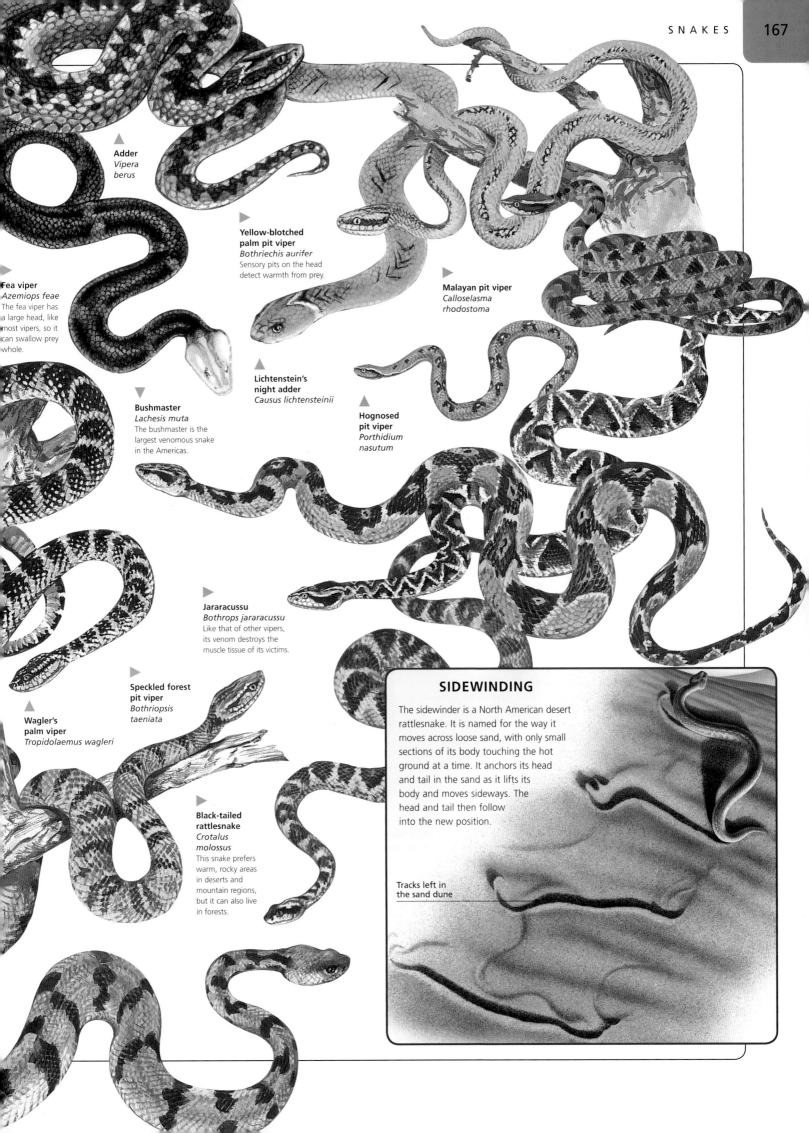

Adder
Vipera berus

Fea viper
Azemiops feae
The fea viper has a large head, like most vipers, so it can swallow prey whole.

Yellow-blotched palm pit viper
Bothriechis aurifer
Sensory pits on the head detect warmth from prey.

Malayan pit viper
Calloselasma rhodostoma

Lichtenstein's night adder
Causus lichtensteinii

Bushmaster
Lachesis muta
The bushmaster is the largest venomous snake in the Americas.

Hognosed pit viper
Porthidium nasutum

Jararacussu
Bothrops jararacussu
Like that of other vipers, its venom destroys the muscle tissue of its victims.

Speckled forest pit viper
Bothriopsis taeniata

Wagler's palm viper
Tropidolaemus wagleri

Black-tailed rattlesnake
Crotalus molossus
This snake prefers warm, rocky areas in deserts and mountain regions, but it can also live in forests.

SIDEWINDING

The sidewinder is a North American desert rattlesnake. It is named for the way it moves across loose sand, with only small sections of its body touching the hot ground at a time. It anchors its head and tail in the sand as it lifts its body and moves sideways. The head and tail then follow into the new position.

Tracks left in the sand dune

Amphibians

3 ORDERS • 10 FAMILIES • 60 GENERA • 472 SPECIES

Amphibians

Male green and black poison frogs make trilling calls to attract females. Males fight with each other for territories, which they defend during the breeding season.

There are three main groups of amphibians: caecilians; salamanders; and frogs and toads. Most species live in water when young and on land as adults. Amphibians are cold-blooded: Their body temperature is controlled largely by their environment. They can also alter their temperature through behavior. Amphibians are usually active at night, but only when the conditions are moist enough to prevent their bodies from losing too much water by evaporation. As adults, amphibians eat small animals, such as insects and worms. They catch prey mostly by waiting until it comes within reach. Their young usually eat different food. Tadpoles,

for example, are often plant-eaters, but become carnivores as frogs. Because they are relatively small, amphibians are often preyed on by larger animals. Many have poison glands in their skin that produce bad-tasting or poisonous substances to protect them from predators. When threatened, frogs often lie motionless on their backs and play dead until a predator passes. To frighten away predators, toads may puff up, making themselves look larger. Male and female amphibians usually live apart. To find each other to breed, salamanders leave scent trails. Male frogs and toads call and croak to attract females during the breeding season.

AMPHIBIAN SKIN

Mucus glands keep the skin moist so amphibians can breathe through their skin. Many species produce substances that kill bacteria or fungi, which are common in moist environments. Poison glands deter predators. Cells called chromatophores produce bright colors.

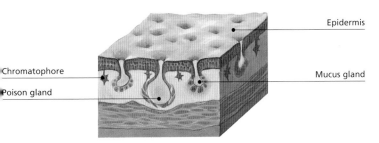

Epidermis

Chromatophore

Mucus gland

Poison gland

The colorful underside of the poisonous fire-bellied toad warns off potential predators.

HOW AMPHIBIANS REPRODUCE

Most frogs leave eggs to develop, but male marsupial frogs carry tadpoles in hip pouches.

A male frog guards his hatching froglets in a tropical Papua New Guinean forest.

Amphibian eggs lack waterproof shells. To stay moist, eggs are usually deposited in or near water. Embryos are surrounded by protective jelly-like membranes. Most frogs' eggs contain just enough nutrients for tadpoles to grow into free-swimming larvae. But the yolks of some species nourish embryos through the tadpole stage.

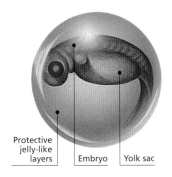

Protective jelly-like layers

Embryo

Yolk sac

---

1 ORDER • 6 FAMILIES • 33 GENERA • 149 SPECIES

Caecilians

Caecilians are amphibians that look like worms. They do not have limbs and almost always live underground. They dig with their strong, bullet-shaped heads to create burrows. Adults range in length from just under 3 inches (8 cm) to 5¼ feet (1.6 m). Caecilians reproduce by internal fertilization, which means males deposit sperm inside females. Most species give birth to live young. Adults eat earthworms and insects.

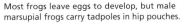

☐ Caecilians

Caecilians are found only in tropical and subtropical areas of India, southern China, Malaysia, the Philippines, Africa, Central America, and South America.

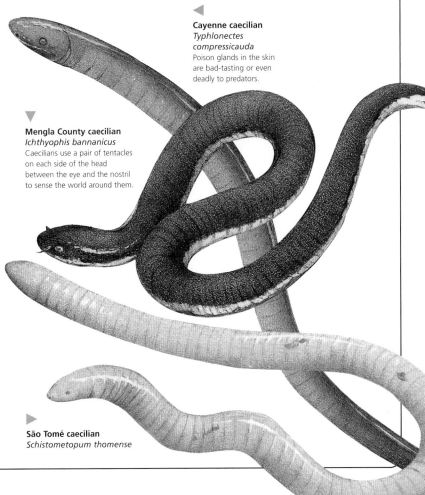

◄
Cayenne caecilian
Typhlonectes compressicauda
Poison glands in the skin are bad-tasting or even deadly to predators.

▼
Mengla County caecilian
Ichthyophis bannanicus
Caecilians use a pair of tentacles on each side of the head between the eye and the nostril to sense the world around them.

▶
São Tomé caecilian
Schistometopum thomense

1 ORDER • 10 FAMILIES • 60 GENERA • 472 SPECIES

Salamanders

Salamanders, newts, mudpuppies, waterdogs, and sirens belong to an order called caudates. They all have long tails as adults. Most have four limbs, but a few have only two. They look like lizards, but they are easy to distinguish from reptiles because they do not have scales. Salamanders are secretive animals. Although they are common, they are rarely seen. All species are carnivores. They eat mostly insects, worms, and other small animals. Their skin contains different kinds of glands. Some glands produce mucus, which prevents the skin from drying out while on land. Others produce poison. Salamanders breathe through the skin, although many species also breathe through lungs. Many species develop in water as larvae but live on land as adults. A few always live in water.

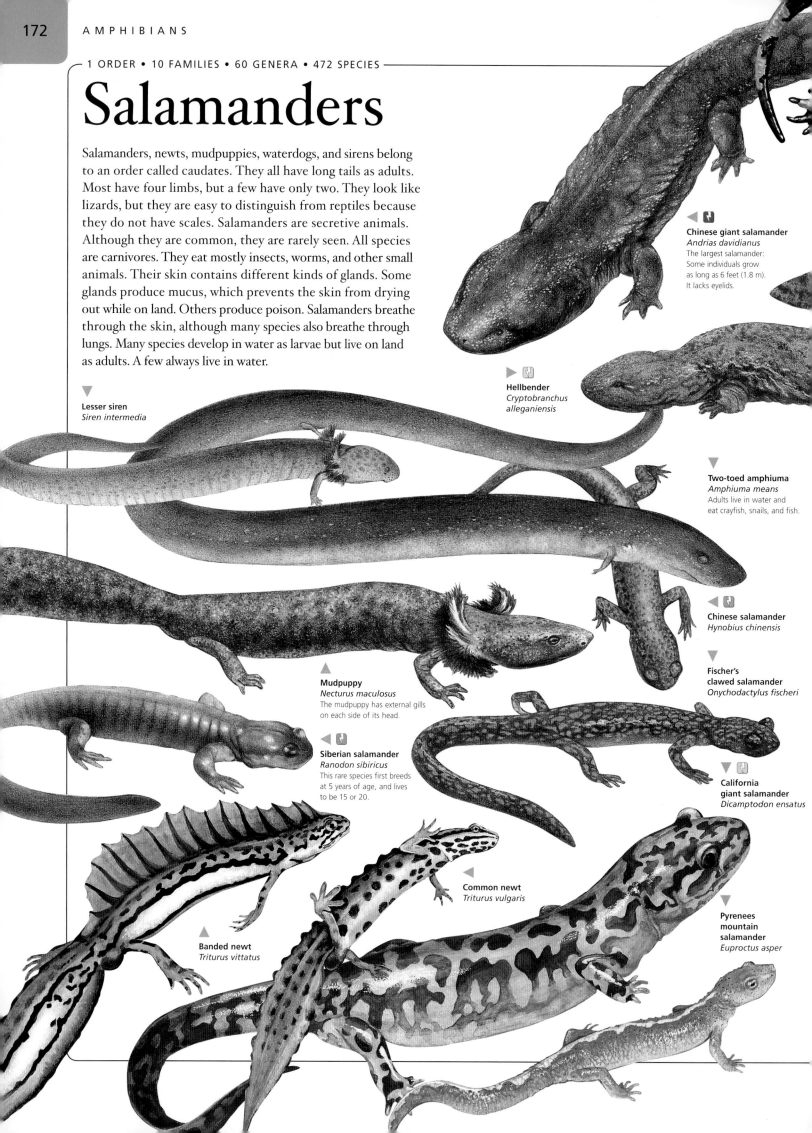

Chinese giant salamander
Andrias davidianus
The largest salamander:
Some individuals grow
as long as 6 feet (1.8 m).
It lacks eyelids.

Lesser siren
Siren intermedia

Hellbender
*Cryptobranchus
alleganiensis*

Two-toed amphiuma
Amphiuma means
Adults live in water and
eat crayfish, snails, and fish.

Chinese salamander
Hynobius chinensis

Mudpuppy
Necturus maculosus
The mudpuppy has external gills
on each side of its head.

**Fischer's
clawed salamander**
Onychodactylus fischeri

Siberian salamander
Ranodon sibiricus
This rare species first breeds
at 5 years of age, and lives
to be 15 or 20.

**California
giant salamander**
Dicamptodon ensatus

Common newt
Triturus vulgaris

Banded newt
Triturus vittatus

**Pyrenees
mountain
salamander**
Euproctus asper

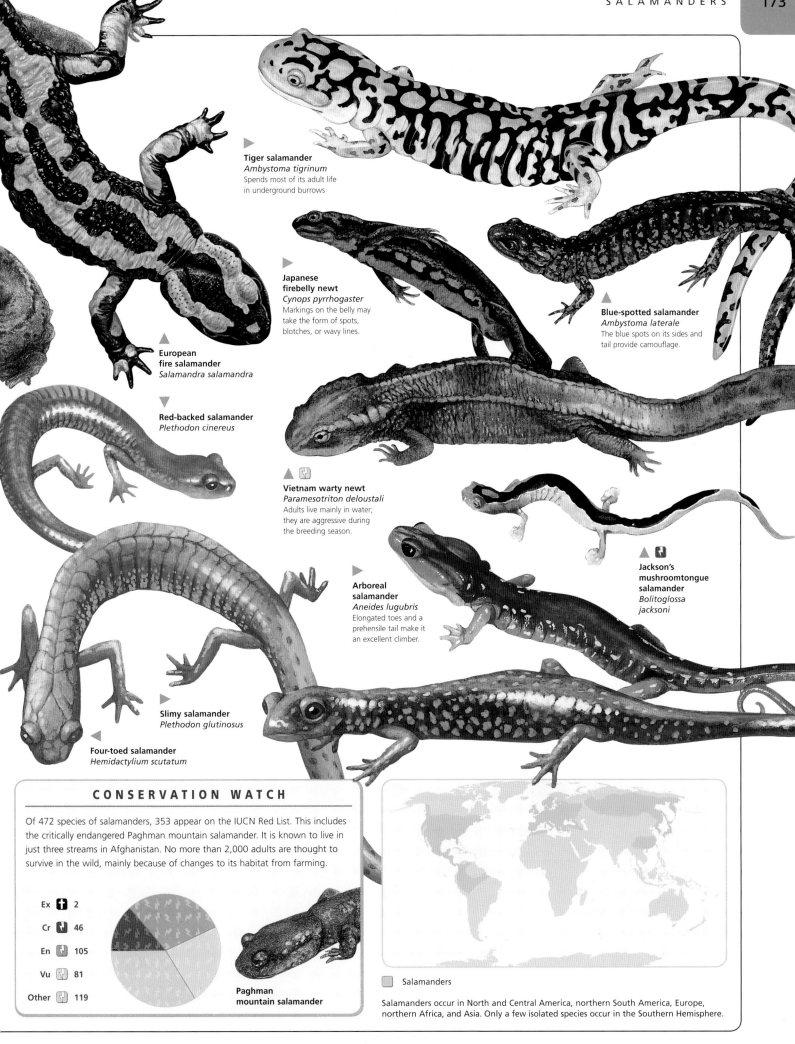

Tiger salamander
Ambystoma tigrinum
Spends most of its adult life
in underground burrows

**Japanese
firebelly newt**
Cynops pyrrhogaster
Markings on the belly may
take the form of spots,
blotches, or wavy lines.

Blue-spotted salamander
Ambystoma laterale
The blue spots on its sides and
tail provide camouflage.

**European
fire salamander**
Salamandra salamandra

Red-backed salamander
Plethodon cinereus

Vietnam warty newt
Paramesotriton deloustali
Adults live mainly in water;
they are aggressive during
the breeding season.

**Jackson's
mushroomtongue
salamander**
*Bolitoglossa
jacksoni*

**Arboreal
salamander**
Aneides lugubris
Elongated toes and a
prehensile tail make it
an excellent climber.

Slimy salamander
Plethodon glutinosus

Four-toed salamander
Hemidactylium scutatum

CONSERVATION WATCH

Of 472 species of salamanders, 353 appear on the IUCN Red List. This includes
the critically endangered Paghman mountain salamander. It is known to live in
just three streams in Afghanistan. No more than 2,000 adults are thought to
survive in the wild, mainly because of changes to its habitat from farming.

Ex		2
Cr		46
En		105
Vu		81
Other		119

**Paghman
mountain salamander**

Salamanders

Salamanders occur in North and Central America, northern South America, Europe,
northern Africa, and Asia. Only a few isolated species occur in the Southern Hemisphere.

1 ORDER • 28 FAMILIES • 338 GENERA • 4,937 SPECIES

Frogs and Toads

Anurans—frogs and toads—make up the largest amphibian order. They have long back legs, short bodies, and moist skin. Most have no tail. Their skeletons are adapted for jumping. The smallest anuran is Brazil's Izecksohn's toad, which is less than ½ inch (1 cm) long. Africa's goliath frog, at 12 inches (30 cm) long and weighing more than 7 pounds (3 kg), is the largest. Frogs and toads capture insects and other small animals by flicking out their long, sticky tongues. They blink their eyes once food is inside the mouth; the movement pushes food down the throat. Frogs are indicators of environmental pollution. Since the 1970s, there has been growing evidence worldwide that frog populations are disappearing. Many species have become extinct, even in apparently pristine areas.

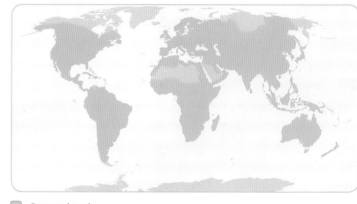

Frogs and toads

Frogs and toads are found on all continents except Antarctica. More than 80 percent of anuran species live in the tropics.

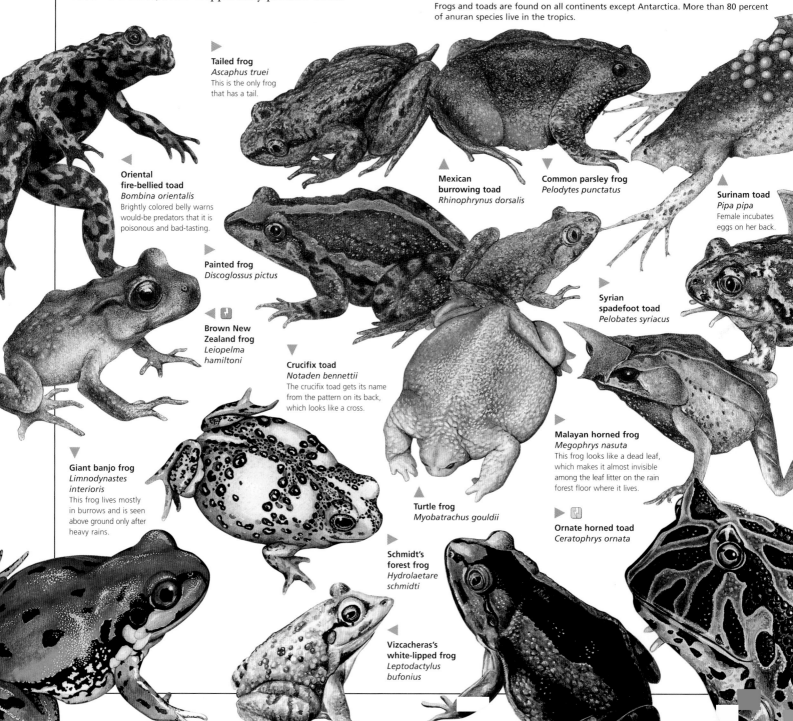

Tailed frog
Ascaphus truei
This is the only frog that has a tail.

Oriental fire-bellied toad
Bombina orientalis
Brightly colored belly warns would-be predators that it is poisonous and bad-tasting.

Mexican burrowing toad
Rhinophrynus dorsalis

Common parsley frog
Pelodytes punctatus

Surinam toad
Pipa pipa
Female incubates eggs on her back.

Painted frog
Discoglossus pictus

Brown New Zealand frog
Leiopelma hamiltoni

Syrian spadefoot toad
Pelobates syriacus

Crucifix toad
Notaden bennettii
The crucifix toad gets its name from the pattern on its back, which looks like a cross.

Giant banjo frog
Limnodynastes interioris
This frog lives mostly in burrows and is seen above ground only after heavy rains.

Malayan horned frog
Megophrys nasuta
This frog looks like a dead leaf, which makes it almost invisible among the leaf litter on the rain forest floor where it lives.

Turtle frog
Myobatrachus gouldii

Ornate horned toad
Ceratophrys ornata

Schmidt's forest frog
Hydrolaetare schmidti

Vizcacheras's white-lipped frog
Leptodactylus bufonius

STAGES OF LIFE

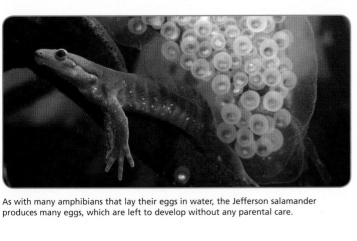

As with many amphibians that lay their eggs in water, the Jefferson salamander produces many eggs, which are left to develop without any parental care.

WATER BABIES

Most frogs, toads, and salamanders have a two-stage life cycle. Usually, young live in the water as larvae that breathe through gills. They then transform into air-breathing adults that live mostly on land. Chemicals called pheromones are important for salamander reproduction. Males release these chemicals to attract females. The males of most salamanders deposit sperm in little packets that the female takes up into her body. Almost all frogs and toads reproduce by external fertilization. This means that sperm and eggs are released and mixed together outside the female's body. Male frogs attract females by calling to them.

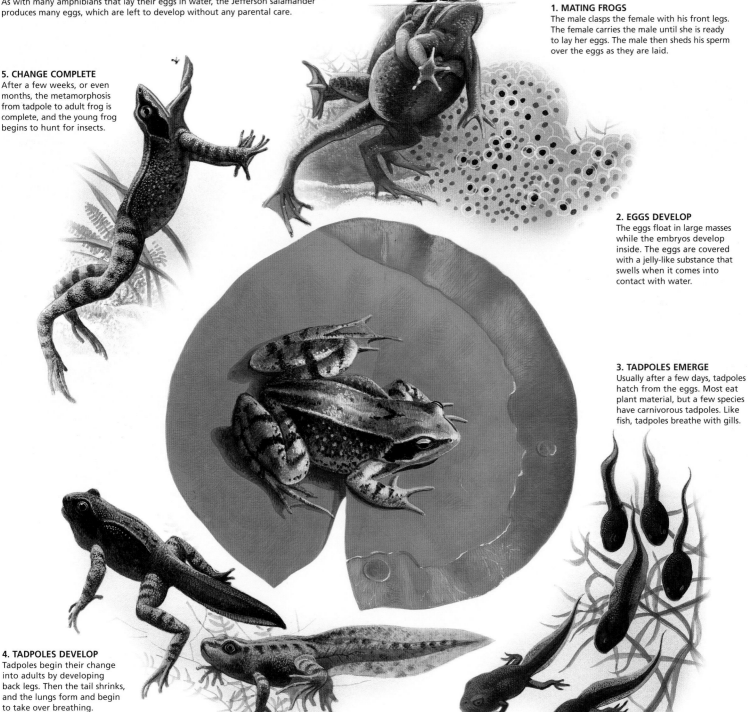

1. MATING FROGS
The male clasps the female with his front legs. The female carries the male until she is ready to lay her eggs. The male then sheds his sperm over the eggs as they are laid.

2. EGGS DEVELOP
The eggs float in large masses while the embryos develop inside. The eggs are covered with a jelly-like substance that swells when it comes into contact with water.

3. TADPOLES EMERGE
Usually after a few days, tadpoles hatch from the eggs. Most eat plant material, but a few species have carnivorous tadpoles. Like fish, tadpoles breathe with gills.

4. TADPOLES DEVELOP
Tadpoles begin their change into adults by developing back legs. Then the tail shrinks, and the lungs form and begin to take over breathing.

5. CHANGE COMPLETE
After a few weeks, or even months, the metamorphosis from tadpole to adult frog is complete, and the young frog begins to hunt for insects.

Frogs and toads

The largest family of anurans is the New World frogs, such as the barking frog of Arizona in the United States. Many species develop entirely in the egg and hatch as miniature adults. Some frogs in this family are adapted to burrowing, with short limbs and spade-shaped back feet for digging. Many New World frogs are small and slender, and suited to life in trees. The hylid family, or tree frogs, are all similar in shape. Their toes are enlarged at the tips and sticky to aid in climbing. Most species live in the Americas. The ranid family, or "true frogs," look like typical frogs with smooth, moist skin and bulging eyes. They live near ponds and other bodies of water. Toads belong to the bufonid family. They tend to be short-legged, with solid bodies, and can be covered in wartlike glands. They do not have teeth.

CONSERVATION WATCH

Of the 4,937 anuran species, 3,034 appear on the IUCN Red List, including the endangered Australian lace-lid frog. A fungus or a virus may be causing it to disappear.

Ex	33
Cr	367
En	623
Vu	544
Other	1,467

Australian lace-lid frog

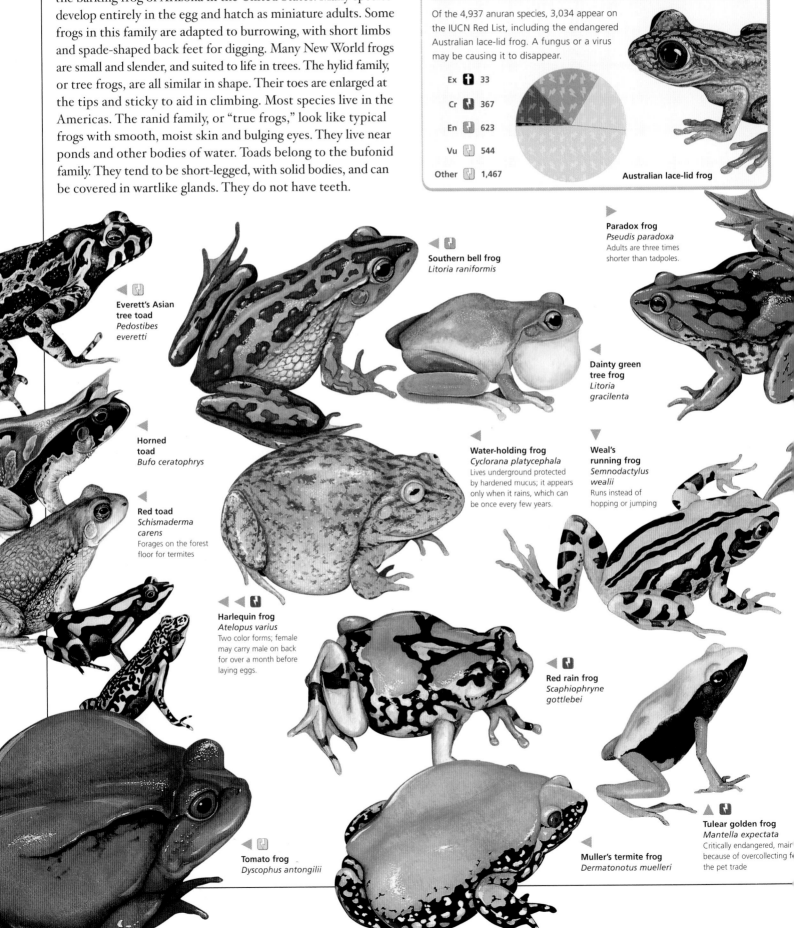

Everett's Asian tree toad
Pedostibes everetti

Southern bell frog
Litoria raniformis

Paradox frog
Pseudis paradoxa
Adults are three times shorter than tadpoles.

Horned toad
Bufo ceratophrys

Dainty green tree frog
Litoria gracilenta

Red toad
Schismaderma carens
Forages on the forest floor for termites

Water-holding frog
Cyclorana platycephala
Lives underground protected by hardened mucus; it appears only when it rains, which can be once every few years.

Weal's running frog
Semnodactylus wealii
Runs instead of hopping or jumping

Harlequin frog
Atelopus varius
Two color forms; female may carry male on back for over a month before laying eggs.

Red rain frog
Scaphiophryne gottlebei

Tomato frog
Dyscophus antongilii

Muller's termite frog
Dermatonotus muelleri

Tulear golden frog
Mantella expectata
Critically endangered, main because of overcollecting fo the pet trade

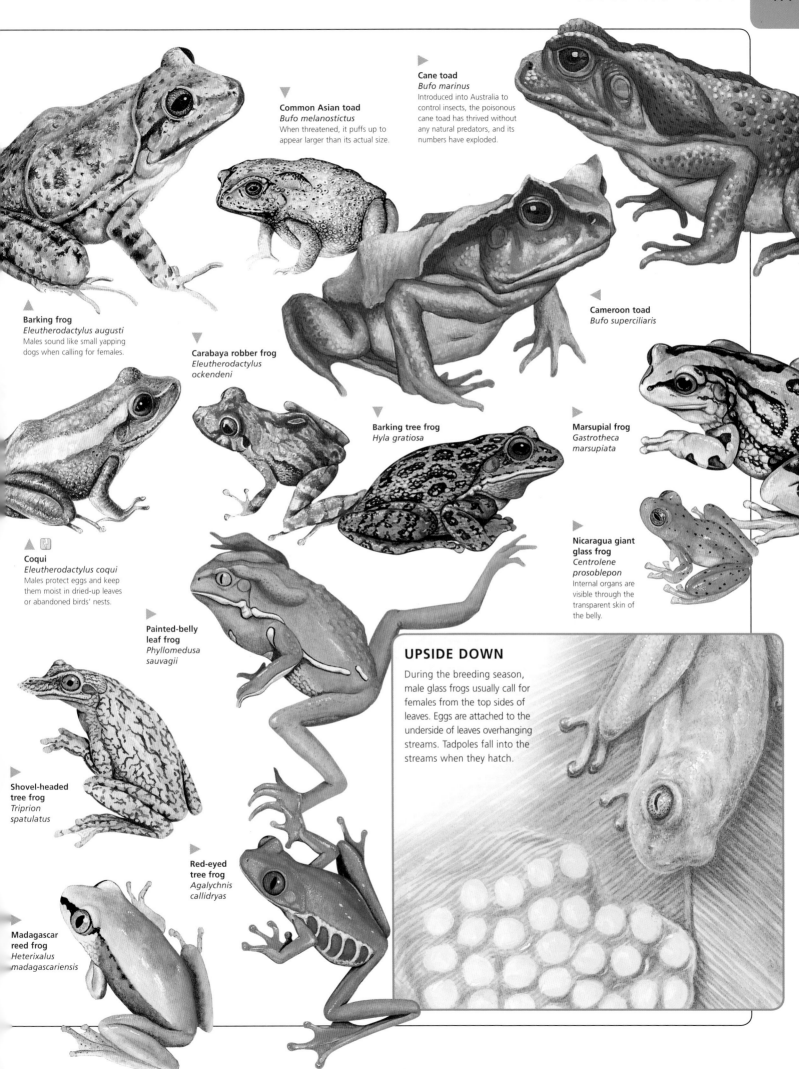

Common Asian toad
Bufo melanostictus
When threatened, it puffs up to appear larger than its actual size.

Cane toad
Bufo marinus
Introduced into Australia to control insects, the poisonous cane toad has thrived without any natural predators, and its numbers have exploded.

Barking frog
Eleutherodactylus augusti
Males sound like small yapping dogs when calling for females.

Carabaya robber frog
Eleutherodactylus ockendeni

Cameroon toad
Bufo superciliaris

Coqui
Eleutherodactylus coqui
Males protect eggs and keep them moist in dried-up leaves or abandoned birds' nests.

Barking tree frog
Hyla gratiosa

Marsupial frog
Gastrotheca marsupiata

Painted-belly leaf frog
Phyllomedusa sauvagii

Nicaragua giant glass frog
Centrolene prosoblepon
Internal organs are visible through the transparent skin of the belly.

Shovel-headed tree frog
Triprion spatulatus

Red-eyed tree frog
Agalychnis callidryas

Madagascar reed frog
Heterixalus madagascariensis

UPSIDE DOWN

During the breeding season, male glass frogs usually call for females from the top sides of leaves. Eggs are attached to the underside of leaves overhanging streams. Tadpoles fall into the streams when they hatch.

Frogs and toads

The frogs most commonly seen in North America and Europe belong to the ranid family, which includes the bullfrog that lives in the eastern United States. Their relatives in Asia and Africa are the racophorid tree frog family. This includes flying frogs that glide on huge webbed feet. The squeakers, so-called because some have high-pitched calls, make up another related family. One member of this family is the hairy frog. Breeding males develop hairlike growths on their back legs. These growths may absorb oxygen from water, allowing males to sit submerged in streams while they guard their egg masses. In dry African regions, shovel-nosed frogs make up a small but distinctive family. These odd-looking frogs, such as the spotted snout-burrower, have small pointed heads with hard snouts for burrowing.

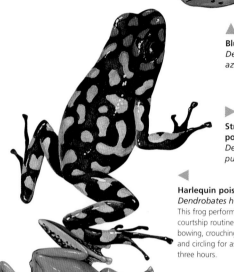

Blue poison frog
Dendrobates azureus

Strawberry poison frog
Dendrobates pumilio

Harlequin poison frog
Dendrobates histrionicus
This frog performs a complex courtship routine of sitting, bowing, crouching, touching, and circling for as long as three hours.

Dahaoping sucker frog
Amolops viridimaculatus

Java flying frog
Rhacophorus reinwardtii
Rarely leaves the upper layer of branches in Indonesian rain forests

Singapore wart frog
Limnonectes malesianus

Hairy frog
Trichobatrachus robustus

Bongon whipping frog
Polypedates otilophus
This huge tree frog produces a distinctive, unpleasant smell.

Pickerel frog
Rana palustris
This North American species hibernates during coldest months; males' calls sound like snores.

Spotted snout-burrower
Hemisus guttatus

African bullfrog
Pyxicephalus adspersus
Bullfrogs eat mice, lizards, and other frogs.

Bullfrog
Rana catesbeiana

FAST FACT
Female African rain frogs dig underground chambers where they lay their eggs. Tadpoles develop inside the eggs, and hatch as froglets. Their mothers watch over the nests until all eggs have hatched.

POISON FROGS

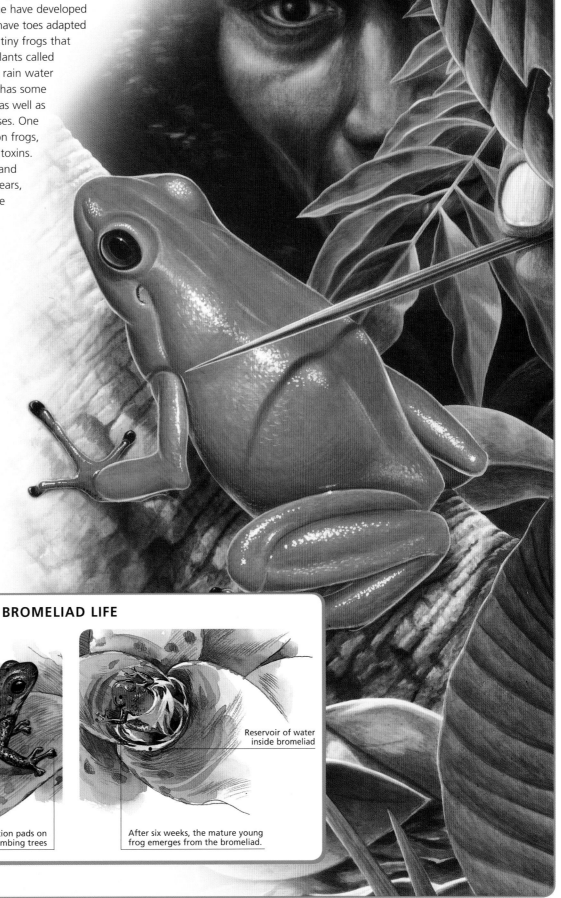

RAIN FOREST BOUNTY

Because rain forests are warm, moist places, they provide ideal habitats for frogs. Many species live high in trees and rarely come down to the forest floor. Some have developed webbing on their feet for gliding. Others have toes adapted for clinging and climbing. There are even tiny frogs that live their entire life cycles inside tropical plants called bromeliads. Their tadpoles develop in the rain water that the plants collect. Life in rain forests has some disadvantages: There are many predators, as well as moisture-loving fungal and bacterial diseases. One group of South American frogs, the poison frogs, has responded by developing deadly skin toxins. Many produce poisons that can paralyze and even kill other animals. For hundreds of years, indigenous people in South America have been coating the tips of their hunting arrows and darts with these poisons.

The yellow-headed poison frog lives in leaf litter on South American rain forest floors. Tadpoles develop in water captured by plants.

BROMELIAD LIFE

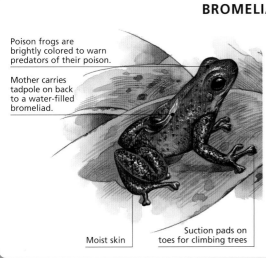

Poison frogs are brightly colored to warn predators of their poison.

Mother carries tadpole on back to a water-filled bromeliad.

Moist skin

Suction pads on toes for climbing trees

Reservoir of water inside bromeliad

After six weeks, the mature young frog emerges from the bromeliad.

Fish

5 CLASSES • 62 ORDERS • 504 FAMILIES • 3,245 GENERA • 25,777 SPECIES

Fish

Butterflyfish live in large groups called schools around the coral reefs that fringe islands in the Pacific Ocean. They have a varied diet that includes algae and small animals.

More than half of all vertebrate animals alive today are fish. At least 25,000 fish species have been identified, but there are probably thousands more still to be discovered. There are three main groups of fish: jawless fish (hagfish and lampreys), cartilaginous fish (sharks and rays), and bony fish (lobe-finned fish and ray-finned fish). They are found in almost every watery habitat, from polar seas to tropical ponds. Fish can be as small as tiny gobies, which grow to be just ⅔ inch (1 cm) long, or as large as whale sharks, which reach 59 feet (18 m) in length. Some fish are vibrantly colored. Others can be silvery-blue, mottled green, or colored and shaded to blend in with their environment. Many fish eat algae or insect larvae and other small animals. However, some fish are fierce predators that hunt large sea mammals. Most fish swim; some have fins adapted for "flying" briefly above water; a few can even "walk," using their fins like feet. Fish have the same basic senses as other vertebrate animals: sight, smell, hearing, touch, and taste. In fish, however, these senses are adapted to work in water. Many fish have an additional sense called the lateral line. This allows them to feel tiny movements and pressure changes in the water around them. The lateral line helps fish find food and avoid obstacles.

FISH ANATOMY

Many fish have streamlined, torpedo-shaped bodies that let them move easily through water. Their skin is usually protected by bony scales. There are four main kinds of scales. The most common interlock like roof tiles. They can have a rough surface (ctenoid) or smoother (cycloid). A few primitive fish have scales like armor (ganoid). Sharks have hollow, toothlike scales (placoid) with an outer layer of enamel.

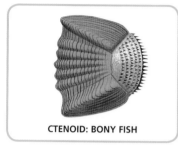

CTENOID: BONY FISH

CYCLOID: BONY FISH

GANOID: ARMORED FISH

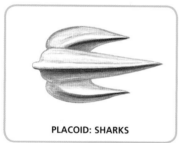

PLACOID: SHARKS

FISH REPRODUCTION

Most bony fish lay a large number of eggs. These are fertilized with the male's sperm outside the female's body, in the surrounding water. The larvae that hatch from these eggs usually look very different from their adult parents. All male cartilaginous fish, such as sharks, place their sperm inside the female's body. The young of these fish may develop inside their mother's body, or inside hard shell cases. They are born looking like miniature copies of their parents.

Male and female mandarinfish swim toward the water's surface, releasing eggs and sperm.

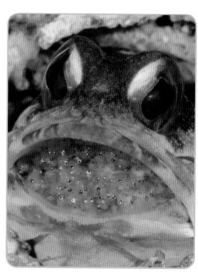

The male gold-specs jawfish incubates eggs in his mouth to protect them from predators.

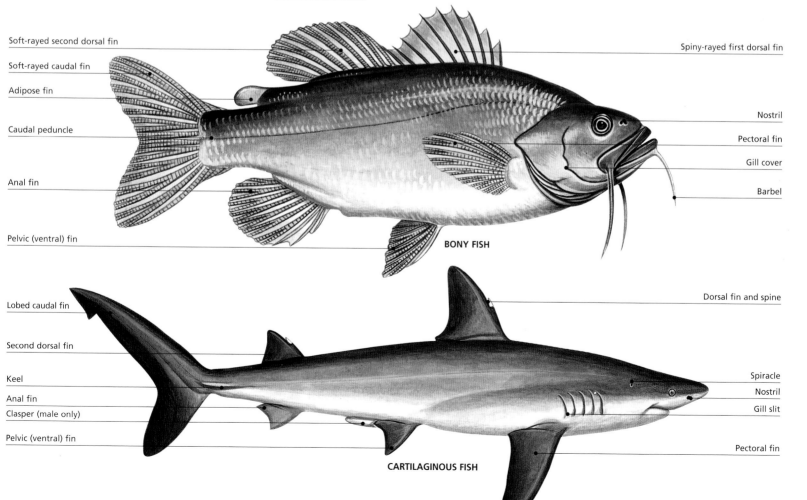

Soft-rayed second dorsal fin

Soft-rayed caudal fin

Adipose fin

Caudal peduncle

Anal fin

Pelvic (ventral) fin

Spiny-rayed first dorsal fin

Nostril

Pectoral fin

Gill cover

Barbel

BONY FISH

Lobed caudal fin

Second dorsal fin

Keel

Anal fin

Clasper (male only)

Pelvic (ventral) fin

Dorsal fin and spine

Spiracle

Nostril

Gill slit

Pectoral fin

CARTILAGINOUS FISH

2 CLASSES • 2 ORDERS • 2 FAMILIES • 105 SPECIES

Jawless Fish

Hagfish and lampreys, or jawless fish, were among the first fish. Most early species became extinct about 360 million years ago, but these two small groups have survived. Hagfish and lampreys have no jaws or scales. Their skeletons are not made of bone but of cartilage—the same kind of flexible material that supports human ears. Their bodies are shaped like those of eels, and they often lack paired fins. Hagfish produce enormous amounts of slime from mucus glands in their skin. This probably makes them too slippery for predators to bite firmly. They eat the flesh of dead or dying fish and invertebrates. Adult lampreys are parasites that attach themselves to larger fish, from which they suck body fluids. Young lampreys spend their first few years as larvae that feed by filtering small food particles from the water.

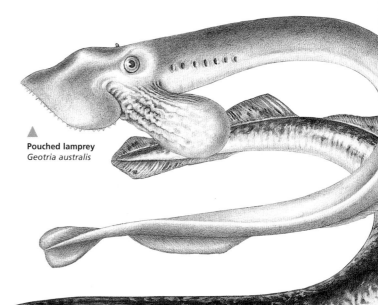

▲ **Pouched lamprey**
Geotria australis

◄ **Pacific lamprey**
Lampetra tridentata
Migrates around the Pacific, attached to whales and large fish

▲ **Sea lamprey**
Petromyzon marinus
Sea lamprey live in rivers as larvae, swim into the sea to live as adults, then migrate back to rivers to breed once and die.

FAST FACT

To feed, a hagfish attaches itself to dead animals with its mouth and ties itself into a knot. By pulling the knot along its slippery, slimy body to its head, it gains enough leverage to tear off pieces of flesh.

▼ **Atlantic hagfish**
Myxine glutinosa
Lampreys and hagfish both have porelike gill openings.

▲ **European river lamprey**
Lampetra fluviatilis
Unlike most lampreys, the river lamprey has sharp teeth.

CONSERVATION WATCH

Of the 105 jawless fish species, 12 appear on the IUCN Red List. The brook lamprey is listed as vulnerable, mostly because of water pollution. It is also threatened by the building of dams. This freshwater species occurs naturally only in Greece.

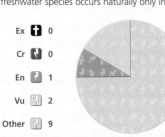

Ex	🛡	0
Cr	🛡	0
En	🛡	1
Vu	🛡	2
Other	🛡	9

Brook lamprey

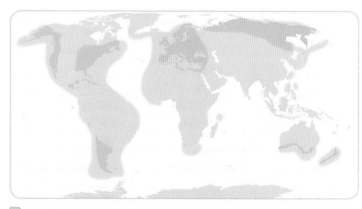

▢ Jawless fish

Jawless fish are found in shallow, temperate waters worldwide, and cool, deep waters in the tropics. Hagfish live only in salt water. Lampreys are found also in fresh water.

2 SUBCLASSES • 12 ORDERS • 47 FAMILIES • 160 GENERA • 999 SPECIES

Cartilaginous Fish

The gray reef shark is well camouflaged. To animals below, its white belly seems to disappear into the light above. From above, its dark back blends into the ocean's depths.

Sharks, rays, and their relatives are cartilaginous fish: They have skeletons of cartilage, not bone. Sharks have existed for about 400 million years; the first rays appeared about 200 million years ago. Most cartilaginous fish live in saltwater habitats. They have strong jaws and feed on other animals. They fertilize their eggs internally, with the male depositing sperm inside the female. Males have firm rods called claspers that look like fins running along the body behind their pectoral fins. They use these to guide sperm into the female. Unlike most fish, cartilaginous fish produce only small numbers of eggs. Some lay eggs with large amounts of yolk that nourish the developing young for months before they hatch. For most of this group, the young are nourished inside their mother's body for long periods before birth.

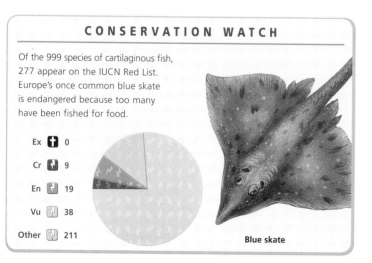

CONSERVATION WATCH

Of the 999 species of cartilaginous fish, 277 appear on the IUCN Red List. Europe's once common blue skate is endangered because too many have been fished for food.

Ex	🐟	0
Cr	🐟	9
En	🐟	19
Vu	🐟	38
Other	🐟	211

Blue skate

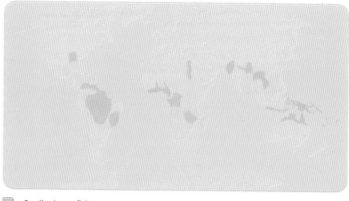

Cartilaginous fish

Cartilaginous fish are found throughout the oceans. Some live in estuaries and freshwater rivers and lakes. Rays and skates live mostly on the bottom of oceans and seas.

Sharks

Just 2 percent of all living fish are sharks, but they are vitally important to the world's oceans. Sharks play a critical role in marine environments because they are apex predators. This means they are at, or near, the top of the food chain. If too many sharks are fished commercially or killed by pollution, all other species further down the food chain are affected. Without sharks some populations swell until there is no more food for them to eat, then they dwindle. Sharks usually occur in smaller numbers than other fish. Most live alone, although a few sometimes gather in large groups. Sharks also reproduce more slowly than other fish, with most females producing fewer than 300 young, called pups, at a time. They usually do not begin to reproduce until 6 years of age; some species are not ready to mate until 18 years.

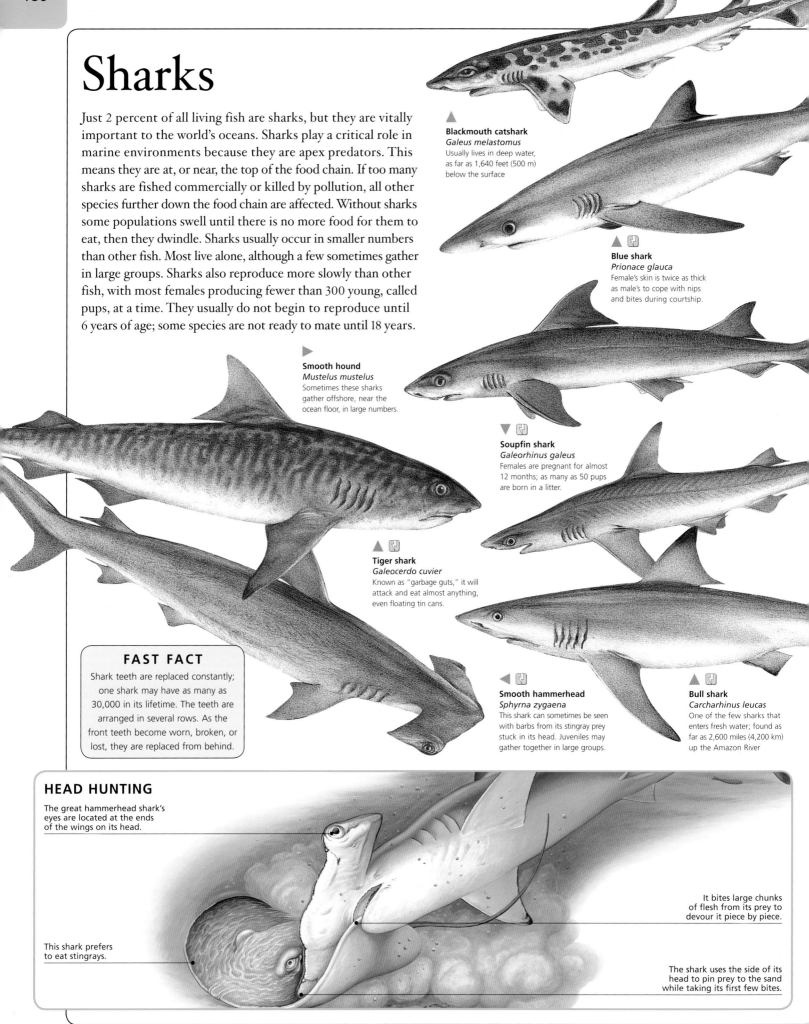

Blackmouth catshark
Galeus melastomus
Usually lives in deep water, as far as 1,640 feet (500 m) below the surface

Blue shark
Prionace glauca
Female's skin is twice as thick as male's to cope with nips and bites during courtship.

Smooth hound
Mustelus mustelus
Sometimes these sharks gather offshore, near the ocean floor, in large numbers.

Soupfin shark
Galeorhinus galeus
Females are pregnant for almost 12 months; as many as 50 pups are born in a litter.

Tiger shark
Galeocerdo cuvier
Known as "garbage guts," it will attack and eat almost anything, even floating tin cans.

FAST FACT
Shark teeth are replaced constantly; one shark may have as many as 30,000 in its lifetime. The teeth are arranged in several rows. As the front teeth become worn, broken, or lost, they are replaced from behind.

Smooth hammerhead
Sphyrna zygaena
This shark can sometimes be seen with barbs from its stingray prey stuck in its head. Juveniles may gather together in large groups.

Bull shark
Carcharhinus leucas
One of the few sharks that enters fresh water; found as far as 2,600 miles (4,200 km) up the Amazon River

HEAD HUNTING

The great hammerhead shark's eyes are located at the ends of the wings on its head.

This shark prefers to eat stingrays.

It bites large chunks of flesh from its prey to devour it piece by piece.

The shark uses the side of its head to pin prey to the sand while taking its first few bites.

THE BIG BITE

SHARK ATTACK

Many people think sharks are senseless killers that hunt just for the sake of it. This is not how they really behave. Sharks hunt only when they are hungry. Most will avoid people. Of the 415 species of sharks, just 27 are known to have attacked either people or boats. The great white shark is usually a daytime predator of fish, squid, turtles, and marine mammals. It has also attacked people who have entered its habitat. Teeth reveal a lot about the food sharks prefer. The flattened back teeth of horn sharks are designed for crushing small hard-shelled animals. Blue sharks have sawlike teeth for catching fish and squid. The teeth of makos are like needles, perfect for grasping large, slippery prey. The great white shark has large, triangular teeth with sharp edges. With one bite, it can take a large chunk out of a dolphin or a seal.

Great white sharks that live off the coast of South Africa can be seen leaping out of the water to snatch prey.

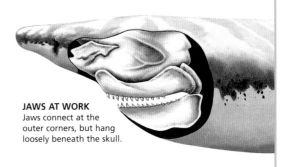

JAWS AT WORK
Jaws connect at the outer corners, but hang loosely beneath the skull.

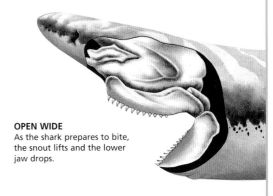

OPEN WIDE
As the shark prepares to bite, the snout lifts and the lower jaw drops.

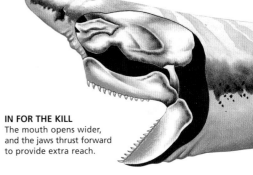

IN FOR THE KILL
The mouth opens wider, and the jaws thrust forward to provide extra reach.

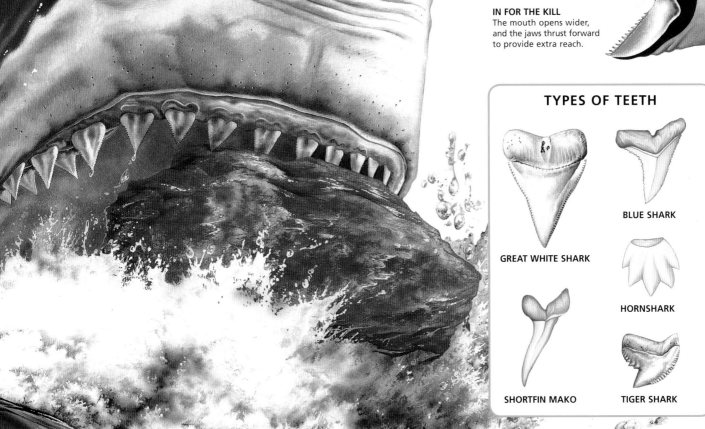

TYPES OF TEETH

GREAT WHITE SHARK

BLUE SHARK

HORNSHARK

SHORTFIN MAKO

TIGER SHARK

Sharks

Most sharks are strong and agile swimmers, which helps them to hunt prey. Some species make long migrations, covering many hundreds of miles in search of food. Sharks do not need to feed as often as other kinds of fish and can go months between meals. They generally eat fish and other small animals, but the largest sharks also hunt sea turtles and mammals, such as seals. Most sharks have good eyesight and a keen sense of smell. Many can detect tiny amounts of blood in the ocean. They are also sensitive to sound waves traveling through water. Most species have a well-developed lateral line system, which detects vibrations in water. Some sharks have special organs, called ampullae of Lorenzi, located around the head. These can detect the weak electrical fields that come from prey.

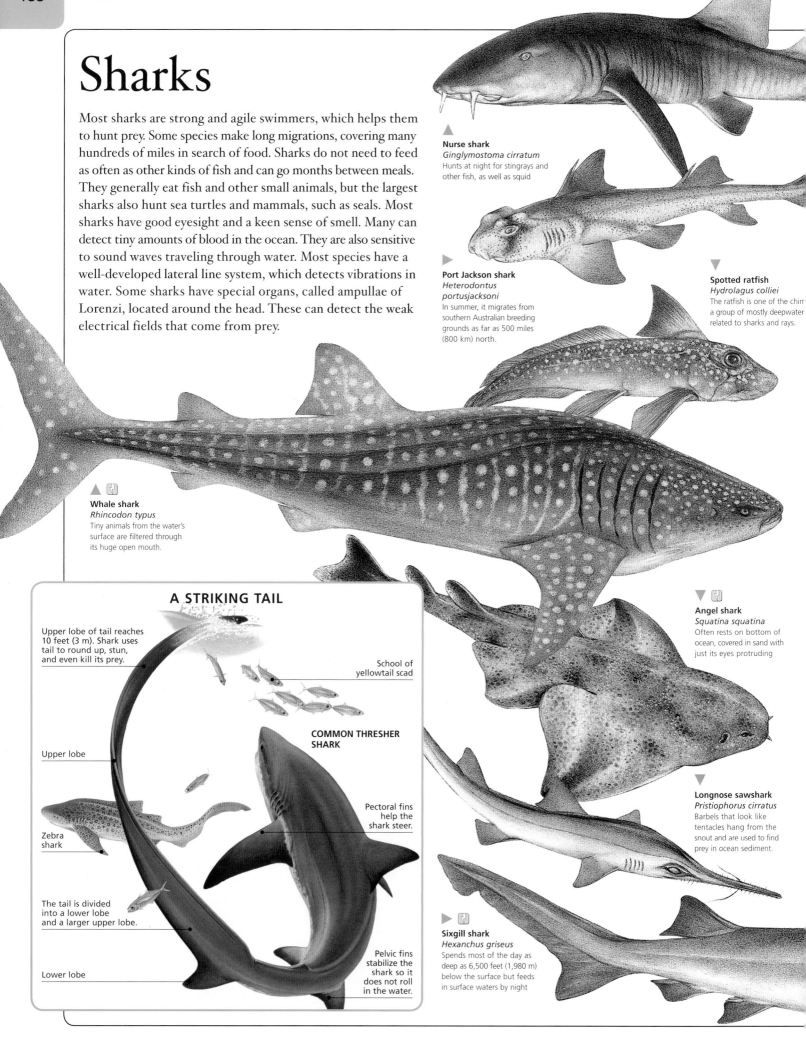

Nurse shark
Ginglymostoma cirratum
Hunts at night for stingrays and other fish, as well as squid

Port Jackson shark
Heterodontus portusjacksoni
In summer, it migrates from southern Australian breeding grounds as far as 500 miles (800 km) north.

Spotted ratfish
Hydrolagus colliei
The ratfish is one of the chim a group of mostly deepwater related to sharks and rays.

Whale shark
Rhincodon typus
Tiny animals from the water's surface are filtered through its huge open mouth.

Angel shark
Squatina squatina
Often rests on bottom of ocean, covered in sand with just its eyes protruding

Longnose sawshark
Pristiophorus cirratus
Barbels that look like tentacles hang from the snout and are used to find prey in ocean sediment.

Sixgill shark
Hexanchus griseus
Spends most of the day as deep as 6,500 feet (1,980 m) below the surface but feeds in surface waters by night

A STRIKING TAIL

Upper lobe of tail reaches 10 feet (3 m). Shark uses tail to round up, stun, and even kill its prey.

School of yellowtail scad

COMMON THRESHER SHARK

Upper lobe

Pectoral fins help the shark steer.

Zebra shark

The tail is divided into a lower lobe and a larger upper lobe.

Lower lobe

Pelvic fins stabilize the shark so it does not roll in the water.

Great white shark
Carcharodon carcharias
The great white shark is a huge predator that may see in color.

Shortfin mako
Isurus oxyrinchus
Makos hunt fast-swimming fish, such as tuna and swordfish.

Basking shark
Cetorhinus maximus
Enormous liver makes up a quarter of its body weight; it is full of oil to keep the shark from sinking. Sometimes this shark is seen in groups of more than 100 members.

Sand tiger shark
Carcharias taurus

Bramble shark
Echinorhinus brucus
This shark's name comes from the unusual thorny scales all over its body. Embryos eat each other while still inside their mother; only two ever survive to be born.

Sharpnose sevengill shark
Heptranchias perlo
Usually found living near the ocean floor, as deep as 3,300 feet (1,000 m) below the surface

Spiny dogfish
Squalus acanthias
Forms large schools of individuals of the same size, age, and often sex; spines on the dorsal fins are used against predators.

CAMOUFLAGE

The tassled wobbegong has a fringe of fleshy lobes on its head and body, which makes it look like a clump of rocks or marine plants even when it is swimming. It rests during the day and swims out at night to snap up fish, crabs, and shrimp with its narrow, sharp teeth.

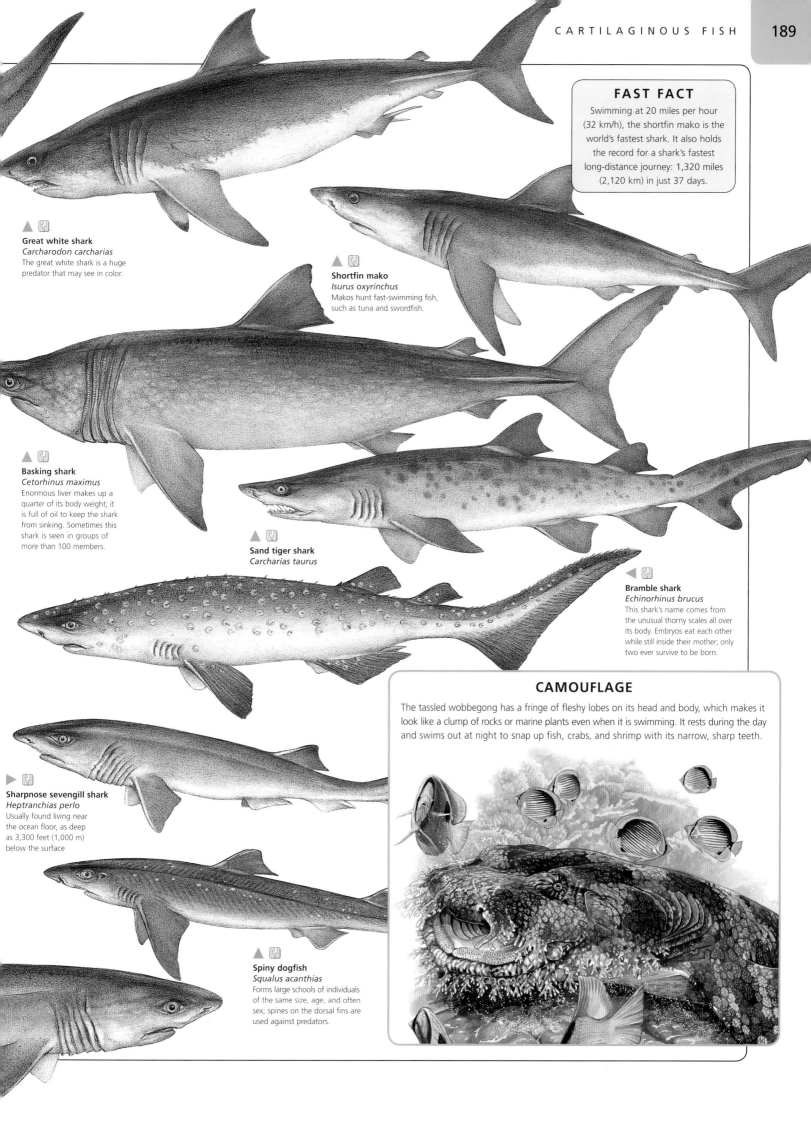

Rays

Rays and their relatives, the skates, are related to sharks. Their distinctive body shape—flattened from top to bottom—suits life on the ocean floor, where most of these fish are found. They have large pectoral fins that extend from near their snouts to the base of their tails. These fins join the body, and often the head, to form a disk that can be triangular, round, or shaped like a diamond. The mouth is underneath the disk and the eyes are on top. Rays and skates also have two openings, called spiracles, located near the front of the head. The spiracles are often mistaken for eyes, but rays and skates use them to breathe. Water is taken in through the spiracles and then passes across the gills. This process allows rays and skates to breathe even when their mouths are buried in sediment. Their teeth are used for crushing prey.

Manta
Manta birostris
Mantas regularly go to "cleaning stations" where small fish remove their external parasites. Their fins can extend 29 feet (8.8 m) from tip to tip.

Marbled electric ray
Torpedo marmorata
Stuns or kills prey with an electric shock produced by organs near its eyes

Largetooth sawfish
Pristis pristis
As many as 20 pairs of needle-like teeth line its long, flat snout. This saw is slashed at fish and squid to stun and kill them.

Atlantic guitarfish
Rhinobatos lentiginosus
The guitarfish looks like a cross between a shark and a ray. It often buries itself in the top layer of mud or sand along beaches.

MANTA RAY FEEDING

Some rays, such as mantas, live in the open ocean. Mantas feed on small animals called zooplankton. They use two special fins on either side of the head to guide zooplankton into the mouth, where they are filtered from the water and swallowed. Groups of feeding mantas may be seen swimming in large loops in surface waters rich with zooplankton.

Thornback ray
Raja clavata

FAST FACT
Devil fish are some of the largest fish on Earth. The devil fish may reach widths of 23 feet (7 m) and weigh as much as 2,200 pounds (1,000 kg). Despite their size, some can leap clear of the water.

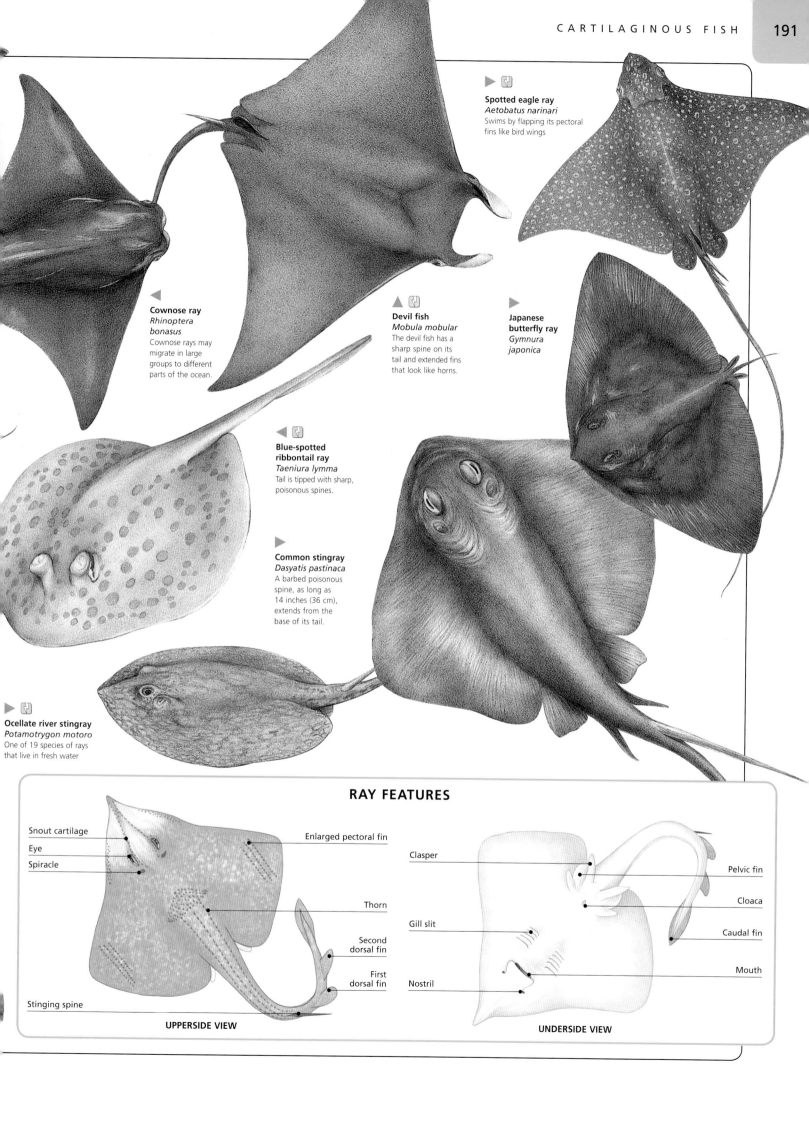

▶ Spotted eagle ray
Aetobatus narinari
Swims by flapping its pectoral
fins like bird wings

◀ Cownose ray
Rhinoptera bonasus
Cownose rays may migrate in large groups to different parts of the ocean.

▲ Devil fish
Mobula mobular
The devil fish has a sharp spine on its tail and extended fins that look like horns.

▶ Japanese butterfly ray
Gymnura japonica

◀ Blue-spotted ribbontail ray
Taeniura lymma
Tail is tipped with sharp, poisonous spines.

▶ Common stingray
Dasyatis pastinaca
A barbed poisonous spine, as long as 14 inches (36 cm), extends from the base of its tail.

▶ Ocellate river stingray
Potamotrygon motoro
One of 19 species of rays that live in fresh water

RAY FEATURES

Snout cartilage

Eye

Spiracle

Enlarged pectoral fin

Thorn

Second dorsal fin

First dorsal fin

Stinging spine

UPPERSIDE VIEW

Clasper

Gill slit

Nostril

Pelvic fin

Cloaca

Caudal fin

Mouth

UNDERSIDE VIEW

2 CLASSES • 48 ORDERS • 455 FAMILIES • 3,080 GENERA • 24,673 SPECIES
Bony Fish

Red lionfish are aggressive predators that hide by day and hunt by night. They stalk small fish and shrimp, which they corner by stretching out their pectoral fins like fans.

L obe-finned and ray-finned fish are the main bony fish classes. Their fins are supported by complex muscles and bones, giving them more control when they swim than other fish. Many can move backward as well as forward, and some can hover. Increasing or decreasing the air in a swim bladder, a gas-filled sac inside the body, changes buoyancy and gives them even more control over their movement.

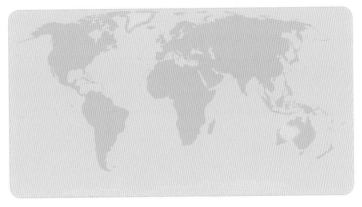

☐ Bony fish

Bony fish are found in almost every available water habitat in the world. Some even live in waterways that have dried up. Species are most numerous and diverse near coastlines.

BONY FISH FEATURES

BLUE-FIN TUNA

Nostril

Spiny first dorsal fin

Soft-rayed second dorsal fin

Caudal

TUNA SKELETON

Gill cover

Pelvic fin

Pectoral fin

Anal fin

Caudal peduncle

Lobe-finned fish

Lobe-finned fish are part of an ancient group that appeared on Earth at the time of the earliest sharks, about 400 million years ago. The first land vertebrates probably developed from this group. Today, the only survivors are nine lungfish and two coelacanth species. All have fleshy fins. These fins have bones and muscles that are more like the limbs of a vertebrate animal than the fanlike fins of most other living fish. In fact, it was once thought that lungfish were amphibians or reptiles. Larval lungfish breathe through gills, but the adults of all but one species survive by breathing air through lungs. Lungfish live in fresh water in the tropics. Most species survive dry seasons inside burrows, in cocoons made of dried mucus. Coelacanths live in the ocean and breathe using gills.

HOW LUNGFISH BREATHE

The Australian lungfish has a single lung. When its gills are clogged with mud, it breathes air through its mouth into its lung. Unlike the African and American lungfish, which each have two lungs, it cannot survive when its environment dries up completely.

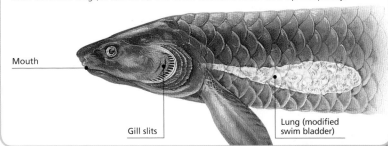

Mouth

Gill slits

Lung (modified swim bladder)

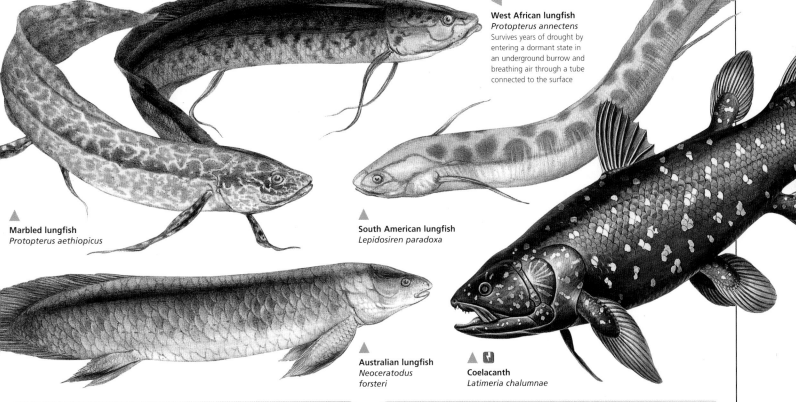

West African lungfish
Protopterus annectens
Survives years of drought by entering a dormant state in an underground burrow and breathing air through a tube connected to the surface

Marbled lungfish
Protopterus aethiopicus

South American lungfish
Lepidosiren paradoxa

Australian lungfish
Neoceratodus forsteri

Coelacanth
Latimeria chalumnae

CONSERVATION WATCH

Of the 11 species of lobe-finned fish, 1 appears on the IUCN Red List. The critically endangered coelacanth lives near the Indian Ocean's Cormoros Islands. It was thought to have become extinct with the dinosaurs, about 65 million years ago, but was rediscovered in 1938.

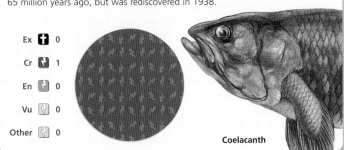

Ex	✝	0
Cr		1
En		0
Vu		0
Other		0

Coelacanth

Lungfish and coelacanths

Lungfish live in fresh water in Africa, South America, and Australia. One coelacanth species occurs off Sulawesi in Indonesian waters; the other is found in the Indian Ocean.

Primitive fish

Most bony fish are ray-finned fish. Sturgeons and paddlefish are among the most primitive of these, with scales that look like armor. They have some features, like spiracles or gill slits, that normally occur only in cartilaginous fish, such as sharks. Like sturgeons and paddlefish, gars probably look similar to early fish, with their primitive, interlocking scales. They are aggressive predators with long rows of sharp teeth. Gars often live in swampy water with low oxygen levels, where they survive by using their swim bladders like lungs to breathe air. Another primitive group includes bonytongues, featherbacks, and elephantfish. These fish are found only in fresh water. The unusual, toothlike bones on their tongues bite against teeth on the roofs of their mouths.

Aba
Gymnarchus niloticus

Blunt-jaw elephantnose
Campylomormyrus elephas
Produces weak electrical currents, which it uses to navigate through murky water

Freshwater butterflyfish
Pantodon buchholzi
This fish catches insects with its large mouth, while camouflaged among floating vegetation.

Clown knifefish
Chitala chitala
Males protect eggs from predators and fan them with their tails to increase oxygen in the surrounding water.

Arapaima
Arapaima gigas

European sturgeon
Acipenser sturio

Beluga
Huso huso
Known as the world's most expensive fish, its caviar is the most prized of the sturgeons.

Atlantic sturgeon
Acipenser oxyrinchus

Mottled bichir
Polypterus weeksi

Longnose gar
Lepisosteus osseus
A predator that suddenly ambushes its prey at great speed

Bowfin
Amia calva
This air-breather survives high temperatures and low oxygen levels in swampy North American lakes and rivers.

Chinese swordfish
Psephurus gladius

CONSERVATION WATCH

Of the 276 primitive fish species, 29 appear on the IUCN Red List. Populations of sturgeons, such as Europe's endangered stellate sturgeon, have been devastated since the late 20th century. Too many have been fished for their flesh, as well as for their unfertilized eggs, which are eaten as caviar.

Ex		0
Cr		6
En		12
Vu		7
Other		4

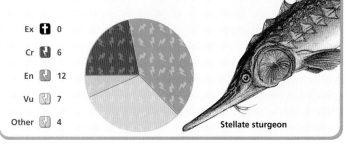

Stellate sturgeon

Gars, sturgeons, and bonytongues

Gars occur in North and Central America, sturgeons in temperate parts of the Northern Hemisphere. Bonytongues are found in tropical America, Africa, Asia, and Australia.

Sardines

Sardines and their relatives are called clupeoids. This order includes some of the most important commercial fish, such as herrings, pilchards, anchovies, and shads, as well as sardines. They have streamlined bodies, large silver scales, and forked tails. Most form large schools in the ocean, near coastlines. Some travel in huge numbers on migrations that can cover thousands of miles and take several years. Most clupeoids feed by filtering small animals called zooplankton from the water. This group experiences "boom–bust" population cycles, based on availability of food. Their numbers may crash, with many dying at once. But these fish reproduce quickly from a young age, so their numbers bounce back when conditions are good.

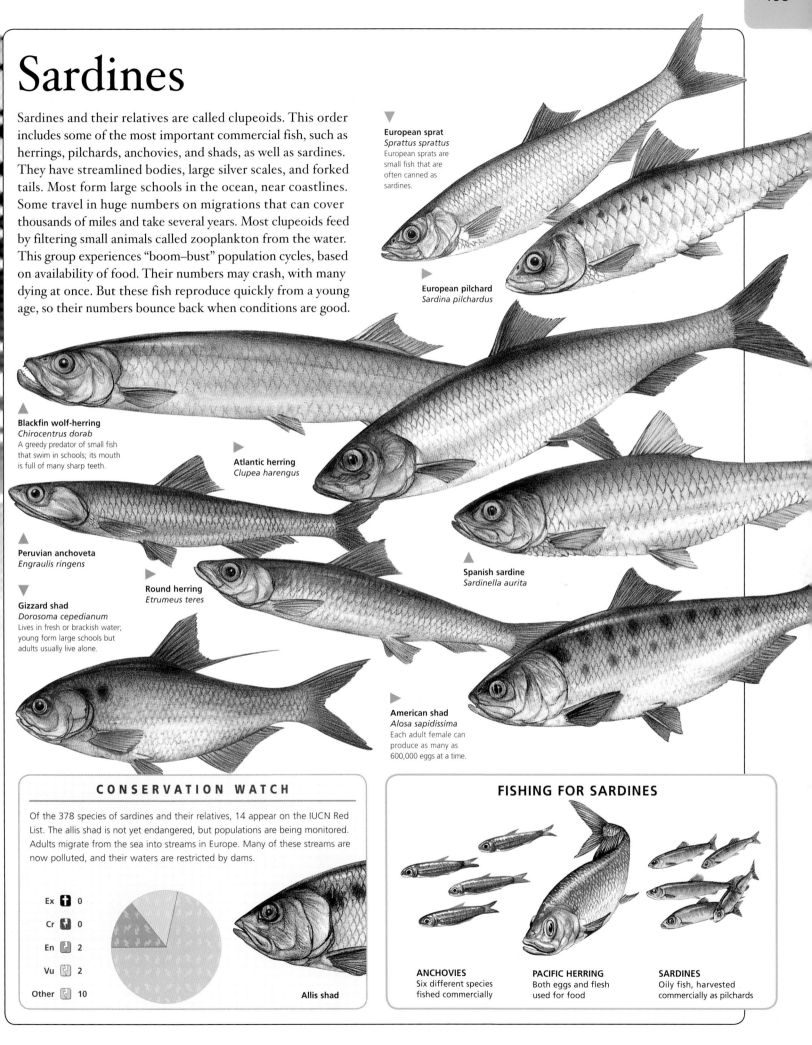

European sprat
Sprattus sprattus
European sprats are small fish that are often canned as sardines.

European pilchard
Sardina pilchardus

Blackfin wolf-herring
Chirocentrus dorab
A greedy predator of small fish that swim in schools; its mouth is full of many sharp teeth.

Atlantic herring
Clupea harengus

Peruvian anchoveta
Engraulis ringens

Round herring
Etrumeus teres

Spanish sardine
Sardinella aurita

Gizzard shad
Dorosoma cepedianum
Lives in fresh or brackish water; young form large schools but adults usually live alone.

American shad
Alosa sapidissima
Each adult female can produce as many as 600,000 eggs at a time.

CONSERVATION WATCH

Of the 378 species of sardines and their relatives, 14 appear on the IUCN Red List. The allis shad is not yet endangered, but populations are being monitored. Adults migrate from the sea into streams in Europe. Many of these streams are now polluted, and their waters are restricted by dams.

Ex	0
Cr	0
En	2
Vu	2
Other	10

Allis shad

FISHING FOR SARDINES

ANCHOVIES
Six different species fished commercially

PACIFIC HERRING
Both eggs and flesh used for food

SARDINES
Oily fish, harvested commercially as pilchards

Eels

There are 900 species of eels and their relatives, the eel-like fish. All begin life as leptocephalus larvae. These larvae are see-through, shaped like a ribbon, and drift on ocean currents for as long as three years. They then change into a small version of their adult form. Most live in the oceans or around the mouths of rivers. The largest group—the true eels—includes moray, conger, and freshwater eels. They have long bodies, and most have no pelvic or pectoral fins. As adults, many eel-like fish look different from true eels. Tarpons and bonefish have forked tails and large, metallic scales. Deep-sea swallowers do not have scales. They have enormous mouths and expandable stomachs that allow them to gulp down large, but infrequent, meals.

Laced moray
Gymnothorax favagineus

European eel
Anguilla anguilla

Geometric moray
Gymnothorax griseus

Oxeye
Megalops cyprinoides
Often seen gulping air at the water's surface when oxygen levels in the water fall

Tarpon
Megalops atlanticus
Sometimes called "the world's greatest gamefish," the tarpon is hard to catch and leaps explosively from the water while fighting fiercely for hours.

Bonefish
Albula vulpes
Uses its protruding snout to dig in sandy and muddy bottoms for small animal prey

EEL GARDENS

At least 20 species of conger, or garden, eels live their entire lives in colonies, "growing" out of sand or mud on the ocean's bottom. The tail and almost half the body is inserted permanently into a burrow lined with mucus. The head normally waves in passing currents but will be withdrawn into the burrow if a predator threatens. Conger eels feed by using their short, turned-up mouths to pluck tiny animals called plankton from the water. Even when mating, they never leave their burrows. Instead, they release eggs and sperm while they wrap their heads and bodies around their nearest neighbors. Garden eel colonies can include thousands of members. They can be found as deep as 1,000 feet (300 m) below the surface.

Conger eel
Conger conger

Swallower
Saccopharynx ampullaceus
Like the other gulper eels, the swallower can live as deep as 10,000 feet (3,000 m).

Spotted garden eel
Heteroconger hassi
Lives in large colonies; it embeds itself in sandy bottoms near coral reefs.

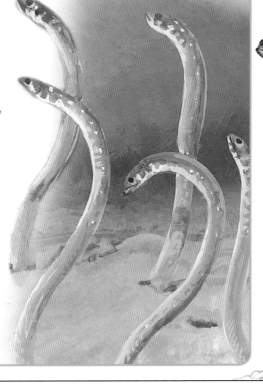

MYSTERIOUS MIGRATION

LIFE OF THE FRESHWATER EEL

The European eel and its relative, the American eel, have complex life cycles that involve migrations over huge distances, traveling as far as 7,000 miles (11,250 km). Both species release eggs and sperm into the salty waters of the Sargasso Sea, in the western Atlantic Ocean. Exactly where this occurs is a mystery. European eels live most of their adult lives in fresh water throughout Europe and parts of northern Africa. American eels head west to North America to live in fresh water, before returning to the Sargasso Sea to breed.

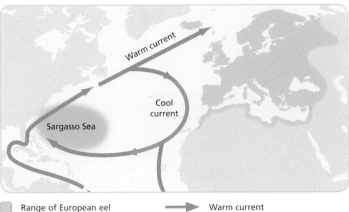

| Range of European eel | | Warm current |
| Spawning grounds | | Cool current |

European eel larvae travel in warm ocean currents from the Sargasso Sea to the coastlines of northwestern Europe. They return as adults in cool currents.

Larvae drift in ocean currents for their first few years. When they reach the coastlines of northwestern Europe, they are tiny eels just 2 to 4 inches (5 to 10 cm) long.

Adult European eels live for 6 to 20 years in freshwater rivers, streams, and lakes connected to the North Atlantic Ocean, as well as the Baltic and Mediterranean Seas.

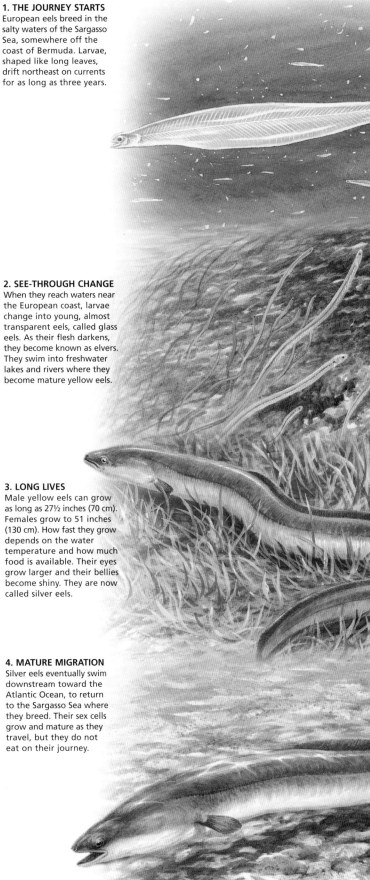

1. THE JOURNEY STARTS
European eels breed in the salty waters of the Sargasso Sea, somewhere off the coast of Bermuda. Larvae, shaped like long leaves, drift northeast on currents for as long as three years.

2. SEE-THROUGH CHANGE
When they reach waters near the European coast, larvae change into young, almost transparent eels, called glass eels. As their flesh darkens, they become known as elvers. They swim into freshwater lakes and rivers where they become mature yellow eels.

3. LONG LIVES
Male yellow eels can grow as long as 27½ inches (70 cm). Females grow to 51 inches (130 cm). How fast they grow depends on the water temperature and how much food is available. Their eyes grow larger and their bellies become shiny. They are now called silver eels.

4. MATURE MIGRATION
Silver eels eventually swim downstream toward the Atlantic Ocean, to return to the Sargasso Sea where they breed. Their sex cells grow and mature as they travel, but they do not eat on their journey.

Catfish

Catfish and their relatives are the most common fish in freshwater habitats worldwide. More than 7,000 species belong to this group. When they face danger, most species produce chemicals from special skin cells, warning other fish nearby of the threat. They also have a set of bones that enhances their hearing. The largest order of catfish includes the goldfish, minnows, and many other fish that are kept as pets in aquariums around the world. Another order, the characins, includes piranhas, which are famous for eating the flesh of animals that stray into the South American rivers where they live. The harmless tetras also belong to this order. True catfish are easily identified by the tentacle-like barbels around their mouths, which they use to find food.

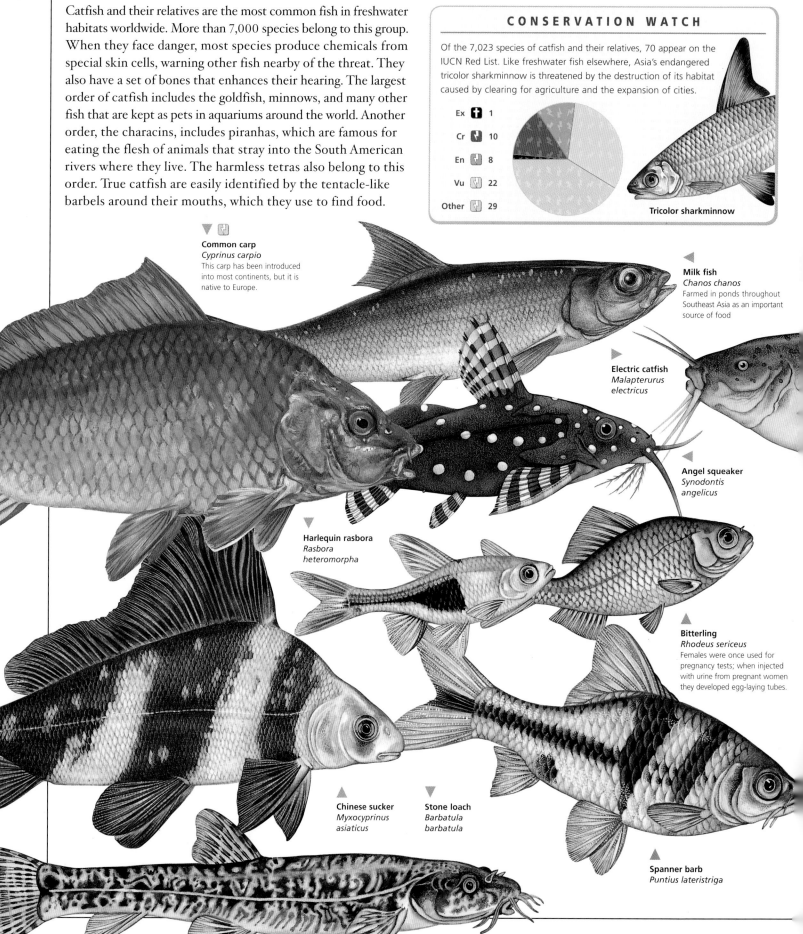

CONSERVATION WATCH

Of the 7,023 species of catfish and their relatives, 70 appear on the IUCN Red List. Like freshwater fish elsewhere, Asia's endangered tricolor sharkminnow is threatened by the destruction of its habitat caused by clearing for agriculture and the expansion of cities.

Ex   1
Cr   10
En   8
Vu   22
Other   29

Tricolor sharkminnow

Common carp
Cyprinus carpio
This carp has been introduced into most continents, but it is native to Europe.

Milk fish
Chanos chanos
Farmed in ponds throughout Southeast Asia as an important source of food

Electric catfish
Malapterurus electricus

Angel squeaker
Synodontis angelicus

Harlequin rasbora
Rasbora heteromorpha

Bitterling
Rhodeus sericeus
Females were once used for pregnancy tests; when injected with urine from pregnant women they developed egg-laying tubes.

Chinese sucker
Myxocyprinus asiaticus

Stone loach
Barbatula barbatula

Spanner barb
Puntius lateristriga

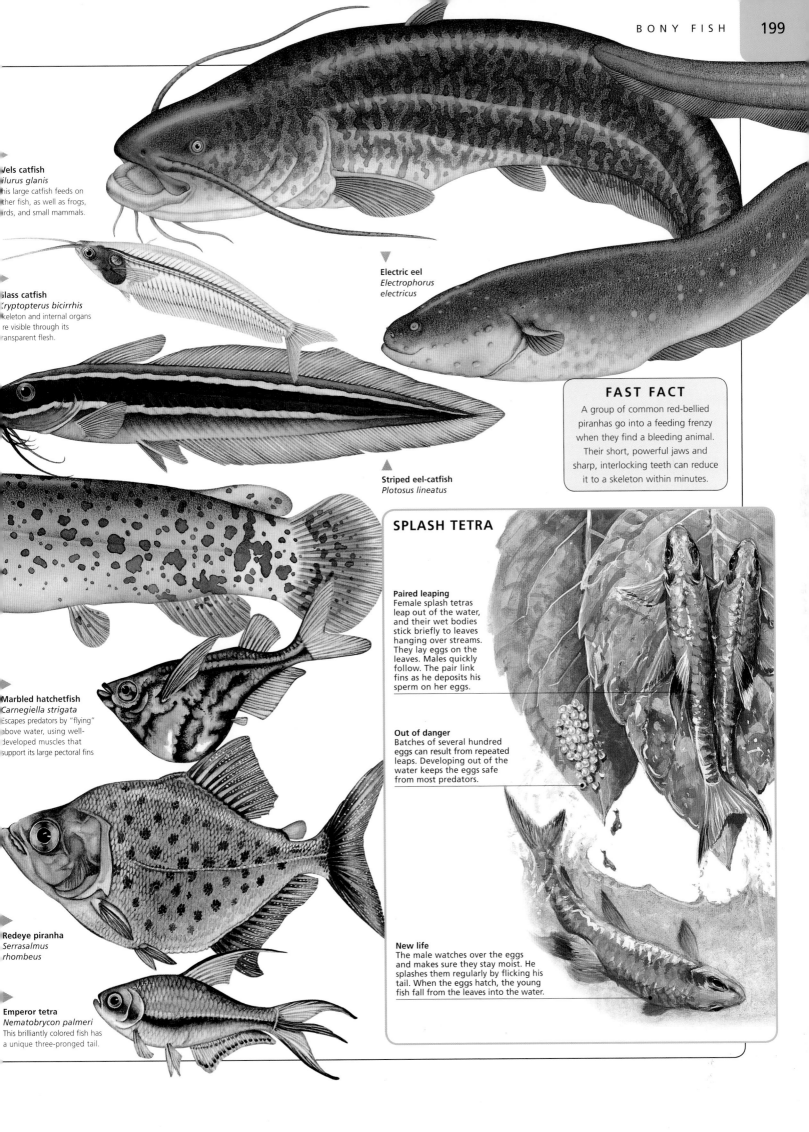

Wels catfish
Silurus glanis
This large catfish feeds on other fish, as well as frogs, birds, and small mammals.

Glass catfish
Kryptopterus bicirrhis
Skeleton and internal organs are visible through its transparent flesh.

Electric eel
Electrophorus electricus

Striped eel-catfish
Plotosus lineatus

FAST FACT
A group of common red-bellied piranhas go into a feeding frenzy when they find a bleeding animal. Their short, powerful jaws and sharp, interlocking teeth can reduce it to a skeleton within minutes.

Marbled hatchetfish
Carnegiella strigata
Escapes predators by "flying" above water, using well-developed muscles that support its large pectoral fins

Redeye piranha
Serrasalmus rhombeus

Emperor tetra
Nematobrycon palmeri
This brilliantly colored fish has a unique three-pronged tail.

SPLASH TETRA

Paired leaping
Female splash tetras leap out of the water, and their wet bodies stick briefly to leaves hanging over streams. They lay eggs on the leaves. Males quickly follow. The pair link fins as he deposits his sperm on her eggs.

Out of danger
Batches of several hundred eggs can result from repeated leaps. Developing out of the water keeps the eggs safe from most predators.

New life
The male watches over the eggs and makes sure they stay moist. He splashes them regularly by flicking his tail. When the eggs hatch, the young fish fall from the leaves into the water.

Salmon

Salmon and their relatives are mostly carnivores, or meat-eaters. Their large mouths and sharp teeth are well designed for catching food. Streamlined bodies and strong tails make them fast, powerful swimmers. They are divided into three orders. One includes the pikes and pickerels, fierce freshwater predators that ambush prey. Another order includes the smelts, which are abundant along ocean coastlines in the Northern Hemisphere. Trout and salmon are in the third order, which also includes whitefish, graylings, and chars. Salmon are strong swimmers. Many make long, difficult migrations to breed. Although salmon and trout are native to the Northern Hemisphere, many species have been introduced around the world, because they are so exciting to catch and good to eat.

Atlantic salmon
Salmo salar

European smelt
Osmerus eperlanus

Capelin
Mallotus villosus
Most produce eggs sperm only once an then die.

Cutthroat trout
Oncorhynchus clarki
Adults migrate from the sea into streams to breed; young fish enter the sea after about two years.

Sea trout
Salmo trutta trutta

Chain pickerel
Esox niger

Mudminnow
Umbra krameri

Alaska blackfish
Dallia pectoralis
Can breathe oxygen from the air so it can survive in stagnant Arctic ponds during summer

Ayu
Plecoglossus altivelis

California slickhead
Alepocephalus tenebrosus

Northern pike
Esox lucius

Sockeye salmon
Oncorhynchus nerka

Cherry salmon
Oncorhynchus masou

Golden trout
Oncorhynchus aguabonita

Lake trout
Salvelinus namaycush
Females are mated with brook trout males in commercial hatcheries to produce fast-growing fish called splakes.

FAST FACT
Salmon probably rely on their sense of smell to find their way back to the streams where they were born. Each waterway has its own distinctive odor, created by the surrounding soil and plants.

Huchen
Hucho hucho

Grayling
Thymallus thymallus
Females lay their eggs in nests dug by males in streams and lakes in northern Europe.

Cisco
Coregonus artedi
Lives in deep, clean, cold waters of North American lakes and rivers

SALMON LIFE CYCLE

Sockeye salmon start their lives in rivers. They hatch with yolk sacs attached. A few days later, they become fry. As parr, they stay in fresh water for several years before becoming smolt that live in salt water. They live at sea as adults, returning to fresh water to breed.

Eggs are laid in gravel nests.

Free-swimming fry

Just-hatched young (with yolk sac attached) are called alevin.

Parr live in fresh water.

Salmon breed and lay eggs in rivers. When breeding, the male sockeye salmon turns a brilliant red color.

Seagoing adults

Smolt

Pink salmon
Oncorhynchus gorbuscha
Female uses her tail to make a deep gravel nest in a streambed; she guards eggs for several weeks but dies after spawning.

Rainbow trout
Oncorhynchus mykiss

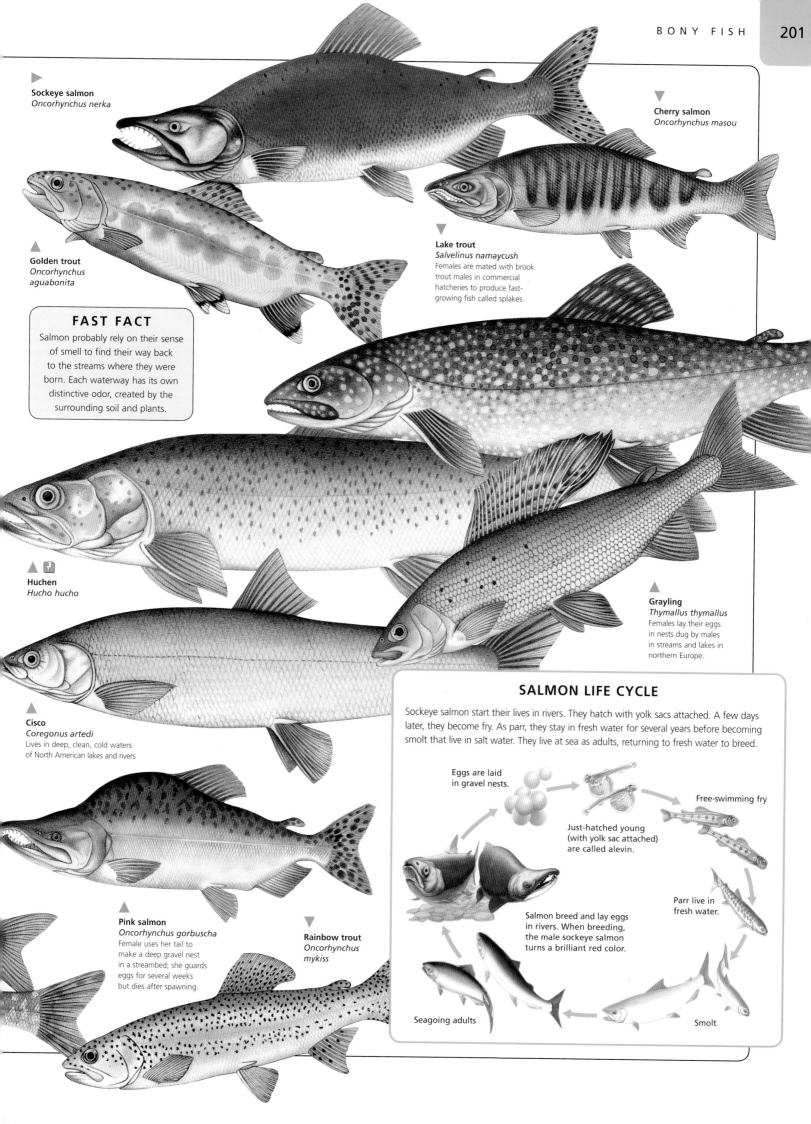

Cod and anglerfish

Most cod and anglerfish live on or near the bottom of seas and oceans. They tend to be most active at night, or live in dark habitats such as underwater caves or the deep sea. Some exceptions include commercially important species—such as haddock, hake, and cod—which form large schools that swim in the open ocean. Some can produce noise with special muscles found on the swim bladder. They may use noises for courting mates or sending distress messages to warn other fish of danger. Many cod are strong swimmers that actively hunt for prey. Anglerfish tend to be slow-moving fish that prefer to wait for food to come to them. Other fish that live in the deep sea are the dragonfish, lizardfish, lanternfish, and beardfish. These have adapted in different ways to life in the dark ocean depths.

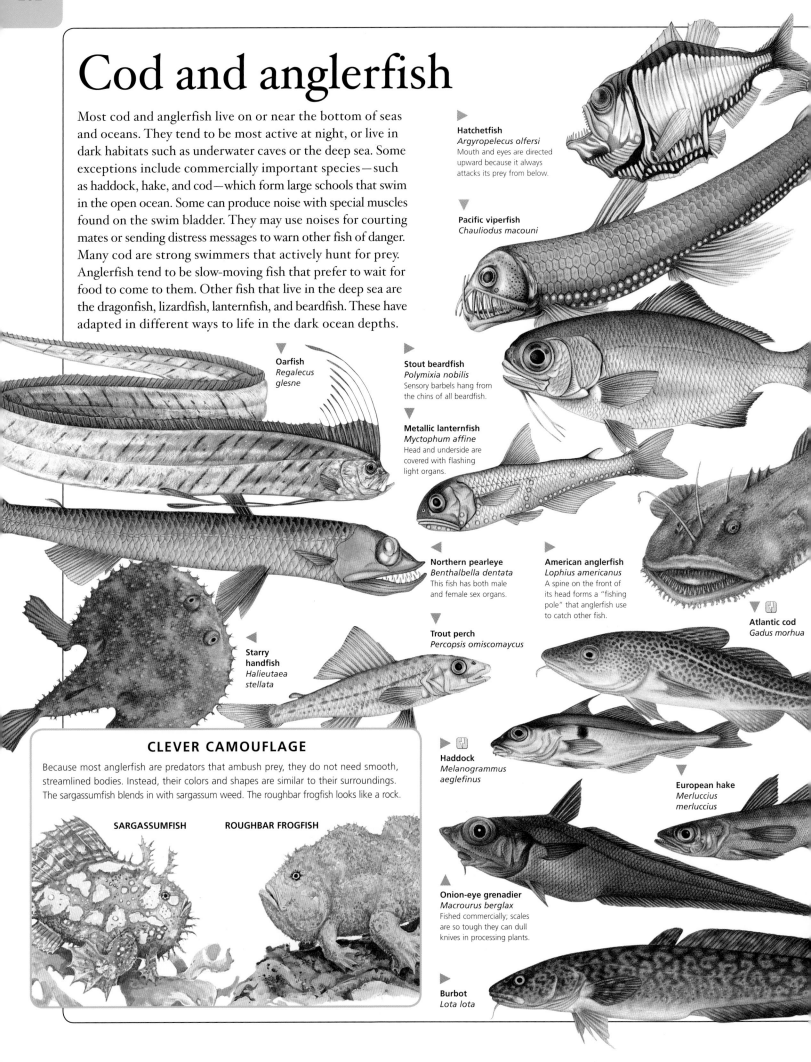

Hatchetfish
Argyropelecus olfersi
Mouth and eyes are directed upward because it always attacks its prey from below.

Pacific viperfish
Chauliodus macouni

Oarfish
Regalecus glesne

Stout beardfish
Polymixia nobilis
Sensory barbels hang from the chins of all beardfish.

Metallic lanternfish
Myctophum affine
Head and underside are covered with flashing light organs.

Northern pearleye
Benthalbella dentata
This fish has both male and female sex organs.

American anglerfish
Lophius americanus
A spine on the front of its head forms a "fishing pole" that anglerfish use to catch other fish.

Atlantic cod
Gadus morhua

Starry handfish
Halieutaea stellata

Trout perch
Percopsis omiscomaycus

Haddock
Melanogrammus aeglefinus

European hake
Merluccius merluccius

Onion-eye grenadier
Macrourus berglax
Fished commercially; scales are so tough they can dull knives in processing plants.

Burbot
Lota lota

CLEVER CAMOUFLAGE

Because most anglerfish are predators that ambush prey, they do not need smooth, streamlined bodies. Instead, their colors and shapes are similar to their surroundings. The sargassumfish blends in with sargassum weed. The roughbar frogfish looks like a rock.

SARGASSUMFISH　　　**ROUGHBAR FROGFISH**

DEEP-SEA FISH

EXPLORING THE DEEP

Deep-sea fish live in a world with no light, where the pressure of the surrounding water pushes in on their bodies. In the darkness, many produce their own light, by a process called bioluminescence. Because it would be difficult to find a member of the opposite sex in the dark, deep-sea fish are often hermaphrodites—they have both male and female sex organs. This means they can play either role when they get the rare opportunity to mate. If necessary, they can even fertilize their own eggs. Prey is also in short supply in the ocean depths. Most deep-sea fish have long teeth, big mouths, and stomachs that can stretch to enormous proportions so that their bodies can cope with even the largest prey.

Deep-sea dragonfish stay hidden in the complete darkness of the ocean depths during the day, but swim upward at night for a better chance of finding prey.

Patterns created by flashing light organs on the bodies of lanternfish may help these fish stay in position within their deep-sea schools.

Tube worms

Eelpout

UNDERWATER HOT SPRINGS

In 1977, scientists were exploring the floor of the Pacific Ocean in a deepwater craft called *Alvin*. At 8,000 feet (2,440 m) below the surface, not far from the Galápagos Islands, they discovered a new habitat: an underwater hot spring called a hydrothermal vent. These vents are surrounded by unusual deep-sea life, such as a fish called an eelpout that eats giant tube worms.

15 ORDERS • 269 FAMILIES • 2,289 GENERA • 13,262 SPECIES

Spiny-rayed Fish

The leafy seadragon, which occurs along the Australian coastline, has frilled, leafy fins that look like the seaweeds and seagrasses among which it lives.

The largest group of bony fish, spiny-rayed fish, show almost every variation on the basic fish body plan. Some are flat, for life on the ocean floor. Bullet-shaped bodies make others among the fastest swimming marine animals. Special fins help a few to glide above water. For others, lightweight, overlapping scales have developed into hard body armor. Spiny-rays usually have flexible mouths that can protrude a long way, letting them eat a huge range of foods.

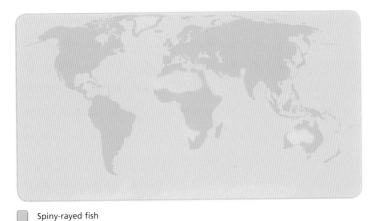

Spiny-rayed fish

Spiny-rayed fish occur almost worldwide. They are found in both fresh and salt water.

SPINY-RAYED FISH FEATURES

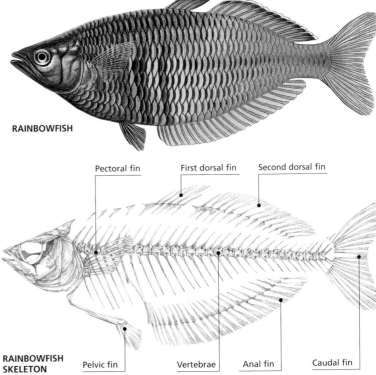

RAINBOWFISH

Pectoral fin   First dorsal fin   Second dorsal fin

RAINBOWFISH
SKELETON   Pelvic fin   Vertebrae   Anal fin   Caudal fin

Spiny-rayed fish

Killifish are some of the best known spiny-rayed fish, because they are among the most popular aquarium fish in the world. They include guppies, mollies, and swordtails. Most killifish occur in the fresh or slightly salty water of rivers and estuaries. Relatives of killifish include silversides. Most silversides live in coastal waters around the world and may form dense schools near the surface over coral reefs. There are also many species that live in fresh water. Silversides are common in the streams, lakes, and swamps of Australia and New Guinea. In contrast, squirrelfish and their relatives live only in salt water. Almost all of this group avoid bright sunlight. They live in deep water, shelter in caves, or hide in other dark places during the day. They become active only at night.

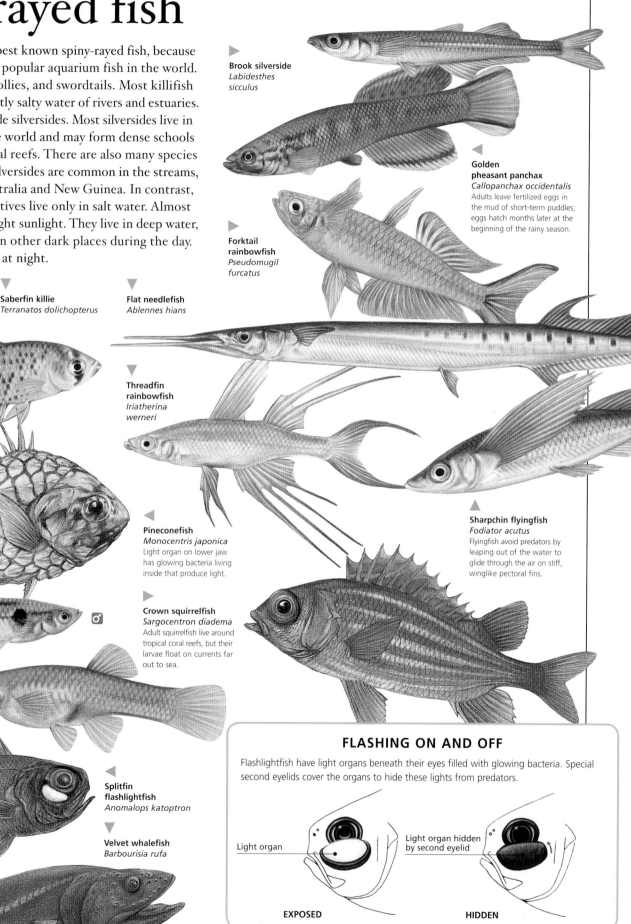

Brook silverside
Labidesthes sicculus

Golden pheasant panchax
Callopanchax occidentalis
Adults leave fertilized eggs in the mud of short-term puddles; eggs hatch months later at the beginning of the rainy season.

Forktail rainbowfish
Pseudomugil furcatus

Saberfin killie
Terranatos dolichopterus

Flat needlefish
Ablennes hians

Threadfin rainbowfish
Iriatherina werneri

Sharpchin flyingfish
Fodiator acutus
Flyingfish avoid predators by leaping out of the water to glide through the air on stiff, winglike pectoral fins.

Pineconefish
Monocentris japonica
Light organ on lower jaw has glowing bacteria living inside that produce light.

Crown squirrelfish
Sargocentron diadema
Adult squirrelfish live around tropical coral reefs, but their larvae float on currents far out to sea.

Guppy
Poecilia reticulata
The guppy is one of the few spiny-rays that gives birth to live young.

Splitfin flashlightfish
Anomalops katoptron

Velvet whalefish
Barbourisia rufa

FLASHING ON AND OFF

Flashlightfish have light organs beneath their eyes filled with glowing bacteria. Special second eyelids cover the organs to hide these lights from predators.

Light organ

Light organ hidden by second eyelid

EXPOSED

HIDDEN

Spiny-rayed fish

One of the most unusual spiny-rayed groups includes pipefish and seahorses. These fish and their relatives—shrimpfish, ghost pipefish, snipefish, trumpetfish, and seamoths—all have long snouts. Many are bizarre in appearance and do not move like most other fish. Dories and their relatives are another group of fish with unusual bodies. The John Dory is so flattened sideways that it is almost impossible to see in the water when viewed from the front. Even more odd are the scorpionfish and their relatives. This group includes pigfish, gurnards, waspfish, and sculpins. Many species in this group live on the seafloor. Their shapes and colors blend into their surroundings to keep them hidden from prey. Some, such as the poisonous stonefish, look like lumps of rock and weeds.

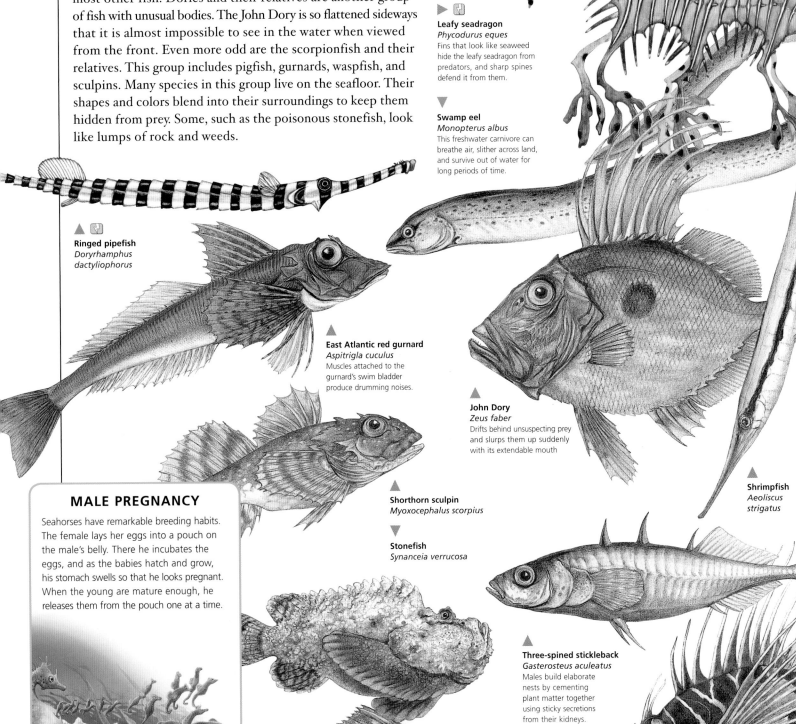

Leafy seadragon
Phycodurus eques
Fins that look like seaweed hide the leafy seadragon from predators, and sharp spines defend it from them.

Swamp eel
Monopterus albus
This freshwater carnivore can breathe air, slither across land, and survive out of water for long periods of time.

Ringed pipefish
Doryrhamphus dactyliophorus

East Atlantic red gurnard
Aspitrigla cuculus
Muscles attached to the gurnard's swim bladder produce drumming noises.

John Dory
Zeus faber
Drifts behind unsuspecting prey and slurps them up suddenly with its extendable mouth

Shrimpfish
Aeoliscus strigatus

Shorthorn sculpin
Myoxocephalus scorpius

Stonefish
Synanceia verrucosa

MALE PREGNANCY

Seahorses have remarkable breeding habits. The female lays her eggs into a pouch on the male's belly. There he incubates the eggs, and as the babies hatch and grow, his stomach swells so that he looks pregnant. When the young are mature enough, he releases them from the pouch one at a time.

Three-spined stickleback
Gasterosteus aculeatus
Males build elaborate nests by cementing plant matter together using sticky secretions from their kidneys.

Sablefish
Anoplopoma fimbria

Radial firefish
Pterois radiata

FISH DEFENSE

This honeycomb cowfish has a protective covering of large, thick scale plates that encases it in boxlike armor.

Some fish defend themselves through strength of numbers: A school of striped catfish form a tight ball when threatened by predators.

STING OF A LION

Stonefish and their relatives are among the most deadly of all sea animals. Poison from venom glands at the base of their fin spines travels up ducts to the tips of the spines. The venom is injected into a predator, such as a ray, when it bites into a stonefish. People can be poisoned when they mistakenly stand on these fish on reef flats. Lionfish (right) are related to stonefish, but they do not hide behind camouflage. Instead, they are beautiful and easy to see—but their bright colors warn that they are dangerous. Long, lacy, and brilliantly colored fins conceal 18 needle-sharp spines that are full of deadly venom.

Spiny-rayed fish

The largest group of spiny-rayed fish is the perchlike fish. It includes snappers, groupers, and drums and croakers, which feed millions of people around the world. Most perchlike fish are ocean dwellers. As adults, they live in schools in coastal waters or around reefs. As larvae, many travel widely on ocean currents, eating plankton. The mainly freshwater cichlids of Africa and South America are attentive parents that watch over their young. Cichlids may have elaborate courtship displays that involve body and fin movements. The sexes of many species are distinguished by different colors and patterns. Damselfish also show complex behavior. Most live in well-defined territories near reefs. Some species behave like fish "farmers," tending mats of algae growing in their territories and feeding on them.

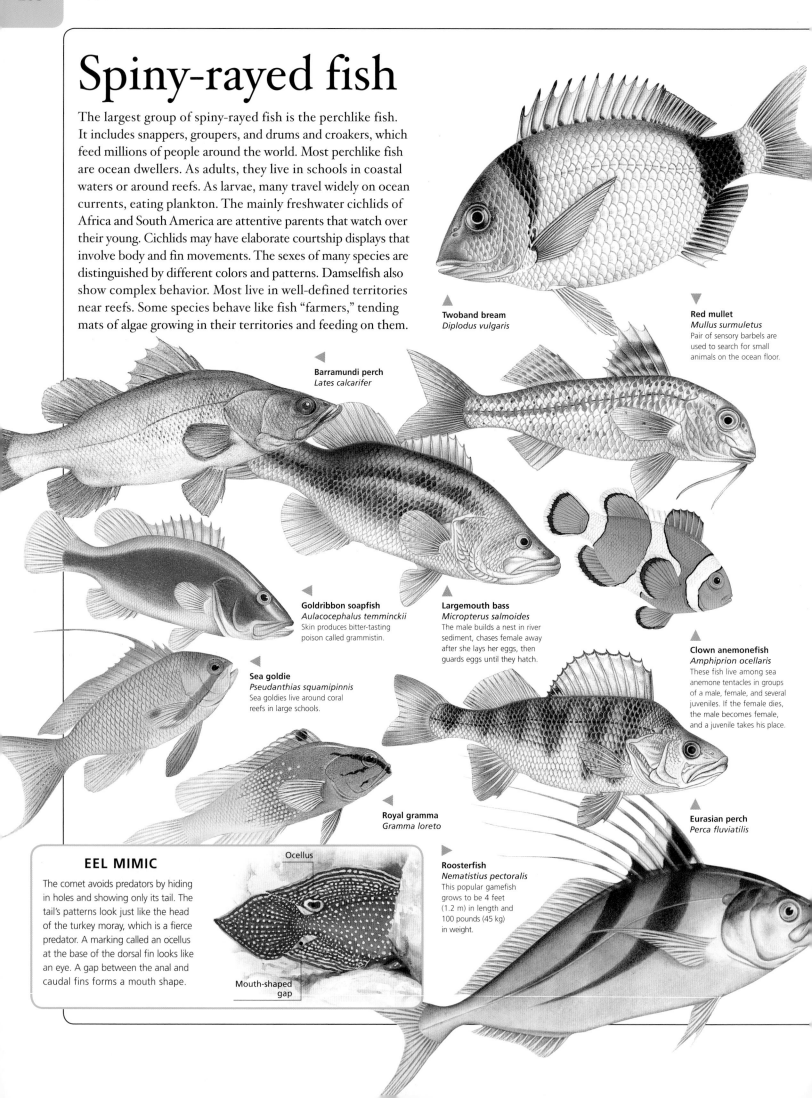

▲
Twoband bream
Diplodus vulgaris

▼
Red mullet
Mullus surmuletus
Pair of sensory barbels are used to search for small animals on the ocean floor.

◀
Barramundi perch
Lates calcarifer

◀
Goldribbon soapfish
Aulacocephalus temminckii
Skin produces bitter-tasting poison called grammistin.

◀
Largemouth bass
Micropterus salmoides
The male builds a nest in river sediment, chases female away after she lays her eggs, then guards eggs until they hatch.

▲
Clown anemonefish
Amphiprion ocellaris
These fish live among sea anemone tentacles in groups of a male, female, and several juveniles. If the female dies, the male becomes female, and a juvenile takes his place.

◀
Sea goldie
Pseudanthias squamipinnis
Sea goldies live around coral reefs in large schools.

◀
Royal gramma
Gramma loreto

▲
Eurasian perch
Perca fluviatilis

▶
Roosterfish
Nematistius pectoralis
This popular gamefish grows to be 4 feet (1.2 m) in length and 100 pounds (45 kg) in weight.

EEL MIMIC

The comet avoids predators by hiding in holes and showing only its tail. The tail's patterns look just like the head of the turkey moray, which is a fierce predator. A marking called an ocellus at the base of the dorsal fin looks like an eye. A gap between the anal and caudal fins forms a mouth shape.

Ocellus

Mouth-shaped gap

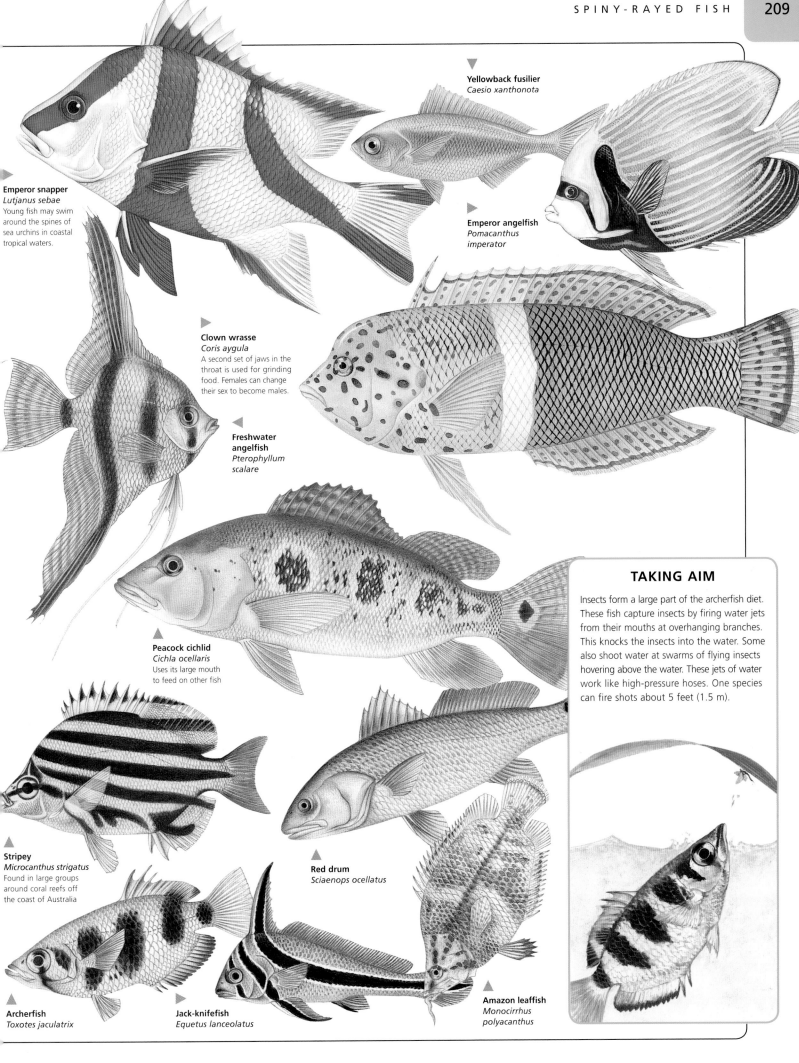

Emperor snapper
Lutjanus sebae
Young fish may swim around the spines of sea urchins in coastal tropical waters.

Yellowback fusilier
Caesio xanthonota

Emperor angelfish
Pomacanthus imperator

Clown wrasse
Coris aygula
A second set of jaws in the throat is used for grinding food. Females can change their sex to become males.

Freshwater angelfish
Pterophyllum scalare

Peacock cichlid
Cichla ocellaris
Uses its large mouth to feed on other fish

Stripey
Microcanthus strigatus
Found in large groups around coral reefs off the coast of Australia

Red drum
Sciaenops ocellatus

Archerfish
Toxotes jaculatrix

Jack-knifefish
Equetus lanceolatus

Amazon leaffish
Monocirrhus polyacanthus

TAKING AIM

Insects form a large part of the archerfish diet. These fish capture insects by firing water jets from their mouths at overhanging branches. This knocks the insects into the water. Some also shoot water at swarms of flying insects hovering above the water. These jets of water work like high-pressure hoses. One species can fire shots about 5 feet (1.5 m).

Spiny-rayed fish

Spiny-rayed fish have adapted to many different habitats and ways of life. Tuna and their relatives, such as mackerel and billfish, are agile predators of the open water. Their streamlined bodies are perfectly designed for speed; many are among the fastest swimming animals in the oceans. Flatfish, such as flounders and soles, have bodies that are compressed sideways so they seem to disappear into the ocean floor. They wait there for prey to come to them. Flatfish are the chameleons of the fish world; some species can modify the color of their skin to match their surroundings perfectly. Gobies, such as mudskippers, are shaped like lizards and live among sediment on the ocean floor. Most gobies are tiny, and many live in cooperative relationships with other animals, such as corals, mollusks, and crustaceans.

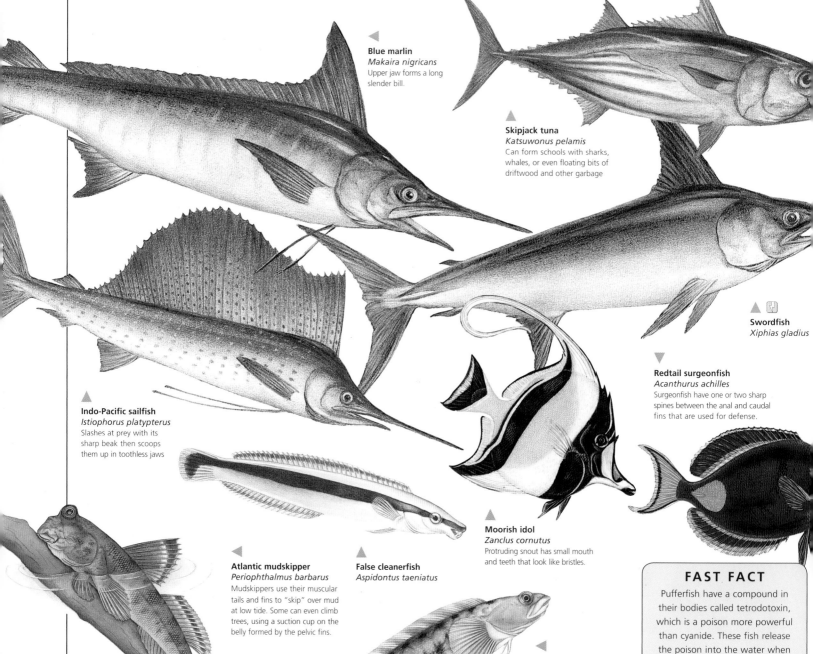

Blue marlin
Makaira nigricans
Upper jaw forms a long slender bill.

Skipjack tuna
Katsuwonus pelamis
Can form schools with sharks, whales, or even floating bits of driftwood and other garbage

Swordfish
Xiphias gladius

Redtail surgeonfish
Acanthurus achilles
Surgeonfish have one or two sharp spines between the anal and caudal fins that are used for defense.

Indo-Pacific sailfish
Istiophorus platypterus
Slashes at prey with its sharp beak then scoops them up in toothless jaws

Atlantic mudskipper
Periophthalmus barbarus
Mudskippers use their muscular tails and fins to "skip" over mud at low tide. Some can even climb trees, using a suction cup on the belly formed by the pelvic fins.

False cleanerfish
Aspidontus taeniatus

Moorish idol
Zanclus cornutus
Protruding snout has small mouth and teeth that look like bristles.

Viviparous blenny
Zoarces viviparus

FAST FACT

Pufferfish have a compound in their bodies called tetrodotoxin, which is a poison more powerful than cyanide. These fish release the poison into the water when threatened by a predator.

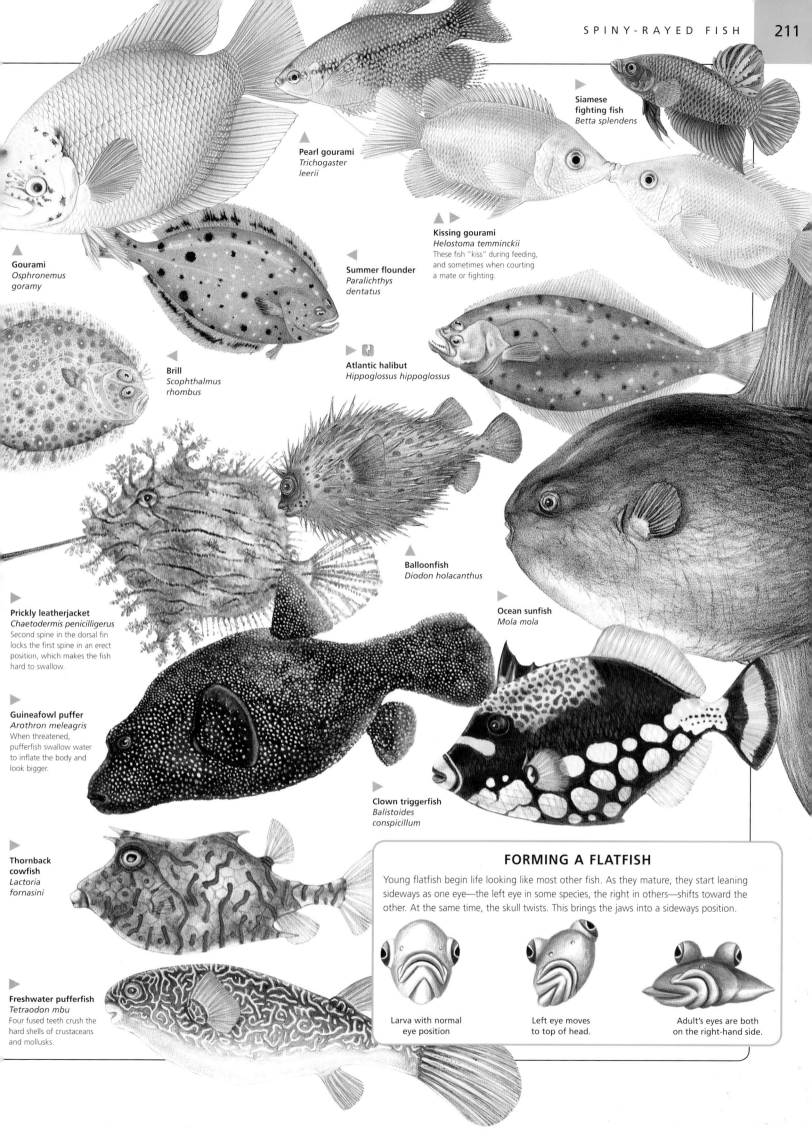

Siamese fighting fish
Betta splendens

Pearl gourami
Trichogaster leerii

Kissing gourami
Helostoma temminckii
These fish "kiss" during feeding, and sometimes when courting a mate or fighting.

Gourami
Osphronemus goramy

Summer flounder
Paralichthys dentatus

Brill
Scophthalmus rhombus

Atlantic halibut
Hippoglossus hippoglossus

Prickly leatherjacket
Chaetodermis penicilligerus
Second spine in the dorsal fin locks the first spine in an erect position, which makes the fish hard to swallow.

Balloonfish
Diodon holacanthus

Ocean sunfish
Mola mola

Guineafowl puffer
Arothron meleagris
When threatened, pufferfish swallow water to inflate the body and look bigger.

Clown triggerfish
Balistoides conspicillum

Thornback cowfish
Lactoria fornasini

Freshwater pufferfish
Tetraodon mbu
Four fused teeth crush the hard shells of crustaceans and mollusks.

FORMING A FLATFISH

Young flatfish begin life looking like most other fish. As they mature, they start leaning sideways as one eye—the left eye in some species, the right in others—shifts toward the other. At the same time, the skull twists. This brings the jaws into a sideways position.

Larva with normal eye position

Left eye moves to top of head.

Adult's eyes are both on the right-hand side.

>30 PHYLA • >90 CLASSES • >370 ORDERS • >1.3 MILLION SPECIES

Invertebrates

The purple jellyfish can grow as wide as 1½ feet (45 cm). It provides a temporary home to fish and young crabs as it floats on the ocean's currents.

Just a fraction of all known species—fewer than 50,000—are vertebrates, such as mammals, reptiles, amphibians, and fish. The rest are invertebrates, including sponges, worms, snails, spiders, and insects. The first invertebrates appeared in Earth's oceans more than 650 million years ago. This was many millions of years before the first vertebrates appeared. Today, most invertebrates still live in the oceans, but they can be found in almost every habitat worldwide. Unlike vertebrates, invertebrates do not have backbones. In fact, they have no bones at all. Invertebrate bodies are usually supported by some sort of skeleton. Some species have a hard casing called an exoskeleton on the outside of their bodies, with the soft tissues contained inside. Others have hard materials scattered through their bodies to provide support. Invertebrates have two basic body plans. Jellyfish and sea anemones have a circular body plan with a mouth at the center. This is known as radial symmetry. Others, such as worms and insects, have bilateral symmetry, meaning they have identical left and right sides. Young invertebrates often look very different from their parents, and must go through a change called a metamorphosis to reach their adult form. This may be a simple, gradual change or a complete transformation.

KINDS OF INVERTEBRATES

At least 1.3 million species of invertebrates have been discovered. Most are small, but a few can be enormous. The giant squid can grow to be as large as a whale. Invertebrates are divided into more than 30 major groups, known as phyla. While they all lack backbones, or vertebrae, most have few features in common. The largest phylum contains the arthropods, such as insects, spiders, and crustaceans. Many, from prawns and lobsters to honeybees, provide humans with food. Some can be a source of lifesaving medicines, whereas others are pests or parasites.

BUG: INSECT

BUTTERFLY: INSECT

BEETLE: INSECT

BEE: INSECT

CRICKET: INSECT

SEA URCHIN: ECHINODERM

EARTHWORM: SEGMENTED WORM

SCORPION: ARACHNID

SPIDER: ARACHNID

SNAIL: MOLLUSK

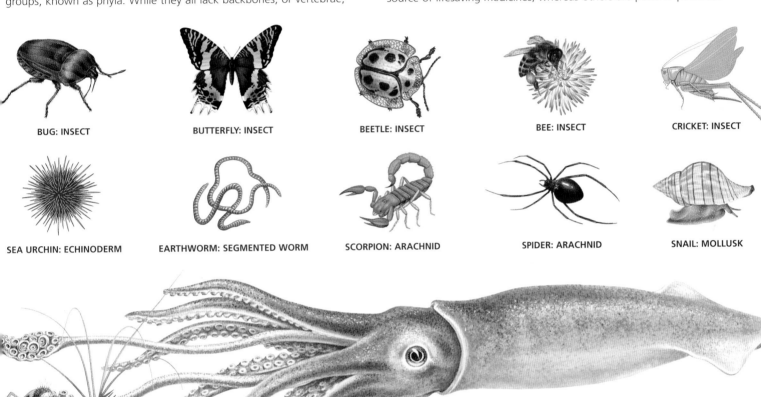

SHRIMP: CRUSTACEAN

SQUID: MOLLUSK

ANEMONE: CNIDARIAN

SPONGE: PORIFERAN

INVERTEBRATE REPRODUCTION

Most invertebrates reproduce sexually. Eggs are fertilized inside the female by sperm from the male. The female then usually lays huge numbers of fertilized eggs. These and the young that hatch from them are generally left to develop without further attention from their parents. However, some invertebrates develop from the female's unfertilized eggs. Others reproduce by "budding": breaking off a piece of their own bodies to create copies of themselves.

Butterflies, like many invertebrates, exist as two sexes that get together to mate.

Male Caribbean reef squid compete with each other for the attention of females.

Invertebrates rarely care for their young, but the female wolf spider protects her egg sac.

7 CLASSES • 27 ORDERS • 127 FAMILIES • >11,000 SPECIES

Sponges and Squirts

People once thought that sponges were plants, not animals. Sponges have a simple structure. They have no tissues or organs, such as a stomach or heart. Instead, different cells are specialized for functions like collecting or digesting food. Sponges are found mostly in the oceans. They range in shape from bushes, vases, barrels, and balls to shapeless masses. Sea squirts are known as tunicates. Most adults live attached to the seafloor and are simple baglike creatures that filter food particles from the water. Sea squirts are linked to vertebrates; this can best be seen in sea squirt larvae. Shaped like tadpoles, they have a flexible rod in their backs called a notochord. Vertebrate embryos share this feature, but their notochords are replaced with backbones as they become adults.

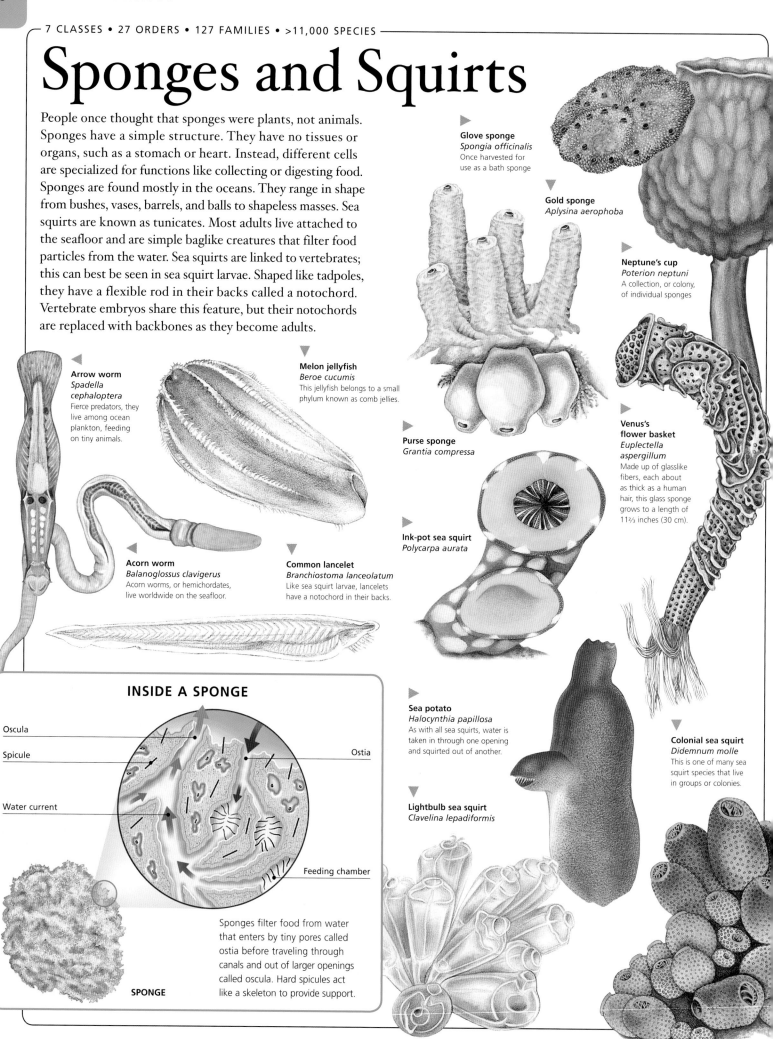

Glove sponge
Spongia officinalis
Once harvested for use as a bath sponge

Gold sponge
Aplysina aerophoba

Neptune's cup
Poterion neptuni
A collection, or colony, of individual sponges

Venus's flower basket
Euplectella aspergillum
Made up of glasslike fibers, each about as thick as a human hair, this glass sponge grows to a length of 11⅔ inches (30 cm).

Arrow worm
Spadella cephaloptera
Fierce predators, they live among ocean plankton, feeding on tiny animals.

Melon jellyfish
Beroe cucumis
This jellyfish belongs to a small phylum known as comb jellies.

Purse sponge
Grantia compressa

Acorn worm
Balanoglossus clavigerus
Acorn worms, or hemichordates, live worldwide on the seafloor.

Common lancelet
Branchiostoma lanceolatum
Like sea squirt larvae, lancelets have a notochord in their backs.

Ink-pot sea squirt
Polycarpa aurata

Sea potato
Halocynthia papillosa
As with all sea squirts, water is taken in through one opening and squirted out of another.

Colonial sea squirt
Didemnum molle
This is one of many sea squirt species that live in groups or colonies.

Lightbulb sea squirt
Clavelina lepadiformis

INSIDE A SPONGE

Oscula

Spicule

Water current

Ostia

Feeding chamber

SPONGE

Sponges filter food from water that enters by tiny pores called ostia before traveling through canals and out of larger openings called oscula. Hard spicules act like a skeleton to provide support.

10 CLASSES • 76 ORDERS • 675 FAMILIES • >45,000 SPECIES

Worms

There are three main kinds of worms: flatworms, roundworms, and segmented worms. Flatworms can be as small as microscopic species found in water or as large as 100-foot (30-m) tapeworms living as parasites inside humans. Because they are flat and thin, gases such as carbon dioxide and oxygen pass through their skin, so they do not need organs for breathing. Roundworms have long, slender bodies. Most are microscopic, so it is hard to imagine they are some of the most abundant animals. Many live in water or soil; others are parasites in plants or animals. Segmented worms look different from other worms. Their long bodies are made of ringlike sections called segments. Each has its own organs for breathing, moving, and getting rid of waste. Other body parts, such as the nervous and digestive systems, are shared.

CONSERVATION WATCH

Of the more than 45,000 species of flatworms, roundworms, and segmented worms, just 11 appear on the IUCN Red List. The medicinal leech is near threatened in its natural habitat, mainly because too many have been collected in past centuries for medical use.

Ex 🕆 2
Cr 2
En 0
Vu 4
Other 3

Medicinal leech

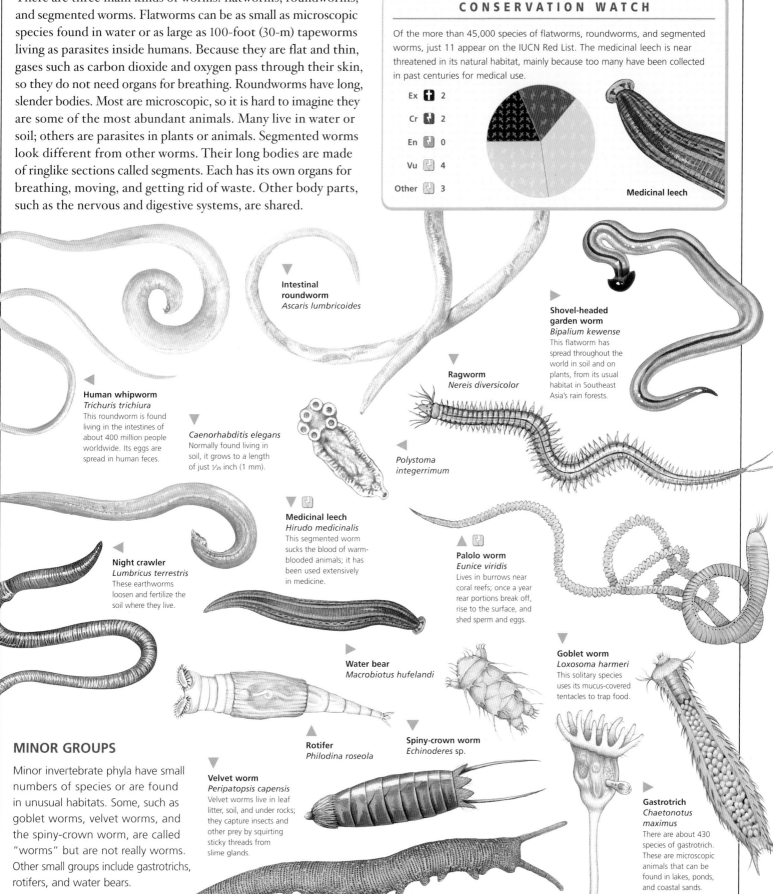

Intestinal roundworm
Ascaris lumbricoides

Shovel-headed garden worm
Bipalium kewense
This flatworm has spread throughout the world in soil and on plants, from its usual habitat in Southeast Asia's rain forests.

Ragworm
Nereis diversicolor

Human whipworm
Trichuris trichiura
This roundworm is found living in the intestines of about 400 million people worldwide. Its eggs are spread in human feces.

Caenorhabditis elegans
Normally found living in soil, it grows to a length of just 1/25 inch (1 mm).

Polystoma integerrimum

Medicinal leech
Hirudo medicinalis
This segmented worm sucks the blood of warm-blooded animals; it has been used extensively in medicine.

Palolo worm
Eunice viridis
Lives in burrows near coral reefs; once a year rear portions break off, rise to the surface, and shed sperm and eggs.

Night crawler
Lumbricus terrestris
These earthworms loosen and fertilize the soil where they live.

Water bear
Macrobiotus hufelandi

Goblet worm
Loxosoma harmeri
This solitary species uses its mucus-covered tentacles to trap food.

MINOR GROUPS

Minor invertebrate phyla have small numbers of species or are found in unusual habitats. Some, such as goblet worms, velvet worms, and the spiny-crown worm, are called "worms" but are not really worms. Other small groups include gastrotrichs, rotifers, and water bears.

Rotifer
Philodina roseola

Spiny-crown worm
Echinoderes sp.

Velvet worm
Peripatopsis capensis
Velvet worms live in leaf litter, soil, and under rocks; they capture insects and other prey by squirting sticky threads from slime glands.

Gastrotrich
Chaetonotus maximus
There are about 430 species of gastrotrich. These are microscopic animals that can be found in lakes, ponds, and coastal sands.

4 CLASSES • 27 ORDERS • 236 FAMILIES • >9,000 SPECIES

Corals and Jellyfish

Corals and jellyfish are known as cnidarians. This phylum also includes sea anemones and hydras. Most cnidarians live in the seas and oceans. All eat other animals and use stinging cells to capture their prey as well as to deter predators. Cnidarians occur in two forms. Some, such as sea anemones and corals, are polyps. Polyps are shaped like cylinders. They have a mouth surrounded by tentacles at one end of their bodies; they attach themselves to a surface with the other end. Other cnidarians, such as jellyfish, are medusae. They have an umbrella shape and swim or float freely in the water with their mouths and tentacles hanging downward. Although there are cnidarians that exist only as a medusa or as a polyp, many species alternate between the two forms during their life cycles.

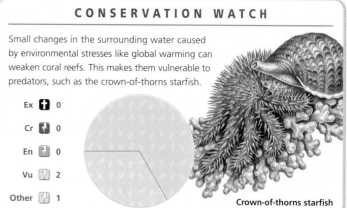

CONSERVATION WATCH

Small changes in the surrounding water caused by environmental stresses like global warming can weaken coral reefs. This makes them vulnerable to predators, such as the crown-of-thorns starfish.

Ex ✝ 0
Cr 🗙 0
En 🗙 0
Vu 🗙 2
Other 🗙 1

Crown-of-thorns starfish

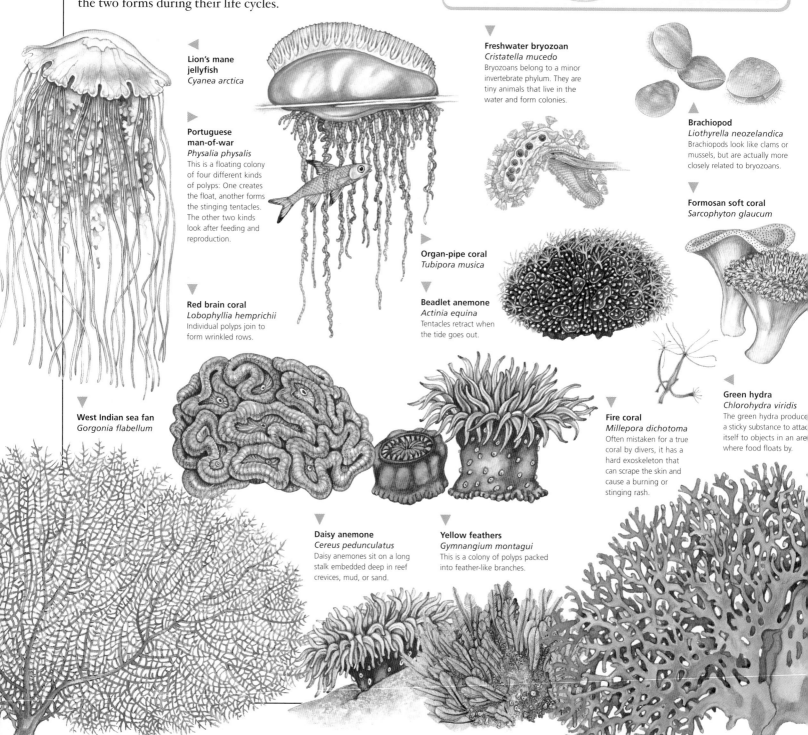

Lion's mane jellyfish
Cyanea arctica

Portuguese man-of-war
Physalia physalis
This is a floating colony of four different kinds of polyps: One creates the float, another forms the stinging tentacles. The other two kinds look after feeding and reproduction.

Red brain coral
Lobophyllia hemprichii
Individual polyps join to form wrinkled rows.

West Indian sea fan
Gorgonia flabellum

Freshwater bryozoan
Cristatella mucedo
Bryozoans belong to a minor invertebrate phylum. They are tiny animals that live in the water and form colonies.

Brachiopod
Liothyrella neozelandica
Brachiopods look like clams or mussels, but are actually more closely related to bryozoans.

Formosan soft coral
Sarcophyton glaucum

Organ-pipe coral
Tubipora musica

Beadlet anemone
Actinia equina
Tentacles retract when the tide goes out.

Fire coral
Millepora dichotoma
Often mistaken for a true coral by divers, it has a hard exoskeleton that can scrape the skin and cause a burning or stinging rash.

Green hydra
Chlorohydra viridis
The green hydra produce a sticky substance to attac itself to objects in an are where food floats by.

Daisy anemone
Cereus pedunculatus
Daisy anemones sit on a long stalk embedded deep in reef crevices, mud, or sand.

Yellow feathers
Gymnangium montagui
This is a colony of polyps packed into feather-like branches.

GREAT BARRIER REEF

Coral reefs are made up of the hard exoskeletons of coral polyps, which exist in interconnected colonies. With the aid of algae living inside them, the polyps produce cups of calcium carbonate, also called limestone, around themselves. As they die, the polyps leave these hard skeletons behind. Following generations build on top of them. This process has been going on for many millions of years on the Great Barrier Reef, a system of coral reefs that stretches for more than 1,400 miles (2,250 km) along the northeast coast of Australia. It is Earth's largest natural feature, supporting 400 coral species, 1,500 fish species, and 4,000 mollusk species. Tropical rain forests are the only other kind of habitat to boast such enormous diversity. Because the algae living inside coral polyps must have sunshine to live, just as other plants do, coral reefs are found only in clear, shallow waters. Sudden increases or decreases in sea level can cause untold damage to the reefs.

Sea anemones, such as this sebae anemone, are commonly found on coral reefs. They spend most of their lives attached to a surface, but can also move around slowly.

Deadly thorns
The crown-of-thorns starfish attacks and eats coral. It spreads its stomach over polyp colonies to liquefy their soft tissues and then absorb them.

Coral refuge
Coral reefs provide shelter, food, and breeding territories for thousands of different species of plants and animals. These include fish, turtles, and sponges.

Special roles
Within some coral colonies, individual polyps can have special roles to play. Some feed, while others act to defend the colony. Others are responsible for breeding.

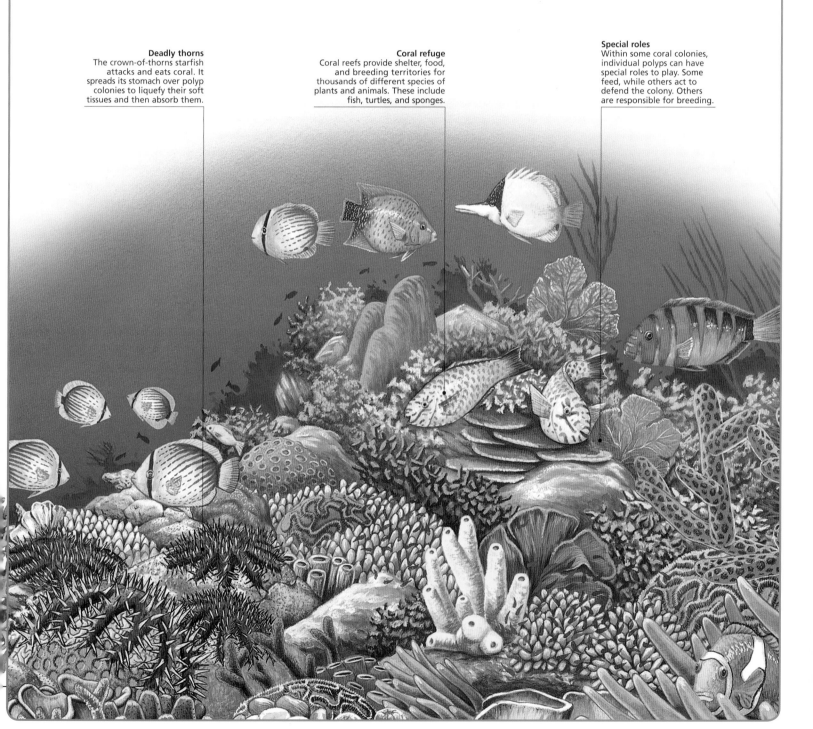

7 CLASSES • 20 ORDERS • 185 FAMILIES • 75,000 SPECIES

Mollusks

Most mollusks are found in the oceans. But many live in fresh water and on land, particularly where conditions are moist. Mollusk bodies have a well-defined head region, a muscular foot that often produces mucus, and an area for organs, such as the stomach. Most have a hard shell of calcium carbonate made by a specialized skin layer called the mantle, which covers the body. In some species, the shell has become very small, is carried inside the body, or has been lost altogether. There are seven classes of mollusks. Bivalves and gastropods are two of the best known. Bivalves include clams, oysters, and mussels. All have a two-part hinged shell and a tiny head. Gastropods are the largest mollusk group, and include snails, slugs, and limpets. Gastropod means "belly foot." Most species have a spiral shell, but some have none.

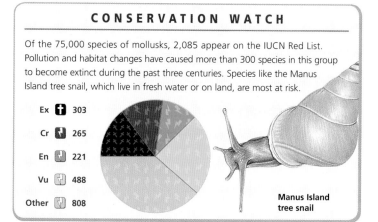

CONSERVATION WATCH

Of the 75,000 species of mollusks, 2,085 appear on the IUCN Red List. Pollution and habitat changes have caused more than 300 species in this group to become extinct during the past three centuries. Species like the Manus Island tree snail, which live in fresh water or on land, are most at risk.

Ex 🕆 303
Cr 🗝 265
En 🗝 221
Vu 🗝 488
Other 🗝 808

Manus Island tree snail

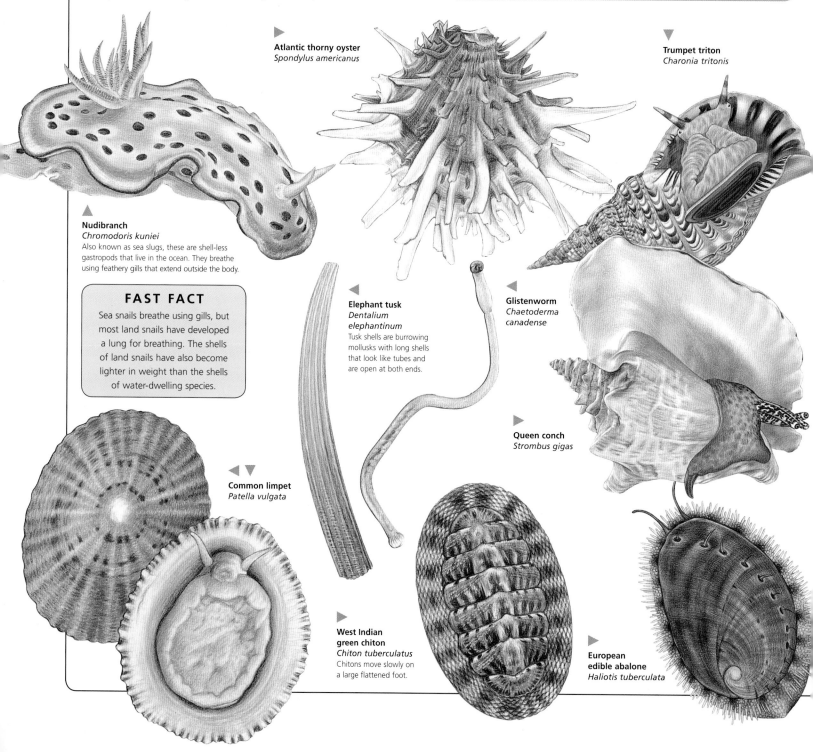

Atlantic thorny oyster
Spondylus americanus

Trumpet triton
Charonia tritonis

Nudibranch
Chromodoris kuniei
Also known as sea slugs, these are shell-less gastropods that live in the ocean. They breathe using feathery gills that extend outside the body.

FAST FACT

Sea snails breathe using gills, but most land snails have developed a lung for breathing. The shells of land snails have also become lighter in weight than the shells of water-dwelling species.

Elephant tusk
Dentalium elephantinum
Tusk shells are burrowing mollusks with long shells that look like tubes and are open at both ends.

Glistenworm
Chaetoderma canadense

Queen conch
Strombus gigas

Common limpet
Patella vulgata

West Indian green chiton
Chiton tuberculatus
Chitons move slowly on a large flattened foot.

European edible abalone
Haliotis tuberculata

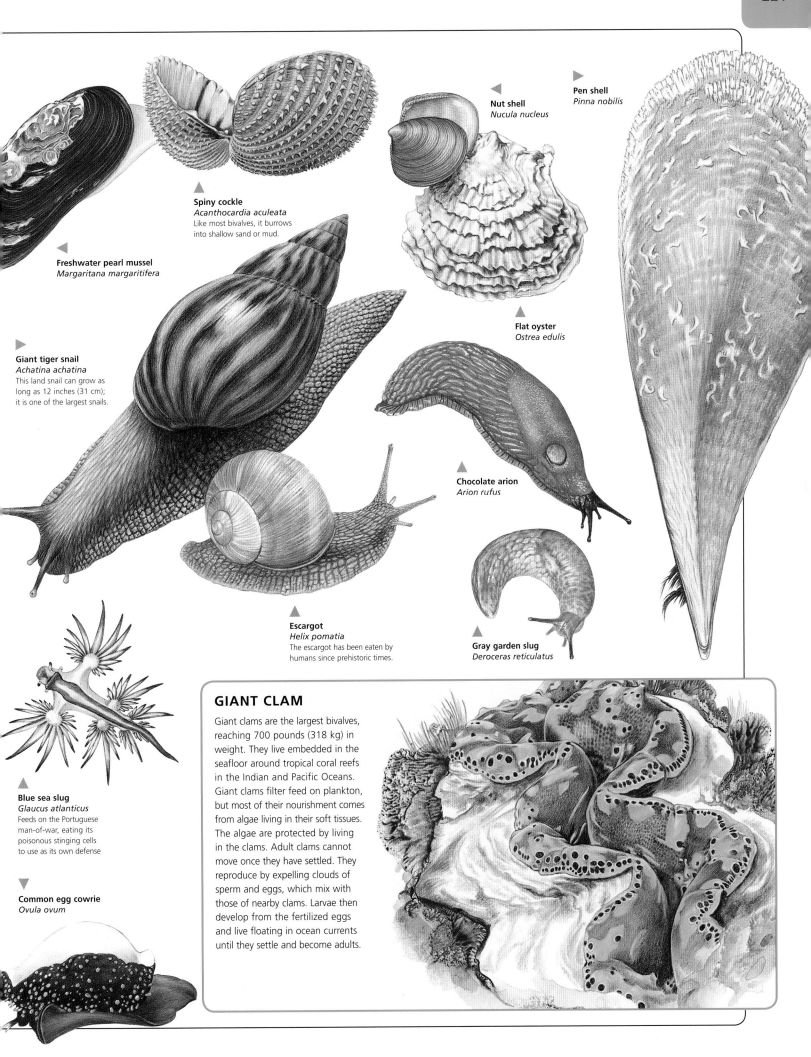

Spiny cockle
Acanthocardia aculeata
Like most bivalves, it burrows into shallow sand or mud.

Nut shell
Nucula nucleus

Pen shell
Pinna nobilis

Freshwater pearl mussel
Margaritana margaritifera

Giant tiger snail
Achatina achatina
This land snail can grow as long as 12 inches (31 cm); it is one of the largest snails.

Flat oyster
Ostrea edulis

Chocolate arion
Arion rufus

Escargot
Helix pomatia
The escargot has been eaten by humans since prehistoric times.

Gray garden slug
Deroceras reticulatus

Blue sea slug
Glaucus atlanticus
Feeds on the Portuguese man-of-war, eating its poisonous stinging cells to use as its own defense

Common egg cowrie
Ovula ovum

GIANT CLAM

Giant clams are the largest bivalves, reaching 700 pounds (318 kg) in weight. They live embedded in the seafloor around tropical coral reefs in the Indian and Pacific Oceans. Giant clams filter feed on plankton, but most of their nourishment comes from algae living in their soft tissues. The algae are protected by living in the clams. Adult clams cannot move once they have settled. They reproduce by expelling clouds of sperm and eggs, which mix with those of nearby clams. Larvae then develop from the fertilized eggs and live floating in ocean currents until they settle and become adults.

Squid and octopuses

Squid, octopuses, nautiluses, and cuttlefish form a class of mollusk called cephalopods. This means "head foot." The foot of these ocean dwellers lies close to the head and is modified to form arms and tentacles. Nautiluses have a large shell; squid and cuttlefish have a shrunken shell located inside the body; and octopuses have lost their shell entirely. Most cephalopods move by jet propulsion: They squirt water out of their bodies to swim either forward or backward. They are the most intelligent invertebrates and show complex behavior. Males may perform courtship displays to attract mates. They pick up sperm in packages called spermatophores, which they place inside females with a special arm. Most females attach fertilized eggs to rocks or seaweed. Their young look like miniature adults when they hatch.

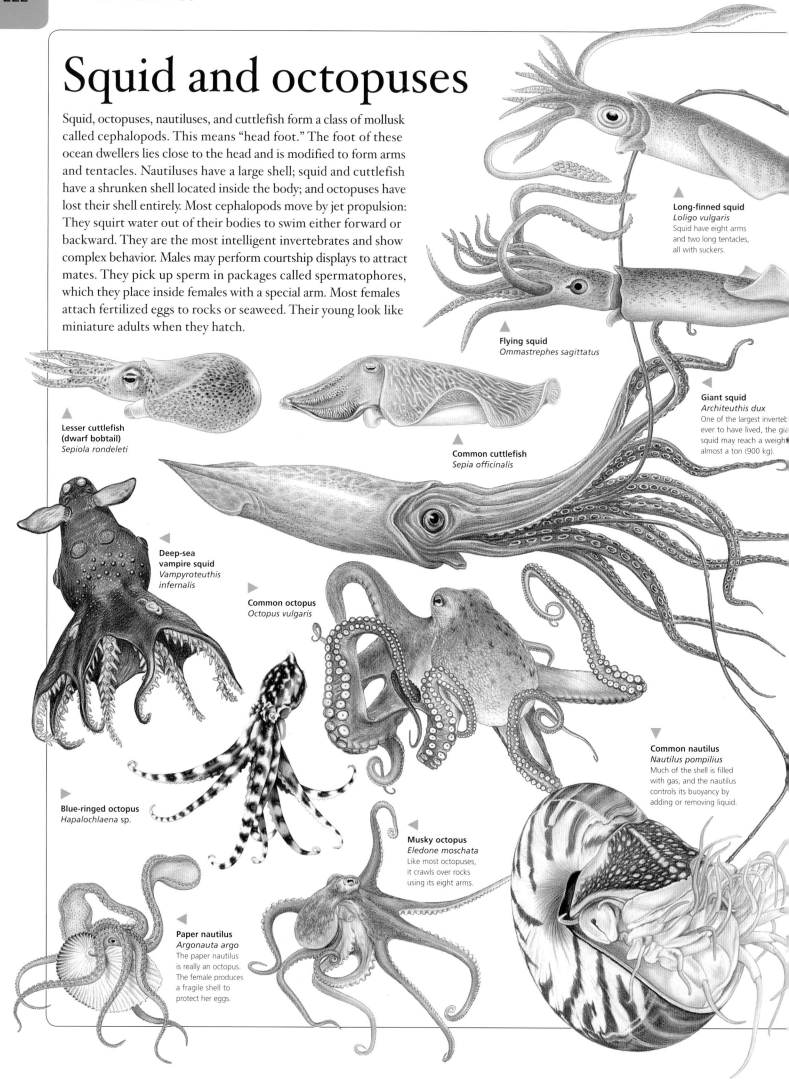

Long-finned squid
Loligo vulgaris
Squid have eight arms and two long tentacles, all with suckers.

Flying squid
Ommastrephes sagittatus

Giant squid
Architeuthis dux
One of the largest invertebrates ever to have lived, the giant squid may reach a weight of almost a ton (900 kg).

Lesser cuttlefish (dwarf bobtail)
Sepiola rondeleti

Common cuttlefish
Sepia officinalis

Deep-sea vampire squid
Vampyroteuthis infernalis

Common octopus
Octopus vulgaris

Common nautilus
Nautilus pompilius
Much of the shell is filled with gas, and the nautilus controls its buoyancy by adding or removing liquid.

Blue-ringed octopus
Hapalochlaena sp.

Musky octopus
Eledone moschata
Like most octopuses, it crawls over rocks using its eight arms.

Paper nautilus
Argonauta argo
The paper nautilus is really an octopus. The female produces a fragile shell to protect her eggs.

GIANT OF THE DEEP

CLASH OF THE TITANS

In September 2005, Japanese scientists made the first confirmed observations of a live giant squid in the wild and took the first photographs of the huge invertebrate swimming. It was at a depth of almost 3,000 feet (915 m), off the coast of Japan, in the North Pacific Ocean. Studies of dead giant squid have shown they eat deep-sea fish, but they may also eat sperm whales. The whales, in turn, may eat giant squid. Sailors, lighthouse keepers, and whalers have reported seeing the two species engaged in fierce battles. There have also been reports of giant squid attacking boats, possibly because the boats looked like whales. Large sucker scars thought to be from giant squid have been recorded on the bodies of dead sperm whales, and giant squid body parts have been found inside the whales.

Until recently, giant squid were known only from dead or dying specimens washed ashore.

Giant squid have the largest eyes of any animal, more than 10 inches (25 cm) across.

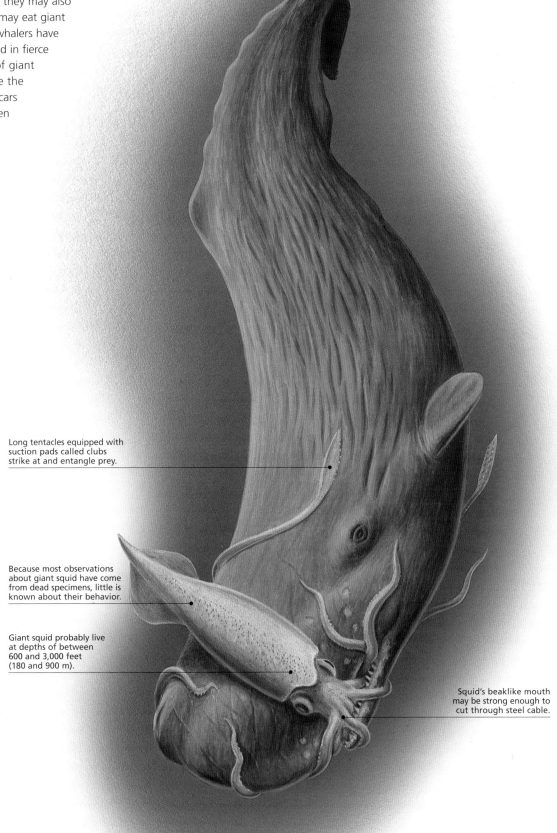

Powerful tail flukes help the sperm whale dive down to the cold ocean depths to hunt giant squid.

Long tentacles equipped with suction pads called clubs strike at and entangle prey.

Because most observations about giant squid have come from dead specimens, little is known about their behavior.

Giant squid probably live at depths of between 600 and 3,000 feet (180 and 900 m).

Squid's beaklike mouth may be strong enough to cut through steel cable.

22 CLASSES • 110 ORDERS • 2,120 FAMILIES • >1.1 MILLION SPECIES

Arthropods

Some spiders, such as this pink-toed tarantula, breathe using book lungs. Book lungs work like gills and are made up of stacked leaves of tissue.

Three-quarters of all animal species are arthropods, which means "jointed feet." All have appendages, such as limbs or antennae, with joints. Arthropods have an exoskeleton, a tough but flexible covering that encloses their soft body parts. Their bodies are divided into segments. In most cases, these segments are arranged into distinct body regions called tagma. For many, these consist of the head, abdomen, and an area in between called the thorax. The first arthropods appeared in the oceans, but they are now found in almost every habitat on Earth.

KINDS OF ARTHROPODS

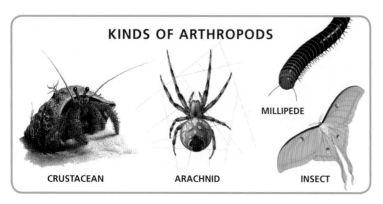

CRUSTACEAN   ARACHNID   INSECT

MILLIPEDE

ARTHROPOD ANATOMY

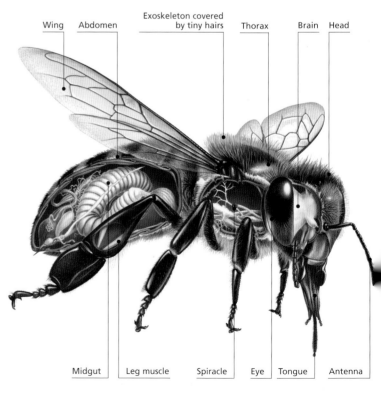

Wing   Abdomen   Exoskeleton covered by tiny hairs   Thorax   Brain   Head

Midgut   Leg muscle   Spiracle   Eye   Tongue   Antenna

Arachnids

Spiders, scorpions, daddy longlegs, mites, and ticks are arachnids. All but a small number live on land, and most are predators that eat other invertebrates. Arachnids are unable to swallow solid food. They liquefy their prey by squirting it with digestive juices, then they suck it up into their mouths. Arachnids have a two-part body: the abdomen and a single section composed of the head and thorax, called the cephalothorax. They have eight jointed limbs and a number of simple eyes that only detect variations in light. Spiders are the best known arachnids. They are noted for having silk glands. These produce webs and protective egg cases. Most spiders are venomous and inject poison into prey or enemies through fanglike mouthparts called chelicerae. The venom of only 30 out of 40,000 species can cause illness in humans.

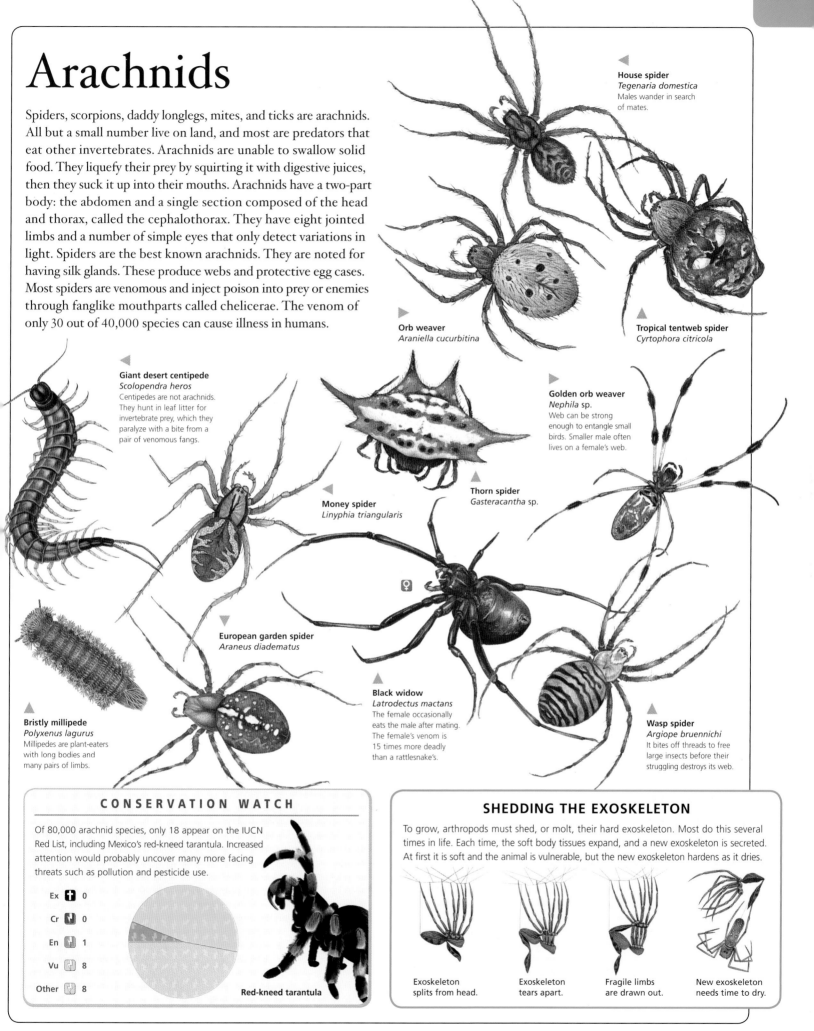

House spider
Tegenaria domestica
Males wander in search
of mates.

Orb weaver
Araniella cucurbitina

Tropical tentweb spider
Cyrtophora citricola

Giant desert centipede
Scolopendra heros
Centipedes are not arachnids.
They hunt in leaf litter for
invertebrate prey, which they
paralyze with a bite from a
pair of venomous fangs.

Golden orb weaver
Nephila sp.
Web can be strong
enough to entangle small
birds. Smaller male often
lives on a female's web.

Money spider
Linyphia triangularis

Thorn spider
Gasteracantha sp.

European garden spider
Araneus diadematus

Black widow
Latrodectus mactans
The female occasionally
eats the male after mating.
The female's venom is
15 times more deadly
than a rattlesnake's.

Wasp spider
Argiope bruennichi
It bites off threads to free
large insects before their
struggling destroys its web.

Bristly millipede
Polyxenus lagurus
Millipedes are plant-eaters
with long bodies and
many pairs of limbs.

CONSERVATION WATCH

Of 80,000 arachnid species, only 18 appear on the IUCN Red List, including Mexico's red-kneed tarantula. Increased attention would probably uncover many more facing threats such as pollution and pesticide use.

Ex	✝	0
Cr		0
En		1
Vu		8
Other		8

Red-kneed tarantula

SHEDDING THE EXOSKELETON

To grow, arthropods must shed, or molt, their hard exoskeleton. Most do this several times in life. Each time, the soft body tissues expand, and a new exoskeleton is secreted. At first it is soft and the animal is vulnerable, but the new exoskeleton hardens as it dries.

Exoskeleton
splits from head.

Exoskeleton
tears apart.

Fragile limbs
are drawn out.

New exoskeleton
needs time to dry.

Arachnids

Arachnids have two pairs of appendages near the mouth. The first pair are the chelicerae, which work like fangs. The second pair are pedipalps, sometimes called pincers. These may be used like antennae to sense the surrounding environment. The pedipalps of scorpions and some other arachnids have developed into large claws. Scorpions also have a stinger at the tip of their tails. Most species hide in crevices or burrows during the day and hunt at night. Although scorpions and spiders are the best known arachnids, the most abundant and varied are the mites and ticks. They occur in almost every habitat, from polar caps to deserts, and from hot springs to ocean depths. Some are parasites, feeding on the fluids of other animals or plants. Many spread bacteria that cause disease in other living things.

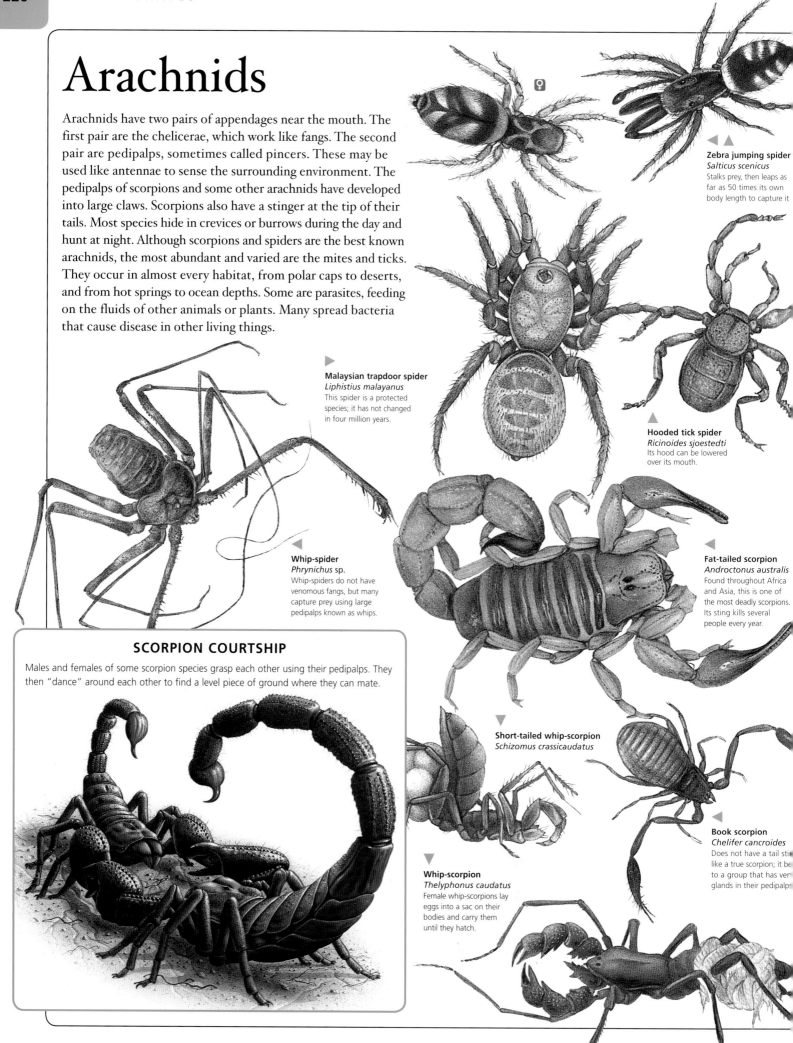

Zebra jumping spider
Salticus scenicus
Stalks prey, then leaps as far as 50 times its own body length to capture it

Malaysian trapdoor spider
Liphistius malayanus
This spider is a protected species; it has not changed in four million years.

Hooded tick spider
Ricinoides sjoestedti
Its hood can be lowered over its mouth.

Whip-spider
Phrynichus sp.
Whip-spiders do not have venomous fangs, but many capture prey using large pedipalps known as whips.

Fat-tailed scorpion
Androctonus australis
Found throughout Africa and Asia, this is one of the most deadly scorpions. Its sting kills several people every year.

Short-tailed whip-scorpion
Schizomus crassicaudatus

Whip-scorpion
Thelyphonus caudatus
Female whip-scorpions lay eggs into a sac on their bodies and carry them until they hatch.

Book scorpion
Chelifer cancroides
Does not have a tail stir like a true scorpion; it be to a group that has ven glands in their pedipalp:

SCORPION COURTSHIP

Males and females of some scorpion species grasp each other using their pedipalps. They then "dance" around each other to find a level piece of ground where they can mate.

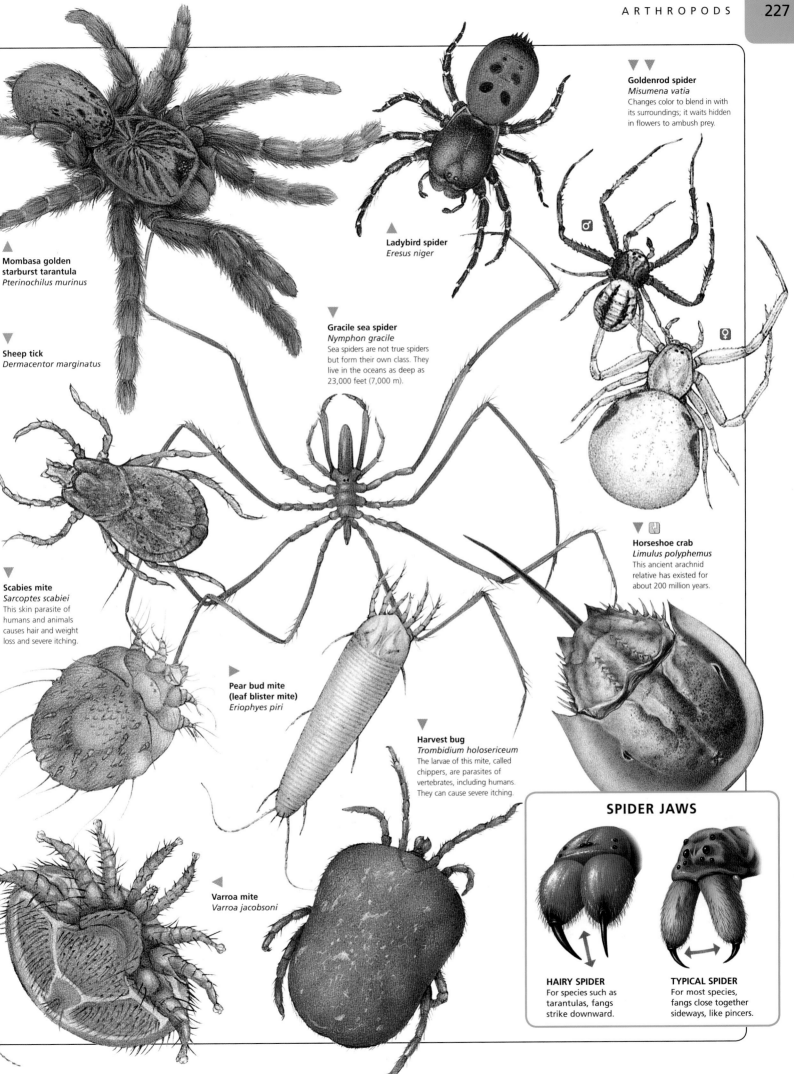

Mombasa golden starburst tarantula
Pterinochilus murinus

Sheep tick
Dermacentor marginatus

Scabies mite
Sarcoptes scabiei
This skin parasite of humans and animals causes hair and weight loss and severe itching.

Varroa mite
Varroa jacobsoni

Pear bud mite (leaf blister mite)
Eriophyes piri

Harvest bug
Trombidium holosericeum
The larvae of this mite, called chippers, are parasites of vertebrates, including humans. They can cause severe itching.

Ladybird spider
Eresus niger

Gracile sea spider
Nymphon gracile
Sea spiders are not true spiders but form their own class. They live in the oceans as deep as 23,000 feet (7,000 m).

Goldenrod spider
Misumena vatia
Changes color to blend in with its surroundings; it waits hidden in flowers to ambush prey.

Horseshoe crab
Limulus polyphemus
This ancient arachnid relative has existed for about 200 million years.

SPIDER JAWS

HAIRY SPIDER
For species such as tarantulas, fangs strike downward.

TYPICAL SPIDER
For most species, fangs close together sideways, like pincers.

Crabs and crayfish

Crabs and crayfish are crustaceans. This group ranges from waterfleas less than 1/100 inch (0.25 mm) in length to giant spider crabs with limbs 12 feet (3.7 m) long. A few crustacean species have adapted to life on land, but most live in salt or fresh water. Their bodies are similar to those of other arthropods, with a segmented body, jointed limbs, and a hard exoskeleton that must be shed to allow the body to grow. The head usually has two pairs of antennae; well-developed eyes, often on stalks; and three pairs of biting mouthparts. The front legs of many species have become claws that are used to collect food, fight off predators, or communicate with each other. Some females lay their eggs in water and leave them to develop on their own. Many, however, keep their eggs on their bodies until they hatch.

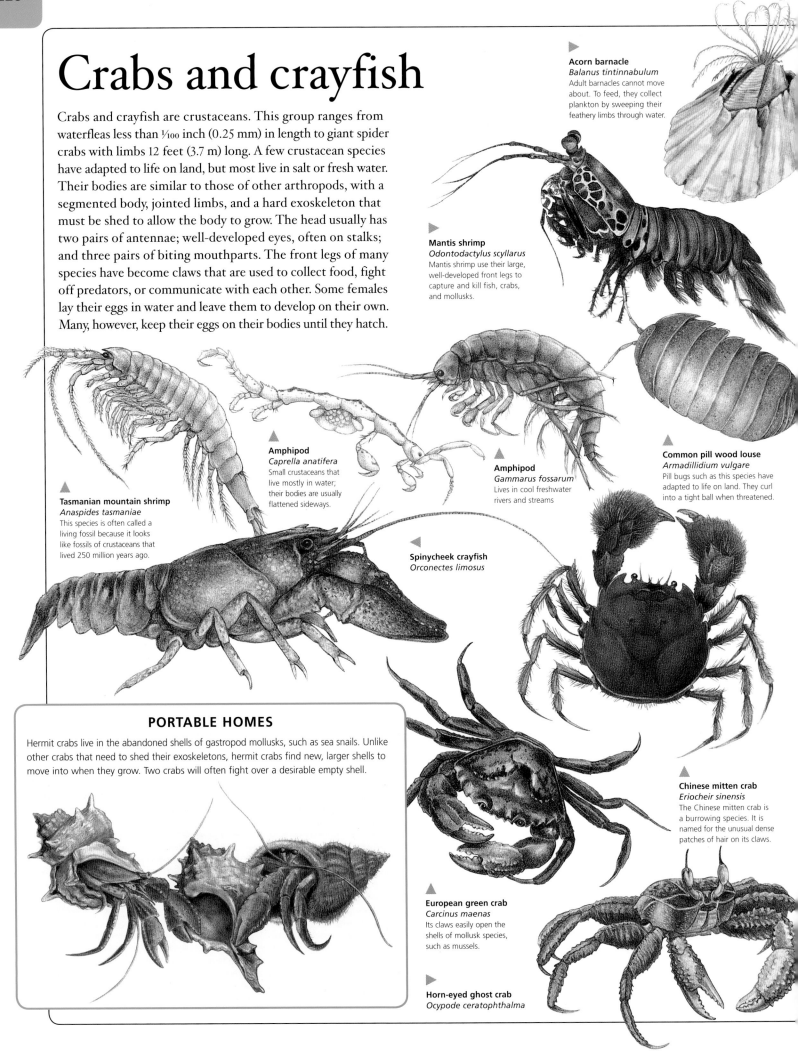

Acorn barnacle
Balanus tintinnabulum
Adult barnacles cannot move about. To feed, they collect plankton by sweeping their feathery limbs through water.

Mantis shrimp
Odontodactylus scyllarus
Mantis shrimp use their large, well-developed front legs to capture and kill fish, crabs, and mollusks.

Amphipod
Caprella anatifera
Small crustaceans that live mostly in water; their bodies are usually flattened sideways.

Amphipod
Gammarus fossarum
Lives in cool freshwater rivers and streams

Common pill wood louse
Armadillidium vulgare
Pill bugs such as this species have adapted to life on land. They curl into a tight ball when threatened.

Tasmanian mountain shrimp
Anaspides tasmaniae
This species is often called a living fossil because it looks like fossils of crustaceans that lived 250 million years ago.

Spinycheek crayfish
Orconectes limosus

Chinese mitten crab
Eriocheir sinensis
The Chinese mitten crab is a burrowing species. It is named for the unusual dense patches of hair on its claws.

PORTABLE HOMES

Hermit crabs live in the abandoned shells of gastropod mollusks, such as sea snails. Unlike other crabs that need to shed their exoskeletons, hermit crabs find new, larger shells to move into when they grow. Two crabs will often fight over a desirable empty shell.

European green crab
Carcinus maenas
Its claws easily open the shells of mollusk species, such as mussels.

Horn-eyed ghost crab
Ocypode ceratophthalma

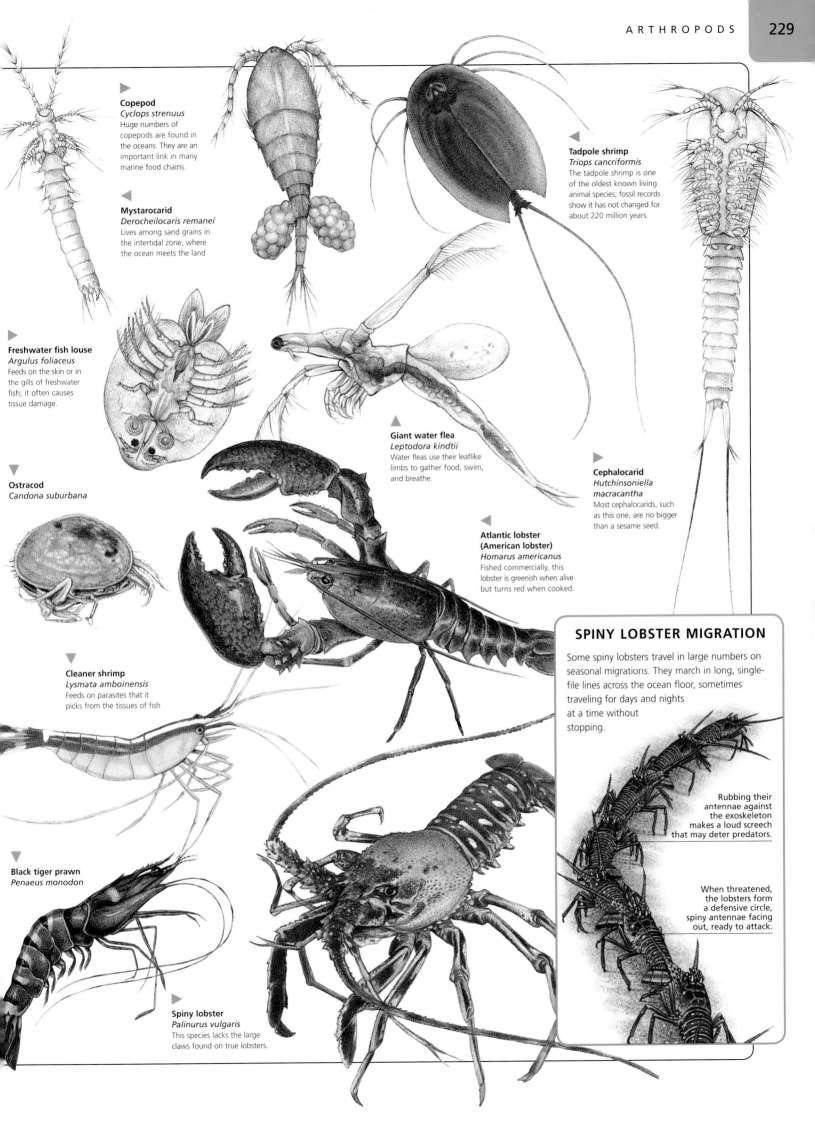

Copepod
Cyclops strenuus
Huge numbers of copepods are found in the oceans. They are an important link in many marine food chains.

Mystarocarid
Derocheilocaris remanei
Lives among sand grains in the intertidal zone, where the ocean meets the land

Tadpole shrimp
Triops cancriformis
The tadpole shrimp is one of the oldest known living animal species; fossil records show it has not changed for about 220 million years.

Freshwater fish louse
Argulus foliaceus
Feeds on the skin or in the gills of freshwater fish; it often causes tissue damage.

Ostracod
Candona suburbana

Giant water flea
Leptodora kindtii
Water fleas use their leaflike limbs to gather food, swim, and breathe.

Cephalocarid
Hutchinsoniella macracantha
Most cephalocarids, such as this one, are no bigger than a sesame seed.

Atlantic lobster (American lobster)
Homarus americanus
Fished commercially, this lobster is greenish when alive but turns red when cooked.

Cleaner shrimp
Lysmata amboinensis
Feeds on parasites that it picks from the tissues of fish

Black tiger prawn
Penaeus monodon

Spiny lobster
Palinurus vulgaris
This species lacks the large claws found on true lobsters.

SPINY LOBSTER MIGRATION

Some spiny lobsters travel in large numbers on seasonal migrations. They march in long, single-file lines across the ocean floor, sometimes traveling for days and nights at a time without stopping.

Rubbing their antennae against the exoskeleton makes a loud screech that may deter predators.

When threatened, the lobsters form a defensive circle, spiny antennae facing out, ready to attack.

29 ORDERS • 949 FAMILIES • >1 MILLION SPECIES

Insects

Most insects, such as this two-spotted lady beetle, are less than 2 inches (5 cm) long. Their size allows them to live in an enormous variety of habitats and develop into many different forms.

In many ways, insects are the most successful animals ever to have lived. More than half of all known animal species are insects. More than a million species have been discovered, but there may be as many as 30 million. There are also many more individuals than in other kinds of animals. The success of insects is partly due to their tough, but flexible, exoskeleton. This lets them move easily, protects them, and stops them from drying out. While some insects spread disease and destroy crops, most cause no harm and play important roles in the environment. About three-quarters of all flowering plants are pollinated by insects, and many animals depend on insects for food.

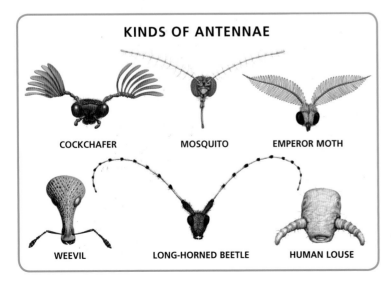

KINDS OF ANTENNAE

COCKCHAFER MOSQUITO EMPEROR MOTH

WEEVIL LONG-HORNED BEETLE HUMAN LOUSE

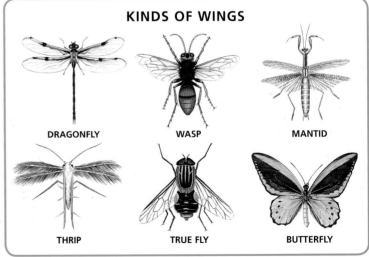

KINDS OF WINGS

DRAGONFLY WASP MANTID

THRIP TRUE FLY BUTTERFLY

Insects

Appearing 300 million years ago, dragonflies and damselflies are among the oldest living insect orders. They have wingspans of as much as 7½ inches (19 cm) across and usually live near water. They are predators that catch other insects while flying. Mantids also prey on other insects. Some of the largest species, which are 10 inches (25 cm) in length, also catch small birds and reptiles. They sit perfectly still, waiting for prey to appear. With lightning-fast reflexes, they then pounce and grasp prey with their strong front legs. Termites and cockroaches do not hunt. Cockroaches usually eat decaying plant matter as well as bird and mammal droppings. Social termites feed on dead wood. This recycles nutrients in their natural habitats but can damage buildings in urban environments. Grasshoppers and crickets are omnivorous: They eat both plants and animals. They are not usually social, but some group together in huge swarms.

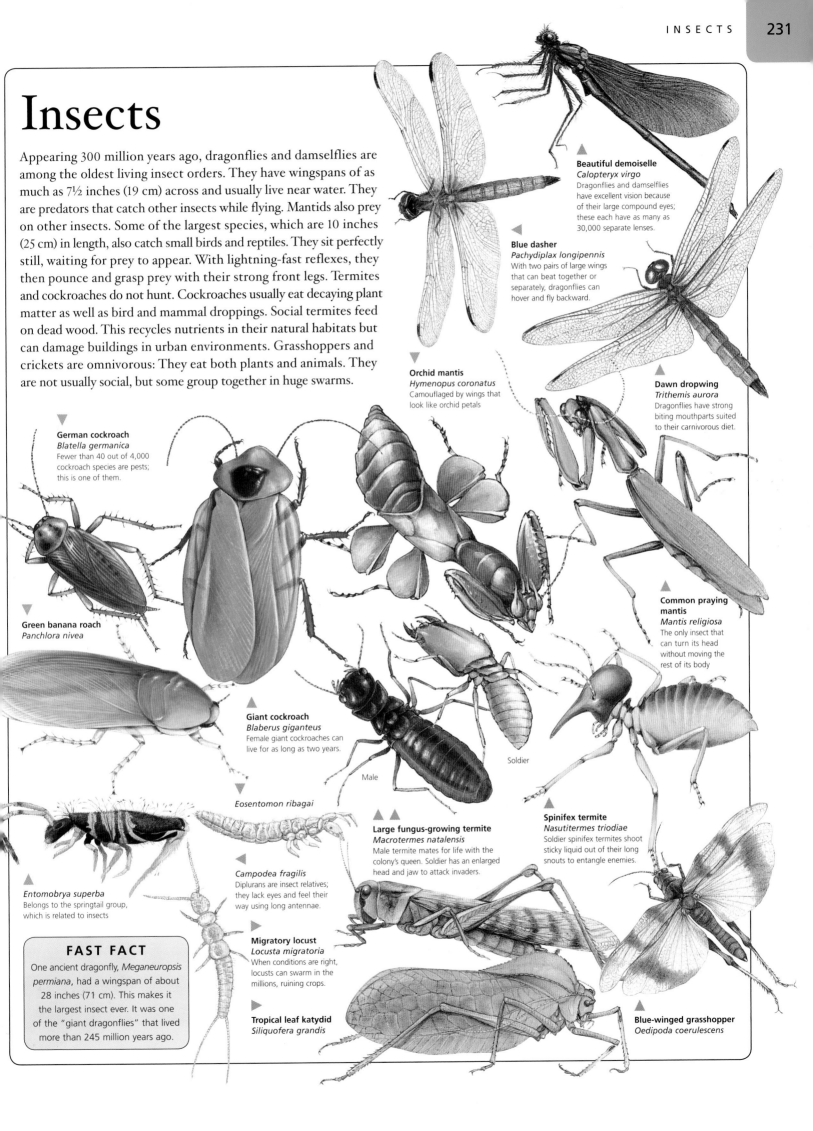

Beautiful demoiselle
Calopteryx virgo
Dragonflies and damselflies have excellent vision because of their large compound eyes; these each have as many as 30,000 separate lenses.

Blue dasher
Pachydiplax longipennis
With two pairs of large wings that can beat together or separately, dragonflies can hover and fly backward.

Orchid mantis
Hymenopus coronatus
Camouflaged by wings that look like orchid petals

Dawn dropwing
Trithemis aurora
Dragonflies have strong biting mouthparts suited to their carnivorous diet.

German cockroach
Blatella germanica
Fewer than 40 out of 4,000 cockroach species are pests; this is one of them.

Green banana roach
Panchlora nivea

Common praying mantis
Mantis religiosa
The only insect that can turn its head without moving the rest of its body

Giant cockroach
Blaberus giganteus
Female giant cockroaches can live for as long as two years.

Male

Soldier

Eosentomon ribagai

Entomobrya superba
Belongs to the springtail group, which is related to insects

Campodea fragilis
Diplurans are insect relatives; they lack eyes and feel their way using long antennae.

Large fungus-growing termite
Macrotermes natalensis
Male termite mates for life with the colony's queen. Soldier has an enlarged head and jaw to attack invaders.

Spinifex termite
Nasutitermes triodiae
Soldier spinifex termites shoot sticky liquid out of their long snouts to entangle enemies.

Migratory locust
Locusta migratoria
When conditions are right, locusts can swarm in the millions, ruining crops.

Tropical leaf katydid
Siliquofera grandis

Blue-winged grasshopper
Oedipoda coerulescens

FAST FACT

One ancient dragonfly, *Meganeuropsis permiana*, had a wingspan of about 28 inches (71 cm). This makes it the largest insect ever. It was one of the "giant dragonflies" that lived more than 245 million years ago.

Bugs

To many people, all insects are bugs. However, true bugs belong to an order of about 80,000 species called hemipterans. This includes cicadas, aphids, scale insects, and shield bugs. Many shield bugs, also known as stink bugs, have glands that produce a smelly substance when threatened. All hemipterans have mouthparts designed for piercing and sucking. These penetrate plant surfaces or animal skin and then inject digestive juices. This breaks down the tissues inside, so they can be sucked up as a liquid. Most bugs feed on plant sap. Others suck the blood of vertebrate animals or prey on other insects. Bugs can be found in most land habitats around the world. There are even some that have adapted to life in or on water. These include sea skaters, which are the only insects that live in the open ocean.

CONSERVATION WATCH

The IUCN has assessed fewer than 800 of all known insect species; most of these are on the Red List. Of the more than 80,000 species of bugs, 5 appear on the IUCN Red List. The unusual life cycle of periodic cicadas, which involves every adult appearing above ground at the same time, makes them vulnerable.

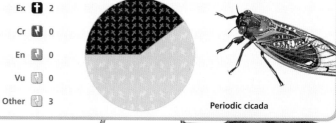

Ex	2
Cr	0
En	0
Vu	0
Other	3

Periodic cicada

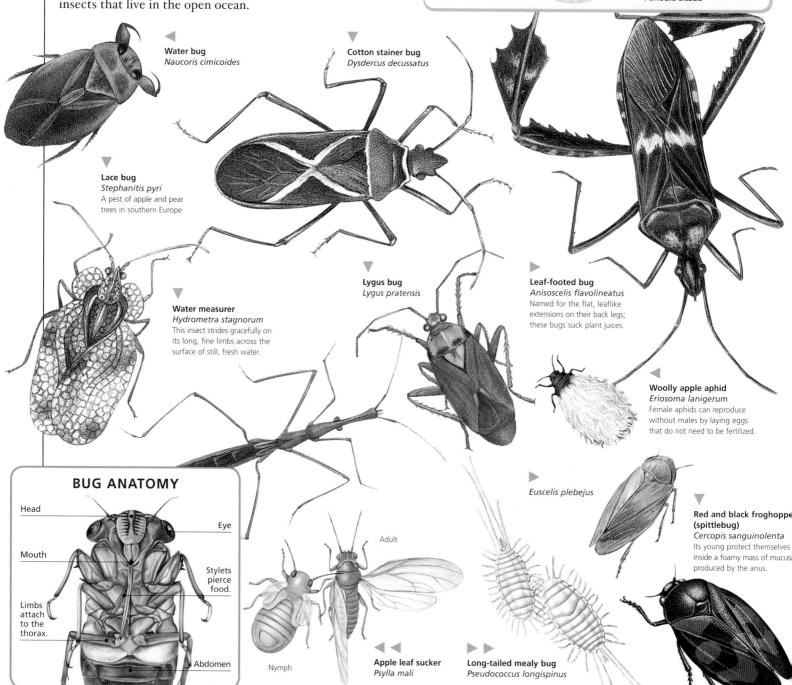

Water bug
Naucoris cimicoides

Cotton stainer bug
Dysdercus decussatus

Lace bug
Stephanitis pyri
A pest of apple and pear trees in southern Europe

Water measurer
Hydrometra stagnorum
This insect strides gracefully on its long, fine limbs across the surface of still, fresh water.

Lygus bug
Lygus pratensis

Leaf-footed bug
Anisoscelis flavolineatus
Named for the flat, leaflike extensions on their back legs; these bugs suck plant juices.

Woolly apple aphid
Eriosoma lanigerum
Female aphids can reproduce without males by laying eggs that do not need to be fertilized.

Euscelis plebejus

Red and black froghopper (spittlebug)
Cercopis sanguinolenta
Its young protect themselves inside a foamy mass of mucus produced by the anus.

BUG ANATOMY

Head

Eye

Mouth

Stylets pierce food.

Limbs attach to the thorax.

Abdomen

Adult

Nymph

Apple leaf sucker
Psylla mali

Long-tailed mealy bug
Pseudococcus longispinus

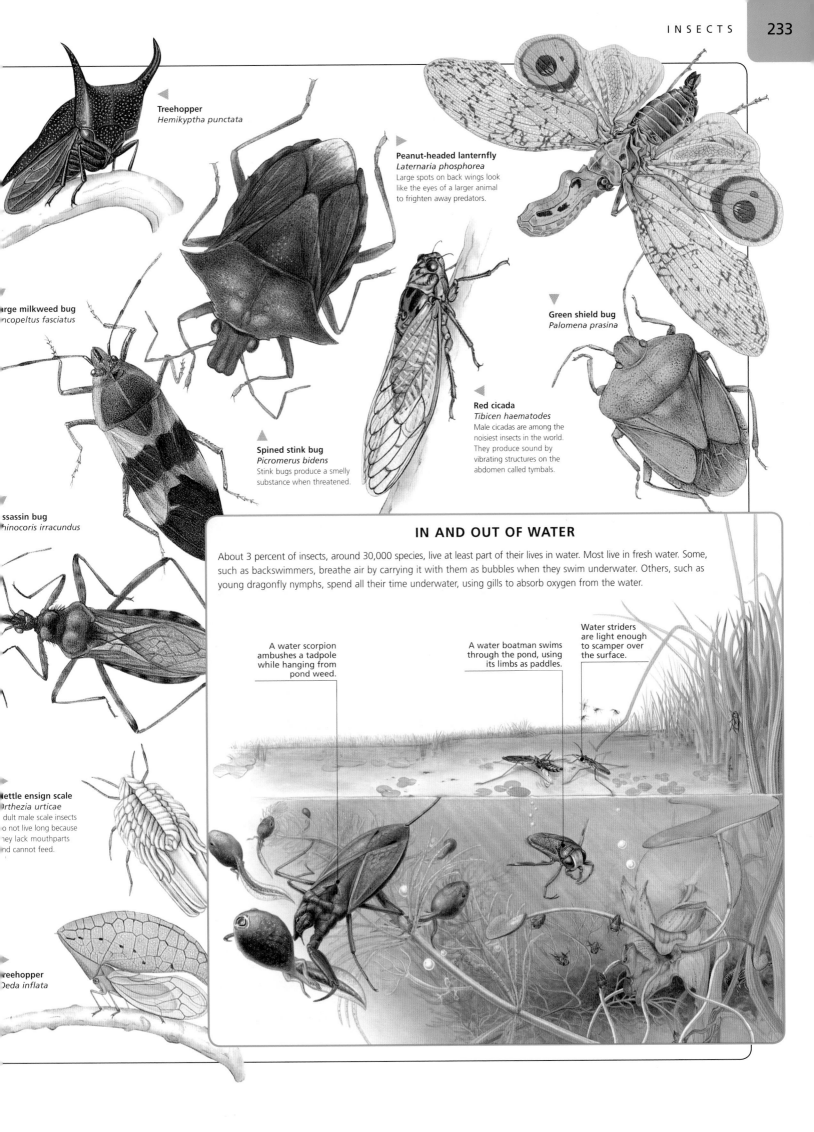

Treehopper
Hemikyptha punctata

Peanut-headed lanternfly
Laternaria phosphorea
Large spots on back wings look like the eyes of a larger animal to frighten away predators.

arge milkweed bug
ncopeltus fasciatus

Green shield bug
Palomena prasina

Spined stink bug
Picromerus bidens
Stink bugs produce a smelly substance when threatened.

Red cicada
Tibicen haematodes
Male cicadas are among the noisiest insects in the world. They produce sound by vibrating structures on the abdomen called tymbals.

ssassin bug
hinocoris irracundus

ettle ensign scale
rthezia urticae
dult male scale insects o not live long because ey lack mouthparts nd cannot feed.

reehopper
Deda inflata

IN AND OUT OF WATER

About 3 percent of insects, around 30,000 species, live at least part of their lives in water. Most live in fresh water. Some, such as backswimmers, breathe air by carrying it with them as bubbles when they swim underwater. Others, such as young dragonfly nymphs, spend all their time underwater, using gills to absorb oxygen from the water.

A water scorpion ambushes a tadpole while hanging from pond weed.

A water boatman swims through the pond, using its limbs as paddles.

Water striders are light enough to scamper over the surface.

Beetles

About one in every four animals on Earth is a beetle. This diverse order, called coleopterans, includes glow worms and fireflies. Beetles can be found in almost every habitat, from Arctic wastelands to lush woodlands and the surface waters of lakes. Most species live in the fertile forests of the tropics. Beetles generally live on the ground, but some live in trees, in water, or underground. One of the smallest is the feather-winged beetle, which is just ¹⁄₁₀₀ inch (0.25 mm) long. The largest is the American longhorn beetle, which can grow longer than 6½ inches (17 cm). The mouthparts of beetles are adapted for biting but can be used in many different ways. Plant-eating beetles may eat roots, seeds, stems, leaves, flowers, fruit, or wood. Predatory beetles usually feed on other invertebrates.

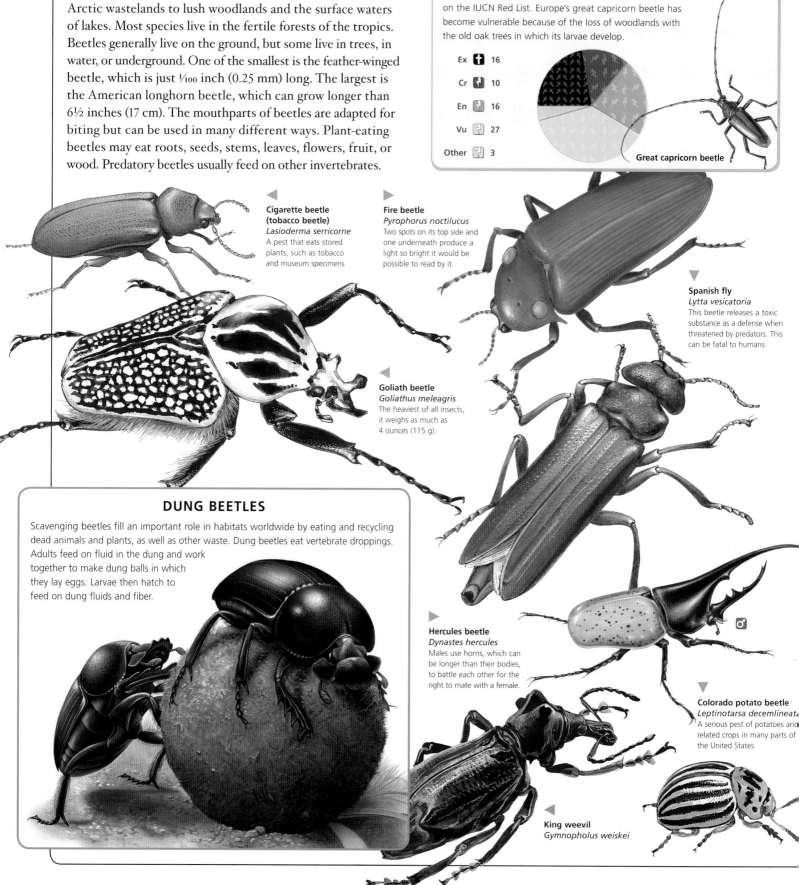

CONSERVATION WATCH

Of the more than 370,000 known beetle species, 72 appear on the IUCN Red List. Europe's great capricorn beetle has become vulnerable because of the loss of woodlands with the old oak trees in which its larvae develop.

Ex	🕆	16
Cr		10
En		16
Vu		27
Other		3

Great capricorn beetle

Cigarette beetle (tobacco beetle)
Lasioderma serricorne
A pest that eats stored plants, such as tobacco and museum specimens

Fire beetle
Pyrophorus noctilucus
Two spots on its top side and one underneath produce a light so bright it would be possible to read by it.

Spanish fly
Lytta vesicatoria
This beetle releases a toxic substance as a defense when threatened by predators. This can be fatal to humans.

Goliath beetle
Goliathus meleagris
The heaviest of all insects, it weighs as much as 4 ounces (115 g).

DUNG BEETLES

Scavenging beetles fill an important role in habitats worldwide by eating and recycling dead animals and plants, as well as other waste. Dung beetles eat vertebrate droppings. Adults feed on fluid in the dung and work together to make dung balls in which they lay eggs. Larvae then hatch to feed on dung fluids and fiber.

Hercules beetle
Dynastes hercules
Males use horns, which can be longer than their bodies, to battle each other for the right to mate with a female.

Colorado potato beetle
Leptinotarsa decemlineata
A serious pest of potatoes and related crops in many parts of the United States

King weevil
Gymnopholus weiskei

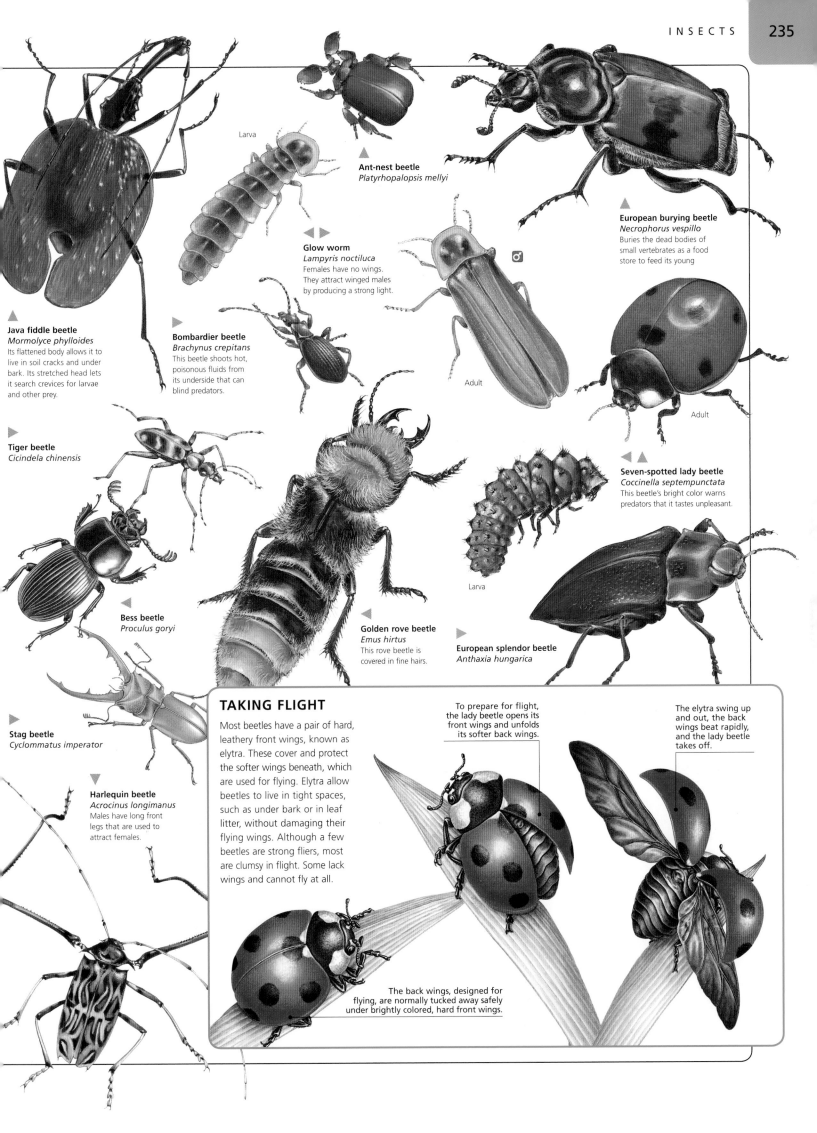

Larva

Ant-nest beetle
Platyrhopalopsis mellyi

European burying beetle
Necrophorus vespillo
Buries the dead bodies of
small vertebrates as a food
store to feed its young

Glow worm
Lampyris noctiluca
Females have no wings.
They attract winged males
by producing a strong light.

Java fiddle beetle
Mormolyce phylloides
Its flattened body allows it to
live in soil cracks and under
bark. Its stretched head lets
it search crevices for larvae
and other prey.

Bombardier beetle
Brachynus crepitans
This beetle shoots hot,
poisonous fluids from
its underside that can
blind predators.

Adult

Seven-spotted lady beetle
Coccinella septempunctata
This beetle's bright color warns
predators that it tastes unpleasant.

Tiger beetle
Cicindela chinensis

Adult

Larva

Bess beetle
Proculus goryi

Golden rove beetle
Emus hirtus
This rove beetle is
covered in fine hairs.

European splendor beetle
Anthaxia hungarica

Stag beetle
Cyclommatus imperator

Harlequin beetle
Acrocinus longimanus
Males have long front
legs that are used to
attract females.

TAKING FLIGHT

Most beetles have a pair of hard,
leathery front wings, known as
elytra. These cover and protect
the softer wings beneath, which
are used for flying. Elytra allow
beetles to live in tight spaces,
such as under bark or in leaf
litter, without damaging their
flying wings. Although a few
beetles are strong fliers, most
are clumsy in flight. Some lack
wings and cannot fly at all.

To prepare for flight,
the lady beetle opens its
front wings and unfolds
its softer back wings.

The elytra swing up
and out, the back
wings beat rapidly,
and the lady beetle
takes off.

The back wings, designed for
flying, are normally tucked away safely
under brightly colored, hard front wings.

CHANGING FORMS

DRAGONFLY LIFE CYCLE

Some insects look like small versions of their parents when they hatch, but most do not. They need to go through a change called metamorphosis to become adults. For some insects, such as bugs and dragonflies, this change occurs gradually. This is called simple metamorphosis. Young dragonflies called nymphs hatch from eggs. They live underwater and do not have wings. To develop into their adult form, they molt several times. During each molt they shed their exoskeleton, growing and changing a little more each time. It can take as long as five years before they finally climb up a plant stem, molt for the last time, and emerge as fully grown adults that can fly.

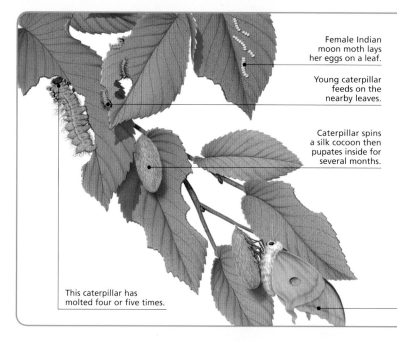

Female Indian moon moth lays her eggs on a leaf.

Young caterpillar feeds on the nearby leaves.

Caterpillar spins a silk cocoon then pupates inside for several months.

This caterpillar has molted four or five times.

MOTH LIFE CYCLE

For butterflies and moths to become adults, they change completely. This is called complex metamorphosis. They hatch from eggs as soft-bodied larvae, or caterpillars. They eat and grow constantly until ready to pupate, or change into adults. During this time, their juvenile larval body parts break down and adult features grow. Finally, an adult moth emerges.

A new adult moon moth hangs to stretch and dry its wings.

Female dragonfly lays her eggs in a plant below the water's surface.

Tiny nymphs hatch by chewing their way out of their egg cases.

Adult male and female dragonflies mate on plants in or near the water.

Nymphs catch and eat tadpoles and worms.

Nymph climbs out of the water for its final molt into adulthood.

Nymph swallows air to burst open its outer skeleton.

New adult dragonfly basks in the sun, extending its wings.

Flies

Houseflies and mosquitoes are known as dipterans. This order includes gnats, midges, blowflies, fruit flies, crane flies, hover flies, and horseflies. Most flying insects use four wings to fly, but dipterans usually fly with just their front pair. The back pair, called halteres, have become very small and look like two tiny clubs instead of wings. During flight, the halteres vibrate up and down in time with the front wings to help balance the insect. Some dipterans have lost their wings completely and cannot fly. Flies eat liquid food with mouthparts that are designed for sucking. Their feet have sticky pads with tiny claws that allow them to walk on smooth surfaces. They can even walk upside down. Most flies have a large head and compound eyes, each with as many as 4,000 lenses. This gives them excellent vision.

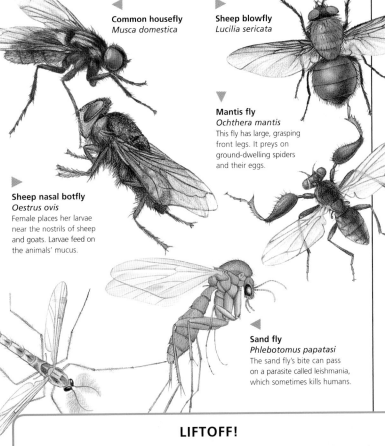

Common housefly
Musca domestica

Sheep blowfly
Lucilia sericata

Mantis fly
Ochthera mantis
This fly has large, grasping front legs. It preys on ground-dwelling spiders and their eggs.

Sheep nasal botfly
Oestrus ovis
Female places her larvae near the nostrils of sheep and goats. Larvae feed on the animals' mucus.

Sand fly
Phlebotomus papatasi
The sand fly's bite can pass on a parasite called leishmania, which sometimes kills humans.

Buzzer midge
Chironomus plumosus
Flies in large buzzing swarms

House mosquito
Culex pipiens
Male feeds on nectar, but the female needs protein from a vertebrate's blood for her eggs to develop.

Adult

Aquatic larva (wriggler)

Robber fly
Laphria flava
Preys on other insects: It injects them with paralyzing saliva, then sucks out their body fluids.

Hover fly
Syrphus ribesii

Greater bee fly
Bombylius major
Adults look like bees; larvae are parasites in some bee species.

Stalk-eyed fly
Diopsis tenuipes
Its eyes and small antennae are carried on long stalks. This probably improves vision.

Horsefly
Tabanus bovinus
Females are bloodsuckers that find mammals to feed on by tracking the carbon dioxide in their breath.

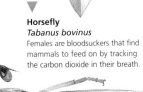

LIFTOFF!

To fly, the deerfly tilts its wings and beats them. This pushes air backward, giving it the thrust it needs for liftoff. It adjusts the angle of its wings' front edges to change the thrust. The more they dip, the stronger the thrust, and the faster the deerfly travels.

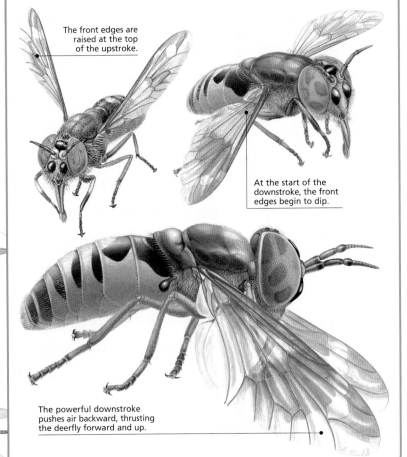

The front edges are raised at the top of the upstroke.

At the start of the downstroke, the front edges begin to dip.

The powerful downstroke pushes air backward, thrusting the deerfly forward and up.

Butterflies and moths

Butterflies and moths are lepidopterans. This means "scale wing" in Greek: Their wings and bodies are covered by tiny, colored, overlapping scales. These are actually hollow, flattened hairs. More than 85 percent of lepidopterans are moths, but butterflies are more easily recognized. Butterflies are diurnal, and their wings are often brightly colored. Moths are nocturnal and usually drab in color. Both butterflies and moths have two pairs of wings. These are linked by tiny hooks so that they beat together when flying. Almost all lepidopterans are plant-eaters. The mouthparts of most butterflies form a long tube called a proboscis. This is usually coiled up, but uncurls to feed on flower nectar. Some lack mouthparts and do not feed at all. Lepidopteran larvae are called caterpillars; most feed on plant matter.

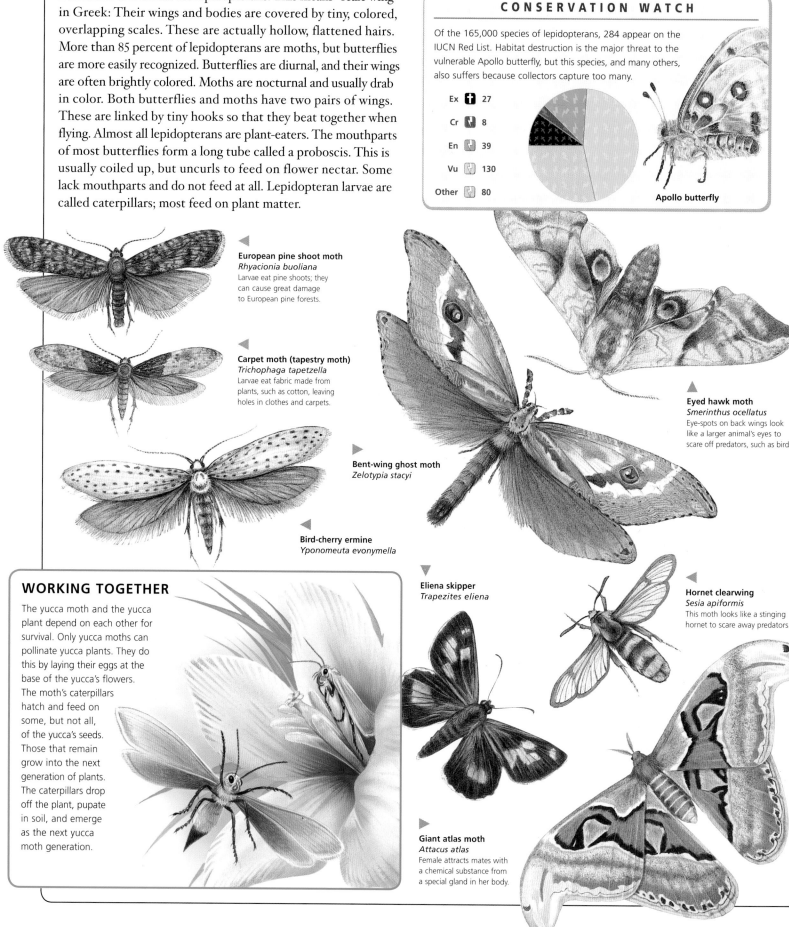

CONSERVATION WATCH

Of the 165,000 species of lepidopterans, 284 appear on the IUCN Red List. Habitat destruction is the major threat to the vulnerable Apollo butterfly, but this species, and many others, also suffers because collectors capture too many.

Ex 27
Cr 8
En 39
Vu 130
Other 80

Apollo butterfly

European pine shoot moth
Rhyacionia buoliana
Larvae eat pine shoots; they can cause great damage to European pine forests.

Carpet moth (tapestry moth)
Trichophaga tapetzella
Larvae eat fabric made from plants, such as cotton, leaving holes in clothes and carpets.

Bent-wing ghost moth
Zelotypia stacyi

Bird-cherry ermine
Yponomeuta evonymella

Eyed hawk moth
Smerinthus ocellatus
Eye-spots on back wings look like a larger animal's eyes to scare off predators, such as bird

Eliena skipper
Trapezites eliena

Hornet clearwing
Sesia apiformis
This moth looks like a stinging hornet to scare away predators.

Giant atlas moth
Attacus atlas
Female attracts mates with a chemical substance from a special gland in her body.

WORKING TOGETHER

The yucca moth and the yucca plant depend on each other for survival. Only yucca moths can pollinate yucca plants. They do this by laying their eggs at the base of the yucca's flowers. The moth's caterpillars hatch and feed on some, but not all, of the yucca's seeds. Those that remain grow into the next generation of plants. The caterpillars drop off the plant, pupate in soil, and emerge as the next yucca moth generation.

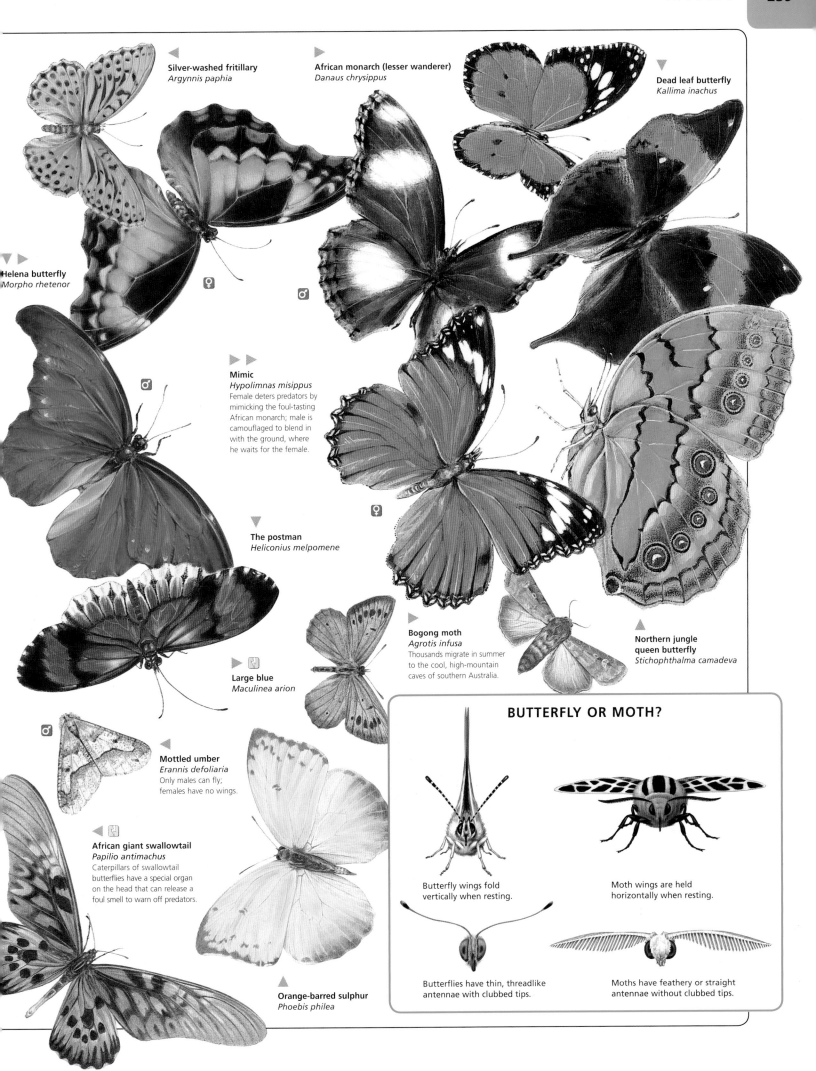

Silver-washed fritillary
Argynnis paphia

African monarch (lesser wanderer)
Danaus chrysippus

Dead leaf butterfly
Kallima inachus

Helena butterfly
Morpho rhetenor

Mimic
Hypolimnas misippus
Female deters predators by mimicking the foul-tasting African monarch; male is camouflaged to blend in with the ground, where he waits for the female.

The postman
Heliconius melpomene

Bogong moth
Agrotis infusa
Thousands migrate in summer to the cool, high-mountain caves of southern Australia.

Northern jungle queen butterfly
Stichophthalma camadeva

Large blue
Maculinea arion

Mottled umber
Erannis defoliaria
Only males can fly; females have no wings.

African giant swallowtail
Papilio antimachus
Caterpillars of swallowtail butterflies have a special organ on the head that can release a foul smell to warn off predators.

Orange-barred sulphur
Phoebis philea

BUTTERFLY OR MOTH?

Butterfly wings fold vertically when resting.

Moth wings are held horizontally when resting.

Butterflies have thin, threadlike antennae with clubbed tips.

Moths have feathery or straight antennae without clubbed tips.

Bees, wasps, and ants

Bees, wasps, ants, and sawflies are hymenopterids, a word that means "membrane wing" in Greek. Hymenopterids usually have two pairs of see-through wings. The back pair is attached to the larger front pair by tiny hooks, so that they beat together during flight. The mouthparts of adult hymenopterids are designed for biting or sucking. They may eat plants or other insects; some are parasites. Apart from sawflies, all species have a slim "waist" between the middle part of the body, the thorax, and the back part, the abdomen. The smallest species is the fairyfly wasp, which is so tiny it could fly through the eye of a needle. The largest is the spider-eating wasp, which is about 2¾ inches (7 cm) long. Although many species live alone, some live and work together in complex societies called colonies.

Larva

Rose sawfly
Arge ochropus

Adult

Sirex parasite (saber wasp)
Rhyssa persuasoria
Female drills through wood with the long, egg-laying appendage at the tip of her abdomen. She lays eggs directly into the wood-boring larvae of other insects.

Weaver ant
Oecophylla smaragdina

Currant sawfly
Nematus ribesii
Larvae are pests that can rapidly strip currant bushes of their leaves.

Common wasp
Vespula vulgaris

Red-tailed bumblebee
Bombus lapidarius
Bumblebees are related to honeybees, but their colonies are much smaller: They consist of only a hundred or so members.

INTO THE POT

Adult potter wasps sting and paralyze caterpillars, then stash them in mud nests shaped like small pots. The female lays an egg in each nest. When the larva hatches, it eats the caterpillar.

Potter wasp
Eumenes pomiformis

Paper wasp
Polistes gallicus
Builds a nest of paper-thin six-sided cells by rolling wood particles around in its mouth with saliva

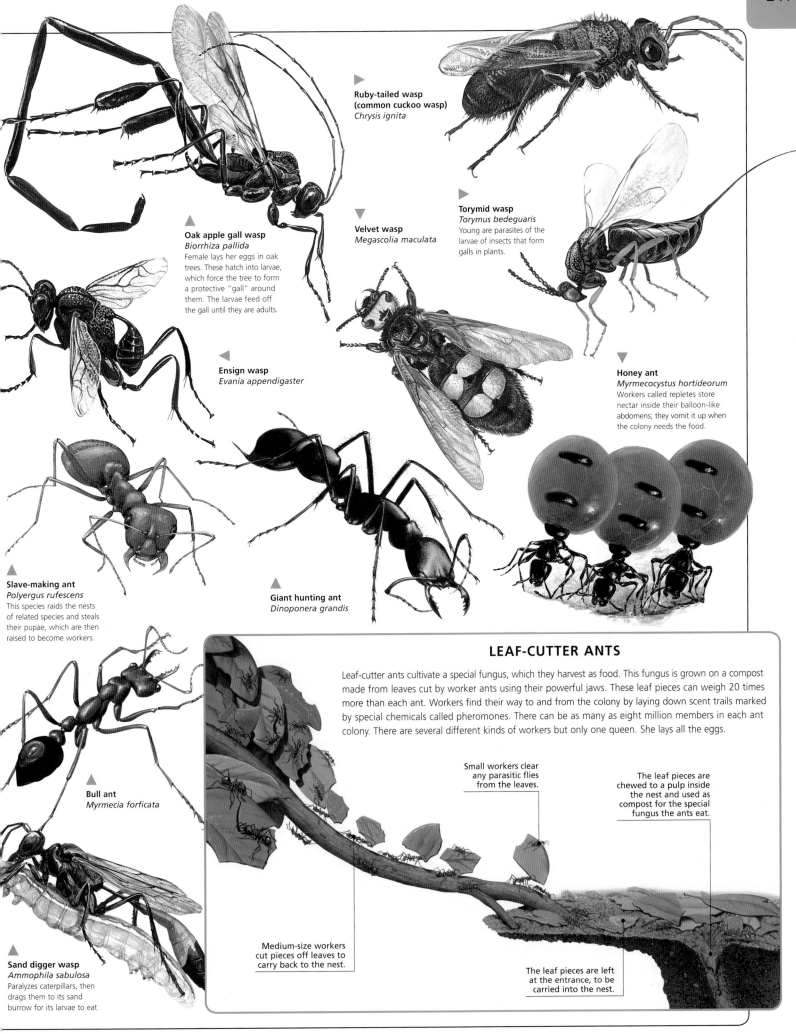

**Ruby-tailed wasp
(common cuckoo wasp)**
Chrysis ignita

Oak apple gall wasp
Biorrhiza pallida
Female lays her eggs in oak trees. These hatch into larvae, which force the tree to form a protective "gall" around them. The larvae feed off the gall until they are adults.

Velvet wasp
Megascolia maculata

Torymid wasp
Torymus bedeguaris
Young are parasites of the larvae of insects that form galls in plants.

Ensign wasp
Evania appendigaster

Honey ant
Myrmecocystus hortideorum
Workers called repletes store nectar inside their balloon-like abdomens; they vomit it up when the colony needs the food.

Slave-making ant
Polyergus rufescens
This species raids the nests of related species and steals their pupae, which are then raised to become workers.

Giant hunting ant
Dinoponera grandis

Bull ant
Myrmecia forficata

Sand digger wasp
Ammophila sabulosa
Paralyzes caterpillars, then drags them to its sand burrow for its larvae to eat

LEAF-CUTTER ANTS

Leaf-cutter ants cultivate a special fungus, which they harvest as food. This fungus is grown on a compost made from leaves cut by worker ants using their powerful jaws. These leaf pieces can weigh 20 times more than each ant. Workers find their way to and from the colony by laying down scent trails marked by special chemicals called pheromones. There can be as many as eight million members in each ant colony. There are several different kinds of workers but only one queen. She lays all the eggs.

Small workers clear any parasitic flies from the leaves.

The leaf pieces are chewed to a pulp inside the nest and used as compost for the special fungus the ants eat.

Medium-size workers cut pieces off leaves to carry back to the nest.

The leaf pieces are left at the entrance, to be carried into the nest.

HIVE OF ACTIVITY

Honeybee colonies produce far more honey than bees need. Humans have been keeping and raiding hives for this sweet food for many thousands of years.

HONEYBEE COLONY

Honeybees live in highly organized colonies that may contain thousands of individuals. Each is ruled by just one queen, the largest bee in the hive. She lays all the eggs—sometimes as many as 1,500 eggs a day. Most fertilized eggs produce female workers, but some can become new queens. Unfertilized eggs develop into male drones. Drones have short lives. Their only purpose is to mate with the ruling queen. Colonies live in hives built by the workers. They construct combs of six-sided wax cells that are water-resistant. Some are used as chambers in which the larvae develop. Other cells store honey to feed the colony when nectar and flowers are scarce. As well as building the hive, workers attend to the young bees and gather food for the colony. Glands in their heads produce a substance called royal jelly, which is fed to the larvae. All larvae are fed this at first, but future queens are fed only this substance. When a colony reaches its maximum size, the old queen flies off to begin a new one, followed by thousands of workers. The first new queen to emerge becomes ruler of the old colony.

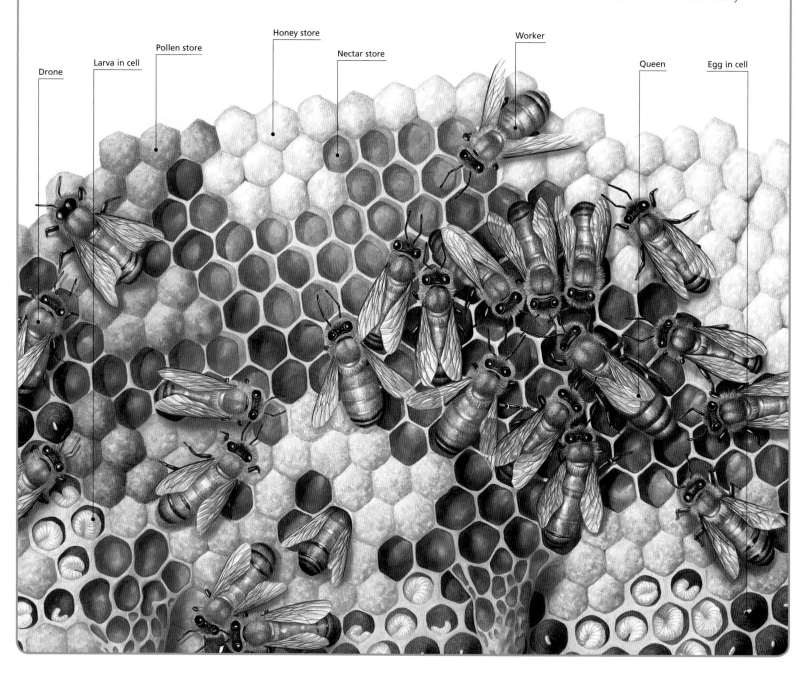

Drone • Larva in cell • Pollen store • Honey store • Nectar store • Worker • Queen • Egg in cell

5 CLASSES • 36 ORDERS • 145 FAMILIES • 6,000 SPECIES

Sea Stars

Sea stars are echinoderms. This phylum also contains sea urchins, brittle stars, feather stars, and sea cucumbers. As adults, these animals have unusual body shapes. Instead of having two sides that look the same, their bodies are usually arranged into five equal parts around a central axis. This is called radial symmetry. Most of the body's organs are organized in this pattern. Sea stars and their relatives have an internal skeleton of plates made from calcium. These often have spines or small lumps. All echinoderms live in marine environments. Most can move across sediment; however, sea lilies are fixed to the seafloor by a long stalk, and some sea cucumbers float in the open ocean. The larvae of many echinoderms look nothing like their parents until they settle onto the seafloor to change into their adult form.

CONSERVATION WATCH

Just 1 of the 6,000 known echinoderm species appears on the IUCN Red List. This is the edible sea urchin. It is at risk because people harvest so many for their eggs, which are prized as a delicacy.

Ex 🕆 0
Cr 🗴 0
En 🗴 0
Vu 🗴 0
Other 🗴 1

Edible sea urchin

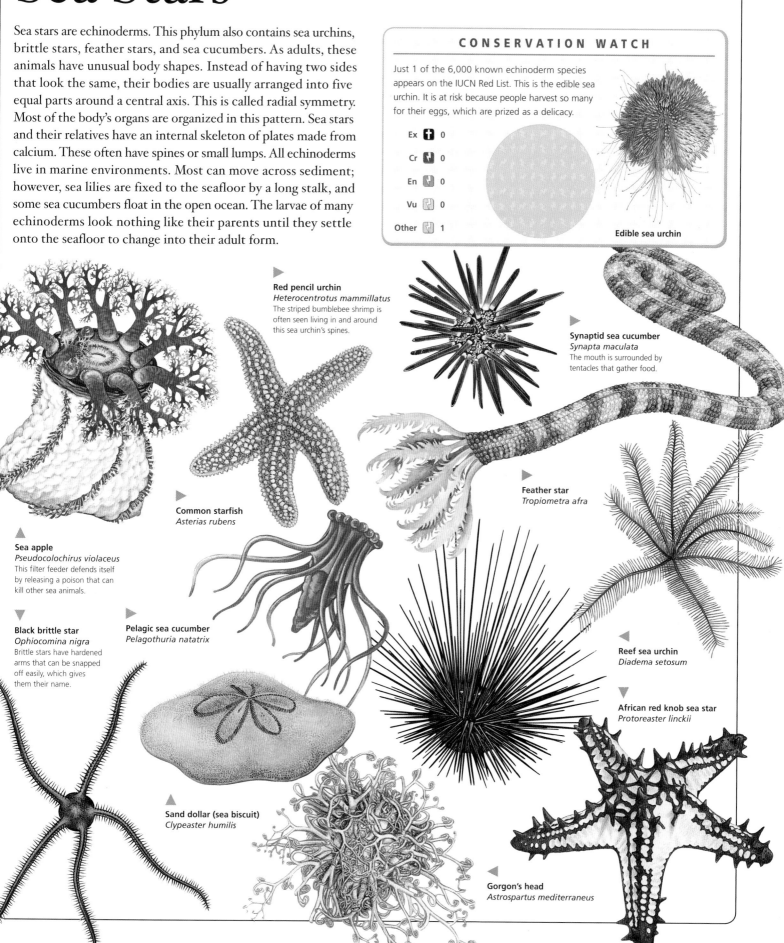

Red pencil urchin
Heterocentrotus mammillatus
The striped bumblebee shrimp is often seen living in and around this sea urchin's spines.

Synaptid sea cucumber
Synapta maculata
The mouth is surrounded by tentacles that gather food.

Common starfish
Asterias rubens

Feather star
Tropiometra afra

Sea apple
Pseudocolochirus violaceus
This filter feeder defends itself by releasing a poison that can kill other sea animals.

Black brittle star
Ophiocomina nigra
Brittle stars have hardened arms that can be snapped off easily, which gives them their name.

Pelagic sea cucumber
Pelagothuria natatrix

Reef sea urchin
Diadema setosum

African red knob sea star
Protoreaster linckii

Sand dollar (sea biscuit)
Clypeaster humilis

Gorgon's head
Astrospartus mediterraneus

Glossary

Abdomen A section of the body where food is usually digested; also the rear section of insects and other arthropods

Albumen Clear, jelly-like fluid between the shell and yolk of an egg; it provides the developing embryo with protection as well as water and nutrition.

Anatomy Structure of an animal; also science concerned with animal structure

Ancestor A related animal that lived in the past

Antenna An insect head organ used to sense information about the surrounding environment (pl. antennae)

Antlers Bony head growths on deer

Aquatic Living in water

Australasia Region consisting of Australia, New Zealand, and Melanesia, a group of Pacific islands

Bacteria Microscopic life-forms that are usually just a single cell. Their simple structure is so different from any other living cells that they belong to their own kingdom: Protista. (sing. bacterium)

Barbels Thin, fleshy growths around an animal's mouth, used to find food; they are common in some fish groups.

Binocular vision Using two eyes at the same time to see; this helps judge how far away an object is.

Bioluminescence Light produced by living organisms

Blubber A thick layer of fat beneath the skin of some mammals helps keep them warm. It is well developed in marine mammals such as whales and seals.

Camouflage Colors and patterns on an animal's outer cover that help it blend into its surrounding environment

Canines Sharp pointed teeth in mammals; they are used for tearing food.

Carapace A hard outer covering, such as a turtle's shell; this provides protection for an animal's body.

Carnassials Special cheek teeth with scissor-like edges in mammal carnivores; they are used to cut through flesh.

Carnivore An animal that eats mostly other animals; it is also an order of mammals.

Cartilage A tough type of body tissue, softer, more elastic, and lighter than bone; it forms the skeletons of cartilaginous fish such as sharks and rays.

Caudal Located on or near the tail or rear of an animal; the caudal peduncle, for

example, is the narrowest part of a fish's body, before it fans into the tail.

Class One of the highest groups into which scientists sort living things; there are one or more classes in a phylum and each class contains one or more orders. Classes can be divided into subclasses.

Cloaca The opening in most vertebrates through which body wastes pass out. Eggs or young leave the body from this opening in females. In males, it is the passageway for sperm.

Cold-blooded See ectothermic

Colony Members of the same species that live together; they may do so to breed or for protection from predators.

Compound eye An eye that is made up of many smaller eyes, found in many insects and some crustaceans; each of these has its own lens and cells that are sensitive to light and can form a weak image.

Courtship Behavior involving males and females of the same species that helps them select or attract a mate

Crop Expanded part of the digestive tract used to store food; it is found in many birds and some insects.

Dermis The second layer of the skin of animals, located beneath the epidermis; it contains nerves, sweat glands, and blood vessels.

Digestion Processes that occur inside an animal to break down food into substances the body can use for energy, growth, or to repair itself

Diurnal Active during the day

Domestication The process of taming and breeding an animal for use by humans; domesticated animals include pets as well as animals used for sport, food, or work.

Dominance The status of certain animals within a group that are treated with more respect and caution than others; this often determines mating rights.

Dormant To be in a sleeplike state, often because of environmental conditions; the body's activity slows for this period.

Dorsal Located on or toward the back of an animal

Dung Hard waste from an animal; this usually refers to mammal waste.

Echolocation A system used by some animals to sense nearby objects and thus find their way and search for food; it relies on sound rather than sight or touch.

Ectothermic Having a body temperature that adjusts to that of the surrounding

environment; fish, reptiles, amphibians, and invertebrates are ectothermic. Also known as cold-blooded

Eggs Reproductive cells of female animals

Embryo The early stage of an animal's development that begins just after an egg has been fertilized

Endothermic Having a body temperature independent to that of the surrounding environment, which is kept stable by sweating to cool down and shivering to warm up; vertebrates such as birds and mammals are endothermic. Also known as warm-blooded

Epidermis The thin, outermost skin layer in animals; it does not contain any blood vessels but provides a barrier to protect the body against diseases.

Equator This imaginary line runs around the center of Earth, separating it into two equal parts—the Northern and Southern Hemispheres.

Estuary Where a river mouth meets the sea or ocean and fresh water mixes with salt water to produce brackish water; at this point the river is under the influence of the tides.

Eurasia Landmass that consists of the continents of Europe and Asia

Evolve To develop gradually over time as a species; this is often in response to changes in the environment.

Exoskeleton A structure located outside an animal that provides support for the soft body tissues inside; it is found on arachnids, insects, crustaceans, and many other invertebrates.

External fertilization Sperm and egg unite to create an embryo outside a female animal's body.

Extinction The death of a species

Family A term used in classifying animals; there are one or more families in an order, and each family contains one or more genera.

Feces Hard waste from an animal

Feral Domesticated animals, such as cats and dogs, that have returned to live in the wild

Fertilization Occurs when a sperm enters an egg successfully to create an embryo

Fetus In mammals, an embryo that has developed its basic structure and major body organs

Food chain A feeding pattern in which energy from food moves in a sequence from one level to the next

Forage To search for and eat food

Fungi Life-forms, such as mushrooms and molds; they are so different from any other living things they belong to their own kingdom: Fungi.

Genus The second lowest group into which scientists sort living things. Animals in the same genus are closely related and share many characteristics. There is at least one genus in each family, and each genus contains one or more species. (pl. genera)

Gestation Length of a pregnancy; this is the time it takes from the moment fertilization occurs to an animal's birth.

Gills Organs used by water-living animals, such as fish and crustaceans, for breathing; they absorb oxygen from water into an animal's bloodstream and give off carbon dioxide as waste.

Glands Special tissues in an animal that secrete substances, such as hormones, tears, or mucus, used by the body

Habitat The natural environment where an animal lives, including plant life, climate, and geology

Harem A group of same-species female animals that breed with a single male

Herbivore An animal that eats mainly plant material

Hermaphrodite An animal that has both male and female sex organs during its life; this can occur at the same time, or at different times in its life cycle.

Hibernate To spend the winter in a kind of deep sleep; in this state, an animal becomes inactive, its breathing rate and body temperature drops, and it lives off fat reserves. It is common among insects, reptiles, and some mammals.

Hormone A chemical produced in one part of an animal's body that is carried by the blood to another part where it causes a response

Incisors The front teeth in either or both the top and bottom jaws of a mammal

Incubate To keep eggs or embryos in the best environment for their development: Birds usually sit on their eggs; crocodiles bury eggs in a protected chamber.

Indigenous people The original human inhabitants of a region or country

Insectivores Animals that eat mainly insects

Internal fertilization This occurs when sperm and egg unite inside a female animal's body to create an embryo.

Introduced Species that do not occur naturally in a place or a region, but

rather arrive by either the accidental or the deliberate actions of humans

Invertebrates Animals without a backbone, such as worms, mollusks, and insects; most animals on Earth are invertebrates.

Jacobson's organ Small pits in the top of the mouth in snakes, lizards, and mammals; these analyze scents picked up by the tongue.

Keratin A lightweight, but tough, colorless protein: This makes up mammal hair, nails, and horns; bird beaks and feathers; and the filter-feeding plates of baleen whales.

Kingdom The highest group into which scientists sort living things; five separate kingdoms are recognized. The Kingdom Animalia contains all animals. Kingdoms are comprised of phyla.

Larva The young of certain animals that hatch from eggs, such as insects and other invertebrates, fish, and amphibians; they usually look different from their adult form and include grubs, caterpillars, and maggots in insects, and tadpoles in frogs and toads. (pl. larvae)

Lateral line System of sensory canals that runs along the sides of fish; it registers movement by detecting pressure changes in the surrounding water.

Marine The ocean environment

Membrane Soft, thin tissue or cell layer in an animal

Metamorphosis The sometimes dramatic transformation that can occur as a young animal becomes an adult; invertebrates, such as insects, spend time as larvae or nymphs before becoming adults. For vertebrates, metamorphosis from a larva to an adult is widespread in amphibians and common in fish.

Micro-organisms Tiny life-forms, such as bacteria, that can be seen only with a microscope

Migration Regular journeys made by animals from one habitat to another; they are usually made with the seasons and for the purpose of finding food, mates, or a place to produce young.

Molars Teeth in the sides of a mammal's mouth used for crushing and grinding

Molt To shed the body's outer layer, such as hair, scales, feathers, or exoskeleton

Monsoon A seasonal wind that brings heavy rain to parts of the world; it is most common in tropical southern and Southeast Asia.

Mucus Thick, slimy substance produced by some parts of animals' bodies; it provides protection and moisture.

New World North, South, and Central America and nearby islands

Nictitating membrane Thin, usually see-through, protective "third eyelid," found in reptiles, birds, and some mammals; it moves across the eye, not up and down.

Nocturnal Active at night

Northern Hemisphere The northern half of Earth; it includes all of North and Central America, the top part of South America, all of Europe, much of Africa, and all but a small portion of Asia.

Notochord A stiff rod of tissue along the back of some animals, including vertebrate embryos; it is replaced by the backbone in vertebrates as they mature.

Nutrients Substances, usually found in food, that are needed for an animal to grow and function

Nymph A juvenile stage in some insect species; a nymph looks much like the adult it gradually will become but is usually wingless and cannot breed.

Old World Europe, Asia, and Africa

Olfactory An animal's sense of smell

Omnivore An animal that eats both plant and animal material

Opposable thumbs Thumbs that can reach around and touch all of the fingers on the same hand; this allows an animal to hold objects.

Order One of the major groups into which scientists sort living things; there are one or more orders in a class and each order contains one or more families. Orders can be divided into suborders.

Organ A group of tissues that comprises a body part with a specific role inside an animal, such as the brain, skin, and heart

Patagium A skin flap forming a winglike structure that is used for flying or gliding in mammals such as bats and squirrels

Pelt The skin and fur of a mammal

Pelvis A structure of basin-shaped bones that joins the spine with the back legs

Pheromone A chemical produced by an animal; pheromones send signals to and influence the behavior of other members of the same species.

Phylum The second highest group into which scientists sort living things; it falls below the kingdom level. Each phylum contains one or more classes. (pl. phyla)

Pigment The chemical substance in cells that gives color to an animal's skin, eyes, hair, fur, or feathers

Plankton Tiny plants and animals floating in oceans, seas, and lakes; they are filtered from the water by large animals as food, and eaten directly by small animals.

Plumage The feathers of a bird

Poach To hunt or capture animals illegally

Predator An animal that hunts, kills, and eats other animals

Prehensile Able to grasp or grip

Prey An animal that is hunted, killed, and eaten by other animals

Primitive A simple or early form of an animal; having features that are ancient

Pupa A stage of development in insects that does not move or feed; it occurs after the larva and before the adult. (pl. pupae)

Quill Long, sharp, stiffened hair of an echidna, porcupine, or anteater; this is used for defense against predators.

Reproduction The process of creating offspring: Sexual reproduction involves sperm from a male joining with the egg of a female; asexual reproduction does not involve sperm or eggs.

Rookery A regular breeding site used by many animals, particularly seabirds

Roost A safe place used by some animals, such as birds or bats, to sleep in groups

Ruminants Hoofed animals, such as cattle, that have a stomach with four chambers; one chamber, the rumen, contains micro-organisms that help to break down the tough walls of plant cells.

Savanna Open grassland with some trees

Sediment The soil, sand, or gravel that covers the bottom of water bodies; this includes rivers, ponds, oceans, and lakes.

Simple eye An eye that can detect light and dark but cannot form an image; they are found in many invertebrate animals, such as worms and snails.

Snout Front, often elongated, part of an animal's head that includes the nose area

Social Animals that live with others of the same species; they may live with a mate, in a family group, or in a herd or colony with thousands of others.

Sonar A system of locating objects by transmitting and detecting sound waves underwater, used by dolphins and whales

Southern Hemisphere The southern half of Earth; this includes all of Australasia and Antarctica, most of South America, part of Africa, and a small portion of Asia.

Species Animals with the same physical and behavioral features that are able to breed with each other to create young that can also breed

Sperm The reproductive cells of some male animals

Spine The backbone of an adult vertebrate animal; it is also a stiff, rodlike extension from the body of an animal that is used for defense against predators.

Symmetrical To be arranged with all sides having the same appearance and structure; bilaterally symmetrical means to have two equal sides.

Syrinx The special organ in the throat of perching birds used to produce songs and other sounds for communication

Talons The sharp claws of birds of prey, such as owls and eagles; they are used to capture, hold, and kill prey.

Territory An area that an animal defends against intruders from its own or other species; it can be permanent, to control food or other resources, or it may be temporary, to breed.

Tissue A group of cells inside an animal's body; they are located together, have the same or a similar structure, and act together to perform the same function.

Torpor A sleeplike state entered by some animals, particularly small mammals and birds, to survive difficult conditions such as cold weather or food shortages; the body's processes are slowed down greatly.

Troop A group of animals, particularly primates such as monkeys or baboons

Umbilical cord The ropelike structure that connects a developing mammal embryo or fetus with its mother's placenta during pregnancy; it carries nutrients and oxygen to the baby and removes waste products such as carbon dioxide.

Urine Liquid waste from an animal's body produced from the blood by the kidneys

Venom Poison injected by an animal into a predator or prey through fangs, spines, or similar structures

Vertebrate Any animal with a backbone, including all mammals, birds, reptiles, amphibians, and fish

Vibrissae Special hairs that are sensitive to touch; they are often present on the face of mammals and are called whiskers.

Warm-blooded See endothermic

Zooplankton Tiny animals that drift on or near the surface of the ocean; they are an important source of food for some whales, fish, and seabirds.

Animal Sizes

Animals come in an amazing variety of sizes and shapes. Every species featured in this book is listed below in its group by common name. Beside every name is the size of that animal. All of the measurements represent the largest size a normal animal in this species can reach. How each animal is measured—whether by height, length, wingspan, or width—is indicated by an icon at the top of each group, or next to each animal's name. A key on page 251 explains what each icon represents.

Mammals

Monotremes		
Long-nosed echidna	31¼ in (80 cm)	2 in (5 cm)
Platypus	16 in (41 cm)	6 in (15 cm)
Short-nosed echidna	14 in (36 cm)	4 in (10 cm)

Marsupials		
Bilby	21½ in (55 cm)	11⅓ in (29 cm)
Brushtail possum	22⅔ in (58 cm)	15⅔ in (40 cm)
Common opossum	16¾ in (43 cm)	17½ in (45 cm)
Common ringtail possum	14¾ in (38 cm)	10½ in (27 cm)
Common wombat	4 ft (1.2 m)	1¼ in (3 cm)
Ecuadorean shrew-opossum	5⅓ in (13.5 cm)	⅛ in (4 mm)
Fat-tailed dunnart	3½ in (9 cm)	2¾ in (7 cm)
Feathertail glider	2½ in (6.5 cm)	3 in (7.5 cm)
Goodfellow's tree kangaroo	24½ in (63 cm)	29⅔ in (76 cm)
Herbert River ringtail possum	15⅔ in (40 cm)	18¾ in (48 cm)
Koala	32 in (82 cm)	None
Leadbeater's possum	6¼ in (16 cm)	7 in (18 cm)
Little water opossum	15⅔ in (40 cm)	12 in (31 cm)
Monito del monte	5 in (13 cm)	5 in (13 cm)
Mountain pygmy-possum	4⅔ in (12 cm)	6 in (15 cm)
Mulgara	7¾ in (20 cm)	4¼ in (11 cm)
Musky rat-kangaroo	11 in (28 cm)	6⅔ in (17 cm)
Numbat	10¾ in (27.5 cm)	8¼ in (21 cm)
Patagonian opossum	5½ in (14 cm)	4 in (10 cm)
Red kangaroo	4½ ft (1.4 m)	38⅔ in (99 cm)
Robinson's mouse opossum	6½ in (16.5 cm)	8¼ in (21 cm)
Rufous bettong	20¼ in (52 cm)	15⅔ in (40 cm)
Scaly-tailed possum	15¼ in (39 cm)	11⅔ in (30 cm)
Southern brown bandicoot	14 in (36 cm)	5½ in (14 cm)
Southern marsupial mole	6¼ in (16 cm)	1 in (2.5 cm)
Southern short-tailed opossum	6 in (15 cm)	3 in (8 cm)
Spotted cuscus	22⅔ in (58 cm)	17½ in (45 cm)
Spotted-tailed quoll	29¼ in (75 cm)	21¾ in (56 cm)
Striped bandicoot	11⅔ in (30 cm)	10 in (26 cm)
Striped possum	11 in (28 cm)	15¼ in (39 cm)
Sugar glider	12½ in (32 cm)	18¾ in (48 cm)
Tasmanian devil	25⅓ in (65 cm)	10 in (26 cm)
Thylacine	4½ ft (1.4 m)	25⅓ in (65 cm)
Western gray kangaroo	4 ft (1.2 m)	3¼ ft (1 m)
Yapok	15⅔ in (40 cm)	16¾ in (43 cm)
Yellow-footed antechinus	6¼ in (16 cm)	5½ in (14 cm)
Yellow-footed rock wallaby	25⅓ in (65 cm)	27⅓ in (70 cm)

Anteaters & pangolins		
Collared anteater	34⅓ in (88 cm)	23 in (59 cm)
Giant anteater	6½ ft (2 m)	35 in (90 cm)
Giant ground pangolin	3¼ ft (1 m)	27⅓ in (70 cm)
Larger hairy armadillo	15⅔ in (40 cm)	6⅔ in (17 cm)
Maned three-toed sloth	19½ in (50 cm)	2 in (5 cm)
Pale-throated three-toed sloth	29⅔ in (76 cm)	2¾ in (7 cm)
Southern three-banded armadillo	10½ in (27 cm)	3 in (8 cm)

Insect-eating mammals		
Cuban solenodon	15¼ in (39 cm)	9⅓ in (24 cm)
Elegant water shrew	5 in (13 cm)	4¼ in (11 cm)
Eurasian common shrew	3 in (8 cm)	1¾ in (4.5 cm)
European mole	6¼ in (16 cm)	¾ in (2 cm)
Giant otter shrew	13¾ in (35 cm)	11⅓ in (29 cm)
Himalayan water shrew	5 in (13 cm)	4⅔ in (12 cm)
Hottentot golden mole	5½ in (14 cm)	None
Mindanao moonrat	6 in (15 cm)	2¾ in (7 cm)
Western European hedgehog	10 in (26 cm)	1¼ in (3 cm)

Flying lemurs & tree shrews		
Common tree shrew	7⅔ in (19.5 cm)	6½ in (16.5 cm)
Large tree shrew	12½ in (32 cm)	9¾ in (25 cm)
Malayan flying lemur	16½ in (42 cm)	10½ in (27 cm)
Pen-tailed tree shrew	5½ in (14 cm)	7½ in (19 cm)

Bats		
American false vampire bat	6 in (15 cm)	None
Common pipistrelle	1¾ in (4.5 cm)	1⅓ in (3.5 cm)
Common vampire bat	3½ in (9 cm)	None
Diadem leaf-nosed bat	4 in (10 cm)	2⅓ in (6 cm)
Eastern tube-nosed bat	4¼ in (11 cm)	¾ in (2 cm)
Egyptian fruit bat	5½ in (14 cm)	¾ in (2 cm)
Gambian epauletted fruit bat	9¾ in (25 cm)	None
Greater bulldog bat	5 in (13 cm)	1½ in (4 cm)
Greater mouse-tailed bat	3 in (8 cm)	2⅓ in (6 cm)
Hammer-headed fruit bat	11⅔ in (30 cm)	¾ in (2 cm)
Indian flying fox	11 in (28 cm)	None
Least blossom bat	2¾ in (7 cm)	⅓ in (1 cm)
Mauritian tomb bat	3¾ in (9.5 cm)	1¼ in (3 cm)
New Zealand lesser short-tailed bat	2¾ in (7 cm)	⅓ in (1 cm)
Noctule	3 in (8 cm)	2¼ in (5.5 cm)
Particolored bat	2½ in (6.5 cm)	1¾ in (4.5 cm)
Pocketed free-tailed bat	4¼ in (11 cm)	2 in (5 cm)
Serotine	3 in (8 cm)	2⅓ in (6 cm)
Straw-colored fruit bat	8½ in (22 cm)	¾ in (2 cm)
Sucker-footed bat	2⅓ in (6 cm)	2 in (5 cm)
Western barbastelle	2⅓ in (6 cm)	1½ in (4 cm)
Wrinkle-faced bat	2¾ in (7 cm)	None
Yellow-winged bat	3 in (8 cm)	None

Primates		
Allen's swamp monkey	19½ in (50 cm)	21½ in (55 cm)
Angwantibo	10 in (26 cm)	⅓ in (1 cm)
Aye-aye	15⅔ in (40 cm)	15⅔ in (40 cm)
Barbary ape	27⅓ in (70 cm)	None
Bear macaque	25⅓ in (65 cm)	3 in (8 cm)
Black gibbon	25⅓ in (65 cm)	None
Black howler	26 in (67 cm)	26 in (67 cm)
Black-headed uakari	19½ in (50 cm)	8¼ in (21 cm)
Bonobo	32⅓ in (83 cm)	None
Brown capuchin	18¾ in (48 cm)	18¾ in (48 cm)
Brown lemur	15⅔ in (40 cm)	21½ in (55 cm)
Chimpanzee	36¼ in (93 cm)	None
Chinese snub-nosed monkey	27⅔ in (71 cm)	29⅔ in (76 cm)
Common marmoset	6 in (15 cm)	13¾ in (35 cm)
Common squirrel monkey	12½ in (32 cm)	16¾ in (43 cm)
Common woolly monkey	22⅔ in (58 cm)	31¼ in (80 cm)
Coquerel's dwarf lemur	9¾ in (25 cm)	12½ in (32 cm)
Demidoff's galago	6 in (15 cm)	8¼ in (21 cm)
Diadem sifaka	21½ in (55 cm)	21¾ in (56 cm)
Douc langur	29⅔ in (76 cm)	29⅔ in (76 cm)
Dusky titi	14 in (36 cm)	18 in (46 cm)
Eastern needle-clawed bushbaby	7¾ in (20 cm)	10 in (26 cm)
Fork-marked lemur	11 in (28 cm)	14½ in (37 cm)
Gelada	35 in (90 cm)	19½ in (50 cm)
Geoffroy's tamarin	11⅔ in (30 cm)	16½ in (42 cm)
Golden lion tamarin	11 in (28 cm)	15⅔ in (40 cm)
Hamadryas baboon	35 in (90 cm)	27⅓ in (70 cm)
Hanuman langur	30½ in (78 cm)	3¼ ft (1 m)
Hoolock	25⅓ in (65 cm)	None
Indri	35 in (90 cm)	15⅔ in (40 cm)
King colobus	28 in (72 cm)	3¼ ft (1 m)
Kloss's gibbon	25⅓ in (65 cm)	None
Lar gibbon	25⅓ in (65 cm)	None
Lesser bushbaby	7¾ in (20 cm)	11⅔ in (30 cm)
Long-haired spider monkey	22⅔ in (58 cm)	35 in (90 cm)
Mandrill	31¼ in (80 cm)	4 in (10 cm)
Mantled howler	22⅔ in (58 cm)	26 in (67 cm)
Mountain gorilla	6¼ ft (1.9 m)	None
Northern night monkey	18⅓ in (47 cm)	16 in (41 cm)
Orangutan	5 ft (1.5 m)	None
Potto	17½ in (45 cm)	4 in (10 cm)
Proboscis monkey	29⅔ in (76 cm)	29⅔ in (76 cm
Pygmy marmoset	6 in (15 cm)	8¼ in (21 cm)
Red colobus	26 in (67 cm)	31¼ in (80 cm)
Redtail monkey	23½ in (60 cm)	35 in (90 cm)
Ruffed lemur	21½ in (55 cm)	4 ft (1.2 m)
Siamang	35 in (90 cm)	None
Slender loris	10 in (26 cm)	None
Slow loris	14¾ in (38 cm)	¾ in (2 cm)
Spectral tarsier	6 in (15 cm)	10½ in (27 cm)
Sykes's monkey	26 in (67 cm)	33 in (85 cm)
Vervet monkey	24¼ in (62 cm)	28 in (72 cm)
Weasel sportive lemur	14 in (36 cm)	11⅔ in (30 cm
Western gorilla	6 ft (1.8 m)	None
Western tarsier	6 in (15 cm)	10½ in (27 cm)
White-cheeked mangabey	28 in (72 cm)	3¼ ft (1 m)
White-faced saki	18¾ in (48 cm)	17½ in (45 cm)
Woolly spider monkey	24½ in (63 cm)	31¼ in (80 cm)

Carnivores		
Aardwolf	26 in (67 cm)	9⅓ in (24 cm)
African golden cat	3¼ ft (1 m)	18 in (46 cm)
African weasel	13¾ in (35 cm)	9 in (23 cm)
American badger	28 in (72 cm)	6 in (15 cm)
American black bear	7 ft (2.1 m)	7 in (18 cm)
American mink	19½ in (50 cm)	7¾ in (20 cm)
Andean cat	33 in (85 cm)	19 in (49 cm)
Andean hog-nosed skunk	13 in (33 cm)	7¾ in (20 cm)
Angolan genet	19½ in (50 cm)	20⅔ in (53 cm)
Arctic fox	27⅓ in (70 cm)	15⅔ in (40 cm)
Asiatic black bear	6¼ ft (1.9 m)	4 in (10 cm)
Asiatic golden cat	3¼ ft (1 m)	21¾ in (56 cm)
Baikal seal	4½ ft (1.4 m)	
Banded linsang	17½ in (45 cm)	16⅔ in (40 cm)
Banded mongoose	17½ in (45 cm)	11⅔ in (30 cm)
Banded palm civet	24½ in (62 cm)	14¾ in (38 cm)
Bat-eared fox	25¾ in (66 cm)	13¼ in (34 cm)
Bengal fox	23½ in (60 cm)	13¾ in (35 cm)
Black-backed jackal	35 in (90 cm)	15⅔ in (40 cm)
Bobcat	3¼ ft (1 m)	7¾ in (20 cm)
Bush dog	29¼ in (75 cm)	5 in (13 cm)
California sea lion	8 ft (2.4 m)	
Canada lynx	3¼ ft (1 m)	5½ in (14 cm)
Cape clawless otter	37 in (95 cm)	26 in (67 cm)
Cape wild dog	35 in (90 cm)	15⅔ in (40 cm)
Caracal	36 in (92 cm)	12 in (31 cm)
Cheetah	4½ ft (1.4 m)	31¼ in (80 cm)
Chinese ferret badger	9⅓ in (24 cm)	7½ in (19 cm)
Common palm civet	27⅔ in (71 cm)	25¾ in (66 cm)
Coyote	37¾ in (97 cm)	14¾ in (38 cm)
Crab-eating fox	29⅔ in (76 cm)	13 in (33 cm)
Culpeo fox	4 ft (1.2 m)	17½ in (45 cm)
Dingo	3¼ ft (1 m)	14 in (36 cm)
Ethiopian wolf	3¼ ft (1 m)	11⅔ in (30 cm)
Eurasian badger	35 in (90 cm)	7¾ in (20 cm)
Eurasian lynx	4¼ ft (1.3 m)	9⅓ in (24 cm)
European brown bear	9 ft (2.8 m)	8¼ in (21 cm)
European mink	16¾ in (43 cm)	7½ in (19 cm)
European otter	27⅓ in (70 cm)	15⅔ in (40 cm)
Falanouc	25⅓ in (65 cm)	9¾ in (25 cm)
Fanaloka	17½ in (45 cm)	8¼ in (21 cm)
Fisher	30¾ in (79 cm)	16 in (41 cm)
Fishing cat	33½ in (86 cm)	13 in (33 cm)
Fishing genet	17½ in (45 cm)	13¼ in (34 cm)
Fossa	29⅔ in (76 cm)	27⅓ in (70 cm)
Giant otter	4 ft (1.2 m)	27⅓ in (70 cm)
Giant panda	5 ft (1.5 m)	4 in (10 cm)
Gray fox	31⅔ in (81 cm)	17 in (44 cm)
Gray wolf (Alaskan)	5 ft (1.5 m)	20 in (51 cm)
Gray wolf (Scandinavian)	5 ft (1.5 m)	20 in (51 cm)
Grison	21½ in (55 cm)	7¾ in (20 cm)
Harp seal	6½ ft (2 m)	
Himalayan brown bear	9 ft (2.8 m)	8¼ in (21 cm)
Hog badger	27⅓ in (70 cm)	6⅔ in (17 cm)
Hooded seal	8¾ ft (2.7 m)	
Hose's palm civet	21 in (54 cm)	13¼ in (34 cm)
Iberian lynx	3⅔ ft (1.1 m)	5 in (13 cm)
Jaguar	6¼ ft (1.9 m)	23½ in (60 cm)
Jaguarundi	25⅓ in (65 cm)	23¾ in (61 cm)
Japanese marten	21½ in (55 cm)	8½ in (22 cm)
Jungle cat	36⅔ in (94 cm)	12 in (31 cm)
Kinkajou	21½ in (55 cm)	22¼ in (57 cm)
Kit fox	20¼ in (52 cm)	12½ in (32 cm)
Kodiak bear	9 ft (2.8 m)	8¼ in (21 cm)
Kodkod	20 in (51 cm)	9¾ in (25 cm)

ANIMAL SIZES 247

Leopard	7 ft (2.1 m)	3⅔ ft (1.1 m)
Leopard cat	23½ in (60 cm)	11⅔ in (30 cm)
Leopard seal	10½ ft (3.2 m)	
Lion	7½ ft (2.3 m)	3¼ ft (1 m)
Long-tailed weasel	10 in (26 cm)	6 in (15 cm)
Maned wolf	3¼ ft (1 m)	15⅔ in (40 cm)
Marbled cat	20⅔ in (53 cm)	21½ in (55 cm)
Marbled polecat	13¾ in (35 cm)	8½ in (22 cm)
Margay	30¾ in (79 cm)	20 in (51 cm)
Masked palm civet	29⅔ in (76 cm)	25 in (64 cm)
Mediterranean monk seal	9 ft (2.8 m)	
New Zealand fur seal	5¼ ft (1.6 m)	
Northern fur seal	7 ft (2.1 m)	
Ocelot	18⅓ in (47 cm)	16 in (41 cm)
Owston's palm civet	28 in (72 cm)	18⅓ in (47 cm)
Pale fox	18 in (46 cm)	11⅓ in (29 cm)
Pampas fox	28 in (72 cm)	5 in (13 cm)
Polar bear	8 ft (2.4 m)	5 in (13 cm)
Polecat	20 in (51 cm)	7½ in (19 cm)
Puma	5 ft (1.5 m)	37½ in (96 cm)
Raccoon	21½ in (55 cm)	16⅔ in (40 cm)
Raccoon dog	23½ in (60 cm)	7 in (18 cm)
Ratel	30 in (77 cm)	11⅔ in (30 cm)
Red fox (North American)	19½ in (50 cm)	13 in (33 cm)
Red panda	25⅓ in (65 cm)	18¾ in (48 cm)
Red wolf	4 ft (1.2 m)	13¾ in (35 cm)
Ribbon seal	5¼ ft (1.6 m)	
Ringed seal	5 ft (1.5 m)	
Ringtail	16½ in (42 cm)	17 in (44 cm)
Sea otter	4 ft (1.2 m)	14 in (36 cm)
Serval	3¼ ft (1 m)	17½ in (45 cm)
Siberian weasel	25¾ in (66 cm)	9¾ in (25 cm)
Sloth bear	6 ft (1.8 m)	4⅔ in (12 cm)
Small-eared zorro	3¼ ft (1 m)	13¾ in (35 cm)
Snow leopard	4¼ ft (1.3 m)	3¼ ft (1 m)
Southern elephant seal	19⅔ ft (6 m)	
Spectacled bear	6½ ft (2 m)	4⅔ in (12 cm)
Spotted hyena	4¼ ft (1.3 m)	9¾ in (25 cm)
Spotted skunk	13 in (33 cm)	11 in (28 cm)
Steller's sea lion	10¾ ft (3.3 m)	
Stoat	12½ in (32 cm)	5 in (13 cm)
Striped hog-nosed skunk	19½ in (50 cm)	12½ in (32 cm)
Striped hyena	3⅔ ft (1.1 m)	7¾ in (20 cm)
Striped polecat	14¾ in (38 cm)	11⅔ in (30 cm)
Striped skunk	31¼ in (80 cm)	15¼ in (39 cm)
Sun bear	4½ ft (1.4 m)	2¾ in (7 cm)
Suricate	12 in (31 cm)	9⅓ in (24 cm)
Swift fox	20⅔ in (53 cm)	10 in (26 cm)
Tayra	27⅓ in (70 cm)	17½ in (45 cm)
Three-striped palm civet	20⅔ in (53 cm)	25¾ in (66 cm)
Tibetan fox	27⅓ in (70 cm)	18¾ in (48 cm)
Tiger	12 ft (3.6 m)	3¼ ft (1 m)
Walrus	11½ ft (3.5 m)	
Weddell seal	9½ ft (2.9 m)	
White-nosed coati	27 in (69 cm)	24¼ in (62 cm)
Wildcat	29¼ in (75 cm)	13¾ in (35 cm)
Yellow mongoose	13¾ in (35 cm)	9¾ in (25 cm)
Yellow-throated marten	27⅓ in (70 cm)	17½ in (45 cm)

Hoofed mammals

Aardvark	4 ft (1.2 m)	21½ in (55 cm)
Ader's duiker	28 in (72 cm)	4⅔ in (12 cm)
African elephant	24½ ft (7.5 m)	5 ft (1.5 m)
African manatee	13 ft (4 m)	
Alpaca	6½ ft (2 m)	7¾ in (20 cm)
Amazonian manatee	9 ft (2.8 m)	
Aoudad	5½ ft (1.7 m)	9¾ in (25 cm)
Arabian tahr	4½ ft (1.4 m)	4⅔ in (12 cm)
Asiatic elephant	21 ft (6.4 m)	5 ft (1.5 m)
Ass (wild)	6½ ft (2 m)	17½ in (45 cm)
Babirusa	3⅔ ft (1.1 m)	12½ in (32 cm)
Bactrian camel	11½ ft (3.5 m)	20⅔ in (53 cm)
Baird's beaked whale	43 ft (13 m)	
Barasingha	6 ft (1.8 m)	7¾ in (20 cm)
Beluga	16½ ft (5 m)	
Bison	11½ ft (3.5 m)	23½ in (60 cm)
Black rhinoceros	12½ ft (3.8 m)	23½ in (60 cm)
Blackbuck	4 ft (1.2 m)	7 in (18 cm)
Blesbok	5¼ ft (1.6 m)	17½ in (45 cm)
Blue whale	110 ft (33.5 m)	
Bongo	8 ft (2.5 m)	25⅓ in (65 cm)
Bottle-nosed dolphin	13 ft (4 m)	
Bowhead whale	59 ft (18 m)	
Brazilian tapir	6½ ft (2 m)	3¼ ft (1 m)
Bush pig	4¼ ft (1.3 m)	14¾ in (38 cm)
Caribbean manatee	14¾ ft (4.5 m)	
Caribou	7 ft (2.2 m)	9¾ in (25 cm)
Chaco peccary	3⅔ ft (1.1 m)	4 in (10 cm)
Chamois	4¼ ft (1.3 m)	1½ in (4 cm)
Chinese water deer	3¼ ft (1 m)	3 in (8 cm)
Chiru	4½ ft (1.4 m)	4 in (10 cm)
Collared peccary	3¼ ft (1 m)	2¼ in (5.5 cm)
Common dolphin	8 ft (2.4 m)	
Common duiker	3⅔ ft (1.1 m)	7½ in (19 cm)
Common hartebeest	6¼ ft (1.9 m)	27⅓ in (70 cm)
Common porpoise	6¼ ft (1.9 m)	
Dall sheep	6 ft (1.8 m)	4⅔ in (12 cm)
Dromedary	11½ ft (3.5 m)	19½ in (50 cm)
Dugong	13 ft (4 m)	
Fallow deer	6 ft (1.8 m)	9¾ in (25 cm)
False killer whale	19⅔ ft (6 m)	
Fin whale	82 ft (25 m)	
Finless porpoise	6½ ft (2 m)	
Ganges dolphin	10 ft (3 m)	
Gemsbok	5¼ ft (1.6 m)	35 in (90 cm)
Giant eland	11½ ft (3.5 m)	35 in (90 cm)
Giant hog	7 ft (2.1 m)	17½ in (45 cm)
Giant muntjak	3¼ ft (1 m)	6⅔ in (17 cm)
Gray whale	49 ft (15 m)	
Greater kudu	5 ft (1.5 m)	18¾ in (48 cm)
Guanaco	6½ ft (2 m)	10½ in (27 cm)
Gulf porpoise	5 ft (1.5 m)	
Hippopotamus	13¾ ft (4.2 m)	21¾ in (56 cm)
Horse (wild)	9 ft (2.8 m)	23½ in (60 cm)
Humpback whale	49 ft (15 m)	
Impala	5 ft (1.5 m)	15⅔ in (40 cm)
Indian muntjak	3⅔ ft (1.1 m)	7½ in (19 cm)
Indian rhinoceros	12½ ft (3.8 m)	31¼ in (80 cm)
Irrawaddy dolphin	9 ft (2.8 m)	
Javan rhinoceros	10½ ft (3.2 m)	27⅓ in (70 cm)
Kenyan giraffe	26¼ ft (8 m)	5 ft (1.5 m)
Kiang	8 ft (2.5 m)	19½ in (50 cm)
Klipspringer	35 in (90 cm)	5 in (13 cm)
Lesser Malay chevrotain	18¾ in (48 cm)	2 in (5 cm)
Little red brocket	3¼ ft (1 m)	4 in (10 cm)
Llama	7 ft (2.2 m)	9¾ in (25 cm)
Long-finned pilot whale	28 ft (8.5 m)	
Malayan tapir	4 ft (1.2 m)	4 in (10 cm)
Markhor	6 ft (1.8 m)	5½ in (14 cm)
Minke whale	36 ft (11 m)	
Mongolian wild ass	8 ft (2.5 m)	19 in (49 cm)
Moose	11½ ft (3.5 m)	4 in (10 cm)
Mountain anoa	5 ft (1.5 m)	9⅓ in (24 cm)
Mountain goat	5¼ ft (1.6 m)	7¾ in (20 cm)
Mountain reedbuck	4¼ ft (1.3 m)	7¾ in (20 cm)
Mountain zebra	8½ ft (2.6 m)	15⅔ in (40 cm)
Musk ox	7½ ft (2.3 m)	4 in (10 cm)
Narwhal	19⅔ ft (6 m)	
Northern right whale	59 ft (18 m)	
Nubian giraffe	15½ ft (4.7 m)	3¼ ft (1 m)
Okapi	6½ ft (2 m)	16½ in (42 cm)
Onager	4½ ft (1.4 m)	19½ in (50 cm)
Orca	32 ft (9.8 m)	
Pampas deer	4¼ ft (1.3 m)	6 in (15 cm)
Peruvian guemal	5½ ft (1.7 m)	5 in (13 cm)
Pronghorn	5 ft (1.5 m)	7 in (18 cm)
Pygmy hippopotamus	6½ ft (2 m)	6 in (15 cm)
Pygmy hog	27⅔ in (71 cm)	1¼ in (3 cm)
Pygmy sperm whale	10 ft (3 m)	
Red river hog	5 ft (1.5 m)	16¾ in (43 cm)
Reticulated giraffe	15½ ft (4.7 m)	3¼ ft (1 m)
Risso's dolphin	12½ ft (3.8 m)	
Rock hyrax	22⅔ in (58 cm)	12 in (31 cm)
Roosevelt elk	8 ft (2.4 m)	6⅔ in (17 cm)
Rusa	3⅔ ft (1.1 m)	9¾ in (25 cm)
Saiga	4½ ft (1.4 m)	4⅔ in (12 cm)
Saola	6½ ft (2 m)	5 in (13 cm)
Serow	6 ft (1.8 m)	6¼ in (16 cm)
Southern giraffe	15½ ft (4.7 m)	3¼ ft (1 m)
Southern pudu	32⅓ in (83 cm)	2 in (5 cm)
Southern tree hyrax	27⅓ in (70 cm)	1¼ in (3 cm)
Spanish ibex	4½ ft (1.4 m)	6 in (15 cm)
Spectacled porpoise	7 ft (2.1 m)	
Sperm whale	60⅔ ft (18.5 m)	
Springbok	4½ ft (1.4 m)	11⅔ in (30 cm)
Steenbok	33 in (85 cm)	3¼ in (8 cm)
Sumatran rhinoceros	10½ ft (3.2 m)	25⅓ in (65 cm)
Thomson's gazelle	3⅔ ft (1.1 m)	7¾ in (20 cm)
Tufted deer	5¼ ft (1.6 m)	6¼ in (16 cm)
Vicuña	6¼ ft (1.9 m)	9¾ in (25 cm)
Warthog	5 ft (1.5 m)	19½ in (50 cm)
Water chevrotain	37 in (95 cm)	5½ in (14 cm)
Waterbuck	8 ft (2.4 m)	17½ in (45 cm)
White rhinoceros	13¾ ft (4.2 m)	27⅓ in (70 cm)
White-beaked dolphin	9 ft (2.8 m)	
White-lipped peccary	3¼ ft (1 m)	2⅓ in (6 cm)
White-tailed deer	8 ft (2.4 m)	11⅔ in (30 cm)
Wild boar	6 ft (1.8 m)	11⅔ in (30 cm)
Wildebeest	7½ ft (2.3 m)	21¾ in (56 cm)
Yak	10¾ ft (3.3 m)	23½ in (60 cm)
Yellow-spotted hyrax	14¾ in (38 cm)	None
Zebra (northern)	8 ft (2.5 m)	21¾ in (56 cm)

Rodents

African brush-tailed porcupine	22¼ in (57 cm)	9 in (23 cm)
Black rat	9⅓ in (24 cm)	10 in (26 cm)
Black-tailed prairie dog	13¼ in (34 cm)	3½ in (9 cm)
Botta's pocket gopher	11⅔ in (30 cm)	3¾ in (9.5 cm)
Brazilian porcupine	20¼ in (52 cm)	20¼ in (52 cm)
Capybara	4½ ft (1.4 m)	¾ in (2 cm)
Chinchilla	9 in (23 cm)	6 in (15 cm)
Chinchilla-rat	7½ in (19 cm)	2¾ in (7 cm)
Coypu	25 in (64 cm)	16½ in (42 cm)
Crested porcupine	27⅓ in (70 cm)	4⅔ in (12 cm)
Dassie rat	8¼ in (21 cm)	6 in (15 cm)
Deer mouse	4 in (10 cm)	4⅔ in (12 cm)
Demarest's hutia	23½ in (60 cm)	11⅔ in (30 cm)
Desert kangaroo rat	6 in (15 cm)	7¾ in (20 cm)
Eastern chipmunk	6⅔ in (17 cm)	4⅔ in (12 cm)
Eurasian beaver	31¼ in (80 cm)	17½ in (45 cm)
Eurasian red squirrel	11 in (28 cm)	9⅓ in (24 cm)
European hamster	12½ in (32 cm)	2⅓ in (6 cm)
European souslik	8½ in (22 cm)	3 in (7 cm)
Fawn hopping mouse	4⅔ in (12 cm)	6¼ in (16 cm)
Garden dormouse	6⅔ in (17 cm)	5 in (13 cm)
Gray agouti	29⅔ in (76 cm)	1½ in (4 cm)
Gray climbing mouse	2¾ in (7 cm)	3 in (8 cm)
Great gerbil	7¾ in (20 cm)	6¼ in (16 cm)
Greater bandicoot rat	14 in (36 cm)	11 in (28 cm)
Greater stick-nest rat	10 in (26 cm)	7 in (18 cm)
Gundi	7¾ in (20 cm)	1 in (2.5 cm)
Harvest mouse	3 in (7.5 cm)	3 in (7.5 cm)
Hispid cotton rat	7¾ in (20 cm)	6¼ in (16 cm)
Hoary marmot	22¼ in (57 cm)	9¾ in (25 cm)
Large bamboo rat	18¾ in (48 cm)	7¾ in (20 cm)
Long-clawed mole-vole	6¼ in (16 cm)	2¾ in (7 cm)
Long-tailed pocket mouse	4 in (10 cm)	4⅔ in (12 cm)
Malayan porcupine	28½ in (73 cm)	4¼ in (11 cm)
Meadow jumping mouse	4 in (10 cm)	5 in (13 cm)
Mountain beaver	16½ in (42 cm)	2 in (5 cm)
Muskrat	13 in (33 cm)	11⅔ in (30 cm)
North American porcupine	3⅔ ft (1.1 m)	9¾ in (25 cm)
Northern three-toed jerboa	6¼ in (16 cm)	7½ in (19 cm)
Paca	30½ in (78 cm)	1¼ in (3 cm)
Pacarana	30¾ in (79 cm)	7½ in (19 cm)
Plains viscacha	25¾ in (66 cm)	7¾ in (20 cm)
Prevost's squirrel	11 in (28 cm)	10 in (26 cm)
Siberian collared lemming	6 in (15 cm)	⅓ in (1 cm)
Smooth-tailed giant rat	14½ in (37 cm)	16 in (41 cm)
Southern flying squirrel	5½ in (14 cm)	4⅔ in (12 cm)
Springhare	16¾ in (43 cm)	18⅓ in (47 cm)
Striped grass mouse	5½ in (14 cm)	6 in (15 cm)
Striped ground squirrel	15⅔ in (40 cm)	11⅔ in (30 cm)
Vlei rat	8½ in (22 cm)	4¼ in (11 cm)
White-bellied tuco-tuco	6⅔ in (17 cm)	3 in (8 cm)

Rabbits & elephant shrews

American pika	8½ in (22 cm)	None
Arctic hare	23½ in (60 cm)	3 in (8 cm)
Asiatic brown hare	26½ in (68 cm)	4 in (10 cm)
Black-tailed jackrabbit	24½ in (63 cm)	4¼ in (11 cm)
Brown hare	26½ in (68 cm)	4 in (10 cm)
Central African hare	17½ in (45 cm)	2 in (5 cm)
Checkered elephant shrew	12½ in (32 cm)	10 in (26 cm)
Daurian pika	7¾ in (20 cm)	None
Eastern cottontail	19½ in (50 cm)	2⅓ in (6 cm)
European rabbit	18 in (46 cm)	3 in (8 cm)
Forest rabbit	15⅔ in (40 cm)	1½ in (4 cm)
Four-toed elephant shrew	9 in (23 cm)	6⅔ in (17 cm)
Golden-rumped elephant shrew	11 in (28 cm)	9⅓ in (24 cm)
Hispid hare	19½ in (50 cm)	1½ in (4 cm)
Northern pika	7¾ in (20 cm)	None
Pygmy rabbit	11 in (28 cm)	¾ in (2 cm)
Royle's pika	7¾ in (20 cm)	None
Rufous elephant shrew	6 in (15 cm)	6¼ in (16 cm)
Snowshoe hare	18⅓ in (47 cm)	2 in (5 cm)
Sumatran rabbit	15⅔ in (40 cm)	⅗ in (1.5 cm)
Volcano rabbit	12½ in (32 cm)	1¼ in (3 cm)

Birds

Ratites & tinamous

Elegant crested tinamou	16 in (41 cm)
Emu	6½ ft (2 m)
Great tinamou	18 in (46 cm)
Greater rhea	5¼ ft (1.6 m)
Little spotted kiwi	17½ in (45 cm)
Ostrich	9½ ft (2.9 m)
Southern cassowary	6½ ft (2 m)
Variegated tinamou	13 in (33 cm)

Gamebirds

California quail	11 in (28 cm)
Gray-striped francolin	13 in (33 cm)
Great argus	6½ ft (2 m)
Great curassow	36 in (92 cm)
Indian peafowl	7 ft (2.1 m)
Koklass pheasant	25 in (64 cm)
Mikado pheasant	33½ in (86 cm)
Ocellated turkey	4 ft (1.2 m)
Red junglefowl	29¼ in (75 cm)
Red spurfowl	14 in (36 cm)
Red-legged partridge	14¾ in (38 cm)
Reeves's pheasant	7 ft (2.1 m)
Rock ptarmigan	14¾ in (38 cm)
Vulturine guineafowl	23½ in (60 cm)
White-crested guan	32⅓ in (83 cm)

Waterfowl

Bean goose	34⅓ in (88 cm)
Black-necked swan	3⅔ ft (1.1 m)
Canada goose	3⅔ ft (1.1 m)
Comb duck	29⅔ in (76 cm)
Common eider	27 in (69 cm)
Common pochard	17½ in (45 cm)
Common shelduck	25⅔ in (65 cm)
Coscoroba swan	3¾ ft (1.1 m)
Freckled duck	23 in (59 cm)
Magpie goose	35 in (90 cm)
Mallard	25⅓ in (65 cm)
Muscovy duck	32¾ in (84 cm)
Mute swan	5 ft (1.5 m)
Northern shoveler	18¾ in (48 cm)
Oldsquaw	16½ in (42 cm)
Orinoco goose	25¾ in (66 cm)
Red-breasted goose	21½ in (55 cm)
Red-crested pochard	22⅔ in (58 cm)
Snow goose	31¼ in (80 cm)
Southern screamer	37 in (95 cm)
Torrent duck	18 in (46 cm)
White-faced whistling-duck	19½ in (50 cm)
Whooper swan	5 ft (1.5 m)
Wood duck	20 in (51 cm)

Penguins

Adelie penguin	23¾ in (61 cm)
Emperor penguin	4 ft (1.2 m)
Jackass penguin	3¼ ft (1 m)
King penguin	3¼ ft (1 m)
Little penguin	17½ in (45 cm)
Royal penguin	27⅓ in (70 cm)
Snares penguin	23½ in (60 cm)
Yellow-eyed penguin	23½ in (60 cm)

Albatrosses & grebes

Arctic loon	26½ in (68 cm)
Band-rumped storm-petrel	9 in (23 cm)
Cape petrel	15¼ in (39 cm)
Common diving-petrel	9¾ in (25 cm)
Common loon	35 in (90 cm)
Eared grebe	13 in (33 cm)
Gray petrel	19½ in (50 cm)
Great crested grebe	25 in (64 cm)
Great grebe	30½ in (78 cm)
Hooded grebe	13¼ in (34 cm)
Jouanin's petrel	12½ in (32 cm)
Little grebe	11 in (28 cm)
New Zealand grebe	11⅔ in (30 cm)
Northern fulmar	19½ in (50 cm)
Red-throated loon	27⅓ in (70 cm)
Royal albatross	4 ft (1.2 m)
Wedge-tailed shearwater	18 in (46 cm)
Western grebe	29⅔ in (76 cm)
Wilson's storm-petrel	7½ in (19 cm)
Yellow-billed loon	35 in (90 cm)
Yellow-nosed albatross	29⅔ in (76 cm)

Herons & flamingos

Andean flamingo	3⅔ ft (1.1 m)
Boat-billed heron	20 in (51 cm)
Cattle egret	20 in (51 cm)
Great blue heron	4½ ft (1.4 m)
Greater flamingo	4¾ ft (1.45 m)
Hamerkop	21¾ in (56 cm)
Sacred ibis	35 in (90 cm)
Whistling heron	23¾ in (61 cm)
White-crested bittern	31¼ in (80 cm)
Wood stork	3¼ ft (1 m)

Pelicans

Anhinga	35 in (90 cm)
Dalmatian pelican	5½ ft (1.7 m)
Darter	37¾ in (97 cm)
Double-crested cormorant	35½ in (91 cm)
European shag	30¾ in (79 cm)
Great cormorant	3¼ ft (1 m)
Great white pelican	5¾ ft (1.75 m)
Lesser frigatebird	31⅔ in (81 cm)
Northern gannet	36 in (92 cm)
Pelagic cormorant	28¾ in (74 cm)
Peruvian booby	3¼ ft (1 m)
Red-tailed tropicbird	19½ in (50 cm)

Birds of prey

African cuckoo-hawk	15⅔ in (40 cm)
African white-backed vulture	36⅔ in (94 cm)
Andean condor	4¼ ft (1.3 m)
Bald eagle	3⅔ ft (1.1 m)
Black baza	13¾ in (35 cm)
Black harrier	19½ in (50 cm)
Black kite	21½ in (55 cm)
Cinereous vulture	3¼ ft (1 m)
Collared falconet	7 in (18 cm)
Common kestrel	14½ in (37 cm)
Crested serpent-eagle	29⅔ in (76 cm)
Crowned eagle	33 in (85 cm)
Dark chanting-goshawk	21 in (54 cm)
Egyptian vulture	27⅓ in (70 cm)
Eurasian griffon	3⅔ ft (1.1 m)
Eurasian sparrowhawk	14¾ in (38 cm)
European honey-buzzard	22⅔ in (58 cm)
Harris's hawk	22⅔ in (58 cm)
Hooded vulture	27 in (69 cm)
Javan hawk-eagle	23¾ in (61 cm)
King vulture	31⅔ in (81 cm)
Martial eagle	32⅓ in (83 cm)
Mississippi kite	13¾ in (35 cm)
Osprey	22⅔ in (58 cm)
Palm-nut vulture	19½ in (50 cm)
Red-footed falcon	12 in (31 cm)
Scissor-tailed kite	13¾ in (35 cm)
Secretary bird	5 ft (1.5 m)
Short-toed eagle	27 in (69 cm)
Snail kite	16¾ in (43 cm)
Turkey vulture	31⅔ in (81 cm)
Variable goshawk	21½ in (55 cm)
Yellow-headed caracara	16¾ in (43 cm)

Cranes

African finfoot	23 in (59 cm)
Barred buttonquail	6⅔ in (17 cm)
Black crowned crane	3¼ ft (1 m)
Corncrake	11⅔ in (30 cm)
Demoiselle crane	35 in (90 cm)
Denham's bustard	3¼ ft (1 m)
Hoatzin	27⅓ in (70 cm)
Horned coot	20⅔ in (53 cm)
Lesser florican	20 in (51 cm)
Limpkin	27⅓ in (70 cm)
Sunbittern	18¾ in (48 cm)
White-breasted mesite	4 ft (1.2 m)

Waders & shorebirds

Atlantic puffin	14 in (36 cm)
Beach stone curlew	21¾ in (56 cm)
Black skimmer	18 in (46 cm)
Black-faced sheathbill	16 in (41 cm)
Black-tailed godwit	16½ in (42 cm)
Black-winged stilt	15⅔ in (40 cm)
Collared pratincole	9¾ in (25 cm)
Common redshank	11 in (28 cm)
Common snipe	10½ in (27 cm)
Common tern	14¾ in (38 cm)
Crested auklet	10½ in (27 cm)
Curlew sandpiper	8½ in (22 cm)
Eurasian curlew	23½ in (60 cm)
Fairy tern	10½ in (27 cm)
Great black-backed gull	29⅔ in (76 cm)
Herring gull	25¾ in (66 cm)
Ibisbill	16 in (41 cm)
Little tern	11 in (28 cm)
Long-tailed jaeger	20⅔ in (53 cm)
Pied avocet	16¾ in (43 cm)
Red-necked phalarope	7¾ in (20 cm)
Ruff	12½ in (32 cm)
Southern lapwing	14¾ in (38 cm)
Spotted redshank	12½ in (32 cm)
Tufted puffin	14¾ in (38 cm)

Pigeons & sandgrouse

Banded fruit dove	13¼ in (34 cm)
Chestnut-bellied sandgrouse	13 in (33 cm)
Emerald dove	10½ in (27 cm)
Pallas's sandgrouse	15⅔ in (40 cm)
Pied imperial pigeon	16 in (41 cm)
Rock dove	13 in (33 cm)
Seychelles blue pigeon	9⅓ in (24 cm)
Victoria crowned pigeon	29⅔ in (76 cm)
Zebra dove	8¼ in (21 cm)

Cuckoos & turacos

Common cuckoo	13 in (33 cm)
Dideric cuckoo	7 in (18 cm)
Great blue turaco	29¼ in (75 cm)
Greater coucal	20¼ in (52 cm)
Greater roadrunner	21¾ in (56 cm)
Hartlaub's turaco	16¾ in (43 cm)
Jacobin cuckoo	13¼ in (34 cm)
Rufous-vented ground cuckoo	17½ in (45 cm)
Smooth-billed ani	14½ in (37 cm)
Violet turaco	19½ in (50 cm)

Parrots

Blue-fronted parrot	14½ in (37 cm)
Buff-faced pygmy parrot	4 in (10 cm)
Burrowing parakeet	18 in (46 cm)
Eclectus parrot	14 in (36 cm)
Fischer's lovebird	6¼ in (16 cm)
Galah	13¾ in (35 cm)
Ground parrot	11⅔ in (30 cm)
Hyacinth macaw	3¼ ft (1 m)
Kakapo	25 in (64 cm)
Kea	18¾ in (48 cm)
Maroon-faced parakeet	9 in (23 cm)
Military macaw	27⅓ in (70 cm)
Plum-headed parakeet	13 in (33 cm)
Rainbow lorikeet	10 in (26 cm)
Scarlet macaw	34¾ in (89 cm)
Senegal parrot	9¾ in (25 cm)
Swift parrot	9¾ in (25 cm)
White-crowned parrot	9⅓ in (24 cm)
Yellow-collared lovebird	5⅔ in (14.5 cm)

Nightjars & owls

Barn owl	17 in (44 cm)
Barred owl	20⅔ in (53 cm)
Black-banded owl	17½ in (45 cm)
Boreal owl	9¾ in (25 cm)
Burrowing owl	9⅓ in (24 cm)
Common pauraque	11 in (28 cm)
Common poorwill	7¾ in (20 cm)
Common potoo	14¾ in (38 cm)
Elf owl	6 in (15 cm)
Eurasian pygmy owl	6⅔ in (17 cm)
European nightjar	11 in (28 cm)
Great horned owl	21½ in (55 cm)
Long-eared owl	14¾ in (38 cm)
Northern saw-whet owl	7¾ in (20 cm)
Oilbird	19½ in (50 cm)
Snowy owl	23 in (59 cm)
Spectacled owl	18 in (46 cm)
Spotted nightjar	11⅔ in (30 cm)
Tawny frogmouth	20⅔ in (53 cm)
Tropical screech owl	9⅓ in (24 cm)
Ural owl	24¼ in (62 cm)
Verreaux's eagle-owl	25⅓ in (65 cm)

Hummingbirds & swifts

Alpine swift	8½ in (22 cm)
Asian palm swift	5 in (13 cm)
Collared Inca	5⅔ in (14.5 cm)
Festive coquette	3⅓ in (8.5 cm)
Fiery-tailed awlbill	4 in (10 cm)
Giant hummingbird	9 in (23 cm)
Gray-rumped treeswift	9 in (23 cm)
Purple-throated carib	4⅔ in (12 cm)
Ruby topaz	2 in (5 cm)
Sword-billed hummingbird	9 in (23 cm)

Kingfishers

African pygmy kingfisher	4⅔ in (12 cm)
Banded kingfisher	7¾ in (20 cm)
Belted kingfisher	13 in (33 cm)
Carmine bee-eater	10½ in (27 cm)
Common hoopoe	12½ in (32 cm)
Common kingfisher	6¼ in (16 cm)
Cuban tody	4¼ in (11 cm)
Cuckoo-roller	19½ in (50 cm)
Dollarbird	12½ in (32 cm)
European roller	11⅔ in (30 cm)
Great hornbill	3⅔ ft (1.1 m)
Green kingfisher	8½ in (22 cm)
Hook-billed kingfisher	10½ in (27 cm)
Laughing kookaburra	16¾ in (43 cm)
Lilac-cheeked kingfisher	11 in (28 cm)
Narina's trogon	12½ in (32 cm)
Pied kingfisher	11 in (28 cm)
Red-headed trogon	13¾ in (35 cm)
Resplendent quetzal	15⅔ in (40 cm)
Speckled mousebird	15⅔ in (40 cm)
White-headed mousebird	13¾ in (35 cm)
White-tailed trogon	11 in (28 cm)

Woodpeckers

Acorn woodpecker	9 in (23 cm)
Black-rumped woodpecker	11⅓ in (29 cm)
Blue-throated barbet	9 in (23 cm)
Channel-billed toucan	21¾ in (56 cm)
Curl-crested aracari	18 in (46 cm)
Emerald toucanet	14½ in (37 cm)
Golden-tailed woodpecker	9 in (23 cm)
Gray woodpecker	7¾ in (20 cm)
Gray-breasted mountain toucan	18¾ in (48 cm)
Greater honeyguide	7¾ in (20 cm)
Green woodpecker	13 in (33 cm)
Ground woodpecker	11⅔ in (30 cm)
Northern wryneck	6¼ in (16 cm)
Paradise jacamar	13¼ in (34 cm)
Pileated woodpecker	18 in (46 cm)
Red-and-yellow barbet	9 in (23 cm)
Rufous woodpecker	9¾ in (25 cm)
Spotted puffbird	7 in (18 cm)
Yellow-bellied sapsucker	8¼ in (21 cm)

Perching birds

American goldfinch	5 in (13 cm)
American robin	9¾ in (25 cm)
Asian paradise-flycatcher	19½ in (50 cm)
Australian magpie	15⅔ in (40 cm)
Bananaquit	4 in (10 cm)
Bar-bellied cuckoo-shrike	12½ in (32 cm)
Barred antshrike	6¼ in (16 cm)
Black phoebe	7½ in (19 cm)
Black-bellied gnateater	6¼ in (16 cm)
Black-capped vireo	4¼ in (11 cm)
Black-crowned sparrow-lark	4¼ in (11 cm)
Black-thighed grosbeak	7¾ in (20 cm)
Black-throated accentor	6 in (15 cm)
Black-throated huet-huet	9 in (23 cm)
Black-throated thrush	10½ in (27 cm)
Blue-crowned manakin	3½ in (9 cm)
Blue-faced parrotfinch	5 in (13 cm)
Bluethroat	5½ in (14 cm)
Bohemian waxwing	7¾ in (20 cm)
Brown-throated sunbird	5½ in (14 cm)
Cape sugarbird	18 in (46 cm)
Chestnut-crowned babbler	8½ in (22 cm)
Collared redstart	5 in (12.5 cm)
Crested tit	4½ in (11.5 cm)
Crimson chat	4⅔ in (12 cm)
Crimson-breasted flowerpecker	3½ in (9 cm)
Eastern paradise whydah	13 in (33 cm)
Eastern whipbird	10⅓ in (26.5 cm)
Eurasian golden oriole	8½ in (22 cm)
Fairy gerygone	4¼ in (11 cm)
Fluffy-backed tit-babbler	6¼ in (16 cm)
Goldcrest	3½ in (9 cm)
Golden bowerbird	9¾ in (25 cm)
Golden-headed manakin	3½ in (9 cm)
Gouldian finch	5½ in (14 cm)
Greater short-toed lark	6 in (15 cm)
Green broadbill	7½ in (19 cm)
Icterine warbler	5⅓ in (13.5 cm)
Madagascan wagtail	7½ in (19 cm)
Marsh wren	5 in (13 cm)
Northern scrub robin	8½ in (22 cm)
Orange-bellied leafbird	7½ in (19 cm)
Oriental white-eye	4¼ in (11 cm)
Penduline tit	4¼ in (11 cm)
Red-backed shrike	7 in (18 cm)
Red-bellied pitta	6¼ in (16 cm)
Red-billed blue magpie	27⅓ in (70 cm)
Red-billed buffalo weaver	9 in (23 cm)
Red-billed scythebill	10½ in (27 cm)
Red-browed treecreeper	6¼ in (16 cm)
Red-headed honeyeater	4⅔ in (12 cm)
Red-throated pipit	6¼ in (16 cm)
Red-whiskered bulbul	7¾ in (20 cm)
Red-winged blackbird	8½ in (22 cm)
Ruddy treerunner	6¼ in (16 cm)
Satin bowerbird	11⅔ in (30 cm)
Scarlet minivet	9 in (23 cm)
Scarlet tanager	6⅔ in (17 cm)
Shining starling	8½ in (22 cm)
Snow bunting	6⅔ in (17 cm)
Southern red bishop	4⅔ in (12 cm)
Spotted pardalote	3½ in (9 cm)
Standardwing	10½ in (27 cm)
Streak-chested antpitta	5½ in (14 cm)
Superb lyrebird	35 in (90 cm)
Three-wattled bellbird	11⅔ in (30 cm)
Tropical gnatcatcher	3½ in (9 cm)
Tufted flycatcher	5⅓ in (13.5 cm)
Turquoise cotinga	7¼ in (18.5 cm)
Variegated fairy-wren	6 in (15 cm)
Wallcreeper	6⅔ in (17 cm)
Western parotia	13 in (33 cm)
White-banded swallow	6 in (15 cm)
White-browed shortwing	5 in (13 cm)
White-browed woodswallow	7¾ in (20 cm)
White-capped dipper	6½ in (16.5 cm)
White-necked picathartes	15⅔ in (40 cm)
White-necked raven	21½ in (55 cm)
White-winged swallow	5½ in (14 cm)
Yellow-bellied fantail	4⅔ in (12 cm)

Reptiles

Tuatara

Tuatara	23½ in (60 cm)

Turtles & tortoises

African tent tortoise	6¼ in (16 cm)
Alligator snapping turtle	31¼ in (80 cm)
Australian pig-nosed turtle	29⅔ in (76 cm)
Bell's hinge-back tortoise	8½ in (22 cm)
Big-headed turtle	7 in (18 cm)
Black-breasted leaf turtle	4½ in (11.5 cm)
Central American river turtle	25¾ in (66 cm)
Common snapping turtle	18¾ in (48 cm)
Diamondback terrapin	9⅓ in (24 cm)
European pond turtle	7¾ in (20 cm)
Fitzroy turtle	10 in (26 cm)
Flatback turtle	37½ in (96 cm)
Gopher tortoise	10½ in (27 cm)
Green turtle	5 ft (1.5 m)
Hawksbill turtle	35½ in (91 cm)
Hilaire's toadhead turtle	15⅔ in (40 cm)
Indian softshell turtle	27⅓ in (70 cm)
Leatherback turtle	7 ft (2.1 m)
Loggerhead	4 ft (1.2 m)
Malayan snail-eating turtle	7¾ in (20 cm)
Nile softshell turtle	37 in (95 cm)
Painted terrapin	23½ in (60 cm)
Painted turtle	9¾ in (25 cm)
Ringed sawback	8¼ in (21 cm)
River terrapin	23½ in (60 cm)
Smooth softshell turtle	13¾ in (35 cm)
South American red-footed tortoise	19½ in (50 cm)
Twist-necked turtle	6⅔ in (17 cm)
Victoria short-necked turtle	10 in (26 cm)

Crocodiles & alligators

African dwarf crocodile	6¼ ft (1.9 m)
American alligator	14¾ ft (4.5 m)
American crocodile	16½ ft (5 m)
Black caiman	13 ft (4 m)
Chinese alligator	6½ ft (2 m)
Cuvier's dwarf caiman	5 ft (1.5 m)
False gharial	16½ ft (5 m)
Gharial	23 ft (7 m)
Mugger	13 ft (4 m)
Nile crocodile	19⅔ ft (6 m)
Orinoco crocodile	16½ ft (5 m)
Saltwater crocodile	23 ft (7 m)
Siamese crocodile	13 ft (4 m)
Spectacled caiman	8½ ft (2.6 m)

Lizards

Banded galliwasp	7¾ in (20 cm)
Banded tree anole	3½ in (9 cm)
Black iguana	3¼ ft (1 m)
Borneo earless monitor	18 in (46 cm)
Burton's snake-lizard	23¾ in (61 cm)
Carpet chameleon	9¾ in (25 cm)
Chinese crocodile lizard	18 in (46 cm)
Chinese water dragon	29⅔ in (76 cm)
Chuckwalla	16½ in (42 cm)
Collared lizard	14 in (36 cm)
Common agama	9¾ in (25 cm)
Common leopard gecko	9¾ in (25 cm)
Common Mediterranean chameleon	15⅔ in (40 cm)
Common wall gecko	6 in (15 cm)
Crocodile monitor	9 ft (2.8 m)
Desert rainbow skink	9 in (23 cm)
Desert spiny lizard	11⅔ in (30 cm)
Eastern bearded dragon	19½ in (50 cm)
Emerald skink	9¾ in (25 cm)
Five-lined flying dragon	10½ in (27 cm)
Frilled lizard	29¼ in (75 cm)
Gallot's lizard	12½ in (32 cm)
Giant Madagascar chameleon	23½ in (60 cm)
Green basilisk lizard	29¼ in (75 cm)
Green iguana	6½ ft (2 m)

Green thornytail iguana	7 in (18 cm)
Horned leaf chameleon	3½ in (9 cm)
Indo-Chinese forest lizard	15⅔ in (40 cm)
Jackson's chameleon	11⅔ in (30 cm)
Karoo girdled lizard	7 in (18 cm)
Knysna dwarf chameleon	6 in (15 cm)
Komodo dragon	10 ft (3 m)
Kuhl's flying gecko	6 in (15 cm)
Leopard lizard	11⅔ in (30 cm)
Lesser chameleon	11⅔ in (30 cm)
Madagascar day gecko	11⅔ in (30 cm)
Malthe's elephant-eared chameleon	12 in (31 cm)
Menorca wall lizard	7 in (18 cm)
Merrem's Madagascar swift	7¾ in (20 cm)
Mexican beaded lizard	3¼ ft (1 m)
Milo's wall lizard	7 in (18 cm)
Northern leaf-tailed gecko	13¾ in (35 cm)
Northern spiny-tailed gecko	7¾ in (20 cm)
Northwestern sandslider	4 in (10 cm)
Ocellated tegu	25⅓ in (65 cm)
Otago skink	11⅔ in (30 cm)
Parson's chameleon	23½ in (60 cm)
Prehensile-tailed gecko	7 in (18 cm)
Rainbow lizard	9⅓ in (24 cm)
Rhinoceros iguana	4 ft (1.2 m)
Rough-scaled plated lizard	18¾ in (48 cm)
Sawtail lizard	5 in (12.5 cm)
Snake-eyed lizard	7¾ in (20 cm)
Spiny-tailed monitor	25¾ in (66 cm)
Sumatra nose-horned lizard	8½ in (22 cm)
Tiger lizard	9¾ in (25 cm)
Tokay gecko	14 in (36 cm)
West Indian iguana	3½ ft (1.05 m)

Snakes

Adder	27⅓ in (70 cm)
Aesculapian snake	7 ft (2.2 m)
Amazon false fer-de-lance	4 ft (1.2 m)
Anaconda	21⅔ ft (6.6 m)
Arafura file snake	6 ft (1.8 m)
Arizona coral snake	20⅔ in (53 cm)
Black mamba	9 ft (2.8 m)
Black-headed python	9 ft (2.8 m)
Black-tailed rattlesnake	4¼ ft (1.3 m)
Blood python	10 ft (3 m)
Blue-lipped sea krait	3¼ ft (1 m)
Boomslang	5¼ ft (1.6 m)
Bushmaster	14 ft (4.3 m)
Cantil	3¼ ft (1 m)
Chinese rat snake	8½ ft (2.6 m)
Common boa constrictor	10 ft (3 m)
Common bronze-back snake	3¼ ft (1 m)
Common death adder	29⅔ in (76 cm)
Copperhead	4 ft (1.2 m)
Coral cylinder snake	36 in (92 cm)
Drummond Hay's earth snake	13 in (33 cm)
Eastern coral snake	29⅔ in (76 cm)
Emerald tree boa	5 ft (1.5 m)
European grass snake	6½ ft (2 m)
False water cobra	9 ft (2.8 m)
Fea viper	29⅔ in (76 cm)
Forest flame snake	3¼ ft (1 m)
Gaboon viper	4½ ft (1.4 m)
Green whip snake	6½ ft (2 m)
Hognosed pit viper	19½ in (50 cm)
Isthmian dwarf boa	3¼ ft (1 m)
Jararacussu	7 ft (2.2 m)
King cobra	16½ ft (5 m)
Lichtenstein's night adder	3¼ ft (1 m)
Malayan pit viper	3¼ ft (1 m)
Mangrove snake	8 ft (2.5 m)
Masked water snake	4 ft (1.2 m)
Massasauga	29⅔ in (76 cm)
Mexican burrowing python	4½ ft (1.4 m)
Milk snake	35 in (90 cm)
Mojave rattlesnake	4 ft (1.2 m)
Monocled cobra	6 ft (1.8 m)
Mulga snake	9 ft (2.8 m)

Natal black snake	3¼ ft (1 m)
Northern water snake	3½ ft (1.05 m)
Persian horned viper	35 in (90 cm)
Red cylinder snake	3¼ ft (1 m)
Rhinoceros viper	4 ft (1.2 m)
Rhombic egg-eating snake	12 in (31 cm)
Ringed hognose snake	23½ in (60 cm)
Ring-neck snake	25¾ in (66 cm)
Saw-scaled viper	27⅓ in (70 cm)
Schokari sand racer	5¼ ft (1.6 m)
Speckled forest pit viper	4¼ ft (1.3 m)
Striped kukri snake	25¾ in (66 cm)
Sunbeam snake	5 ft (1.5 m)
Taipan	9 ft (2.8 m)
Tatar sand boa	4 ft (1.2 m)
Tiger snake	8 ft (2.4 m)
Timber rattlesnake	5 ft (1.5 m)
Turtle-headed sea snake	4 ft (1.2 m)
Wagler's palm viper	3¼ ft (1 m)
Western brown snake	6 ft (1.8 m)
Western diamondback rattlesnake	6 ft (1.8 m)
Wood snake	3¼ ft (1 m)
Yellow-blotched palm pit viper	9¾ in (25 cm)

Amphibians

Caecilians

Cayenne caecilian	23½ in (60 cm)
Mengla County caecilian	16½ in (42 cm)
São Tomé caecilian	12½ in (32 cm)

Salamanders

Arboreal salamander	4 in (10 cm)
Banded newt	6¼ in (16 cm)
Blue-spotted salamander	5 in (13 cm)
California giant salamander	14 in (36 cm)
Chinese giant salamander	4½ ft (1.4 m)
Chinese salamander	4 in (10 cm)
Common newt	4½ in (11.5 cm)
European fire salamander	9¾ in (25 cm)
Fischer's clawed salamander	5 in (13 cm)
Four-toed salamander	4 in (10 cm)
Hellbender	20⅔ in (53 cm)
Jackson's mushroomtongue salamander	3 in (7.5 cm)
Japanese firebelly newt	5 in (13 cm)
Lesser siren	19½ in (50 cm)
Mudpuppy	13¾ in (35 cm)
Pyrenees mountain salamander	6¼ in (16 cm)
Red-backed salamander	5 in (13 cm)
Siberian salamander	9¾ in (25 cm)
Slimy salamander	6¼ in (16 cm)
Tiger salamander	9¾ in (25 cm)
Two-toed amphiuma	29⅔ in (76 cm)
Vietnam warty newt	7¾ in (20 cm)

Frogs & toads

African bullfrog	9 in (23 cm)
Barking frog	3¾ in (9.5 cm)
Barking tree frog	2¾ in (7 cm)
Blue poison frog	2 in (5 cm)
Bongon whipping frog	3¾ in (9.5 cm)
Brown New Zealand frog	2 in (5 cm)
Bullfrog	7¾ in (20 cm)
Cameroon toad	3 in (8 cm)
Cane toad	9⅓ in (24 cm)
Carabaya robber frog	9 in (23 cm)
Common Asian toad	6 in (15 cm)
Common parsley frog	2 in (5 cm)
Coqui	2¼ in (5.5 cm)
Crucifix toad	2¼ in (5.5 cm)
Dahaoping sucker frog	4 in (10 cm)
Dainty green tree frog	1¾ in (4.5 cm)
Everett's Asian tree toad	11⅔ in (30 cm)
Giant banjo frog	3½ in (9 cm)

Hairy frog	4¼ in (11 cm)
Harlequin frog	2 in (5 cm)
Harlequin poison frog	1½ in (4 cm)
Horned toad	3 in (8 cm)
Java flying frog	3½ in (9 cm)
Madagascar reed frog	1½ in (4 cm)
Malayan horned frog	5 in (12.5 cm)
Marsupial frog	2¾ in (7 cm)
Mexican burrowing toad	3½ in (9 cm)
Muller's termite frog	3 in (7.5 cm)
Nicaragua giant glass frog	1 in (2.5 cm)
Oriental firebelly toad	2⅓ in (6 cm)
Ornate horned toad	7¾ in (20 cm)
Painted frog	3 in (8 cm)
Painted-belly leaf frog	3⅓ in (8.5 cm)
Paradox frog	3 in (7.5 cm)
Pickerel frog	3 in (7.5 cm)
Red rain frog	1½ in (4 cm)
Red toad	5 in (13 cm)
Red-eyed tree frog	3 in (7.5 cm)
Schmidt's forest frog	4 in (10 cm)
Shovel-headed tree frog	3 in (7.5 cm)
Singapore wart frog	4 in (10 cm)
Southern bell frog	4 in (10 cm)
Spotted snout-burrower	2⅓ in (6 cm)
Strawberry poison frog	1 in (2.5 cm)
Surinam toad	7¾ in (20 cm)
Syrian spadefoot toad	3 in (8 cm)
Tailed frog	2 in (5 cm)
Tomato frog	4 in (10 cm)
Tulear golden frog	1¼ in (3.2 cm)
Turtle frog	2⅓ in (6 cm)
Vizcacheras's white-lipped frog	4 in (10 cm)
Water-holding frog	3⅓ in (8.5 cm)
Weal's running frog	1¾ in (4.5 cm)

Fish

Jawless fish

Atlantic hagfish	23¾ in (61 cm)
European river lamprey	19 in (49 cm)
Pacific lamprey	29⅔ in (76 cm)
Pouched lamprey	24¼ in (62 cm)
Sea lamprey	35 in (90 cm)

Cartilaginous fish

Angel shark	8 ft (2.4 m)
Atlantic guitarfish	29⅔ in (76 cm)
Basking shark	32 ft (9.8 m)
Blackmouth catshark	35 in (90 cm)
Blue shark	13 ft (4 m)
Blue-spotted ribbontail ray	27⅓ in (70 cm)
Bramble shark	10¼ ft (3.1 m)
Bull shark	11½ ft (3.5 m)
Common stingray	4½ ft (1.4 m)
Cownose ray	7 ft (2.1 m)
Devil fish	13 ft (4 m)
Great white shark	23⅔ ft (7.2 m)
Japanese butterfly ray	3¼ ft (1 m)
Largetooth sawfish	16½ ft (5 m)
Longnose sawshark	4½ ft (1.4 m)
Manta	22 ft (6.7 m)
Marbled electric ray	3¼ ft (1 m)
Nurse shark	14 ft (4.3 m)
Ocellate river stingray	3¼ ft (1 m)
Port Jackson shark	5½ ft (1.65 m)
Sand tiger shark	10½ ft (3.2 m)
Sharpnose sevengill shark	4½ ft (1.4 m)
Shortfin mako	13 ft (4 m)
Sixgill shark	15¾ ft (4.8 m)
Smooth hammerhead	16½ ft (5 m)
Smooth hound	6½ ft (2 m)
Soupfin shark	6⅓ ft (1.95 m)
Spiny dogfish	5¼ ft (1.6 m)
Spotted eagle ray	9 ft (2.8 m)
Spotted ratfish	37 in (95 cm)
Thornback ray	4 ft (1.2 m)
Tiger shark	24¼ ft (7.4 m)
Whale shark	59 ft (18 m)

Bony fish

Aba	5½ ft (1.7 m)
Alaska blackfish	13 in (33 cm)
American anglerfish	4 ft (1.2 m)
American shad	29⅔ in (76 cm)
Angel squeaker	21½ in (55 cm)
Arapaima	14¾ ft (4.5 m)
Atlantic cod	5 ft (1.5 m)
Atlantic herring	16¾ in (43 cm)
Atlantic salmon	5 ft (1.5 m)
Atlantic sturgeon	14 ft (4.3 m)
Australian lungfish	5½ ft (1.7 m)
Ayu	27⅓ in (70 cm)
Beluga	13 ft (4 m)
Bitterling	4¼ in (11 cm)
Blackfin wolf-herring	3¼ ft (1 m)
Blunt-jaw elephantnose	15⅔ in (40 cm)
Bonefish	3¼ ft (1 m)
Bowfin	3⅔ ft (1.1 m)
Burbot	5 ft (1.5 m)
California slickhead	23¾ in (61 cm)
Capelin	7¾ in (20 cm)
Chain pickerel	38⅔ in (99 cm)
Cherry salmon	27⅔ in (71 cm)
Chinese sucker	23½ in (60 cm)
Chinese swordfish	10 ft (3 m)
Cisco	22¼ in (57 cm)
Clown knifefish	4 ft (1.2 m)
Coelacanth	6½ ft (2 m)
Common carp	4 ft (1.2 m)
Conger eel	8¾ ft (2.7 m)
Cutthroat trout	38⅔ in (99 cm)
Electric catfish	4 ft (1.2 m)
Electric eel	8 ft (2.4 m)
Emperor tetra	2¼ in (5.5 cm)
European eel	3¼ ft (1 m)
European hake	4½ ft (1.4 m)
European pilchard	9¾ in (25 cm)
European smelt	11⅔ in (30 cm)
European sprat	6¼ in (16 cm)
European sturgeon	11½ ft (3.5 m)
Freshwater butterflyfish	4⅔ in (12 cm)
Geometric moray	25⅓ in (65 cm)
Gizzard shad	22¼ in (57 cm)
Glass catfish	6 in (15 cm)
Golden trout	27⅔ in (71 cm)
Grayling	23½ in (60 cm)
Haddock	35 in (90 cm)
Harlequin rasbora	1¾ in (4.5 cm)
Hatchetfish	3½ in (9 cm)
Huchen	5 ft (1.5 m)
Laced moray	10 ft (3 m)
Lake trout	4 ft (1.2 m)
Longnose gar	6 ft (1.8 m)
Marbled hatchetfish	1⅓ in (3.5 cm)
Marbled lungfish	6½ ft (2 m)
Metallic lanternfish	3 in (8 cm)
Milk fish	6 ft (1.8 m)
Mottled bichir	21 in (54 cm)
Mudminnow	5 in (13 cm)
Northern pearleye	9⅓ in (24 cm)
Northern pike	4½ ft (1.4 m)
Oarfish	26¼ ft (8 m)
Onion-eye grenadier	3¼ ft (1 m)
Oxeye	5 ft (1.5 m)
Pacific viperfish	9¾ in (25 cm)
Peruvian anchoveta	7¾ in (20 cm)
Pink salmon	29⅔ in (76 cm)
Rainbow trout	3¾ ft (1.15 m)
Redeye piranha	16½ in (42 cm)
Round herring	9¾ in (25 cm)
Sea trout	4½ ft (1.4 m)
Sockeye salmon	32¾ in (84 cm)
South American lungfish	4¼ ft (1.3 m)
Spanish sardine	12 in (31 cm)
Spanner barb	7 in (18 cm)
Spotted garden eel	14 in (36 cm)
Starry handfish	11⅔ in (30 cm)
Stone loach	8¼ in (21 cm)
Stout beardfish	18¾ in (48 cm)
Striped eel-catfish	13 in (33 cm)
Swallower	5¼ ft (1.6 m)
Tarpon	8 ft (2.4 m)
Trout perch	7¾ in (20 cm)
Wels catfish	10 ft (3 m)
West African lungfish	3¼ ft (1 m)

Spiny-rayed fish

Amazon leaffish	3 in (7.5 cm)
Archerfish	11⅔ in (30 cm)
Atlantic halibut	8 ft (2.5 m)
Atlantic mudskipper	9¾ in (25 cm)
Balloonfish	19½ in (50 cm)
Barramundi perch	6 ft (1.8 m)
Blue marlin	15 ft (4.6 m)
Brill	29¼ in (75 cm)
Brook silverside	5 in (13 cm)
Clown anemonefish	4 in (10 cm)
Clown triggerfish	19½ in (50 cm)
Clown wrasse	4 ft (1.2 m)
Crown squirrelfish	6⅔ in (17 cm)
East Atlantic red gurnard	19½ in (50 cm)
Emperor angelfish	15⅔ in (40 cm)
Emperor snapper	3¼ ft (1 m)
Eurasian perch	20 in (51 cm)
False cleanerfish	4½ in (11.5 cm)
Flat needlefish	4½ ft (1.4 m)
Forktail rainbowfish	2 in (5 cm)
Freshwater angelfish	3 in (7.5 cm)
Freshwater pufferfish	26 in (67 cm)
Golden pheasant panchax	3 in (7.5 cm)
Goldribbon soapfish	15⅔ in (40 cm)
Gourami	27⅓ in (70 cm)
Guineafowl puffer	19½ in (50 cm)
Guppy	2 in (5 cm)
Indo-Pacific sailfish	11½ ft (3.5 m)
Jack-knifefish	9¾ in (25 cm)
John Dory	25¾ in (66 cm)
Kissing gourami	11⅔ in (30 cm)
Largemouth bass	37¾ in (97 cm)
Leafy seadragon	15⅔ in (40 cm)
Moorish idol	9 in (23 cm)
Ocean sunfish	10¾ ft (3.3 m)
Peacock cichlid	28¾ in (74 cm)
Pearl gourami	4⅔ in (12 cm)
Pineconefish	6⅔ in (17 cm)
Prickly leatherjacket	12 in (31 cm)
Radial firefish	9⅓ in (24 cm)
Red drum	5 ft (1.5 m)
Red mullet	15⅔ in (40 cm)
Redtail surgeonfish	9⅓ in (24 cm)
Ringed pipefish	7½ in (19 cm)
Roosterfish	4 ft (1.2 m)
Royal gramma	3 in (8 cm)
Saberfin killie	1½ in (4 cm)
Sablefish	3¼ ft (1 m)
Sea goldie	6 in (15 cm)
Sharpchin flyingfish	9⅓ in (24 cm)
Shorthorn sculpin	23½ in (60 cm)
Shrimpfish	6 in (15 cm)
Siamese fighting fish	2½ in (6.5 cm)
Skipjack tuna	3⅔ ft (1.1 m)
Splitfin flashlightfish	13¾ in (35 cm)
Stonefish	14 in (36 cm)
Stripey	6¼ in (16 cm)
Summer flounder	36⅔ in (94 cm)
Swamp eel	18 in (46 cm)
Swordfish	16 ft (4.9 m)
Thornback cowfish	9 in (23 cm)
Threadfin rainbowfish	1⅓ in (3.5 cm)
Three-spined stickleback	2¾ in (7 cm)
Twoband bream	17½ in (45 cm)
Velvet whalefish	14 in (36 cm)
Viviparous blenny	20¼ in (52 cm)
Yellowback fusilier	15⅔ in (40 cm)

Invertebrates

Sponges & squirts

Acorn worm	11⅔ in (30 cm)
Arrow worm	⅛ in (4 mm)
Colonial sea squirt	4 in (10 cm)
Common lancelet	2 in (5 cm)
Glove sponge	23½ in (60 cm)
Gold sponge	2⅓ in (6 cm)
Ink-pot sea squirt	6 in (15 cm)
Lightbulb sea squirt	¾ in (2 cm)
Melon jellyfish	6 in (15 cm)
Neptune's cup	29¼ in (75 cm)
Purse sponge	2 in (5 cm)
Sea potato	4 in (10 cm)
Venus's flower basket	11⅔ in (30 cm)

Worms

Caenorhabditis elegans	1/25 in (1 mm)
Gastrotrich	⅛ in (3 mm)
Goblet worm	⅕ in (5 mm)
Human whipworm	2 in (5 cm)
Intestinal roundworm	15⅔ in (40 cm)
Medicinal leech	4 in (10 cm)
Night crawler	9¾ in (25 cm)
Palolo worm	23½ in (60 cm)
Polystoma integerrimum	1/25 in (1 mm)
Ragworm	7¾ in (20 cm)
Rotifer	1/100 in (0.4 mm)
Shovel-headed garden worm	11⅔ in (30 cm)
Spiny-crown worm	1/25 in (1 mm)
Velvet worm	2¾ in (7 cm)
Water bear	1/25 in (1 mm)

Corals & jellyfish

Beadlet anemone	3 in (8 cm)
Brachiopod	1⅓ in (3.5 cm)
Daisy anemone	6 in (15 cm)
Fire coral	27⅓ in (70 cm)
Formosan soft coral	3¼ ft (1 m)
Freshwater bryozoan	7¾ in (20 cm)
Green hydra	1/25 in (1 mm)
Lion's mane jellyfish	6½ ft (2 m)
Organ-pipe coral	3¼ ft (1 m)
Portuguese man-of-war (float)	4⅔ in (12 cm)
(tentacles)	33 ft (10 m)
Red brain coral	15⅔ in (40 cm)
West Indian sea fan	36 in (92 cm)
Yellow feathers	6 in (15 cm)

Mollusks

Atlantic thorny oyster	5½ in (14 cm)
Blue sea slug	1½ in (4 cm)
Blue-ringed octopus	7¾ in (20 cm)
Chocolate arion	6 in (15 cm)
Common cuttlefish	23½ in (60 cm)
Common egg cowrie	5 in (13 cm)
Common limpet	2⅓ in (6 cm)
Common nautilus	7¾ in (20 cm)
Common octopus	3¼ ft (1 m)
Deep-sea vampire squid	11 in (28 cm)
Elephant tusk	6 in (15 cm)
Escargot	2 in (5 cm)
European edible abalone	3½ in (9 cm)
Flat oyster	3 in (8 cm)
Flying squid	3¼ ft (1 m)
Freshwater pearl mussel	4 in (10 cm)
Giant squid	60 ft (18.3 m)
Giant tiger snail	12 in (31 cm)
Glistenworm	½ in (1.2 cm)
Gray garden slug	2 in (5 cm)
Lesser cuttlefish	2⅓ in (6 cm)
Long-finned squid	19½ in (50 cm)
Musky octopus	21½ in (55 cm)
Nudibranch	2 in (5 cm)
Nut shell	⅓ in (1 cm)
Paper nautilus	11⅔ in (30 cm)
Pen shell	3¼ ft (1 m)
Queen conch	11⅔ in (30 cm)

Spiny cockle	🐚	4½ in (11.5 cm)
Trumpet triton	🐚	17½ in (45 cm)
West Indian green chiton	🐚	3 in (8 cm)

rachnids

Black widow	⅓ in (1 cm)
Book scorpion	⅛ in (4 mm)
Bristly millipede	⅛ in (3 mm)
European garden spider	¾ in (2 cm)
Fat-tailed scorpion	4⅔ in (12 cm)
Giant desert centipede	3 in (8 cm)
Golden orb weaver	2 in (5 cm)
Goldenrod spider	⅓ in (1 cm)
Gracile sea spider	⅓ in (1 cm)
Harvest bug	⅕ in (5 mm)
Hooded tick spider	⅓ in (1 cm)
Horseshoe crab	23½ in (60 cm)
House spider	⅓ in (1 cm)
Ladybird spider	⅕ in (5 mm)
Malaysian trapdoor spider	4 in (10 cm)
Mombasa golden starburst tarantula	2 in (5 cm)
Money spider	⅕ in (5 mm)
Orb weaver	¼ in (6 mm)
Pear bud mite	<1/100 in (0.2 mm)
Scabies mite	1/100 in (0.4 mm)
Sheep tick	⅗ in (1.5 cm)
Short-tailed whip-scorpion	⅛ in (3 mm)
Thorn spider	⅗ in (1.5 cm)
Tropical tentweb spider	1 in (2.5 cm)
Varroa mite	1/25 in (1 mm)
Wasp spider	⅔ in (1.7 cm)
Whip-scorpion	11⅔ in (30 cm)
Whip-spider	¾ in (2 cm)
Zebra jumping spider	¼ in (7 mm)

abs & crayfish

Acorn barnacle	★	1¼ in (3 cm)
Amphipod (Caprella sp.)	🐚	¼ in (7 mm)
Amphipod (Gammarus sp.)	🐚	⅔ in (1.8 cm)
Atlantic lobster	🐚	11⅔ in (30 cm)
Black tiger prawn	🐚	13 in (33 cm)
Cephalocarid	🐚	1⅓ in (3.5 cm)
Chinese mitten crab	★	3 in (8 cm)
Cleaner shrimp	🐚	2 in (5 cm)
Common pill wood louse	🐚	⅔ in (1.7 cm)
Copepod	🐚	1/50 in (0.5 mm)
European green crab	★	3 in (8 cm)
Freshwater fish louse	🐚	¼ in (7 mm)
Giant water flea	🐚	⅔ in (1.8 cm)
Horn-eyed ghost crab	★	3 in (8 cm)
Mantis shrimp	🐚	4 in (10 cm)
Mystarocarid	🐚	1/100 in (0.4 mm)
Ostracod	🐚	1/50 in (0.6 mm)
Spiny lobster	🐚	23½ in (60 cm)
Spinycheek crayfish	🐚	6¼ in (16 cm)
Tadpole shrimp	🐚	4 in (10 cm)
Tasmanian mountain shrimp	🐚	2 in (5 cm)

agonflies, mantids, cockroaches, rmites & crickets

Beautiful demoiselle	2 in (5 cm)
Blue dasher	1¾ in (4.5 cm)
Blue-winged grasshopper	4 in (10 cm)
Common praying mantis	2½ in (6.5 cm)
Dawn dropwing	1½ in (4 cm)
Dipluran	⅕ in (5 mm)
German cockroach	⅔ in (1.6 cm)
Giant cockroach	3 in (8 cm)
Green banana roach	¾ in (2 cm)
Large fungus-growing termite	⅔ in (1.8 cm)
Migratory locust	2½ in (6.5 cm)
Orchid mantis	2 in (5 cm)
Proturan	1/12 in (2 mm)
Spinifex termite	¼ in (6 mm)
Springtail	1/10 in (2.5 mm)
Tropical leaf katydid	11⅔ in (30 cm)

Bugs

Apple leaf sucker	⅛ in (3 mm)
Assassin bug	¾ in (2 cm)
Cotton stainer bug	⅖ in (1.1 cm)
Green shield bug	½ in (1.4 cm)
Lace bug	1/10 in (2.5 mm)
Large milkweed bug	⅗ in (1.5 cm)
Leaf-footed bug	1 in (2.5 cm)
Leaf-hopper	⅗ in (1.5 cm)
Long-tailed mealy bug	⅛ in (3 mm)
Lygus bug	⅓ in (8 mm)
Nettle ensign scale	⅓ in (4 mm)
Peanut-headed lanternfly	3½ in (9 cm)
Red and black froghopper	⅓ in (1 cm)
Red cicada	2 in (5 cm)
Spined stink bug	½ in (1.4 cm)
Treehopper (Hemikyptha sp.)	¾ in (2 cm)
Treehopper (Oeda sp.)	½ in (1.2 cm)
Water bug	1 in (2.5 cm)
Water measurer	⅓ in (1 cm)
Woolly apple aphid	1/12 in (2 mm)

Beetles

Ant-nest beetle	⅗ in (1.5 cm)
Bess beetle	2½ in (6.5 cm)
Bombardier beetle	1¼ in (3 cm)
Cigarette beetle	⅛ in (4 mm)
Colorado potato beetle	⅓ in (1 cm)
European burying beetle	¾ in (2 cm)
European splendor beetle	⅓ in (8 mm)
Fire beetle	1¾ in (4.5 cm)
Glow worm	¾ in (2 cm)
Golden rove beetle	¾ in (2 cm)
Goliath beetle	4⅔ in (12 cm)
Harlequin beetle	3 in (8 cm)
Hercules beetle	7 in (18 cm)
Java fiddle beetle	4 in (10 cm)
King weevil	1 in (2.5 cm)
Seven-spotted lady beetle	⅓ in (8 mm)
Spanish fly	¾ in (2 cm)
Stag beetle	3 in (8 cm)
Tiger beetle	¾ in (2 cm)

Flies

Buzzer midge	⅓ in (1 cm)
Common housefly	¼ in (6 mm)
Greater bee fly	½ in (1.2 cm)
Horsefly	1 in (2.5 cm)
House mosquito	⅕ in (5 mm)
Hover fly	½ in (1.2 cm)
Mantis fly	⅕ in (5 mm)
Robber fly	1 in (2.5 cm)
Sand fly	⅛ in (3 mm)
Sheep blowfly	⅓ in (1 cm)
Sheep nasal botfly	½ in (1.4 cm)
Stalk-eyed fly	¼ in (6 mm)

Butterflies & moths

African giant swallowtail	9¾ in (25 cm)
African monarch	2⅓ in (6 cm)
Bent-wing ghost moth	9¾ in (25 cm)
Bird-cherry ermine	1 in (2.5 cm)
Bogong moth	2 in (5 cm)
Carpet moth	1 in (2.5 cm)
Dead leaf butterfly	2¾ in (7 cm)
Eliena skipper	1⅓ in (3.5 cm)
European pine shoot moth	1 in (2.5 cm)
Eyed hawk moth	3 in (8 cm)
Giant atlas moth	11⅔ in (30 cm)
Helena butterfly	6 in (15 cm)
Hornet clearwing	1½ in (4 cm)
Large blue	1½ in (4 cm)
Mimic	2⅓ in (6 cm)
Mottled umber	1¾ in (4.5 cm)
Northern jungle queen butterfly	5 in (13 cm)

Orange-barred sulphur	2¾ in (7 cm)
Postman, the	3 in (8 cm)
Silver-washed fritillary	2¾ in (7 cm)

Bees, wasps & ants

Bull ant	¾ in (2 cm)
Common wasp	1¾ in (4.5 cm)
Currant sawfly	⅓ in (7.5 mm)
Ensign wasp	⅗ in (1.5 cm)
Giant hunting ant	1¼ in (3 cm)
Honey ant	⅓ in (9 mm)
Oak apple gall wasp	1/10 in (2.5 mm)
Paper wasp	⅔ in (1.6 cm)
Potter wasp	¾ in (1.9 cm)
Red-tailed bumblebee	1¼ in (3 cm)
Rose sawfly	⅓ in (1 cm)
Ruby-tailed wasp	½ in (1.2 cm)

Sand digger wasp	1 in (2.5 cm)
Sirex parasite	1½ in (4 cm)
Slave-making ant	¼ in (7 mm)
Torymid wasp	⅛ in (4 mm)
Velvet wasp	1⅓ in (3.5 cm)
Weaver ant	¼ in (7 mm)

Sea stars

Black brittle star	★	9¾ in (25 cm)
Common starfish	★	19½ in (50 cm)
Feather star	★	9¾ in (25 cm)
Gorgon's head	★	15⅔ in (40 cm)
Pelagic sea cucumber	🐚	3 in (8 cm)
Red pencil urchin	★	11 in (28 cm)
Reef sea urchin	★	27⅓ in (70 cm)
Sand dollar	🐚	2½ in (6.5 cm)
Sea apple	🐚	7 in (18 cm)
Synaptid sea cucumber	🐚	10 ft (3 m)

Key

The icons below show at a glance how each animal is measured. When each animal within a group is measured the same way, the icon is placed at the top of the measurement column. Most ratites are measured by height rather than length. They have an icon next to each measurement. Invertebrates are so diverse that even within the same group they are often measured differently. In these cases, too, a smaller icon appears next to each measurement.

Mammals

Length

Most mammals' head and body lengths are measured excluding the tail. Aquatic mammals are measured from the head to the tip of the tail.

Tail

The length of the mammal's tail is measured. For mammals that do not have tails, this is indicated by the word "None."

Birds

Length

The bird's length is measured from the tip of its bill to the tip of its tail feathers. Most birds are measured by length.

Height

Some flightless birds—rheas, ostriches, emus, cassowaries, and penguins—are measured by height, from head to feet.

Reptiles

Length

Because turtles and tortoises can draw their heads and limbs back into their shells, only the length of the shell is measured.

Length

All other reptiles—crocodilians, lizards, snakes, and tuatara—are measured from the head to the tip of the tail.

Amphibians

Length

The amphibian's head and body length is measured. For species that have tails, such as salamanders, the tail is included.

Fish

Length

The fish's head and body length is measured, from the front of the head to the tip of the tail fin.

Invertebrates

Length

Most invertebrates, including bugs and beetles, are measured by head and body length, excluding antennae.

Height

Some invertebrates, such as coral, grow upward. These species are measured by the height they reach.

Width

Some invertebrates, such as sea stars and crabs, have shells or bodies that are measured across rather than lengthwise.

Wingspan

Butterflies and moths are measured by wingspan, from wingtip to wingtip, at the widest point.

Index

Credits

Key t=top; l=left; r=right; tl=top left; tcl=top center left; tc=top center; tcr=top center right; tr=top right; cl=center left; c=center; cr=center right; b=bottom; bl=bottom left; bcl=bottom center left; bc=bottom center; bcr=bottom center right; br=bottom right

AAP = Australian Associated Press; APL = Australian Picture Library; APL/CBT = Australian Picture Library/Corbis; APL/MP = Australian Picture Library/Minden Pictures; AUS = Auscape International; COR = Corel Corp.; DV = Digital Vision; GI = Getty Images; IQ3D = imagequestmarine.com; NHPA = Natural History Photographic Agency; NPL=Nature Picture Library; PD = Photodisc; PL = photolibrary.com; WA = Wildlife Art Ltd

Front cover and endpapers Stuart Armstrong

Photographs 1 bc bl c GI, br DV, cl APL, cr APL/MP 12 c GI 13 bcl GI 14 t GI 15 bc NHPA, bl GI, br PL 16 bc PL, bl APL/CBT, br APL/Corbis, tl COR 17 bc bl GI, br APL/CBT, c PL, tl COR, tr Doug Perrine/Seapics.com 18 t PL 19 b br APL/Corbis 20 bl APL/CBT, cr tl APL/Corbis, tr GI 21 bc br PD, tl GI, tr APL/CBT 22 t APL/Corbis 23 bc APL/CBT, bl APL/MP, br IQ3D/Chris Parks 26 t APL/CBT 27 bl APL/MP, br GI 28 tc GI, tl APL/CBT, tr APL 29 bl tl GI, br cr tr APL/CBT 42 t AAP 52 t APL 67 t APL/CBT 70 t GI 80 tl GI 89 bl PL, t AUS 93 tl PL, tr Bruce Coleman 100 t GI 101 bc bl COR 103 bl br tl tr GI 109 tl tr COR 117 bl cl PL 129 bc cr APL/MP 134 t APL/CBT 139 tl tr APL/MP 144 t APL/MP 145 tc tr APL/CBT 152 t APL/MP 160 t APL/MP 164 c cr AUS 170 t GI 171 cl tr GI, tc PL 175 tl APL/CBT 179 cl APL/MP 182 t GI 183 tc tr APL/MP 185 t GI 187 t PL 192 t AUS 197 tl NPL, cl PL 203 cl PL, tl AUS 204 t APL/MP, tl GI 214 t APL/MP 215 bc GI, bl br COR 219 tr APL/MP 223 bl cl NPL 224 t DV 230 t DV 242 tl APL/CBT

Illustrations All illustrations © MagicGroup s.r.o. (Czech Republic) – www.magicgroup.cz
– except for the following:
Susanna Addario 16cl, 242bl, **Alistair Barnard** 201br, 175b, **Sally Beech** 215tl, 230br, 232bl, 233br, 237b bc cr, **Bernard Thornton Artists UK/John Francis** 147br, 154bl, 166bl, **Bernard Thornton Artists UK/Tim Hayward** 79br, **Andre Boos** 61br, 65cr, **Martin Camm** 69bcr br, 187bc bcr cr, 191b, **Creative Communications** 13br, **Simone End** 61br, 75br, 146bl cl, 157br, 215c, 218tr, 235bc bl br, **Christer**

Eriksson 5c, 28b, 32bl, 66bl, 67c, 76bl, 155t, 224bl, 226bl, **Folio/John Mac** 39c cl cr, 82cl bcl bl tl, 83br, **Folio/Martin Macrae** 20c, **Lloyd Foye** 129c, 215cl, **Jon Gittoes** 35cr, 47tl, 74bl, **Ray Grinaway** 73cl, 195bl, 215c cl tr, 224cr, 225bc bcl, 230bcr, **Gino Hasler** 15cl, 101tr, **Robert Hynes** 156bl, 240bl, **Illustration Ltd/Mike Atkinson** 104bl, **David Kirshner** 15tr, 19bl, 33br, 41br, 42br, 44tr, 53bl, 57r bl, 69tc, 70bc bcr br, 79cl, 86tr, 91br, 102t tcr, 108cr, 120tr, 122bl, 127bc, 145c cl cr tl, 146bl, 151br, 164l, 171cr, 179r, 183b c cl cr tcl tl, 196tr, 204cr, 205br, 211br, 223r, 224r, **Frank Knight** 39t, 52br, 54bcl bcr bl br c, 55b, 56bcl bl, 57br, 58tr, 66br cl cr r t tl, 68br c cl cr tc tcr tl, 69bc bl c cl l r tcl tcr tl tr, 71b, 161br, 175b, 206bl, **Rob Mancini** 3c, 16r, 89c, 102tcl, 127br, 133tr, 179bc bl, 215tcl, 224bc, 227br, 239bc bcr, **James McKinnon** 93b, 145bcr bl, **Matthew Ottley** 73b, **Peter Bull Art Studio** 216bl, **Tony Pyrzakowski** 88bl, 116b, 150bl, **John Richards** 121b, **Barbara Rodanska** 59br, 215tcr, **Trevor Ruth** 2l, 65br, 80b, 163br, 167br, 203b, 229br, **Claudia Saraceni** 73c cr, **Peter Schouten** 45tr, 50bl, 158bl, **Rod Scott** 80tr, **Marco Sparaciari** 222bl, **Kevin Stead** 30cl, 102br, 215r, 224br, 230bcl, 236b tr, 239bl, 241br, **Roger Swainston** 188bl, 215cr, **Bernard Tate** 207r, **Thomas Trojer** 195bc, **Guy Troughton** 13tl, 30br cl cr tr, 31br, 32bc c cl, 34cl, 37bl c cl cr tl tr, 39b tl, 40bl br, 43br, 47bc br, 49br, 50c cl cr tr, 51bc bl br tr, 53br, 55tcl tcr tl tr, 58b, 64bc bl cl cr, 65bl, 66tr, 71tr, 73t, 78br, 84bl, 85bcl bcr bl br c cl tr, 87br, 97br, 137br, 139b, 141br, **WA/Priscilla Barret** 116bc bl c cl, **WA/Dan Cole** 107b, 111br, **WA/Tom Connell** 101c, **WA/Marc Dando** 186b, 189br, **WA/Sandra Doyle** 15tc, 125br, **WA/Ian Jackson** 15cr, 187bcl bl br cr r tr, 215cl, 230bl, 239br, **WA/Ken Oliver** 165br, 167tr, 173tl, **WA/Steve Roberts** 15tl, 234bl, 238bl, **WA/Peter Scott** 102bc bl c cl, 109c, **WA/Chris Shields** 215cr, 225bl, 232tr, **WA/Mark Stewart** 218br, **WA/Chris Turnbull** 190bl, **Trevor Weekes** 126bl, 131r, **Ann Winterbotham** 195br

Montages Created by Domenika Markovtzev and John Bull. All images by artists listed above.

Maps/Graphics All pie charts by Domenika Markovtzev. All maps by Domenika Markovtzev and Map Illustrations except for the maps appearing on p. 19 and p. 23 by Andrew Davies and Map Illustrations

The publishers wish to thank Helen Flint, Jennifer Losco, and Dr. Richard Schodde for their assistance in the preparation of this volume.

One of the world's largest nonprofit scientific and educational organizations, the National Geographic Society was founded in 1888 "for the increase and diffusion of geographic knowledge." Fulfilling this mission, the Society educates and inspires millions every day through its magazines, books, television programs, videos, maps and atlases, research grants, the National Geographic Bee, teacher workshops, and innovative classroom materials. The Society is supported through membership dues, charitable gifts, and income from the sale of its educational products. This support is vital to National Geographic's mission to increase global understanding and promote conservation of our planet through exploration, research, and education.

For more information, please call 1-800-NGS LINE (647-5463) or write to the following address:

National Geographic Society
1145 17th Street N.W.
Washington, D.C. 20036-4688 U.S.A.

Visit the Society's Web site at www.nationalgeographic.com.